# WITHOUT A

# WOMAN

# TO READ

SUNY Series in Radical Social and Political Theory
Roger S. Gottlieb, editor

# WITHOUT A

*Toward the Daughter*

# WOMAN

*in Postmodernism*

# TO READ

DANIEL PRICE

STATE UNIVERSITY OF NEW YORK PRESS

Published by
State University of New York Press, Albany

© 1997 State University of New York

For information, address the State University of New York Press,
State University Plaza, Albany, NY 12246

Production design by David Ford
Marketing by Nancy Farrell

Library of Congress Cataloging-in-Publication Data
Price, Daniel, 1965–
        Without a woman to read : toward the daughter in postmodernism /
    Daniel Price.
              p.        cm. -- (SUNY series in radical social and political
    theory)
        Includes bibliographical references and index.
        ISBN 0-7914-3459-1 (hc : alk. paper). -- ISBN 0-7914-3460-5 (pbk.
    : alk. paper)
        1. Women--Philosophy.   2. Postmodernism.   I. Title.   II. Series.
    BD450.P6127   1997
    305.4'01--dc20                                      96-43583
                                                        CIP

10  9  8  7  6  5  4  3  2  1

# C o n t e n t s

# Acknowledgments

Writing this book has, in many ways, been both an exercise in patience and a continually startling reawakening to the generosity of others. Eight years ago, I decided somewhat precipitously that I had a book to write—the intervening years have shown me exactly what lies between the evocative certainty of having the kernel of an idea and the laborious (and repetitive) process of allowing it to take shape on the page. Most of that time was spent without academic affiliation, but still in sustained academic work, a contradiction that makes it necessary for me to thank a number of people for either financial or intellectual support, and sometimes both. I have bounced back and forth between Houston, Bhopal, Mexico City, and Chicago, trying to find some way of honestly encountering the diversity of those situations (sometimes as student, sometimes as teacher, other times just as a writer); this book, with its multiple trajectories and frequently violent juxtapositions, is the record, in many senses, of those bouncings.

It's somewhat tempting, then, to thank everyone who helped me in any way during those times. Instead, I will limit myself to thanking only those people who in one way or another helped directly with the writing of the book. In alphabetical order, then, I would like to thank Steven Crowell, Andrew Cutrofello, Carol Denson, Charles Denson, Margie Denson and Scott Denson, David Mikics, Jane Price, Monty Price, and Stephen Streiffer.

In addition, I am grateful to the following publishers and/or authors for permission to reprint from their works:

Hans Blumenberg, *The Legitimacy of the Modern Age*. (R. Wallace, trans.). © 1983 by MIT Press. Reprinted by permission of MIT Press.

Jacques Derrida, *Margins of Philosophy*. (A. Bass, trans.). © 1982 by the University of Chicago. This work was published in Paris under the title *Marges de la philosophie*, © 1972, by Les Editions de Minuit. Reprinted by permission of the University of Chicago.

Jacques Derrida, *Specters of Marx*. (P. Kamuf, trans.). © 1994 by Routledge. Reprinted by permission of Routledge.

Jacques Derrida, *Writing and Difference*. (A. Bass, trans.). © 1978 by the University of Chicago. Reprinted by permission of the University of Chicago.

René Girard, *The Scapegoat*. (Y. Freccero, trans.). © 1986. Reprinted by permission of the Johns Hopkins University Press.

Jorie Graham, *Hybrids of Plants and Ghost*. © 1980 by PUP. Reprinted by permission of Princeton University Press.

H. D., *Collected Poems*. 1912–1944. © 1982 by the Estate of Hilda Doolittle. Reprinted by permission of New Directions Publishing Corporation.

Jürgen Habermas, *The Philosophical Discourse of Modernity*. (F. Lawrence, trans.). © 1987 by MIT Press. Reprinted by permission of MIT Press.

Jürgen Habermas, *The Theory of Communicative Action,* vol. 1. (T. McCarthy, trans.). © 1987 by Beacon Press. Reprinted by permission of Beacon Press.

© Oxford University Press 1977. Reprinted from Hegel's *Phenomenology of Spirit* translated by A. V. Miller (1977) by permission of Oxford University Press.

Margaret Homans, *Bearing the Word*. © 1986 by the University of Chicago. Reprinted by permission of the University of Chicago.

Luce Irigaray, *Speculum of the Other Woman*. (G. Gill, trans.). © 1985 by Cornell University Press. Reprinted by permission of Cornell University Press.

Reprinted by permission of Farrar, Strauss & Giroux, Inc., for the United States, its dependencies, the Philippines and Canada and the open market throughout the world excluding the United Kingdom and British Commonwealth, and by permission of Faber and Faber Ltd., for the United Kingdom and British Commonwealth:

Excerpts from "The Sphinx's Riddle" from *The Complete Poems* by Randall Jarrell. © 1969 by Mrs. Randall Jarrell.

Excerpts from "Midsummer, Tobago" from *Collected Poems* 1948–1984 by Derek Walcott. © 1986 by Derek Walcott.

From *Écrits: A Selection* by Jacques Lacan, translated by Alan Sheridan. © 1966 by Editions du Seuil. English translation © 1977 by Tavistock Publications. Reprinted by permission of W. W. Norton & Company, Inc.

From *The Four Fundamental Concepts of Psycho-Analysis* by Jacques Lacan, translated by Alan Sheridan. © 1973 by Editions du Seuil. English translation © 1977 by Alan Sheridan. Reprinted by permission of W. W. Norton & Company, Inc.

From *Typography* by Philippe Lacoue-Labarthe, translated by R. Eisenhauer. © 1989 by the President and Fellows of Harvard College. Reprinted by permission of Harvard University Press.

"Revenant," from *Clamor* by Ann Lauterbach. © 1991 by Ann Lauterbach. Used by permission of Viking Penguin, a division of Penguin Books USA Inc.

Emmanuel Levinas, *Collected Philosophical Papers*. (A. Lingis, trans.). © 1987 by Martinus Nijhoff Publishers, Dordrecht. Reprinted by permission of Martinus Nijhoff Publishers.

Emmanuel Levinas, *Otherwise than Being*. (A. Lingis, trans.). © 1981 by Martinus Nijhoff Publishers, The Hague. Reprinted by permission of Martinus Nijhoff Publishers.

Emmanuel Levinas, *Time and the Other*. (R. Cohen, trans.). © Duquesne University Press, 1987. Reprinted by permission of Duquesne University Press.

Emmanuel Levinas, *Totality and Infinity*. (A. Lingis, trans.). © Duquesne University Press, 1969. Reprinted by permission of Duquesne University Press.

Claude Lévi-Strauss, *The Elementary Structures of Kinship*. (J. Bell and J. von Sturmer, trans.). (R. Needham, ed.). © 1969 by Beacon Press. Reprinted by permission of Beacon Press.

Jean-François Lyotard, *The Lyotard Reader*. (A. Benjamin, ed.). © 1989 by Basil Blackwell. Reprinted by permission of Basil Blackwell.

Martha C. Nussbaum, *The Fragility of Goodness*. © Cambridge University Press, 1986. Reprinted by permission of Cambridge University Press.

Ezra Pound, *The Cantos of Ezra Pound*. © 1948 by Ezra Pound. Reprinted by permission of New Directions Publishing Corporation.

Paul Ricoeur, *Freud and Philosophy*. (D. Savage, trans.). Copyright © 1970 by Yale University Press. Reprinted by permission of Yale University Press.

Reiner Schürmann, *Heidegger on Being and Acting: From Principles to Anarchy*. (C. M. Gros, trans.). © 1987 by Indiana University Press. Reprinted by permission of Indiana University Press.

Poems written by Walt Whitman. Excerpted from *Complete Poetry and Selected Prose of Walt Whitman* edited by J. Miller. © 1959 by Houghton Mifflin Company.

# Introduction—Regarding Silence

*Waxing in confrontation with the matter itself,*
*we must become capable of the capable word.*

—*Heidegger,* Nietzsche

Why write? Why read? Before we ever get to ask such questions, we are already inextricably bound up in the textuality of our society. Contemporary illiterates are in a strange position of power because of this—at least so the story goes. Completely marginalized, only they can see the entirety of the structures of literacy, of the exclusions and violences perpetrated in the name of the legitimacy of literacy. This is a true account of our present social and epistemological thinking concerning the marginalized, but there is something specious about it. Ask a group of illiterates about writing and they will tell you that writing is precisely what they don't know.

Do I write, then, to teach people how to write? Do I presume to rectify the ills of literate violence from within? Simply put, I don't (can't) go that far. My goal is, merely, to provide the space for all of us to ask of our writing—and of our reading—that it have a reason. Accordingly, I would want to provide a theory of meaningful life, a reason for going to school, for learning to write, that extends beyond the parental command.

I write, it seems, out of a failure to speak. My spoken words have not done justice to the ideas they represent—not because of a failure of vocabulary, but because of a failure of representation. I write not of a result but of a possibility—allegorically, it's the possibility of new ways of learning how to read, but I am not content with metaphors. This restlessness itself is the reason to write.

Take as a marker of my indecisiveness Zora Neale Hurston's *Their Eyes Were Watching God*, a short book, easy to read, with no stylistic gymnastics. The dramatic action culminates in a trial scene where the central character, a black woman named Janie, has been charged with murder. This accusation seems a rather accidental fact to the accused—she does not feel herself to be guilty and therefore fears no retribution. The reader shares her dismay; the whole idea of the trial is unbelievable. She is, however, passionately, desperately, believably, involved in the effort to speak.

Janie had married three times, and Hurston uses these marriages to speak of a woman's search for meaning in life—a meaning that cannot be reduced to the roles she plays. Only the last marriage, the life of an itinerant farm hand, provides the meaning she had been searching for; yet, explicitly, this meaning arises from the absence of the typical structures associated with meaning. All that Janie wanted to convey to the court was the fact of having led a meaningful life. But people don't say such things in a court of law. Where do they speak? Is there political or legal recourse for people who have been denied meaning? What could Janie, who had no complaints, possibly want of the people in the courtroom? There is no aphorism, no result, at the end of Hurston's book. The power of her answering comes from this failure to speak. But this failure comes at the end of a book, at the end of a writing. In the end, it respects a silence.[1] As a writing, it generates its own silences. It succeeds in its failures.

Other commentators approaching Hurston's book would look in other directions:

1. But it is also the case that the matter of thinking is not achieved in the fact that talk about the "truth of Being" and the "history of Being" is set in motion. Everything depends on this alone, that the truth of Being come to language and that thinking attain to this language. Perhaps, then, language requires much less precipitous expression than proper silence. But who of us today would want to imagine that his attempts to think are at home on the path of silence? At best, thinking could perhaps point toward the truth of Being, and indeed toward it as what is to be thought. It would thus be more easily weaned from mere supposing and opining and directed to the now rare handicraft of writing. Things that really matter, although they are not defined for all eternity, even when they come very late, still come at the right time. (Heidegger, "Letter on Humanism" [1947], *Basic Writings*, p. 223)

Full bibliographic information regarding all the citations in this book can be found at the back.

Trying to talk the poor into believing they are happy right where they are is only a way of subverting the revolutionary possibility of the working classes. Or, further and analogously, the literary model of finding happiness in marriage merely reinforces the old stereotypes of a woman's destiny lying in the home. Love, for bourgeois and revolutionary, is inherently conservative by these lights, even unpolitical.

Class (and race) analyses such as these always presuppose that the political destiny of women lies with their husbands, lies with the publicly defined roles typical of one style of life or another. To think of the political destiny of women, of women before they are anything else, is precisely the possibility of thinking a politics that is neither based on class conflict nor class oppression, that is neither bourgeois nor revolutionary—not revolutionary because it is not satisfied with the half steps of revolution—with the mere redistribution of possessions or power; I am intent, instead, on thinking through those very relations to possessions and power which have made revolutions thinkable/necessary. Yet I'm not even claiming to free society of gender or gender-based biases; I'm not addressing the *problem* of women. Woman's place is exactly the question we are trying not to have to ask: places and roles are the current paradigms for theorizing personal identity; postmodernism, at its best, when it is least of all merely "after" modernism, starts somewhere else. Which is not to say that we must ever remain silent about the oppressions suffered by real women in real places; this book, instead, is about how to start such questioning without presupposing an answer. Without presupposing that woman's current place is the problem and another place for woman is the answer. It is in this sense, perhaps, that this book is not *about* women at all.

A modernist feminism might say that feminine love is a contextualized, caring type of knowing instead of the isolated and abstract knowledge of science. Accordingly, the feminine is a solution. Just as the masculine has been advanced as a solution. Supposedly, masculine and feminine are provisional technologies, to be taken up or discarded by either gender—although, as with literacy, the individual may not *experience* a moment of choice. On the other hand, the knowledge that divides choices from experience, that refuses the model of justifying choices in terms of experience, that questions whether experience is to be the referent and measure of all truth, would be precisely that type of knowing which doesn't ignore class antagonism or gender violence, would be precisely that type of knowing which would not settle for lifting all women, all others, up to the status of the white, bourgeois male, all vacuously the same. To speak, to give voice at such a court, would be to assume the role of the white male lawyer representing the black woman's plight to other white, educated males.

Writing, embodying the various functions of the author in our society, presumedly carries the full presence of voice to an audience. Hurston's writing, Janie's trial, carries—without sorrow or nostalgia—the failure of voice to an audience used only to hearing what has been directed at it. Used to hearing only the facts of experience—of that experience which humanity is said to share. Hurston's writing becomes, in a way that is not easily translatable into polling booths, political, even revolutionary. The political here represents the death of a monarchy and not the son's ascendency to the throne. A diffuse authority, an inclusive theory of meaning in reading—a reading which can hear and respect Janie's silence—translates into the possibility of efficacious political activity based on neither individual nor national greed—an activity postmodern in that it strives after ends outside itself, acquiescent in the face of the other, of the beloved. An activity that is nothing but this acquiescence; an acquiescence which calls forth all the powers of our thought. Allegorically (that is, untruthfully), the father's voice no longer dominates the family; the familiar—conservation and possession—no longer dominates politics.

What does this heirless death of authority imply? That Janie—and Hurston—will be caught, unable to speak or defend or attack, and yet go free—alive in an almost infinite moment of undecideability, of being read and reread, again and for the first time. For my *polemical* purposes, we are taking Hurston as an example of that which cannot be simply appropriated. I wish to position myself in the space of literature—that is, in the space where spatiality and positions are themselves merely fictions. I wish to put forth a style which affirms, which aligns my writing within a tradition, orchestrating the possibility of a reception among those who share that tradition. But, within that reception will be found silences that the text itself can't support: silences that did not arise from the failure of alignments, from the overdetermination of subject-positions or the indetermination of words. Rather, like the use of any word, I will take a few of these overdetermined words from our tradition (like woman, or God), and use them to begin to speak (of/from/against) the tradition. The goal of my speaking is not the speaking, but rather the silences (which cannot serve as ends in themselves). My purpose is not to hear myself speak (to recognize the meaning of my life as arising from the role I have played out); but to speak towards a silence, towards a meaning that is not dependent on my previous understanding of a system of typifications. Such would be the ethics of speaking to another who comes without need of explanation, without being able to justify herself to me.

Recognizing the interplay of social, political, and philosophical in the experience of a life, one wishes to speak of life itself as the product of that play. Fiction, supposedly, expresses the sense, or meaningfulness, of that interplay. In disagreeing with that definition of fiction, I'm also arguing with the received understanding of what it means to use a word. The essence, or meaning, of a word does not come from its use within my experience (this I will be arguing for throughout the book) but from the silences always within the audience to whom I write. Postmodernism's rejection of meaning, accordingly, need not be the abnegation of the responsibility to speak; rather, it is the call not to merely speak to oneself. This, I realize, goes against the dominant understanding of postmodernism, but postmodernism, too, should be taken as one of the terms from our tradition which, although overdetermined, is still possible to use when we need to begin, when it becomes necessary (and it is always necessary) to provide the space from within which the other of tradition—that which doesn't ceaselessly refer to its own tradition—may arise, always as if for the first time. In this way my writing will, of necessity and incessantly, skirt an essentialism that stems from the necessity of referring to a tradition. When we speak, there are no first times; there are only the habits acquired through learning a language. When we begin, there are no traditions; there are only the silences that an essentially metaphorical use of language depends on and leaves behind.

Writing, when it plays with an essentialism already found within the trajectories of a tradition, references that tradition so that it can be heard as meaningful. Yet, when it is new, it has stopped being the habit that makes understanding complete and scientific; when it is new, it is because the writing has reached towards a silence within (or as possibility, other than) the articulated tradition. We do not speak of a previously unspoken fact in need of articulation, but of the bases of articulation in that which is spoken towards and not about—and here I would mark the inadequacy of the term metaphorical. The silence that a metaphor brushes up against is the silence a science of reference would deny at all costs. This not even denotable, merely literary, or metaphorical space isn't the silence of a mind ready to hear, nor of a space already prepared for time to happen to it; instead, it is the very obligation to speak which we always find to have been silent. At the same time, the silence of this obligation is all that enables us to escape the domination of words already spoken; the silence of obligation alone grants the possibility of the new.

The newness of this writing ensures that it cannot find an audience already ready for action. The political ramifications of postmodernism, as with radical feminism, are not to be sought at elections—they are found, politically, outside of the realms of representation, after the death of the author, after the end of the tyranny of great men. To abandon the discourse of the sane self, monadic and virile, is rigorous sanity. Such a writing questions the technologies of inscription and alphabet, writes without control. To phrase this questioning, in a writing more polemical—less regardfully silent—than Hurston's, is the somewhat contradictory goal of the present effort.

# Iphigenia and Other Elisions

> *. . . And hither am I come,*
> *A Prologue arm'd, but not in confidence*
> *Of author's pen or actor's voice, but suited*
> *In like conditions as our argument,*
> *To tell you, fair beholders, that our play*
> *Leaps over the vaunt and firstlings of those*
> *broils,*
> *Beginning in the middle, starting thence away*
> *To what may be digested in a play.*
> *Like, or find fault: do as your pleasures are:*
> *Now good, or bad, 'tis but the chance of war.*
>
> —*Shakespeare,*
> Troilus and Cressida

We fight wars on poverty, on drugs, against communism, against capitalism, for our daily bread. We fight for our right to be heard in the various forums of the world. Even our intimate relations seem dominated by the metaphors and facts of war: we are called to fight against codependency, children turn in their parents for smoking pot, and war after war pits actual or figurative siblings against each other. No life remains untouched; all deaths are wasted. Metaphorically, we belong to a motherland or fatherland so that we might constitute a family ready for war: children who will reflect the will of the patriarchs. The son and the father are tied together—allegorically and in reality—by the suppositions and facts of war, of a competition of man against man, family against family, nation against nation. This is true both insofar as we consider the family every man's private haven held apart from the public world and in the way that we constitute the forces of good and evil, spiritual and fleshly, God and Devil. Christ the Son, for a privileged example, is thus construed as the culmination of the law of the Father: not the birth of something new, but the bringing into becoming, into time, of the eternal. God the True Being is something hidden made manifest only through the coming of Christ, made true only through the violence of crucifixion. God's externalization in Hegel, the creation of gods in Nietzsche, the creation of mortals (the loss of immortality) in *Paradise Lost*, are all seen, through the Patriarch's eyes, as products of war itself—in fact, all existence blends into the same war-time production: the very world is a product which expresses the internal (the manifestation of truth; the product of the forming powers or universal structures of consciousness), an internal created by the conditions of the external world (consciousness as reflection of, or combatant in, experience).

This mediation of outside and inside is man's first bow to the necessary existence of women (and the first tear in the fabric of war/production's self-interpretation). The individual must pass between the sperm of one generation and the actual fact of the next—without, if all goes well, polluting the pure intention of the father's ejaculation. Here the dialectic, the interdependence, of inner and outer mirrors the philosophical conflict of freedom and necessity, human volition and destiny, particular and universal, part and whole: all dialectical oppositions, all cast as war. The place, the locus or battlefield, has come to be identified as the human subject. Perhaps postmodernism, in so far as it is identified with the decentered subject, is the attempt to think after the wars: though we cannot (and would not want to) say war never happened, it remains to ask if it represents the true, to ask if violence is to be our future as well as our past.

Thought invokes a memory of wars, but—in a utopic world of nonviolence—it might as easily have been the memory, the songs, of the vanquished as of the victor. Postmodern thought opens up the possibility of thinking yet a different appointment of time, without a tyrannical past, without the weight of previous battles. Meaning, having meaning, is the way human life defines itself—it is the technology humanity uses to capture the multiplicity of experience. However, only within the system defined by this technology is all truth exhausted in meaning, all meaning completed in truth. For example, for most of us, death is merely the opposite condition to life, that is, meaninglessness. If a previously spoken word continues to be used by us in our appropriation of a tradition, we tend to say that it is still alive for us—the dead, when they were great creative authors, continue to inhabit our present speaking. This book, instead of questioning the life that continues in a tradition of words appropriated, questions the meaning of death that continues and death that inhabits—especially as it is not appropriated. I will argue that tradition, even the very use of words (which always in itself approaches a certain essentialism), is neither dead nor alive. The word does not bear a violence of itself, the death is always silent, the violence always already a referencing towards a silence—called violent to the extent that it wishes to enforce that silence. The style I am advocating, eschewing the technological faith in the sufficient word, is to accentuate the silence of a death: in this case, the metaphorical (but not inconsequential) death of a woman. Thus, in the particular example with which I am beginning, I am asking of the manner of enunciating the universal in the act of denotation, of asking what it means to take a particular woman and say, "This." To take a sacrificial virgin and say, "Let her death signify our devotion, let her death be our life." Accordingly, we look to the often forgotten beginning of modern warfare: the Greek Agamemnon, chained to harbor before unfavorable winds, sacrifices his daughter, Iphigenia, to the gods—all in return for a quick voyage to Troy.[2] Other strategies are available; it is merely my timidity that causes me to start with war, looking for peace.

Iphigenia's sacrifice can be seen, among the many literary and polemical uses it can fulfill, as merely a metaphor for the various acts of exclusion committed in the name of masculine projects. Her name remains in this function, but I find there is more to her death as well—just as there is more to sexism than the domination of the masculine pronoun and unequal pay; they are symptoms and not causes, however much they may contribute to the reproduction of the cause itself. We are asking if a name—or a metaphor or an allegory—can do other than serve an end, can be other than a nodal point within some exterior economy. What is at stake is a signification that neither signifies nor falls on deaf ears. Not a Sade-like attempt to offend your undoubtedly bourgeois sensibilities, not Breton's pistol shot into the crowd: I do not force you to come to some new, enlightened resolution of contradictory positions. No synthesis is necessary, no understanding. No recognition of self or other. Something more like forgiving—but such words sound banal to the modern ear.

2. Some Greek hero is cheated
And your mother's court
Of its bride.

And we ask this—where truth
is,
Of what use is valour and is
worth?
For evil has conquered the
race,
There is no power but in base
men,
Nor any man whom the gods
do not hate.

(H.D., trans., "From the *Iphigenia of Aulis* in Euripides," in *Collected Poems 1912–1944*, pp. 80–81)

Perhaps all the more reason to speak them again, to begin—with them—again.

If one takes the eye of a god, all things stand in relation, all things have their reason and meaning, are either right or wrong. Instead, as mortals, there are some things we merely forgive, without reason. Allegorically, and this is a surprisingly hard position to maintain philosophically, I'm merely saying that Iphigenia was more alive, held more of whatever value we associate with life, before she was sacrificed to the greater causes of Greek glory. Unallegorically, we question how many deaths are acceptable to ensure the smooth operations of industrial plants, how many of a nation's children should die for the nation's sovereignty.

Martha Nussbaum, in *The Fragility of Goodness*, uses the sacrifice of Iphigenia in Aeschylus's *Agamemnon* (along with the death of Antigone in Sophocles' Theban trilogy) to outline a complicated (and complicating) view of death and value in Attic Greece. The play finds Agamemnon in a bind of responsibilities (he is finite in face of the infinity of his responsibilities). Nussbaum poses the question of whether the contingent fact that another obligation supersedes the first may serve to release a moral actor from the bonds of ethical relations:

> A duty not to kill is a duty in all circumstances. Why should this circumstance of conflict make it cease to be a duty? But if a law is broken, there has to be a condemnation and a punishment. That is what it means to take the law seriously, to take one's own autonomy seriously. Kant's view [that all conflicts of interest can be decided in favor of a single duty] does, ironically, just what Kant wishes it to avoid: it gives mere chance the power to remove an agent from the binding authority of the moral law. We can claim to be following a part of the deep motivation behind Kant's own view of duty when we insist that duty does not go away because of the world's contingent interventions. Greek polytheism, surprisingly, articulates a certain element of Kantian morality better than any monotheistic creed could: namely it insists upon the supreme and binding authority, the divinity so to speak, of *each* ethical obligation, in all circumstances whatever, including those in which the gods themselves collide.
>
> Aeschylus, then, shows us not so much a 'solution' to the 'problem of practical conflict' as the richness and depth of the problem itself. (This achievement is closely connected with his poetic resources, which put the scene vividly before us, show us debate about it, and evoke in us responses important to its assessment.)(p. 49)[3]

In short, the form of the play has outdone the philosophical form of the resolution: it has posed a question and not posited an answer to some previously articulated question. This is the ethical advantage of the artistic representation over the philosophical reserve (although it doesn't exhaust the distinction). The tragedy causes us (the viewers) to ask a hard question, without taking away the responsibility for answering. The structural doubling and tripling I merely gesture at here—life and death, freedom and necessity, subject and object, poetry and reason (all understood as structural and structuring moments)—would be the nexus of any writing, whether art, philosophy, polemic, or technology. It is a well-known oddity that in an artistically crafted dialogue Plato proposed throwing the poets out of the ideal city. Nussbaum, on the other side of written history, writes a logically coherent book of philosophy (partly) for the purpose of freeing the poets to their truth-finding mission. We can't ignore the division between stylistic means and projectural goals; this division is the call to self-consciousness itself—the urgency of understanding how we think of the 'what' of knowledge.

Self-consciousness is knowing that we know—knowing that not only do we see, we are seen: active and passive. Hegel saw this far but conceived of passivity as only the silent counterpart to the active: the slave who recognizes, and glorifies, the master. Against Hegel, becoming aware of the contents and structure of passivity, and not just the contents of our activity, is the first step towards a new type of moral order. All ethical decisions are begun, as the Old Testament points out, when God says, 'Hear me, O Israel!' Unable to stop their ears, the chosen have heard. The kerygmatic voice, the voice that commands from elsewhere, unattainable,

3. For Nussbaum, as she continues, both the solution and the problem still belong to the region of words and the appropriateness of their judgments:

> Voicing no blame of the prophet or his terrible message, Agamemnon now begins to cooperate inwardly with necessity, arranging his feelings to accord with his fortune. From the moment he makes his decision, itself the best he could have made, he strangely turns himself into a collaborator, a willing victim. Once he had stated the alternatives and announced his decision, Agamemnon might have been expected to say something like, "This horrible course is what divine necessity requires, though I embark on it with pain and revulsion." What he actually says is very different: "For it is right and holy (*themis*) that I should desire with exceedingly impassioned passion the sacrifice staying the winds, the maiden's blood. May all turn out well" (214–17). We notice two points in this strange and appalling utterance. First, his attitude towards the decision itself seems to have changed with the making of it. From the acknowledgement that a heavy doom awaits him either way, and that either alternative involves wrongdoing, he has moved to a peculiar optimism: if he has chosen the *better* course, all may yet turn out well. (*The Fragility of Goodness* [1986], p. 35)

The irony that sustains the

movement I am writing lies in denying both answers—the outward certainty Agamemnon conforms himself to and the inward certainty Nussbaum calls for Agamemnon to maintain—in favor of a delaying tactic, of questioning the necessity of her death. Such a questioning of course, requires both a new theory of the necessary within sociohistorical contexts and, in what Heidegger has shown is the same problem, a new theory of the question.

determines the structure of passivity. The particular content is a question of historical, or critical, ontology. Philosophy, for the most part, hasn't taken notice of this passivity—the bare fact of our consciousness—as a call of obligation. The function of this book is to show obligation as obligation—an obligation to question the function and activity of showing (of bringing meaning to presence, mine or the other's).

Marx used the Hegelian framework, the Hegelian conception of world history and transhistorically active forces, to structure a systematic critique of the world's progress. Any destruction of the precepts of metaphysics—of activity, presence, recognition, world history—has to accept the loss of the tool Marxist analysis provides. The various attempts to recoup this technology for the forces of good have either returned to one of the individualistic grounds of traditional philosophy or ignored the strength of the philosophical destruction of metaphysics by invoking some sort of pragmatism. Those convinced by the destroyers have turned to a glib insistence on absolute indeterminacy. This book, instead, by turning to the place (or better: the 'how') of obligation, to the figure of passivity and woman, repositions what used to be called the acting subject—strips him of his virility, of the masculine pronoun—such that old questions, questions of social justice, distributive economics, meaningful personal relationships, can be asked again without presupposing the patriarchal answer, without assuming that truth is possession, that possession is inheritance.

Accordingly, I have both a concrete purpose and a diffuse, overdetermined means, like any writer of allegories. Thus will I ask to be read like a fiction and not as the truth. I will not write the result of previous thinking (its truth measured by its adequacy to the matter to be thought). Not that I have hidden what is plain to see or dressed up an ugly truth, but that our truths are no longer simply monistic; you (singular) cannot come to the text with an expectation of exchange, of spending time in return for results, or maxims, possessed. In fact, insofar as you may want to understand, the text must require that you come to it as a host. You must welcome it and all those whom the text carries. You (plural) are multitudes, even as you (singular) sit alone, and you must come all together, satisfied merely to sit with a friend in a moment of enjoyment. Still, you will know that essential things were not touched, perhaps not even guessed at. Even your closest friends and lovers are other than you; that is simplest common knowledge. So much more so the actors on the stage or the words of a book. Correspondingly, I do not present a vocabulary to be adopted. I use 'truth', for example, in at least three recognizably different ways: all of them familiar to the average speaker. You may be able to trace my concepts of 'truth' back to supposed singularities in master texts, but that will cheat thinking with a catalogue of thoughts. Rather, try not to think too far behind the words: there is a certain surface you are being asked to see. Similarly, the death of a woman, the metaphor I am presenting here, is neither normative nor strictly descriptive. You are not being asked to judge whether my intentions are honorable, whether my words adequately represent the truth of 'woman'—exactly because I do not wish to refer to something other than

4. And, of course, the structure of presentation (insofar as it implicates the *structure* of addressing, of being addressed, of writing for an audience or being in the audience of a writing) is what the metaphor of the literary/metaphorical itself contests and reinstates. But the question is not exactly new:

> Icons—the Christ in triumph in the vault at Daphnis or the admirable Byzantine mozaics—undoubtedly have the effect of holding us under their gaze. We might stop there, but were we to do so we would not really grasp the motive that made the painter set about making this icon, or the motive it satisfies in being presented to us. It is something to do with the gaze, of course, but there is more to it than that. What makes the value of the icon is that the god it represents is also looking at it. It is intended to please God. At this level, the artist is operating on the sacrificial plane—he is playing with those things, in this case images, that may arouse the desire of God. (Lacan, *The Four Fundamental Concepts of Psycho-Analysis* [1973], p. 113)

5. This translation is from Nussbaum, *The Fragility of Goodness* (1986), pp. 36–37.

6. *The gaze is at stake from the outset.* Don't forget, in fact, what "castration," or the knowledge of castration, owes to the gaze, at least for Freud. The gaze has always been involved. Now the little girl, the woman, supposedly has *nothing* you

can see. She exposes, exhibits the possibility of a *nothing to see.* Or at any rate she shows nothing that is penis-shaped or could substitute for a penis. This is the odd, the uncanny thing, as far as the eye can see, this nothing around which lingers in horror, now and forever, an overcathexis of the eye, of appropriation by the gaze, and of the *phallomorphic* sexual metaphors, its reassuring accomplices. (Irigaray, *Speculum of the Other Woman* [1974], p. 47)

7. Because human intuition as finite "takes in stride" and because the possibility of a "receiving" which takes-in-stride [*eines hinnehmenden "Bekommens"*] requires affection, therefore organs of affection, "the senses," are in fact necessary. Human intuition, then, is not "sensible" because its affection takes place through "sense organs," but rather the reverse. Because our Dasein is finite—existing in the midst of beings that already are, beings to which it has been delivered over—therefore it must necessarily take this already-existing being in stride, that is to say, it must offer it the possibility of announcing itself. Organs are necessary for the possible relaying of the announcement. The essence of sensibility exists in the finitude of intuition. The organs that serve affection are thus sense organs because they belong to finite intuition, i.e., sensibility. (Heidegger, *Kant and the Problem of Metaphysics* [1929], p. 18)

my own saying, and its (possible) reception, in its own time; exactly to the extent that I write—by presenting it again, by writing my doubts within it—from a tradition of speaking about women which has both determined the trajectories of our 'real' experience and is open to literary and political interventions. To what extent is it 'open'? To the extent that its presentation already depends on the space of a questioning—a space which is perhaps best thought not as a vacuum, but as a propensity for the literary which makes being in an audience a (possibly) communal experience. We sit together, turning our attention to the complex priorities of questions over answers and the location (or the time?) of the responsibility for an answer—and I, the organizer of the event, offer to you: a screen.[4]

Silently the screen plays a ritual sacrifice—father slays daughter; no priest holds the blade—while the Shakespearean prologue (in my epilogue to this section) tells us we have skipped a few things. She is lifted into the air, her voice stifled "by the force and voiceless power of the bridle" (l.238–39). You, of the audience, will undoubtedly want to speak for her, but you do not know what claim can be made for her. If she lives, and this we are sure of, all the Greek men must die and (more importantly) the expedition to avenge Paris's crime against hospitality will fail. (Agamemnon has a choice but the decision is clear. Let him be demagogue or snivelling coward: the decision is still clear.) The gods have spoken with thunderous voice and no other claimant will be heard. Instead, as Shakespeare's prologue continues, invoking our duty as audience/judges, we see, inscribed on the sacrificial screen, the distanced, unvoiced words of

Aeschylus's chorus:

> Her Saffron robes streaming to the ground,
> she shot each of the sacrificers with a pitiful arrow from her eye,
> standing out as in a picture,
> wanting to speak to them by name—
> for often in her father's halls, at the rich feasts given for men,
> she had sung, and, virginal, with pure voice,
> at the third libation, had lovingly honored
> her loving father's paean of good fortune.
>
> $(239-44)$[5]

Close-up: the darting arrows of her eyes[6]—individual, individuating. The knife will be offered to you, and one of you might say, "No, let her live, I have never enjoyed the unfettered hospitality of the Mediterranean, I have no stake in her death." But you say the 'is' of a universal, you praise the laws of the this and now. We cannot close our eyes to the fact of war. Accepting the obligation of our passivity may not require us to take up the knife, but we must—at least—keep our eyes open. We are all living destinies, results of others' decisions, which precede us; it takes more than a lifetime to live a destiny: a destiny consummated in the moment over and over again. And the truth lies here (although the truth is not what we are seeking). We are, in every instant, always already read. And we are always already reading. We are constituted as same—as a community of sorts—before you start, before I start, as if you had finished, exactly in so far as you had given yourself over to being in an audience, exactly insofar as you had given up the pretension of 'having' a destiny. 'Hear me', a voice said, and we could not help but hear.

Small circles of rephrasing the question, stranding the answering. The time of our questions—and this says as much as any sentence in this book—is neither simultaneous nor linear, in precisely the same fashion that an object is neither form nor content; they are given in time, as time, with past, present, future, part, and whole. For the rest of the book, as far as we are capable of holding ourselves within the 'matter itself', this one picture, all that I will speak to, and more, will fill the screen. The book stands within the emblem—and yet there is no representation, no icon, to consume. The book stands within the viewing itself—without a subject's eyes yet claiming the scene (or determining its meaning).[7] To speak metaphorically of the metaphor is to approach not speaking at all; to continue to speak in the approach of that nothingness is to question the falling of the sacrificial knife.

# A Woman's Death

*I read this and I tell myself how terrible it is
that we spend precious months of our
existence trying to give 'proofs,' falling into
the trap of critical interpellation, allowing
ourselves to be led before the tribunal where
we are told: give us proof, explain to us what
feminine writing or sexual difference is. And
if we were more courageous than I am, we
would say: a flute for your proof, I am alive.
I am not serene enough, except when I write.
And when I write I tell myself that it is not
enough, we need to do something else.
However, it is true that the truest is like this:
either you know without knowing, and this
knowledge which does not know is a flash of
joy which the other shares with you, or else
there is nothing. We will never convert
someone who is not already converted. We
will never touch the heart that lives on
another planet. I would no longer continue
with my seminar if I knew that a sufficiently
wide world was reading Clarice Lispector. A
few years ago, when her texts began to
circulate here, I said to myself, I am no
longer going to give a seminar, all that is left
to do is to read her, everything is said, it is
perfect. But as usual everything has been
repressed, she has even been transformed in
the most extraordinary way, they have
embalmed her, had her stuffed as a Brazilian
bourgeois with varnished fingernails. So I
carry on my vigil, accompanying her through
my vigil.*

—Cixous, "Extreme Fidelities,"
Writing Differences

I t will serve well to briefly point to the breadth of the problem of judgment
and impartiality. It has long been argued that there is no outside from which
one judges truly dispassionately—for example, Nietzsche sees that to judge,

or think in any way, without interest is not to think at all.[8] This claim has been taken to extremes unsupported by the nature of the arguments: it is, to begin with, a misconception of the nature of existence and language to invoke a reified private (and therefore irreproachable) belief.[9] What is interesting to me here as a starting point is how often these questions of true and moral judgment revert to a question of women; my answer, eventually, will have to come down to the problem of how to speak of women, of the powerful history of that speaking, without avoiding speaking to the actually living women who may take up this book to read. The *locus classicus* of this avoidance, insofar as it is later taken up into the philosophical tradition in ways that are no longer simply sexist, is Kant's *Critique of Judgment* where the truth of the universal aesthetic judgment can only be decided in the absence of desire, in the distancing of the self from the meaning, or interest, of the words: where, accordingly, the beautiful woman is excluded from the world of pragmatic activity (and activity's necessary precursor, desire) so that her beauty may remain an unsullied object of contemplation, an escape from the trials and tribulations of man's true activity. Kantians may respond that Kant himself specifically thinks treating a human as an object is immoral. The problem is that this is a rule for regulating public life while private life (the individual in *his* preexisting mode of belief, if not in his particular beliefs) becomes correspondingly unassailable precisely where the freedom of separation that establishes critique as a possibility of thought is the freedom to separate oneself

8. That Nietzsche sees judgment as necessarily an act of violence is one of the central features of his thought and a locus of considerable argument. One is often tempted to see Nietzsche as the founder of an absolute relativism which cannot even comment on (make moral judgments about) its own activity. Mark Warren, in *Nietzsche and Political Thought* (1988), argues far more convincingly that Nietzsche's genealogy is not "Nietzsche's alternative to ontology" (p. 103) but that will to power is best seen as a "critical ontology of practice" (Warren's chapter 4). Warren exemplifies the difference: "Where Kant gives the necessary conditions of synthesizing objects, Nietzsche gives the necessary conditions of unifying agency" (p. 123). I think it is reasonable to see Nietzsche as standing in a particular line of thinkers, including Kant and Heidegger, who while minutely interested in the 'individual' have nothing to do with an idiosyncratic perspectivalism. This reading understands Nietzsche as in concert with the search for an understanding based on the concrete situation. However, and with this point we may be going beyond Nietzsche, the 'concrete' cannot be interpreted in advance—and especially not as the correlate of categories as broadly construed as 'life' or 'experience'. Experience and the life which claims to be its sum (either individual or communal) can only be thought after thinking the conditions for the possibility of the act of unification—conditions which are not transcendent of the act and its

enacted unifications. We are thus, however, at the space where the very language of "conditions for the possibility of" stops being usefully opposed, as structure, to the event. Speaking would be a violence, then, in so far as it unifies, and would be just only in accordance with the givens of that unification. The implicit (and unquestioned) sense of justice here, unnoticed by the vast majority of commentators, seems to me to be precisely what Heidegger is (appropriately) arguing against in his criticism of Nietzsche in "Nietzsche's Word: God is Dead" [and I will take this matter up, obliquely, later].

9. For the most famous example, "obeying a rule is a practice. . . . it is not possible to obey a rule privately" (Wittgenstein, *Philosophical Investigations*, [1945], #202). Levinas, whose response I will be following later, sees the other not as a guarantor of rule-guidedness (although it may, in fact, serve that end), but as being the very possibility of the obligation to speak (or think): what remains to be thought after Levinas, the question of Levinas's style or, more specifically, of his metaphors, is the problem of characterizing the speech which that obligation calls for. If it is merely a judgment, as *Totality and Infinity* implies, then existence would still culminate in (or call for) a set of descriptions. *Otherwise than Being*, however, much better explicates the fact that language, at its inception, is not a belief, but a patience. In this, although hardly a Nietzschean, Levinas too is searching

from the desired world of objects.[10] Woman becomes the aesthetic object *par excellence* in the cultural configuration which makes any passivity (as a correlate of activity) into an objectivity (the correlate of a production). That is, as conscious human being and complement of the male, woman becomes the figure for passivity understood as withdrawal from activity and not as the active separation of self from object that would make the rationality of the self superior to its desires—and we note first of all that this forced inactivity took on numerous guises, such as that classification of work which finds housework, and many other types of work to which women are socially relegated, not to be part of a nation's productive activity. In a reiteration of the classic configuration of religious salvation as escape from life, *she* becomes *the* figure for death. In the same iteration, desire for her, since all desire is understood as the will to reach a goal, becomes *the* figure for life—life understood as the will to death. It will take a while to sort out the full implications of these statements, especially to the extent that we will eventually be questioning the appropriateness of characterizing speech in terms of judgment; however, in the interest of beginning from where we find ourselves currently situated, I am going to begin with the question of how our thinking of passivity and activity, and of private and public, structures our thinking of gender.

Carol Gilligan's *In a Different Voice* is the literal chronicle of how a woman's moral and judicial decision-making process is different from a man's. Duration—the relation of the present to the eternal—is key here;

the typically male decision is based on the invocation of abstract eternal rights, reducing the moment to an infinitely small point on an infinitely large, abstractly uniform, line; the typically female decision is based on the existing state of affairs and its extended temporal implications. Here lies the man's difference between science and gossip, technology and narrative. Gilligan reflects the feminist appropriation of a particular side of recent arguments over the nature of knowledge—or, perhaps more appropriately, the reappropriation by a woman of a traditionally feminine way of knowing. Our task, as philosophers, is to think through the situation Gilligan presents without essentializing either the feminine or the traditional.

Sadly, one does not take such a book seriously as a work of philosophy (it is supposed to be sociology, psychology, or less, women's studies). This fact, self-referentially, refers (as supporting instance) to the reason and reasoning of her book and more broadly to the call for a different type of argumentation. It calls for argument which is no longer argument. No longer can we have, at least in the realm of moral decision making, thesis, antithesis, and synthesis—two litigants and a judge, two particular claims and a universal rule: knowledge is an intimate affair which requires considerations of shadings far more subtle than the black and white rules of formal logic. (Which, of course, no one believes in, but the point is to begin to question even its value as an ideal.) With such an invocation of the philosophical importance of Gilligan's work, however, I am not claiming that she has somehow already finished all philosophical questions for us;

for "the conditions for the possibility of unifying agency" (see my preceding note). The fact that he doesn't see these 'conditions' as themselves either powers or practices, instead seeing them in terms of their impotence and impracticality, provides the founding aporia of this book. Indeed, Levinas's distance from Kant, precisely here, points to a radical reconceptualization of the role of possibility in relation to actuality, a reconceptualization, I argue below, that grants us a thinking of ethics that extends beyond a mere respect for the other's existing truths and articulations as a subject.

10. The universality of the aesthetic judgment rests on the object's beauty apart from any subjectively determined concept; it becomes important to place the beautiful beyond the public world of a given culture to the extent that otherwise beauty cannot vouchsafe the transcendence of morality. The fact that ideal beauty (sec. 17) must rest with the human, and the human understood in his undetermined finality, completes the connection of beauty with the European ideal of the human (that is, the human seen as a separate individual who possesses qualities and faculties). This story would have to be greatly complicated by adding any of the various attempts to retrieve Kant from the history of a "bad reading" (and here I think especially of Heidegger's defense of Kant in the first volume of the Nietzsche books, based on his 1936–37 winter semester lecture course, *The Will*

to *Power as Art*). My critique of 'disinterestedness', although it will shift ground, is based very much on the possibilities of 'bad readings' becoming dominant ones, and philosophy prevailing in its thoughtlessness as the history of a misunderstanding, or even as the story of a deliberate, and powerful, deformation. Kant's intentions were never other than dispersed; our task is to understand our desire to individuate as our desire to erect our subjectivity in terms of a separation from, and violence against, the dispersed fields from which we grew. The deliberation of our deformations may be our only response—the call to the original or pure intention may be the problem itself.

11. "I knew it was night, yet the moon and the sun were in the sky at the same time and were struggling for dominance. I had been appointed judge (by whom it was not stated): Which of the two heavenly bodies could shine more brightly? . . . 'The most important thing about your dream, Cassandra, was that faced with a completely perverted question, you nevertheless tried to find an answer. You should remember that when the time comes'" (C. Wolf, *Cassandra* [1983], p. 87 [my ellipsis]). Cassandra's madness, it would seem, lies in insisting on making a judgment—or, in what would possibly be the same thing, in having to occupy the role where judgment is deemed impossible, yet still demanded.

rather, she should be taken as having opened onto a different kind of questioning. No question is more properly philosophical than the one that asks how a question is to be properly phrased, before moving towards any of its possible answers.[11]

The supposed essentialism of any use of the term "woman" is usually criticized on one of two grounds: (1) As a consequence of the Kantian paradigm of judgment, one is supposed to achieve a stance outside our given social situation before gaining the right to speak—this stance would have to precede any true speaking. To essentialize women, in those terms, would be to speak of the existing characteristics of the situation women find themselves in as if it were the essential determinant of all women without first achieving a critical distance. (2) That one should never make the claim that whatever term is being used is in fact valid beyond the given cultural and social situation. Although they seem to stem from contradictory impulses, in a certain sense, the second merely radicalizes the first: the idea of freedom finds itself, as the possibility of possibility, to be the condition for speaking in general, but each act of speaking will be irrevocably tied to a previously given whole. My rejection of the Kantian paradigm of judgment, the rejection of the style of speaking which thinks of judgment as if it were outside of a situation, cannot avoid engaging in the first type of essentializing (and my *right* to speak could never be gained in as much as the critical distance would always be illusory, or at least merely partial). It is only possible, furthermore, to avoid the second kind of essentializing by abandoning the paradigm of judgment itself (or, as with Nietzsche, by multiplying essentialisms in order to fight the old, established essences).[12] Modernism, I would claim, found its morality in (supposedly) avoiding the essentialism specific to a particular culture while postmodernism should find its morality in the refusal to withdraw from the obligation a situation already entails, an obligation to commence speaking for the first time.

One thus does not want to stage a war of subject positions, a dissemination of words as if they were mere markers of presence. The greater disseminating force, the textual move no avant-garde can complete, lies in replacing the very form of the historical subject, in creating a text that wants to read and be read.[13] Such would be a writing that does not place itself in opposition to the reader, a writing that does not speak about or for the reader, that does not express some truth or some point of view. It would be a writing that begins, foregoing the teleologies necessary for judgment, refusing the pretension to unify in the name of some end, refusing the temptation to proclaim ourselves masters of a style.

Accordingly, we do not stake our honor on a bout—or encounter—with the text; neither do we join with it on equal terms; we invite it to engulf us. Hegel is guilty of the opposite of this tactical maneuver, famously, when he argues in his preface against prefaces: there are no shortcuts, one must argue the whole of the *Phenomenology* or none of it. Hegel wrote to engulf others and saw this engulfing as the model of truth itself (as writing). Likewise, Benjamin, in the unfinished *Passagen-Werk* (*Arcades Project*), proposed a radical montage style, a dialectical

12. This multiplication of identities has recently been celebrated in Nietzsche, but I wonder if even Nietzsche's masterful ambiguities truly capture what could be radical about a style that avoids the centering power of judging. In Judith Butler's *Bodies that Matter* (1993), especially the chapter "Phantasmatic Identification and the Assumption of Sex," one can find an extremely sophisticated and wide-ranging application of the strategy of playing with identity. Political, sexual, racial, and corporeal identities are all seen as subservient to the citational practice (as opposed to the founding speech-act) that undergirds the legitimacy of judgments. Following clues from Foucault and Lacan, among others, she is claiming a site of liberation already lies within the necessary structure of citation (of a repetition which creates, by referencing, its own legitimacy): the overdetermination of judgments gives a person caught within the framework the space to play with that framework itself. I mention her work because she is acutely aware of what I will be criticizing in identity politics: "The despair evident in some forms of identity politics is marked by the elevation and regulation of identity-positions *as* a primary political policy. When the articulation of coherent identity becomes its own policy, then the policing of identity takes the place of a politics in which identity works dynamically in the service of a broader cultural struggle toward the rearticulation and empowerment of groups that seeks to overcome the dynamic of

repudiation and exclusion by which 'coherent subjects' are constituted" (p. 117). The problem I have with this conception, and in this her work is serving as an advanced and sophisticated example of a certain (prevalent) poststructuralism, is that the time of citation is still configured as the freedom (albeit essentially finite) over speaking—identity, as I will argue later, demands that we think in terms of this time filled by instantaneous positionings and counterpositionings; the demands of the coherent subject are already implicit in a thinking of time as an assertion (or a performance) of positionality (including as an assumption of a subject-position). The possibility of a style which is not merely a multiplication of *identities*, of a style which is not concerned with the self's identity, reaches toward a speaking to (and not about) the other. This would be a time of passivity, or endurance, which does not culminate in inaction or despair—precisely because the style of the questioning, and the time of that style of questioning, precludes the self-absorption which characterizes modernity. In other words, although I am deeply impressed by the ambition and clarity of her critique, its conclusions about the nature of speaking—"the melancholic reiteration of a language that one never chose" (p. 242)—run exactly contrary to the understanding of the ethical foundation of thought I will be proposing here. Not that I have gained a pure moment of choice, but that I am obligated not to reiterate words as roles. Stylistically, then, the commencement that follows this obligation not to merely repeat the history of violence, is not enacted in respect for the other, or for the other's position, but in the speaking which allows a range of concerns to resonate without being fused together. Concurrently, my attempt, in the practice of these notes, is to affirm the words of others without thereby speaking in their place.

13. And, I would guess, this same problem motivates Lyotard's attempt to save Kant's theory of aesthetic judgment from the critiques leveled at his *Critique of Pure Reason* (although the separation would not be absolute) in *Lessons on the Analytic of the Sublime* (1991). My doubt, expanding on the need to think of the deformative misreading I evoked above, would be directed against the value of separating 'Kant' from his social and political reception. That is, even if a new theory of the judgment is to be proposed, and even if that theory avoids the reified 'subject of synthesis', we need also to ask whether the function of judging—as it is presently, and polemically, given within our society—would be changed at the level of its functioning. That is, even if Kant is separable from the history of his reception, and any name would be, does the reworking of 'judgment' break the tyranny of thought conceived on the model of a judging? The possibility of that question being phrased philosophically is the sense of following a surface instead of looking for some underlying truth. We shouldn't ask on what basis the functioning would (or would not be) justified, but rather on what bases it might be questioned and changed in general—a turn towards the possibility of questioning which abandons the necessity of an organizing trope such as 'judgment'. *The Differend*, I would also argue, and despite its obvious brilliance, is open to the same critique as well because it wishes to characterize the response to the call of obligation as itself a judgment. Everything returns, tautologically, to the necessity of the economy of violence.

encounter between the reader and the un-simplifiable truth of the field of the image, which was to be resolved, revealed, in the reader who engulfs the text which had pre-viously threatened to engulf him (or her). The reader recognizes the primordial (com-munal) desire for harmonious unity in the jumbled images of the montage created by the artist struggling with the same fragmen-tation of modern urban life. She (or he), too, has known the confusion of the contempo-rary urban milieu and dreamed of its resolu-tion (how this dream is instituted in the au-dience is itself open to question). The community of readers recognizes itself in the montage, and recognizing itself as a commu-nity the self of the community then effaces the trace of the work, engulfing the object seen, the montage.[14] The powerful work of art would thus be the site of an engulfing and an effacement: either the readers are en-gulfed by the work itself or by the structure of the recognition the work articulates.

Writing a powerful book, a book that confronts the reader with the pure argu-ment, with the necessity of its thesis, inex-tricably links all possible readers with the discourse of naked power. The terms of the game are already granted within the dialec-tic: activity, power itself, wins. What is the prize? The identity of subject and object: the subject becomes an object, *the* subject possesses, bodily is, all objects. Private ex-perience is found to be commensurate with public experience; all individuals (once they have found their personal truth) live in happy contentment with the Spirit of their time. Hegel, here, is more logically consis-tent, more intrepid, than Marx or his fol-lowers: the concept of absolute experience

14. Buck-Morss gives us a sense for how complicated the question is:

> Materially, the technologically produced "new" nature ap-pears in the fantastic form of the old, organic nature. The *Passagen-Werk* gives repeated documentation of how the modernity that was emerging in the nineteenth century evoked both of these realms, in what might seem to be a collective expression of nostal-gia for the past and the out-moded. But Benjamin leads us to understand a different motivation. On the one hand, it is an 'attempt to master the new experiences of the city' and of technology "in the frame of the old, traditional ones of nature" and of myth. On the other hand, it is the distorted form of the dream "wish," which is not to re-deem the past, but to redeem the desire for utopia to which humanity has persistently given expression. This utopia is none other than the com-munist goal stated by Marx in the 1844 "Economic and Philosophic Manuscripts": the harmonious reconciliation of subject and object through the humanization of nature and the naturalization of hu-manity, and it is in fact an ur-historical motif in both Bibli-cal and classical myth. Greek antiquity, no heaven-on-earth in reality, achieved such a rec-onciliation symbolically in its cultural forms. To replicate these forms, however, as if some 'truth' were eternally present within them, denies

the historical particularly [*sic*] which is essential to all truth. Rather, the ur-utopian themes are to be rediscovered not merely symbolically, as aesthetic ornamentation, but actually, in matter's most modern configurations.

It is with the new, technological nature that human beings must be reconciled. . . . The paradox is that precisely by giving up nostalgic mimicking of the past and paying strict attention to the new nature, the ur-images are reanimated. Such is the logic of historical images, in which collective images are negated, surpassed, and at the same time dialectically redeemed. This logic does not form a discursive system in a Hegelian sense. The moment of sublation reveals itself visually, in an instantaneous flash wherein the old is illuminated precisely at the moment of its disappearance. This *fleeting* image of truth "is not a process of exposure which destroys the secret, but a revelation which does it justice." (*The Dialectics of Seeing* [1989], pp. 145–46)

She is quoting from the notes for Benjamin's *Passagen-Werk* (The Arcades Project), published as volume 5 of his *Gesammelte Schriften*. My point, echoing my contention against Butler, in a preceding note, is that the time of recognition is always still my time (time understood subjectively, and also methodologically, as the making mine of recognition). With Benjamin, the justice

begins with the formless identity of Being and Nothingness in pretextual (borrowing Derrida's sense for textuality in Hegel)[15] preexperience and is fulfilled in the posttextual void, the absolute identity and passivity, of death. This is the death, like a woman, that we men are all said to desire (attracted to her negative, and negating, qualities). This is the death, that as a woman, as passivity, as the dialectical opposite of mastery, the culminating moment of (male) desire—ejaculation as death—is said to seek/represent.

Within this paradigmatically modern dyad, the activity of understanding may rest with the writer who presents *the* answer in writing for the passive audience to accept or with the reader who is forced to make present *the* answer within his (or her?) individual consciousness.[16] Passivity never becomes a field of investigation; it is always merely the faithful and silent (or at least subjugated) counterpart to the active pole.

Readers familiar with the critique of the metaphysics of experience will recognize the course of my writing as deconstructive, as the negation of the simple privileges of activity. Other readers may recognize the urban academic's montage, the unity of a written activity, presented for consumption. I would delay these moments of recognition. Deconstruction understood negatively is merely a greater technology in the service of understanding, a tool for grasping the interior movements of the Spirit more effectively, a better fork for eating with. I delay, I defer the moment of the knife, because I deny the *work* of the understanding. Instead, my writing, with its montage of notes and digressions, seeks to maintain the privilege of passivity, to swell within and as the infinitely unfulfillable obligations of a world of writings (and, in that, to stop being 'mine'). Such a style resents *the* answer because that answer only responds to one question. Style alone, mimicking, parodying, and destroying what was once called experience or consciousness, opens onto an infinity of questions. In such a book, the reader merely wanders from path to path, like Beckett's tramps, devoid of reference points. The work fails understanding; it fails the ground. It refuses to reference a privileged experience. We, who are used to thinking of ourselves as experiencing machines, are left with nowhere to stand, nothing to process.

How are we to respond if we are allowed no footing? The point is there is no court to appeal to, no response to be voiced. The end of a line of questioning is not the end of questioning; to no longer ask, first and foremost, of ourselves and our identities is not to cease to exist as a questioner (the affirmation of questioning is not dependent on the identity of the self who questions—to that extent, postmodernism need not be, in fact is the opposite of, a despairing negation of the world). This affirmation without identity is the sense of Nietzsche's inscription on the title page of *Zarathustra*, "A book for everyone and no one." The text—a word that means that words mean—is not a dialogue we are expected to engage in, a series of logical steps we are supposed to reproduce, nor in fact, is it any type of exchange at all (except when viewed from the outside, with an eye toward turning some profit). When we begin to ask critically (suspiciously), and this question can be asked in

of the revelation can only be given in the reconciliation which is mine.

15. Derrida, "The Pit and the Pyramid: Introduction to Hegelian Semiology" (1968), *Margins of Philosophy*.

16. "In contrast, Benjamin's dialectical images are neither aesthetic nor arbitrary. He understood historical 'perspective' as a focus on the past that made the present, as revolutionary 'now-time,' its vanishing point" (Buck-Morss, *The Dialectics of Seeing* [1989], p. 339).

many ways, what it might mean to possess knowledge, much less actually propose (as I want to do) an alternative to exclusive individual possession of exclusive individuated knowledge, we have stopped being able to argue before a judge: like Solomon slicing up babies, questions of possession, of division and exclusion, are all that can be asked in court—a whole and happy child would be just a fortunate (and completely accidental) by-product (happiness itself, after all, being typically defined by possessions).

Most importantly for my analysis, and inseparable from any of the moral, political, or epistemological positions I intend to question, is woman's place as other to man. This is, in some ways, the easiest part of my writing. A lot of work has been done recently on the subject, some of which I take advantage of. The nature of woman's position as other will inundate this entire text in rather twisting ways: giving us, for example, different ways of conceptualizing thinking without the economies of possession, of working for human freedom and justice without the horrifying 'necessity' of 'purifying' and 'just' wars. The act of suspension, the duplicitous activity (the lie) within passivity, opposes the singular activity (the truth) of analytic exclusion and reduction. By the latter logic there is no reason—it is in fact sexist—to identify the active as masculine and the passive as feminine. I would still like to learn to speak from within (albeit also against) this sexism. With a thinking, as mine wants to be, which remains within its time, any investigation into the world that denies the fact of the systematic subjugation of women that exists because of this dyad can be seen to both deny existing women's claims to life (who have, in fact, lived before any male-sponsored liberation) and humanity's claim (which is not a right) to a public life not dominated by war and its metaphors. 'Woman' here is used in an attempt to displace and question its traditional and contemporary uses as a metaphor—and my writing cannot occupy the space of allegory's conclusion—as an allegory for the exclusions perpetrated in the name of virility (against all races, classes, and genders) as well as for all of the inclusions performed without name or resentment. One begins thinking, with the allegorical, as with the parody of the allegorical's tradition, *within* the time of the allegory; one thinks the beginning, in the metaphor, by writing towards that which is not (or those who are not) already referenced *within* the tradition. I do not represent the claims of the excluded in front of the traditional judges (although there are times when such a representation is called for); I do nothing more than recognize that the time of my speaking, any speaking, requires an audience which I speak to (and not about). That audience alone makes time meaningful. Time, similarly, is not a product of the tradition, but its condition. Or rather: time is the very style of a tradition—and the style that might open onto, or itself be, the other(ness) of that tradition is my question

(I am asking about how time, or style, comes to function as a condition of a tradition).

The division of private and public, which philosophically is merely a reformulation of the dyad of passive and active, is widely acknowledged to be the foundation of modern (some say all) sexism. Traditionally, this sexism is to be overcome by allowing women to join the public world of men (all enfranchisements of the subjugated presuppose that 'they' want that which has already been systematically defined as good by, and for, 'us'). That tradition can find sexism in any *division*, allegorical or polemical, between genders. Rather, borrowing from Derrida's famous summation, "there is no outside the text," I would claim (in all too preliminary a fashion) that there is no outside the specificity of the articulations of the metaphor—no outside, in this particular case, the woman. The category of man has failed us, this is the lesson of our century, taught in the various critiques of metaphysics—philosophical, literary, and social upheavals all forming a continuous web, all doubting the very sense of modernity's masculine project. The category of woman is all tradition has left us. One can appropriate this category in the name of a new man, some variation on Nietzsche's *Übermensch*, or take a lesson from the metaphor itself, and learn the transcendence of patience. Such is the entirety, the unity of this present book.

And yet, because I lack the subtlety of the infinite delay, because time is escaped in neither abstraction nor concretion, the unity dissolves before its readers (which is fortunate, since without such a dissolution no reading would be possible). Nothing is presented; no truth remains to be grasped. But, in our simple passivity, in our reading, we begin to think our obligation to the words, to the text. Our passivity cannot be a self-subjugation to an eternal essence; our obligation must come as a serious commitment to begin questioning anew, to commence without referencing the unity implicit in an assertion. Which does not mean that assertion and unity are impossible, but rather implies that we do not start from a unity of the assertive self which is always presupposed. Thus do we avoid thinking the question as if it were transcendent, as if questioning were a faculty of the human as such.[17]

As a beginning, in an attempt to guide the reader through this book, I offer shadowings, summations, and reductions of those things which I want to accompany the presentation. One adumbration among several I have tried to privilege, a reading of this writing which emphasizes its concrete relation to the metaphor and the social situation of women at the expense of its relation to other entwined emblems (reader and writer, for example) and other inseparable concrete social situations (the tradition, writers and their readerships, international capitalism), runs thus:

17. This, I feel, is a key to Heidegger's self-critique after *Being
and Time*. Questioning must be
thought from that which originates the question (in Heidegger's
case, being; in Levinas's case, the
face of the other). *Being and
Time* still thought of the question
as subservient to Dasein's ek-sta-
sis; his later conception of being,
contrary to Levinas's critical reading, is no longer (if it ever was)
the correlate of a self's project.
Instead, we are asked to see certain epochs of being instructing
our questioning (and not just our
projects); we are asked to see the
human as such, and our interpretation of the human as a substance with faculties, as merely a
moment within one of these
epochs—a moment, now having
reached its full extent, whose
time has passed.

'Woman' as evil other serves to create a community of fraternity. The classic function of scapegoat, *pharmakos*, is to cleanse the city of internal impurities by externalizing, exiling, the impure (reunifying those who remain). Men have *sought* to define them-selves through the expulsion of women from the public sphere: this actively enforced ex-clusion is the point where the allegory in-fringes on the real (and this point calls to be thought not just in its activity, but in its in-fringing). I would further make use, how-ever, of a move in Girard's *The Scapegoat* to-ward speaking of writing as the subversion of this process of expulsion—as the subver-sion of the simple translation of allegorical prejudice into real exclusions. (He uses Christ as the example of a *pharmakos* who becomes internalized, thus subverting the order of violence previously considered es-sential to narration). The conception of woman, like Christ, as a scapegoat begins to define a strange tropological space: Woman, as mother/wife, is paradigmatically the inner sanctum, or family, of a society or an indi-vidual, as well as the site of reproduction and reiteration; Woman, as sexual object, as object of the man's outward reaching glance, is the site of the destruction of the security of the internal, the loss of the surety of truth. Woman represents Man's possession and si-multaneous loss of self; *she*, as allegory, speaks the postmodern predicament. I be-lieve it would be artificial within this schema to try to separate a 'Good Woman' from a 'Bad Woman'—more importantly, it isn't en-abling to do such. Rather, we should take advantage of the fact that in this play of dou-bling and tripling of metaphorical functions we can begin to map two faces of a single object: the unity of subject-centered thought, war, and writing, and the unity of the internal, the external, and time. Taken together they approach being a tropological map of modernity, a map which, I hope to show, provides some clues for thinking after the wars, thinking the postmodern; a thought which is capable of the words it speaks (that commences without recourse to the validation of maps and functions). It is writing a poetry of Auschwitz, not merely after Auschwitz; a thinking which is neither postcritical nor naive.

# The death of the literal,
# the death of a woman

*I beg you!—beg you for my father, beg you*
*with eyes that can still look into your eyes.*

—Antigone in Sophocles,
Oedipus at Colonus

*Another thing that she is thinking is this: she is*
*going to die. Antigone is young. She would*
*much rather live than die. But there is no help*
*for it. When your name is Antigone, there is*
*only one part you can play; and she will have*
*to play hers through to the end.*

—Chorus in Anouilh,
Antigone

The death of a particular woman as the man's loss of childhood literality and innocence is such a persistent trope in Western and Eastern literatures, in various guises of violence, contemplation, and naiveté, that it requires some justification for me to pick one approach as representative or to exclude other texts and approaches as frivolous. It crosses a variety of literary spectrums, which are more or less self-conscious, from (and only particular exemplars are appropriate) Robert Hass's "Meditation at Lagunitas" or Rilke's *Duino Elegies* to the violent private diaries and quasi-historical fictions of proto-Nazi stormtroopers (as chronicled, for example, in Theweleit's *Male Fantasies*). It has been perhaps the central trope of our (male) discomfort in the world, especially since the romantics began writing two centuries ago. It seems to transcend philosophical history, or be coterminous with it, inhabiting the form/matter distinction itself since early cosmologies—the death of the earth in the (Greek) winter, for the most obvious example, is a woman's death. Abstraction, generalization, it would seem, is a man's work, and accordingly a little bloody. If one is to master the blooming, buzzing, confusion of infinite singularities he must take to naming, to putting individuals into categories; it doesn't matter so much how well they fit as long as they fit according to man's utilization, his domination, of the particulars. The utopic hope of not doing violence to the other individual, as I would agree, leaves the subject at the hands of chance and the other. Perhaps, however, one can decide on friendly hands: the utopia of women choosing their husbands. Unfortunately, this would be a simple regress to the modern, a reification of the faculty of freedom. Something different mediates abstract and concrete other than the simple questions of choice and restraint, domination and subjugation.

Perhaps, and only perhaps, it is not a mediation at all, but the immediacy of the revealed word, the abundance of the infinite weave of the text. How to address something found everywhere, in everything—the mystic's question of God and Heidegger's question of being—is the question of style as philosophy itself. It is the question of poetry, irony, parody, mythology, structural linguistics, positivist logic and the death of God. To adopt the standpoint of passivity is to abandon the claim, the history, of great men. It is to abandon the striving singularity of the world-historical man and his followers, the village patriarch and his sons. But to abandon the tradition of glorious activity is also to redefine passivity. This redefinition—the possibility of a thinking not merely after modernity—will not be achieved in a single act (nor in a collection of singular acts); but it can't be achieved through the extended labor of an individual either. That is, passivity cannot be understood as a moment in the history of a set of definitions (in the story which explains their externalizing, or internalizing, production), although it still must be understood to bear (essentially) on the meaning of the individual's life and activity. We are neither primary nor secondary sources; we are not even allowed the fidelity of only reading the canon (no matter how limited our reading, it is always mediated by a throng of supplementary opinions). Nor can we simply appropriate the position of the master; our only choice, in one way or another, is to organize ourselves among the notes, enabling questions to form out of the failures of previous questionings, the fissures in our speech. Thus again, with the problem of passivity, we broach the question of time and the relation of time to the possibility of questioning. Does the question itself grant the form in which time will appear as the content of the answer (the present as synonymous with appearance)? Or is time the transcendent continuity and discontinuity of trajectories (or traditions) which will make questions arise for us as they collide? Postmodernism's limits, I believe, are given with its present inability to answer these questions satisfactorily; the style of the digression, inasmuch as it posits the strange time of instituting silences, will have to serve (within this text, at least) as an approximation to a first answer.

For reasons of its acute awareness of intertextuality as a question of the subject (indeed, specifically the gendered subject), the literary critical *Bearing the Word*, by Margaret Homans, will give us (somewhat later in this text) an opportunity to introduce the present text into Freudian questions (through her use of Lacan's "the unconscious is radically structured like a language"); feminist questions (via the particularity of women's experiences as daughters, mothers, and sisters); and importantly, questions of the production of literary texts in/as cultural meaning. It is also important that she privileges the prosaic over the poetic as a woman's issue, where much of the male heritage I will address sees the rights of woman as equivalent to the rights of the poetic over the literal. The ways in which the glorifications of woman still work against the interests of particular women are interesting because they speak directly to the need for a political language outside of the simple dichotomies of liberty and constraint, consumption and deprivation.

Later in this text, we will delve into the question of meaning, the relation of literal to figurative, of word to object, in some minutia. Until that point, and for my own rather obvious polemical reasons, we must be satisfied with a somewhat broad metaphorical understanding of meaning based, reflectively, on the organization of a family (that is, the Hegelian conception, especially as developed in *The Philosophy of Right*, but found throughout his literary career and, as Hegel argues, throughout philosophical history). In brief, the physiological view of parenting is modeled on and provides the model for the epistemological interplay of form and matter; it is itself an exemplar of the complexities of ideal and actual, their always already relatedness. Homans offers a (privileged) summary of the model:

> Aristotle believed that an embryo formed in the uterus only when menstrual blood was activated by semen. The woman's part is thus entirely passive, the man's active; and she contributes only the matter, while he contributes the soul and the form, so that nothing material passes between them. Given Aristotle's hierarchized opposition between matter and spirit, which denigrates matter, this view gives women a decidedly inferior role in reproduction. Aristotle's view constitutes a defense against the obvious visual evidence of women's powerful and active role in childbearing. (*Bearing the Word* [1986], p. 154)[18]

Homans, then, comes to question not whether women also create (following the model of men), but whether there is an opportunity for rethinking a woman's creativity already present within the existing structures. This other type of modeling is reenacted by women who—within powerful social constraints on their writing—see the potential for taking the given roles and transforming them into their 'own' creations. The appropriation of the feminine metaphor by Homans as a consciously manipulated self-conception produces a woman's literary self-consciousness with Hegelian structural overtones (I mean the self-consciousness of self as identical with the site of the production of the object/ other which is the main theme of the *Phenomenology of Spirit*) without the corresponding Hegelian contents. She identifies the processes of literary creation for women as the specific identification of self with male literary creations (of female characters). These recognitions, in Hegelian fashion, take place as appropriate re-creations that enable women to encompass and understand the entire process of their creation and their creations (that is their selves). More easily than men, women can see themselves as the unity of subject and object, creator and created. To be a masculine writer, as Homans argues of the romantics, is to consider one's *self* as invisible to the gaze of others. To be a woman is to be stared at. To be a woman is to be forced into a role. I haven't done justice to Homan's arguments, nor will I when I return to her work later within my text; rather, this question of children, of their parents, has to be seen as an origin, as something we (the present readers of this book) are always asking, always answering—without being willing to establish new master texts. To argue with Hegel is to argue with the whole idea of the son who becomes a father, of the appropriate circle, of the progress of our knowledge, slowly filling in the gaps in an initially complete, but not completely self-conscious, act of possession (knowing). An act always controlled by the tradition of a metaphor's reception, the knowing which possesses

18. It may be a measure of how complex the question of identifying sexism's origins within any social/philosophical/literary tradition is if we consider, as Aristotle does, the soul as feminine in knowledge and masculine in contemplation. The passivity of matter then takes a central role within the conception of our epistemology in general—and, as Aristotle proves in extending this dyad to other realms, the metaphor of a woman, embedded within such an epistemology, takes on the force of a metaphysics, an ontology, and a social program. This plays itself out in a trajectory far beyond Aristotle's work, and did not begin in Aristotle's writing, but has found a certain exemplification there as it has been taken up by successive generations.

19. With the important proviso that even this statement, that is, even the very idea of following a role, may be androcentric, we should note again that the question of gender is asked at the same time as the question of the typical role articulated in society, literature, or philosophy. Chodorow enacts one side of the question:

> Sociologically, boys in father-absent and normally father-remote families develop a sense of what it is to be masculine through identification with cultural images of masculinity and men chosen as masculine models. Boys are taught to be masculine more consciously than girls are taught to be feminine. When fathers or men are not present

would be the knowing which is certain that it can circumscribe the individual inside her/his role; to argue the metaphor against itself is to question the logic of circumscription. Homans, without being a romantic or a Hegelian, has stolen a possibility which was only supposed to be a male's (the question of the woman as heir is her question). Through her text she can never (would not want to) make herself a legitimate heir, but she will not be denied the fruits of the inheritance either. I haven't done justice to Homans's writing, but perhaps exactly what lies at stake here is the idea that justice can be located in my positioning myself in relation to her articulations, to the boundaries of her presence.

The field of the argument is all of history, natural and human, individual and world. The point lies in between sociology and myth—at the level of psychological plays, of novels, of allegories. To say a woman plays a type of role as daughter, another as sister, and yet another as mother, even if one wants to be as literal as possible, depends on numerous assumptions of how socialization works and what it means to describe that process. To practice sociology, as the Heidegger of "The Origin of the Work of Art" could claim against his many materialist detractors, is to have already decided what it means to be art—what it means to describe experience—what it means to experience: attaching attributes to a subject, to use two Heideggerian examples, no more captures the 'experience' of truth than correctly naming its use-value relative to man.

The names and roles attached by literature to its characters seem to have the possibility of functioning relatively free of their real-world significations. Neither realm is quite free of the other since we often garner our expectation of the typical activities of a person from the simplified representations of that role in books, plays, film, or television—which are never free of philosophical assumptions and allegorical or moralizing overtones—and none of the representations of roles would make sense or be believable if they didn't overlap with the generally accepted view of the type.[19] The following divisions (daughters, mothers, and sisters) within this book are meant to exemplify the political/philosophical contours of assuming (or embracing) a role in society—of living life 'as' a subject and an object. Homans, introduced prematurely, asks the question of a woman bearing daughters. Such questioning must be delayed, within this presentation, because the allegorical form of 'Woman' has not been questioned in terms of its patriarchal moorings.

The destruction of a patriarchal base has no philosophical value; it is purely political, a mere polemic and a detriment to the smooth functioning of rational society. But unlike the academic disciplines (also polemical) which would invoke a specialized jargon or expertise as appropriate to specialized parts of an ideally achievable whole, I will claim that all academic disciplines are, as are all nonacademic questionings, implicated in the search for an answer to a single, but not unified, questioning: that is, in the face of what is, what should we do? Which is not to say that we share a common experience of the problem. We are not even at the philosophical stage where we can adequately separate individuals from collectivities or name which collectivities individuals belong to. At this preliminary level, the question asks of the proper and common noun. Consciousness of species-being, recognizing one's own interests in class interests, is preceded, in terms of its explication, by an investigation into the process of naming, of typification. This question comes to the fore with artistic creation (the constant difficulty of genre or of classifying art and artists) in a different way than with the work of science or logic which is precisely why we find so many calls for the aestheticization of politics and science alongside the insistence on an art grounded in concrete experience and the scientific method. It is my task, however, to think the priority of the literary (which I would argue converges with the ethical) over the scientific in this point.

To a large extent, in terms of the broadest polemical goals, the course of this book is set; however, within a certain philosophical trajectory, the polemic has already (and without my participation) attained a certain level, or rather style, of articulation. It is also part of my purpose to enter at the level of this already existing, academically articulated, debate—although I would like that entry to be shaped by the broader (more polemical) goals and not the other way around. I ask, to begin such an entry and following a certain modernist impulse

much, girls are taught the heterosexual components of their role, whereas boys are assumed to learn their heterosexual role without teaching, through interaction with their mother. By contrast, other components of masculinity must be more consciously imposed. Masculine identification, then, is predominantly a gender role identification. By contrast, feminine identification is predominantly *parental*. Males tend to identify with a cultural stereotype of the masculine role; whereas females tend to identify with aspects of their own mother's role specifically. Girls' identification processes, then, are more continuously embedded in and mediated by their ongoing relationship with their mother. They develop through and stress particularistic and affective relationships to others. A boy's identification processes are not likely to be so embedded in or mediated by a real affective relation to his father. At the same time, he tends to deny identification with and relationship to his mother and reject what he takes to be the feminine world; masculinity is defined as much negatively as positively. Masculine identification processes stress differentiation from others, the denial of affective relation, and categorical universalistic components of the masculine role. (*The Reproduction of Mothering* [1978], p. 176)

20. Schutz succinctly expresses a phenomenology of the lifeworld; that is, he joins two currents of thought that are both still alive within our thinking. Although I will be questioning the underlying assumptions of his approach, my interest here is in the self-conscious explanation of the individual's relation to the habitual and the cultural, the material and the spiritual.

(Common sense thinking) is intersubjective because we live in it as men among other men, bound to them through common influence and work, understanding others and being understood by them. It is a world of culture because, from the outset, the world of everyday life is a universe of significance to us, that is, a texture of meaning which we have to interpret in order to find our bearings within it and come to terms with it. This texture of meaning, however—and this distinguishes the realm of culture from that of nature—originates in and has been instituted by human actions, our own and our fellow-men's, contemporaries and predecessors. All cultural objects—tools, symbols, language systems, works of art, social institutions, etc.—point back by their very origins and meaning to the activities of human subjects. (Schutz, "Common Sense and Scientific Interpretation of Human Action" [1953], *Collected Papers*, vol. 1, p. 10)

within the structures of how we presently talk about ourselves, about the bare meaning of our experience—knowing full well that the language of experience is precisely what I am questioning. Alfred Schutz, for example, asks about our socially derived knowledge, our knowledge of and from the other[20]—a type of knowledge which, as we shall see later, is not completely separable from Freud's conception of the unconscious. Maurice Natanson, expanding on Schutz's work, comments on the platitudes of our understanding:

> Such "platitudes" are, in many cases, condensed "recipes" whose ingredients and instructions for mixing and preparation can be set aside in favor of what is deemed a typical result. The platitude becomes an instant recipe. It is typicality, however, which emerges as the dominant term of discourse in this discussion. Whether the recipe for action in the social world is precisely mastered by the actor is not a decisive consideration; most recipes are themselves typified, so that the individual "more or less" understands how to utilize them effectively. In fine, typicality is itself typified. The urgent consideration, for Schutz, is that the intersubjectivity of the social world does not depend on the individual's knowing his fellow-man's subjective meanings in their uniqueness; it is enough to grasp them in their exemplification. We begin to see anonymity as the great signifier. (*Anonymity* [1986], p. 29)

My interest here, and this is less in

Natanson's work itself than in the general approach to culture and individual of which it is a representative (if not exactly an anonymous one since it is in some sense a culmination and a divergence), lies in broaching the question of the uses we make of typification. Typification is clearly possible—perhaps it is even necessary—but is it the very ground from which we must explain life, meaning, and experience? We are still working within a tradition, introducing the terms of an argument I will only be making much later (and in stages throughout the book). Natanson's book is provocative in that it represents something of a closure within our thinking of culture (and is itself very literary, written in a completely atypical, almost nonphilosophical, voice). My quoting, or citing, of his work, is then nothing like a typification (and, as such, is the stylistic argument against the secondary source understood as a codification of some originary schema). No true authority can be granted from typification, this Descartes already understood. Our responses to the structures of a shared language, understood as an anonymous functioning (or as a functioning of anonymity) have often followed a nostalgic reinvocation of self-responsibility. There is, admittedly, a certain logic to this invocation; on the other hand, and this is the path I am trying to enter into, responsibility need not always refer to the self exactly to the extent that typification need not be the primary purpose of language. To that extent (and even after many more pages are spent on the explication of various aspects of these texts, this will continue to be true) my style of engagement with a text refuses the typification which could close a pathway, or announce the completion of a thought or a trajectory. Without recourse to the certainty of either experience or truth, writing is always just now beginning. Without being true to another's work, or its intentions, one brings it forth as an area of inquiry, as a space (perhaps we could call it a time, or an event?) structured by its own writing and its own citational practices. Typification again becomes (and was always) possible, but it stops being the very trope of possibility and truth. In a strong sense, the anonymity of typification already questions Aristotle's claims about matter and form, about the passivity and activity appropriate to a role. But only as a question. For we are used to reabsorbing this anonymity into a trajectory that makes of it a step on the way to a self—taking a philosophical moment which is already well-defined and making it work within a different trajectory is the strategy necessary to any reshaping of the tradition. It is also a strategy which the tradition cannot recognize (exactly inasmuch as a tradition is supposed to represent a single trajectory).

I am well aware that my style at this point annoys some people, although that type of disruption is not my goal. My purpose is not to antagonize a complacent audience; rather, I write in order to approximate the multiplicity of an indeterminate belonging, of a writing not even secure in its right to begin. A certain fragmentation, not within my own control, is enacted in risking par-

21. Which is, I think, the key insight and underlying substrate of Habermas in *The Theory of Communicative Action* (1981): "Reaching understanding is the inherent telos of human speech. . . . (T)he use of language with an orientation to reaching understanding is the *original mode* of language use, upon which indirect understanding, giving something to understand or letting something be understood, and the instrumental use of language in general, are parasitic" (1: 287–88). See, also, my critique of Habermas's position in "Sisters as token of exchange," below.

22. Heidegger, as well as Nietzsche, has often been read as an elitist who merely resents being included in the everyday lists of people who know in an everyday way. It is my belief that the opposite is true. The modernist search for self-certainty is designed to remove knowledge from its dubious intersubjective origins and it is precisely the hubris of this false transcendence that Nietzsche (in his critique of the "Last Man" and his decision to affirm the small man) and Heidegger (in his discussion of truth as disclosure of Being and not the adequation of representations) object to. Thus readings which look for modes of authentic production within Heidegger overlook the importance of Dasein as an open comportment. The act of creation—as in art and poetry—is not transcendent truth (it does not escape the typified world). Creation, if productive, could be measured by its products. Dasein (literally there-being, that which exists) cannot *be*; it isn't measured.

ticipation in a multitude of interminable pathways. It is this fragmentation which speaks of our current situation without nostalgically referencing some supposedly precedent whole. I make an issue of typification, as I had made an issue of the metaphor of woman, so that I may repeat them as issues within contexts where they no longer function anonymously, no longer serve exterior trajectories, because they no longer serve to make sense of themselves and the tradition from which they might have claimed legitimacy.

Natanson's (and Schutz's) works depend on Husserl's in many ways, and I plan to deal with the Husserlian approach to intersubjectivity, and Levinas's interpretation of that approach, at some length later. But for now, attempting to adumbrate the trajectory of the book as a whole, as a response to this typified thinking of language and our relations within language, we should merely note (in outline form) some of the typified results of our thinking about society in terms of typifications: (1) the structure of typification on the part of the individual is based on being able to reduce (comprehend or understand) others to the results, typical from a social standpoint, of their actions, especially those actions which express their understanding of a situation;[21] (2) our socially derived knowledge rests on an ideal iterability of already learned typifications[22] (metaphorically, the importance of woman in the role of reproduction); (3) the way in which we speak of typification and alienation usually assumes that the reliance on typification produces alienation. I would argue, instead, that typification, as a way of participating in language, marks our previous belonging to a discourse which demands that subject positions be occupied according to an overarching economic/symbolic rationality. That is, meaninglessness and inhumanity are not born of the typified individual (understood as a tragic necessity of our world), just as the dyad of subject and object is not born of grammatical analysis. These moments do, however, share a common ground; they are moments, results, of an epoch of the world defined by a technological (use-oriented and anthropocentric) appropriation of language. I begin my writing with an explication of naming, technologically conceived (i.e., thought as a typification), in order to contest this explanation of our alienation. And finally, (4) a standard analysis of typical meanings differs from Heidegger's *Being and Time* mostly in its final object: that is, Heidegger asks of the 'who' instead of the 'what' of language (although a certain 'how' mediates the two). For now, and because it encompasses the other problems, we need to look at this fourth point more closely. Attempting a small excursion into the Heideggerian analyses of the they-self, my hope is to have prepared the possibility of, and announced the need for, the main part of the book.

Heidegger readily admits that everydayness, the realm of platitudes, is the positive mode in which we "always already" are. This is why he can never speak of a society of authentic individuals. It is also where many criticisms of Heidegger rest on a fundamental misunderstanding. As an example, Adorno complains:

> For Heidegger the They becomes a cloudy mixture of elements which are merely ideological products of the exchange relationship. The mixture contains the *idola fori* of condolence speeches and obituaries, as well as that humanity which does not identify the other, but identifies itself with the other, breaks through the circle of abstract selfness and recognizes the latter in its mediation. The general condemnation of that sphere, which philosophy dubiously enough called intersubjectivity, hopes to overcome reified consciousness by means of a primary subject that is supposedly untouched by reification. Yet in truth such a subject is as little something immediate and primary as is anything else. (*Jargon of Authenticity* [1964], p. 151)[23]

For many philosophers, a critique of Heidegger rests on a critique of the individual as conceived by subject-centered metaphysics. Under this revised materialist view (which has its foundations in Marx but not its final word), it is incorrect to assume that anyone is free to choose what they believe or desire, being the products, themselves, of a system of exchange. Postsubjective thinking, for them, is thinking which is conscious of the systems that form our beliefs and is thinking that recognizes its authentic home in the objective expres-

23. I think Adorno is right to see that this becomes a political question. In opposition to Adorno, I feel that it would be possible to access this political problematic through the same question of the creation of an intersubjective time that I address with Levinas, below.

24. Any attentive reader familiar with Heidegger will recognize a sloppiness in my use of his language. On the other hand, by not relying on any single category, any previously understood relation, to carry philosophical weight, by consistently displacing the terminology and style of these categorizations, the reader—and the reader/author in particular—is denied a reliance on (freed from the logic of) a possessed singularity of/within the said. Even after we comprehend the death of the subject or the deconstruction of the metaphysics of presence, we are wrapped in a language which speaks of presence and actors. It is imprecise; it is the style and content of everyday life, of lived experience as the absence of comprehended presence, the absence of simple activity, of owned experience.

sion of material relations. Heidegger himself has an argument against subject-centered metaphysics. His argument, however, applies both to individual subjects/actors and transhistorical processes (subjects) as actors. Both traditional conceptions of activity subscribe to technology's concept of the object (opposed to the subject) which is merely the product of the subject's acting. This implies the subsequent degradation of creativity— one (the individual in the service of self or history) creates only products. The essence of subjective being, for individual or class, is production. Unlike Adorno, Heidegger doesn't conceive of thought from the typical viewpoint of a social scientist observing how others think (how we happen to be constrained as a society to societal belief-structures), but as a person who questions how, as an individual, he/she is to act and understand her/his own activity in relation to the world which surrounds and engulfs.[24] It is a question put to the individual reader as individual facing decisions and not to the social scientist (or anonymous subject functioning within an intersubjectivity) cataloging how others face (or should face) decisions. It is no less philosophy for this reason: questioning doesn't become *merely* polemical just because it abandons that objectivity which science demands of us. Typification, the problem of the name and of conforming ourselves and the objects of our world to those names, is thus a privileged point of intersection for philosophy, science, and literature. By taking this intersection itself seriously we can ask, in general, what it means to respond to the felt obligation to provide (true) names. This question, too, has its epochal constraints, but it is primarily played out for the individual *as* individual. For Adorno, all the determinants of any decision are nameable objects, structures of the material, social world; the decision is individual but so constrained as to make any talk of the originary creative power of the individual equally subject to ideology, reification, or myth.

I think a good way of understanding this issue, putting aside Heidegger's terminology for the second, is in terms not of what we choose but who chooses—that is, it becomes a question of an individual's responsibility for an existence she hasn't 'freely' chosen, for an existence which is not merely a self, either communal or individual (and this distance from the humanistic understanding of the self becomes increasingly clear after *Being and Time*).[25]

Naming as a typifying activity exemplifies the difference. To accept a name—of self or other—as simply given, as authentically true because it originates from an authentic collective, individual, or artistic experience, is to accept an empty meaning. It ignores the contexts of individuality and assumes absolute anonymity as the truth of history (which Natanson, for one, doesn't do)—correspondingly, and as ground for this truth, all-consuming time would be, as the process of consumption, the motor of history. To counterpose this anonymity to the striving world-historical figure—as Nietzsche is wrongly assumed to do—would be to reify the individual as origin or source, either misunderstanding the true nature of (Marxist) social being (which depends on the concept of naming as an anonymous act of history) or maligning the way Heidegger's concept of Dasein functions as being-with and being-in-

25. Such at least is the result of Heidegger's deconstructing the received concept of responsibility. He abolishes neither of the two traits: neither the rendering of the reckoning, nor the authority before which accounts are to be rendered. But as deconstructed, these two traits find themselves displaced. Once humanistic, once corollaries of the dispositions of 'moral' faculties, they turn economic [i.e., not anthropocentric but organized around the symmetries of ontology, the conceptual results of a genealogy of ontology], corollaries of the dispositions of 'ontological' presencing. This twofold incidence of the turning strikes a twofold blow at freedom. Firstly, the accounting for occurs in a place other than the subject. The discharge of conduct and the answering for it do not originarily emanate from freedom understood as the faculty of choice. Neither initially nor essentially does to render a reckoning mean to assume the consequences of one's choices. With the turning, moral freedom, the capacity for practical spontaneity, appears as a derived freedom. Secondly, the measuring can no longer be construed as transcending our acts. Originarily, responsibility as an accounting to cannot mean to go before some authority that limits freedom understood as absence of constraint. As deconstructed, both the rendering of a reckoning and the reference to a

mensurating tribunal are thus to be understood in terms of the economies. (R. Schürmann, *Heidegger on Being and Acting: From Principles to Anarchy* [1982], p. 261)

Part of my task, in later sections, will be to question to what extent the economic here (as in Schurmann's reading of Heidegger) is also implicated in my more general critique of the priority of economic thinking.

26. And one of our central questions would have to be: what sense does destiny have without a grounding logic of the home (or at least of a spatiality, or presence, preceding time)?

the-world. Heidegger's later terminology tries to distance itself even further from simplistic stances concerning individual and history—rather, a mortal dwells within language. To accept a name as emptily given—I am a philosopher, a worker, a teacher, etc.—is to experience life as a collector of objects. Instead, to dwell is to live within a world, a world where these typifications, like all words, have the possibility of being spoken authentically, in the sense of shepherding their truth as language, not as part of *your* destiny and meaning, but as destiny and meaning no longer tied to the trajectories of possession and self; perhaps, then, no longer properly a 'destiny', or a 'destining', at all.[26] The individual thinks, but not from out of its function 'as' individual. Even further, one cannot tie the creation of language to the human faculty for language—such a project would fix all possible articulations within the field of a possible control. Without arguing for the possibility or impossibility of such a project of control, one must see how the development of a language first determines how any truth may be considered enacted within that language and, second, how the initial gesture of philosophy (in terms of its appropriative approach to language) has tended to restrict the field of the self's possible activities (and not to think towards a language which is of itself creative of new possibilities).

Of course, the turn away from the self and towards the 'matter itself' already characterized Husserl's theory of fulfilling intentionalities—worked into a social program in *Crisis of the European Sciences*. Husserl, however, has an idea of the transcendental subject based on the generalized possibilities of individually lived experience that makes possible the singularity of truth—the singularity which is the essential step of appropriating technology. Heidegger, with a different priority of questions, sees beyond the technological fact of being able to name and classify all things (the technology which supports the sciences) to the ethical question of the appropriateness of naming in general. For Husserl this question is simply answered by an analysis of the experiential history of naming—is it true, is it consistent, across time (across various intentional acts, mine and others)? Heidegger here broaches the question, without referring to God, of whether man has not been insufferably arrogant in his claims to subjectivity, experience, and the production of the objects of the world, of whether man, as an idea or process, can rightly claim to be the center of all meaning.[27] Rather, and here I can only speak approximately, one must conceive of the task of thinking in terms of its approach—its initial gesture—toward language itself. How will we best be true to the confusion of voices that the world, and the languages of the world, announce? How can we best articulate a relation to language which respects the other, and the other ways of being, that these languages are constantly expressing? The trick, it seems, is the resolve to live towards that truth of being (and its other ways of being)—one thus moves around within the confusion, writes the uncanniness of such a movement. That which alone separates thinking from the mere repetition of the confusion (and this is a lesson postmodernism still needs to learn) is thinking towards the creation of the field (the space of play) within which such confusion plays itself out.

27. It is far too easy to overstate the difference between Husserl and Heidegger on exactly this point. Neither entertains the facile division between inside and outside which calls for an interior integrity to vouchsafe an external validity claim. Both understand the primacy of appearance within *eidos*, within the construction of the idea. Both understand the crisis of modernity in terms of a crisis in the relationship to meaning. The relationship of meaning to appearance, the possibility of meaning, relies, for Husserl, on the possibility of repetition: simply, of being able to repeat the same word and be certain of its meaning being identical across time. Heidegger's conception of time—which is further radicalized in Levinas—allows for meaning within time that is not certain of transcending, or escaping, time (see the division under "Mothers," below).

Such considerations can only serve to adumbrate the full range of the discussion: its final importance may yet lie in such experiences—of anonymity, typification, responsibility. It will lie, more concretely, in the field of what those typifications come together to be: the system (or path) we call language. Echoing the movements merely sketched above, I will begin with the basis of many of our existing conceptions of language in the Hegelian explication of productive experience and then turn increasingly away from that mode of determination toward a more open idea of participation within a language (or an economy) in general.

Briefly mapping the rest of the book in the terms of language (and other maps would also be possible):

A) "Daughters" is an account of language, particularly language acquisition but not on a psychological level. Part of this will include the ethical question of on what terms we can 'choose' to enter into a language, into an economy of thought.

B) "Sisters" describes the possibility of a meaningful life in relation to a language.

The Christ sections are meant to show the connection of language—of meaning as a whole—to the individual acts of signification: that is, the connection of language and writing. Christ is seen to be, like writing, a challenge to simple interiority.

B) "Sisters, part 2" criticizes the interpretation of society based on exchange (the idea that society is formed from the exchange of goods, women, or language) and its meaning structures.

C) "Mothers" begins to question our relation to passivity and our ability to question our language's assumptions.

A) "Daughters, part 2" is an attempt to look at the ethical implications of language.

If I were forced to name one sentence as the point of the book, within this trajectory, it would be merely that the fields of our enjoyment imply preexisting and corresponding obligations which in their turn even bring the sense of the previous enjoyment into question.

# A) DAUGHTERS—
# part 1

*All this, I believe, converged on the following idea: What classical academic psychology calls "functions of cognition"—intelligence, perception, imagination, etc.—when more closely examined, lead us back to an activity that is prior to cognition properly so called, a function of organizing experiences that imposes on certain totalities the configuration and the kind of equilibrium that are possible under the corporeal and social conditions of the child himself.*

*In another course, moreover, we examined the problem of the acquisition of language, and there again we reached the same kind of conclusion: The acquisition of language appeared to us to be the acquisition of an open system of expression. That is, such a system is capable of expressing, not some finite number of cognitions or ideas, but rather an indeterminate number of cognitions or ideas to come. The system that is speech is learned by the child, not at all by a genuine intellectual operation (as though by means of intelligence the child understood the principles of speech, its morphology, and its syntax). Rather, what is involved is a kind of habituation, a use of language as a tool or instrument. The employment of language, which is an effect and also one of the most active stimuli of intellectual development, does not appear to be founded on the exercise of pure intelligence but instead on a more obscure operation—namely, the child's assimilation of the linguistic system of his environment in a way that is comparable to the acquisition of any habit whatever: the learning of a structure of conduct.*

—Merleau-Ponty,
*"The Child's Relations with Others,"*
The Primacy of Perception

$A$ field of study has recently opened under the somewhat inadequate heading "Feminist Psychoanalysis." It is a diverse field, but far from being coterminous with all work done critically, philosophically, or popularly by or about women. A complete summary (if at all scholarly) would have to include an account of its applications in (and routes through) anthropology, science, literary criticism, politics, fiction, and poetry as well as its theoretical roots in object cathexis theory, existential psychology, and Freud's Oedipus mythology, through both French and American philosophical and psychoanalytic thought. Let me say immediately that I am incapable of that summary; luckily, it's not necessary to be exhaustive here, just as exhaustion won't be necessary within the phenomenological, Marxist, structuralist, religious, or existentialist schools. Such a claim to scholarly eclecticism could not be supported inside any of these academic settings; my style itself is offensive (at least to the standard academic expectations); it argues against the academy and eventually, in the place of the academy—not as a more rigorous foundation, in the sense of a singularity towards which all thought refers, but as a broader base, in the place vacated by the failure of all attempts at exclusion and the ethical bankruptcy of those ideals which continually reinstate that excision. That is, with language, and with philosophy, we are still asking of the space left over by previous failures, by previous attempts to philosophically articulate the meaning of our participation in the public. Such failures are not remnants of uncompleted tasks, but openings left in/by the very structures of our inheritance (and our finitude).

Following the various strains of feminist psychoanalysis, I am unable to avoid a certain history of philosophy which merely culminates with (on) Freud. It is broadly Hegelian—or is susceptible to Hegelian categories—but specifically scientistic; it has to do with desires and the collective unconscious. The Freudian theory of the Oedipus Complex is widely known and widely disputed, but let us allow it a certain initial space of questioning. There are appropriate ways to act in a society, transcribed seemingly in each individual, at a level beyond the individual's control. The mere fact that the individual may desire that control is even eventually seen to be opaque to the individual: all desires are reducible to a single desiring because they are equally obscure. In the Oedipus story, the son has a time of perfect abstract unity with all of nature (for Freud the son, it is the mother; for Christ the Son, it is God—and this parallel is not accidental) which is disrupted by the intrusion of the (idealized, or dead) Father, a question of disputed ownership, and the child's inability to self-sufficiently ensure the satisfaction of desire (e.g., hunger, castration, or man's separation from divinity/immediacy—thus the equation of castration/

28. The phallus is the privileged signifier of that mark in which the role of the logos is joined with the advent of desire. It can be said that this signifier is chosen because it is the most tangible element in the real of sexual copulation, and also the most symbolic in the literal (typographical) sense of the term, since it is equivalent there to the (logical) copula. It might also be said that, by virtue of its turgidity, it is the image of the vital flow as it is transmitted in generation. All these propositions merely conceal the fact that it can play its role only when veiled, that is to say, as itself a sign of the latency with which any signifiable is struck, when it is raised (*aufgehoben*) to the function of signifier. The phallus is the signifier of this *Aufhebung* itself, which it inaugurates (initiates) by its disappearance. That is why the demon of *Aidos* (*Scham*, shame) arises at the very moment when, in the ancient mysteries, the phallus is unveiled (cf. the famous painting in the Villa di Pompei). It then becomes the bar which, at the hands of the demon, strikes the signified, marking it as the bastard offspring of this signifying concatenation. Thus a condition of complementarity is produced in the establishment of the subject by the signifier—which explains the *Spaltung* in the subject and the movement of intervention in which that splitting is completed. Namely:

crucifixion with abstract language)[28] which tension can only be solved through a painful separation (renouncing the mother; crucifixion) which eventually allows the son to enter the order of the father and its pleasures (actual sexual possession of a woman; divinity). One of the many attractions of this theory is that it is argued from concrete life-world experience; its corresponding fault is its unsatisfying claim to universality. A majority of the population, for what should be the easiest example, doesn't even have a penis. (The phallus in Lacan is equated with desire for the Mother, but how the desire for the mother is denied and repressed is fundamentally different according to gender.) These are much argued issues, but the solution is neither my claim nor goal; I seek rather to question desire itself, not just the desire to reappropriate what is lost (the immediate pleasure of the mother's breast) but also to question the desire, and the structuring of the desire, for what one is looking for (as found in the instinct, compulsions, or desires to eat, to suckle, to fuck, or to breathe), and finally, to learn to ask of the more mundane (learned?) wants: vacations, world peace, leisure time for reading good books.

But I have been pointing to an extant critique of Freud. I trust it will seem only appropriately arbitrary to use a brief summary from Homans:

> A commentator on the implications of Lacanian theory for women has recently written, "The particular tragedy for daughters who identify with their (m)Others along traditional gender/role lines, is that they avoid primary Castration—i.e., difference or psychic

separation—and, in so doing, verify the myths which become secondary Castration." And yet from the daughter's point of view, there might be another and more positive way of viewing this continued attachment to the mother. Only in an androcentric culture would it be considered tragic for a girl not to experience pain, if that pain is preeminently a masculine experience.

This alternative story of human development, this story about a daughter's long continuation of her preoedipal attachment to her mother, and of her embracing the Law of the Father so much less enthusiastically than the son, has important consequences for the writing of daughters, for the ways women rewrite the story of language. Although in this new story, the daughter does enter the symbolic order, she does not do so exclusively. Because she does not perceive the mother as lost or renounced, she does not need the compensation the father's law offers as much as does the son. Furthermore, she has the positive experience of never having given up entirely the presymbolic communication that carries over, with the bond to the mother, beyond the preoedipal period. The daughter therefore speaks two languages at once. Along with symbolic language, she retains the literal or presymbolic language that the son represses at the time of his renunciation of his mother. Just as there is for the daughter no oedipal "crisis," her entry into the symbolic order is only a gradual shift of emphasis. (*Bearing the Word* [1986], p. 13)

(1) that the subject designates his being only by barring everything he signifies, as it appears in the fact that he wants to be loved for himself, a mirage that cannot be dismissed as merely grammatical (since it abolishes discourse); (2) that the living part of that being in the *urverdrängt* (primally repressed) finds its signifier by receiving the mark of *Verdrängung* (repression) of the phallus (by virtue of which the unconscious is language). (Lacan, "The Signification of the Phallus" [1958], *Écrits*, pp. 287–88)

29. One finds this expanded upon in "The Breast-Feeder" (Mahasweta Devi, "Stanadayini," trans. Spivak, in *In Other Worlds*) a short story by an Indian author who wishes to use the analogy between man's exploitation of woman and the colonial powers' exploitation of their colonies to show that 'nationalism' is not the mere (emancipatory) opposite of colonialism.

By Mahasweta Devi's own account, "Stanadayini" is a parable of India after decolonization. Like the protagonist Jashoda, India is a mother-by-hire. All classes of people, the post-war rich, the ideologues, the indigenous bureaucracy, the diasporics, the people who are sworn to protect the new state, abuse and exploit her. If nothing is done to sustain her, nothing given back to her, and if scientific help comes too late, she will die of a consuming cancer. I suppose

As should be obvious, I don't intend to quarantine these 'women's issues' to the front of the book, as problems to be transcended. Instead, I wish to mark the intrusion of a question, under a rubric which announces a previous exclusion, a typification which is not essentialism because it announces—for us as readers of a social, political, and philosophical history/trajectory—the absence of a *proper* essence. As the fault of an appropriate answer it is the space of a new questioning; as the privileged question of from where questioning and questions can be produced (as in psychoanalysis's inquiry into the unconscious, or faith's turn towards God), it may even become the rubric for a reconceptualization of questioning, that is, of consciousness itself. Such a reconceptualization would be, perhaps, merely a slight variation in perspective. Everything will only be a gradual reworking, a returning glance and an appropriative respect, revaluing the phrase, "her entry into the symbolic order is only a gradual shift of emphasis." This gradualness is exemplified in how Homans' writing itself is and is not a break with Lacanian theory. The daughter of a tradition is already other than the son was supposed to have been.

We are, here, already on familiar ground. Beauvoir's *The Second Sex* famously recapitulates the difference between the roles of men and the roles of women on the basis of the difference between Life (the pure continuation of the living) and Existence (the project-oriented life of activity).

> The psychoanalyst describes the female child, the young girl, as incited to identification with the mother and the father, torn between "viriloid" and "feminine" tendencies; whereas I conceive her as hesitating between the role of *object*, *Other*, which is offered her, and the assertion of her liberty. (p. 58)

"Object," "Other," and "Liberty" are here, as for any existentialist, pregnant terms with myriad possibilities of meaning. We can see their locus, however, in the moment that defines species and individual, universal and particular. For the tradition and for the average male-on-the-street, as Beauvoir points out, these poles are easy to name: Woman is Life as passive reproductive ground, receptor of seed, object of desire, and, literally, the continuation of the species (the latter constituting her substantive destiny);[29] Man is Existence as choice and activity, shaping and reshaping, individual and particularized existence in the form of his particular accomplishments. Meaning, valuation, is, as will-to-act, will-to-be (man is his willing); and, for the tradition, it is a matter of war and murder. In a famous passage of *The Second Sex*, which opens up towards the question of Woman, true belief, and war, we find:

> The warrior put his life in jeopardy to elevate the prestige of the horde, the

clan to which he belonged. And in this he proved dramatically that life is not the supreme value for man, but on the contrary that it should be made to serve ends more important than itself. The worst curse that was laid upon woman was that she should be excluded from these warlike forays. For it is not in giving life but in risking life that man is raised above the animal; that is why superiority has been accorded in humanity not to the sex that brings forth but to that which kills.

Here we have the key to the whole mystery. On the biological level a species is maintained only by creating itself anew; but this creation results only in repeating the same Life in more individuals. But man assures the repetition of Life while transcending Life through Existence; by this transcendence he creates values that deprive pure repetition of all value. In the animal, the freedom and variety of male activities are vain because no project is involved. Except for his service to the species, what he does is immaterial. Whereas in serving the species, the human male also remodels the face of the earth, he creates new instruments, he invents, he shapes the future. In setting himself up as sovereign he is supported by the complicity of woman herself.

Woman's passivity, then, is her untruth, her complicity with the male lie (Beauvoir continues):

For she, too, is an existent, she feels the urge to surpass, and her project is

if one extended this parable the end of the story might come to "mean" something like this: the ideological construct "India" is too deeply informed by the goddess-infested reverse sexism of the Hindu majority. As long as there is this hegemonic cultural self-representation of India as a goddess-mother (dissimulating the possibility that this mother is a slave), she will collapse under the burden of the immense expectations that such a self-representation permits. This interesting reading is not very useful from the perspective of a study of the subaltern what must be excluded [in order for Mahasweta's account to emerge as a parable] is precisely the attempt to represent the subaltern as such. (p. 244)

That is, "the attempt to represent"—and paradigmatically as an attempt not directed to but rather about a subaltern position—needs to be thematized within our questioning before the idea of an extended conceit itself can make sense. Spivak's answer, somewhat similar to mine, rests on the way the absence of the child represents the failure inherent in thinking of the world as if it were only made up of products (only made up of the externalized values of our social being):

The Marxian fable of a transition from the domestic to the "domestic" mode of social reproduction has no more than a strained plausibility here. In order to construct it, one must entertain a grounding assumption, that the originary state of "necessary labor" is where the lactating mother produces a use-value. For whose use? If you consider her in a subject-position, it is a situation of exchange, with the child, for immediate and future psycho-social affect. Even if we read the story as a proto-nationalist parable about Mother India, it is the failure of this exchange that is the substance of the story. It is this failure, the absence of the child as such, that is marked by the enigmatic answer-question-parataxis toward the conclusion: "Yet someone was supposed to be there at the end. Who was it? It was who? Who was it? Jashoda died at 11 p.m." (Spivak, "A Literary Representation of the Subaltern: A Woman's Text from the Third World," in *In Other Worlds* [1987], pp. 250–51)

30. And this solitude, it would seem, is what the stories of great men, of monuments rising above the masses, actually invoke as the good.

not mere repetition but transcendence toward a different future—in her heart of hearts she finds confirmation of the masculine pretensions. She joins the men in the festivals that celebrate the successes and the victories of the males. (p. 72)

Feminist psychoanalysts have been concerned to distance themselves from Beauvoir's emphasis on free choice—a fundamentally correct descriptional and political move on their part, as they address areas of analysis and activity which return to the societal group as object of their studies and activity. On the level of the individual who reads, however, there are other fundamental questions that must be asked (questions that must be answered together): What should I do? How is it to be done? The answer lies between hesitation and complicity, in/as the gradualness of entering into the symbolic order; it lies in women, and men as well, not revaluing but valuing for the first time what has always been behind the capable word of activity: that silent subjectivity which strives to speak to us (and not to war with us), which strives to match us (and not to overpower us), which is not pregnant with our son, but capable on its own. Or rather: more than pregnant, silence is capable of its own pregnancy while words, when alone, are forever alone.[30] This is the initial attraction of the daughter. In the terms of the metaphor, then, Beauvoir's mistake lies in adopting the fundamentally androcentric division of passive and active (Life and Existence) itself and not just in her associating these conceptual distinctions with the social divisions between women and men.

I look back at what I have written and fear that I will be accused both of coyly avoiding what should be easy to say and so bluntly announcing the results of complex arguments that I become, myself, illegible. Seductively veiled and abruptly nude, the only thing I (as identical with my style) have in common with myself is that I am unproductive, or worse, merely a producer of bastards, of metaphors without grounds, grounds without references. Despite your kind offer to provide space in your home, I do not belong. I am caught in the same trap as the woman I write about: stuck between stagnation and complicity there is no realm of action which remains open to me. As Foucault has shown in his histories of sexuality and prisons, our rush to control, define, name, and limit a problem has served to constitute the problem itself as such. Our activity, in its viruslike drive for reproduction, creates so that it might destroy, creating its object to ensure its reason and reasoning. My problem: I have chosen not to be complicitous with the mindless continuation of war as Existence *per se*, as the subjugation of otherness (and here otherness is not the 'other' person or the 'other' culture, but the other way of being historically which the warlike structures of valuation—or existence—arise from, and yet rush to betray), and my only alternative, since I have chosen the opposition which doesn't oppose, the complicity which does not continue, is to hesitate, to delay, to rephrase the questions over and over again until a new possibility lies concretely before us, until the repetition of the question itself stands in the place of the representation of an answer, until the thing questioned is allowed to pose its questions without the stabilizing gaze of representational thinking.[31] That is, Beauvoir agrees to make success the proper determining factor—the prizing of success establishes the field as a field of valuation, of each project either succeeding (and outliving the individual through its accession to language/universality) or failing (and falling back to the level of mere, meaningless, life). When, instead, we begin to ask what kind of conceptual topology is left for those of us who are weary of combat itself, we can ask only of previous failures—yet, emphatically, the task is not to succeed where previous generations had failed; the task is to rephrase the question, unstack the deck, so that being alive (albeit singular) is not considered worse than being dead (even when elevated to the highest place of honor within the horde). Here we find the privilege of a questioning over an answer, a failure over a success, a silence over a word.

Another metaphor is needed, perhaps, a way of thinking the human without carrying the old conceptions of sexuality with it.[32] I have thought of naming this new metaphor the privilege of reading over writing or of silence over word: the beginning of this possible thought remains in the way my own words drift through so many discourses without grasping onto them; other people's words, discourses, projects, and activities exist, untamed on 'my'

31. And the sight of a *woman's beauty* affords a true *pleasure* to the imagination and the intellect. Such no doubt is the purpose of a man's relation to such an "object," assuming that he stops to contemplate it disinterestedly, without any representation of a goal—a need?—to be satisfied directly. For then, without his knowledge, that vision *feeds* those inconceivable faculties of knowing that are at work in the reflective judgment and that demand the fullness of aesthetic feeling if they are to live and grow. Thus one can understand the formal subjective purpose of what may be called the "woman-object." She will be asked to be *not simply pretty*—too much obvious symmetry is unexciting—*nor too recognizably female*—the intellect might then reduce her to some concept—*nor too virtuous*—this might arouse reason alone and provoke nothing but a little painful respect. Poised in suspense between the faculties of the male subject, woman cannot be decided about, and her beauty serves to promote the free play of mind. And of course what matters is not the existence of the object—*as such it is indifferent*—but the simple effect of a representation upon the subject, its reflection, that is, in the imagination of a man. (Irigaray, *Speculum of the Other Woman* [1974], p. 207)

32. We are often reminded of the countless procedures which Christianity once employed to make us detest the body; but let us ponder all the ruses that

pages, in quotations, notes, and epigraphs. It gives no object to be appropriated and carried to the next task in your life, but gathers a multitude of a certain type of object—people's words—which are given not as systems of mutually oriented relations (children of the same parent), but as a chorus of voices trying to answer the same (open set of) questions: what am I to do? how is it to be done? who am I who does? The words, which come to us as answers, do not (as words) represent themselves as the truth of another's experience. And neither can I answer these questions by looking at another person; the attempt to contextualize all human (and animal) utterances only pretends to provide an answer by showing us analogous speakers (the problem is, of course, that in the realm of representations, only empty names, like "human," exist). These words, so much more than merely mine, try to free the question of its alien contexts—free it of the author's (my?) answers.[33] This freedom, in a key aspect of postmodernism, is a freedom from a tyranny of the *question of the self*, of that question's pretension to be, first among all questions, the site of the truth (of all possibly true judgments). This freedom, so precariously and laboriously negotiated in every instance, is what makes the metaphor of the daughter, of the slow entry into the public which is not the self's externalization of meaning, resonate and become itself capable of rearticulating the other concerns, the concerns of justice and freedom towards others, in the self's stead.

The philosophical key to this freedom—and I will try to sketch this answer several times throughout this book—is that meaning doesn't come as a whole, at least not in the way that the whole is traditionally conceptualized as the determinants of a past wholly defining the activities of the present. My position, however, doesn't imply some abstract freedom of present activity: that is, that activity is no longer thought of as instantaneous rupture, but rather as the slowly dawning commencement (and recommencement) of the new. In brief, but still too metaphorically, meaning is not contextualized according to the unities of lived experience—resting eventually with individual's lives as a whole movement beginning with birth and closed with a death—but according to the unity of a questioning. This unity cuts across the diversity of modes of answering (including the various identities of questioners; including the celebrations of the hunt and the fertility of the fields) without privileging that which euphemistically gets called the living word.

Life, the more than singularly subjective living of these words, these notes, epigraphs, and fragments, exists only as the advantage of death over life—of reading over writing, silence over word, remains over origins. Meaning is not an opposition between yes and no, being and not-being; death is not the opposite of life nor even its culmination and meaning. Neither is death a metaphor which defines an all-encompassing system: there are things which we will say are neither alive nor dead, just as there are things which are both alive and dead. Not exactly a privilege, nor an end, death will be the object we look to without appropriation: we don't approach with hope of some return—we cannot embrace it—but we do not run from the moment. We take death for what it is but we also forgive death in ways that we cannot forgive life. Nussbaum, working within a

were employed for centuries to make us love sex, to make the knowledge of it desirable and everything said about it precious. Let us consider the stratagems by which we were induced to apply all our skills to discovering its secrets, by which we were attached to the obligation to draw out its truth, and made guilty for having failed to recognize it for so long. These devices are what ought to make us wonder today. Moreover, we need to consider the possibility that one day, perhaps, in a different economy of bodies and pleasures, people will no longer quite understand how the ruses of sexuality, and the power that sustains its organization, were able to subject us to that austere monarchy of sex, so that we became dedicated to the endless task of forcing its secret, of exacting the truest of confessions from a shadow. The irony of this deployment is in having us believe that our 'liberation' is in the balance. (Foucault, *The History of Sexuality* [1976], 1:159)

33. Marguerite Duras comments on her own *India Song* (1973) and its use of multiple voices: "What was a sufficient reason was the discovery, in *The Woman of the Ganges*, of the *means* of exploration, revelation: the voices external to the narrative. This discovery made it possible to let the narrative be forgotten and put at the disposal of memories other than that of the author: memories which might remember, in the same way, any other love story. Memories that distort. That create" (p. 6).

tradition somewhat foreign to psychoanalysis, takes us to the edge of this decision between life and death when she approaches the question of how to face death.

Antigone has been sentenced to death for disobeying Creon's injunction against burying her brother, Polynices. Notice: (1) Antigone is a heroine (not a warrior-hero); (2) unlike the sacrifice of Iphigenia, the drama lives in how she faces her own death, how she sacrifices herself and not how she sacrifices another; and (3) it's not a victory in war:

> There is a complexity in Antigone's virtue that permits genuine sacrifice *within* the defense of piety. She dies recanting nothing; but still she is torn by a conflict. Her virtue is, then, prepared to admit a contingent conflict, at least in the extreme case where its adequate exercise requires the cancellation of the conditions of its exercise. From within her single-minded devotion to the dead, she recognizes the power of these contingent circumstances and yields to them, comparing herself to Niobe wasted away by nature's snow and rain (823ff.). (Earlier she had been compared, in her grief, to a mother bird crying out over an empty nest; so she is, while heroically acting, linked with the openness and vulnerability of the female.) The Chorus here briefly tries to console her with the suggestion that her bad luck does not really matter, in view of her future fame; she calls their rationalization a mockery of her loss. This vulnerability in virtue, this ability to acknowledge the world of nature by mourning the constraints that it imposes on virtue, surely contributes to making her the more humanly rational and the richer of the two protagonists: both active and receptive, neither exploiter nor simply victim. (Nussbaum, *The Fragility of Goodness* [1986], p. 67)

If what I have said up to this point has remained within the fairly familiar, at least until we begin to try to speak of the relation which is not an exchange, the object which is never appropriated, the life which is death, we should remember that all of this has been circumscribed in various discourses before (if never any single discourse). An effort has been made, for example, to think how to give without receiving, to be blessed in poverty, and wise in ignorance. The effort can loosely be described under the rubric of love and, itself, fits into several divisions (not coincidentally overlapping with the divisions of this book): the love for that which one creates (daughters), for that from which you have your language (mothers), and for that which lets your words be heard (sisters). The trick of entering this symbolic order on our own terms will be to think each of these moments from the other side, from the side of the woman "both active and receptive, neither exploiter nor simply victim." Such would be a rethinking of the meaning of being an audience of an injunction or a promise.[34]

Homans, marking the conjunction of tradition and metaphor, slips in the clue about daughters that further gives me access to two realms of love (sex and/as religion, desire and/as possession) without losing the paradigmatic (and valuable) concept of the free subject. The story of Eve and Adam is, as a paradigmatic tragedy, a case of a creature overstepping bounds. It is, as a paradigmatic myth, a violation of sacred genre distinctions, the confusion of man and woman (as well as the fact that via a rib Eve had violated the mortal and much resented attachment to an earthly mother). It is perhaps the foundational myth of our sexuality (as it has been referenced and reworked). As men, we are used to thinking of our desires as being frustrated by the competing desires of others (especially women).

Though designed by God for Adam "exactly to thy heart's desire" (8.451, *Paradise Lost*), Eve once created has a mind and will of her own, and this independence is so horrifying to the male imagination that the Fall is ascribed to it. (Homans, *Bearing the Word* [1986], p. 114)[35]

For us, to follow this metaphor to a different conclusion, the task is to think the meaning of having been created in response, as an answer, to another's desires. For if Adam is the son of God, created from God's love of man, in what way is Eve the daughter? Whose love is she obliged to return? Does her destiny waver between the desires of God and Devil, Adam and another man? Or between Adam and God? What would it mean to live beyond a destiny, or beyond the

34. "All that had been impressed on her from babyhood impelled her to the believing of it. 'Love and marriage—a woman's fulfillment.' 'When you loved, you fulfilled the law of your woman's nature.' You were no longer one of those whom 'God had thought unworthy of every woman's right, to love and be loved'" (T. Olsen, *Silences* [1978], p. 105).

35. Which is interesting in contradistinction to the standard romantic interpretation of the Fall (which pretends not to reference Eve at all): "A number of these thinkers adapted the Christian fable of a lost and future paradise into a theory which neatly fused the alternative views of human history as either decline or progress. This they accomplished by representing man's fall from happy unity into the evil of increasing division and suffering as an indispensable stage on his route back toward the lost unity and happiness of his origin, but along an ascending plane that will leave him immeasurably better off at the end than he was in the distant beginning" (M. H. Abrams, *Natural Supernaturalism* [1971], p. 201).

duality of a choice? What would it mean to live without a destiny? Or more, isn't precisely, destiny only found in death, so that all living is 'without a destiny'? What does it mean to live within a language that offers you no escape from servitude, yet binds you to speech? How can we think of the risk (of the hunt) of speaking (of the continuations, ruptures, and commencements that inhabit language) without privileging the model of warlike forays?

And here we broach the strange ambiguity towards the tradition which marks postmodernism in general. When a feminist (like Irigaray) says we need to reappropriate existing images, or when we turn to non-Western (or pre-modern) traditions or lifestyles for models, it seems as though we are endorsing the necessity of the role model (and of the typifications which follow that thinking). Like Eve, using a language Adam had invented, we still speak. To attain a language is different from inventing one—as reading differs from writing—and perhaps we need to think the world-forming power of language on analogy to attaining a language (on analogy to the woman learning to speak) rather than on analogy to God, or the man who invents words from the simple immediacy of willing that something be so.

My promises are now made (promisory notes are signed, prophecies waiting fulfillment), and I have promised everything; we move in small circles however, and before delivery of goods (do we yet know what arrival might entail?), I will have to inscribe (B), "Sisters" and (C) "Mothers" inside of the workings of the daughter, (A).

# B) SISTERS — part 1

*The fundamental certainty is the* me cogitare
= me esse *that is at any time indubitably
representable and represented. This is the
fundamental equation of all reckoning
belonging to the representing that is itself
making itself secure. In this fundamental
certainty man is sure that, as the representer of
all representing, and therewith as the realm of
all representedness, and hence of all certainty
and truth, he is made safe and secure, i.e.,* is.

—Heidegger, "The Age of the World Picture,"
Question Concerning Technology


*. . . And where each firm beginning
reaches its precarious destination at the tip,
giddy and unable to ascertain whether, having
    been attained,
it is instrument
or cause. From such we emerge, ours
a violence done to that stark line drawing
    before* strictly to *after
and from which we break over and over,
    branching as far
as we can conceive, each image
of ourselves growing increasingly identical like
    these leaves,
and waving like the mirage waves to keep our
    eyes from ever letting go.*

—J. Graham, "New Trees,"
Hybrids of Plants and of Ghosts


It would be odd, if not irresponsible, to talk of the philosophical significations of sisters without speaking of Antigone. The first of Sophocles' three Theban plays, although the last in order of the underlying events, *Antigone* was produced close to the year 441 B.C., eleven years before *Oedipus the King* and thirty-five years before *Oedipus at Colonus*. A political play from the first, it holds my attention, in great part, because of the long literary-critical history (never completely separated from politics) surrounding the play[36] and the way in which the story is used to explicate man's relation to nature. To place it within the critical history of tragedy generally, we begin with the romantic conception of the tragic and the human:

> The recognition of human freedom, the honor which fell due to such freedom, followed from the fact that the criminal, defeated only by the superior power of fate, was nonetheless punished as well. Greek tragedy had to allow the hero to be defeated, but, so as to make good upon the humbling of human freedom—a humbling demanded by art—tragedy also had to let him expiate his crime, even the one which was committed because of fate. . . . A great thought was contained in the hero's suffering the penalty even for an unavoidable crime, so that he might prove his freedom through the loss of that freedom itself, and so as to be defeated even as he declared the rights of free will. (Schelling, *Versuch uber das Tragische* [trans. Robert Eisenhauer and quoted in Lacoue-Labarthe, *Typography*, p. 215])

The classic exposition of tragedy as the embodiment of the human condition—which is interesting to the extent that theories of tragedy have dominated much of the general philosophical thought of the last two hundred years—works better for the men than for the women. The tragic hero in the *Antigone*, following the romantic definition, would have to be Creon (even if his niece is, by far, the more interesting character). Antigone's death is part of his punishment, just as her life had been part of the reward for Polynices and earlier a compensation for

36. This history stretches, at least, to Aristotle. It is intimately involved with the birth of speculative thinking in theories of the tragic generally. Lacoue-Labarthe sketches the breadth of its involvement in all modern thinking, insofar as it stems in some sense from Kant's, or from what Heidegger calls the onto-theological. Lacoue-Labarthe adumbrates a course I will follow throughout the discussion of tragedy:

> It has been known for some time, or at least since Bataille, that the dialectic—the mastering thought of the corruptible and of death, the determination of the negative and its conversion into a force of work and production, the assumption of the contradictory and the *Aufhebung* [*relève*] as the very movement of the auto-conception of the True or the Subject, of absolute Thought—that the *theory* of death presupposes (and doubtless not entirely without its knowledge) a *theater*: a structure of representation and a mimesis, a space which is enclosed, distant, and preserved (that is, safeguarded and true if one hears, as did Hegel, what is said in the German word *Wahrheit*), where death in general, decline and disappearance, is able to contemplate "itself," reflect "itself," and interiorize "itself." This space, this "temple," and this scene were for Bataille the space of the sacrifice—a "comedy," he said. We all know this celebrated analysis. On the other hand, what is a little less

known—and which I would like to emphasize for this reason—is that in the earliest stages of absolute Idealism, we find the speculative process itself (dialectical logic) founded quite explicitly on the model of tragedy. In reconstituting this movement even rapidly (following it, of course, in the very denegation or disavowal of theatricality), one can detect, with a certain precision, the philosophical exploitation (raised to the second power) of the Aristotelian concept of catharsis. So that, presuming this suspicion is justified, it is not simply mimesis, or simply the "structure of representation" that turns out to be surreptitiously involved in the dialectic, but the whole of tragedy, along with what essentially defines it for the entire classical tradition, namely, its proper *effect*: the "tragic effect," the so-called "purifying effect."As might be anticipated, the question in this case would be as follows: What if the dialectic were the echo, or the reason, of a ritual? ("The Caesura of the Speculative" (1978), *Typography*, pp. 208–9)

37.  Irigaray adds:

Woman certainly does not know everything (about herself), she doesn't know (herself to be) anything, in fact. But her relationship to (self)knowledge provides access to a whole of what might be known or of what she might know—that is to God. And here again, by duplicat-

Oedipus after his downfall. Lacoue-Labarthe aptly points out that tragedy is a matter of manifesting freedom in a dialectic—in a move of reflection which shows the self its truth as acting self. Freedom *is* only in connection with its articulation as a concrete problematic (as a play between the free and the constrained); freedom comes to be only insofar as it is the object of an audience.[37] That is woman's position: she is the guarantor of audience. Because of Antigone, the daughter, Oedipus is never alone, never without someone who can testify to his suffering, his truth. Because of Antigone, the sister, Polynices is not buried without testimony. She assures the universality, the transcendence of his particularity, through performing the death rites. Without her, neither Oedipus nor Polynices could have made a 'human' decision. They might have made a 'free' decision, but only universalizing consciousness that retains and remembers can name the decision 'human', can remark the mark for humanity to see.

Why, then, a sister? She speaks of a doubling of the man: she lives the possibility that the same parents could have had a daughter as easily as a son. And the sister, by living a possibility for the brother, will be doing work for him. This opposition is not as simple as the alternative between nature and culture—despite certain affinities, at least as a preliminary marker—nor is it strictly speaking an opposition at all. Although it is not immediately obvious, the need for audience is the critical turn in my discussion of the sister (a turn which gains its final flavor only in relation to/rebuttal of the theories of intersubjectivity and language as exchange discussed below in "Sisters—part 2"). The tragic play, as art, reinstitutes the violence at the site of woman—the fight is between Polynices and Creon—the fight over the determination of the character of the stories a woman is allowed to tell, to believe and to live. More basically, it is a fight to determine how a man is seen (the vision then being validated by the passive—faithfully active—eyes of a woman). Antigone embodies the question of politics, of tradition, of intersubjectivity, of art, and of the meaningful life.

The risking of life, as a conscious attempt to validate an otherwise mechanical existence, is the distinction between human and animal life.[38] To risk a life is to show that your will is greater than the mere accidental fact that you are alive. This formulation is based on a primal metaphor of war—to die for your country (clan, tribe, or family) is to show that the continuation of your ideas and values as expressed in the nation is the essential fact, more important than accidental, individual life. Or, to rework the same metaphor, but still in the general terms of *The Second Sex*, man represents the public and woman the private. The man works downtown; the woman raises the children. The man makes money; the woman's validity is found as the locus and origin of (the man's) domestic security. This is also the point where innocence and guilt become intermingled in their appropriations of woman as metaphor: innocent as unreflective expression of the cultural life of a community and guilty to the same extent that she is held responsible for the possibility of the introduction of the bad—she must always have a man's child, but it may be a bastard. Woman 'expresses', in her function

ing that speculative condition as a kind of caricature, that is, by excluding it—except as phallic proxies—from all individual science, from the appropriation of all knowledge (of self), "History" has manipulated the desire of woman—who is forced to function as an object, or more rarely as a subject—so as to perpetuate the existence of God as the stake in an omniscience quite alien to its determination. God is adored even as He is abhorred in his power. And because God has been set aside in/by female jouissance, He will bring horror and aversion down upon it because of its "un-likeness," because its "not yet" defies all comparison. And if in the attention the "subject" now devotes to defining woman's sexuality, he aims to become identical to the being—the Being—of the other—the Other?—and seeks to resorb otherness into Sameness, wanting that, the Id, her and her . . . knowledge in order to be more like Self, to act more like Self, woman can only reply: not . . . yet. And in fact, in one sense, in this sense, never. For man needs an instrument to touch himself with: a hand, a woman, or some substitute. This mechanism is sublated in and by language. Man produces language for self-arousal. And in the various forms of discourse, the various modes of the "subject's" self-arousal can be analyzed. The most ideal of these would be philosophical discourse, which gives privileged status to "self-representing." This mode of self-arousal reduces the need for an instrument to *virtually* nothing—to the thought (of) the soul: soul defined as a mirror placed inside whereby the "subject," in the most secret as well as the most subtle way, ensures the immortality of his auto-eroticism. (*Speculum of the Other Woman* [1974], pp. 231–32)

38. The leap from animality to humanity, as the leap from feeling to thinking, takes its impulse in a suppression of the pressure. Like the animal, man has pressures, but he can himself inhibit, suppress, restrain, bridle, contain them. This negative power—let one not hasten to name it repression—is his very own. In this power man becomes conscious and thinking. The process of idealization, the constitution of ideality as the *milieu* of thought, of the universal, of the infinite, is the suppression of the pressure. Thus *Aufhebung* is also a suppressive counterpressure, a counterforce, a *Hemmung*, an inhibition, a kind of anti-erection. (Derrida, *Glas* [1974], p. 26)

39. This is why our freedom is not to be sought in spurious discussion on the conflict between a style of life which we have no wish to reappraise and circumstances suggestive of another: The real choice is that of whole character and

as child bearer/raiser, the absolute innocence of the child who lives immediately and, alternately, the pollution of that immediacy by an always already existent culture. Both times, what is inner in the man (his values—good or bad) can only come to actuality through the medium of, the more or less faithful medium of, the woman.

This analysis of the metaphorical is rooted in perceptions of the roles men and women are assigned and actually play in concrete situations (and eventually shows the bankruptcy of analyses of freedom which rely on methodological divisions of individual vs. society).[39]

That women do not fight in wars is seen here as the original sexism—and the discourse of war is inseparable from the discourse of production (Marxist or capitalist, peace or war). What is, after all, the exchange-value that can be assigned to domestic work or to reproduction—to activity which sustains a family or a culture? Sustaining work stretches time out and is thus opposed to the compression of time necessary for exchange.

*The Antigone* is a story of conflicting duties. Oedipus's two sons have just killed each other in mortal combat: Etiocles has been accorded a proper burial by the state (Creon), but Polynices has been left unburied. The ideas of the proper (the unwritten laws) are traceable to the customs of a nation, customs which, although bound by time, tend to stretch beyond the immediate experiences of manifest political, pragmatic, situations. The ideals of a family, filial responsibilities, are held up as transcendent to political expediency.

One need not believe Freud's anthropologically dubious *Totem and Taboo* to see the relation of a community to a family. America continually looks to the 'Founding Fathers' as exemplars of what is 'great and true about the essence of the U.S.' We are not only told to look to their original intentions—as in the unhermeneutical constitutional law of unsuccessful Supreme Court appointee Bork— but we are inundated from our youth with mythical stories of the personal integrity and exemplary moral Americanness of our fathers: George Washington does, in fact, chop down the cherry tree—ever, as all Americans, a slave to immediate gratification, but he does not lie.

Obviously, a lot more hides in this metaphor of the family than we are commonly aware. It bears a particular relation to typification: it relies on everyone already understanding what a good father does and is. It also implies that we, as listeners, are the children: and that we know what good children are. Further, the family is the very explanation of typification. We need not know all of the particulars of a person; we need only know they are children of the same father, products of the same activity: we know the model, insofar as we have internalized all of the lessons, so much more subtle than cherry trees, of TV westerns and hard-boiled detectives, and, therefore, we more or less know all of the offspring of the model—and know them as siblings, as (like me and John Wayne) Americans. That many of us want to identify ourselves along the same lines of typification and nonjudgmental familial belonging (which is an exclusion of the non-family) couldn't be clearer in an age of TV presidents. G. W. F. Hegel, conceptualizing

our manner of being in the world. But either this total choice is never uttered, since it is the silent upsurge of our being in the world, in which case it is not clear in what sense it could be said to be ours, since this freedom glides over itself and is the equivalent of a fate—or else our choice of ourselves is truly a choice, a conversion involving our whole existence. In this case, however, there is presupposed a previous acquisition which the choice sets out to modify and it founds a new tradition: this leads us to ask whether the perpetual severance in terms of which we initially defined freedom is not simply the negative aspect of our universal commitment to a world, and whether our indifference to each determinate thing does not express merely our involvement in all; whether the ready-made freedom from which we started is not reducible to a power of initiative, which cannot be transformed into *doing* without taking up some proposition of the world, and whether, in short, concrete and actual freedom is not indeed to be found in this exchange. (Merleau-Ponty, *Phenomenology of Perception* [1945], pp. 438–39) the very foundations of the nationalist state which, at the time of the *Phenomenology* (1807), was sputtering into being under the strange father figure of Napoleon Bonaparte, pushed the metaphor of the family even further (and he was extraordinarily conscious of the strength of a metaphor, of the possibilities of a word's trajectory as, or transformation into, a tradition).

First (Hegel says), there are two sexes: one that leads the public life of exchange and interaction and one that leads the domestic life which prepares the other, grounds the other, works for the other, so that *he* might sojourn in the world.

> It follows that man has his actual substantive life in the state, in learning, and so forth, as well as in labour and struggle with the external world and with himself so that it is only out of his diremption that he fights his way to self-subsistent unity with himself. . . . Woman, on the other hand, has her substantive destiny in the family, and to be imbued with family piety is her ethical frame of mind.
>
> For this reason, family piety is expounded in Sophocles' *Antigone*—one of the most sublime presentations of this virtue—as principally the law of woman, and as the law of a substantiality at once subjective and on the plane of feeling, the law of the inward life, a life which has not yet attained its full actualization; as the law of the ancient gods, 'the gods of the underworld'; as 'an everlasting law, and no man knows at what time it was first put forth'. This law is there displayed as a law opposed to public law, to the law of the land. This is the supreme opposition in ethics and therefore in tragedy; and it is individualized in the same play in the opposing natures of man and woman. (Hegel, *Philosophy of Right* [1821], pp. 114–15 [my ellipsis])

Hegel shows us, therefore, that it is better to talk of, instead of the opposition of nature and culture, an opposition between the universally held beliefs of the unconscious (unwritten) culture and the publicly externalized, pragmatically conditioned and actively changeable culture of public laws. One could equally say that, at least for Hegel, there is no purely given nature and part of the substantive destiny of domesticity is being tied to and responsible for the exigencies of natural reproduction—childbearing and raising, eating, sleeping, and sheltered dwelling. Hannah Arendt summarizes the Aristotelian terms—once again giving us a feeling for the breadth of the question we must continually ask, "How should we lead our lives?":

> To leave the household, originally in order to embark upon some adventure and glorious enterprise and later simply to devote one's life to the affairs of the city, demanded courage because only in the household was one primarily concerned with one's own life and survival. Whoever entered the political realm had first to be ready to risk his life, and too great a love for life obstructed freedom, was a sure sign of slavishness. Courage therefore became the political virtue par excellence, and only those men who possessed it could be admitted to a fellowship that was political in content and purpose and thereby transcended the mere togetherness imposed on all—slaves, barbarians and Greeks alike—through the urgencies of life. The "good life," as Aristotle called the life of the citizen, therefore was not merely better, more carefree or nobler than ordinary life, but of an altogether different quality. It was "good" to the extent that by having mastered the necessities of sheer life, by being freed from labor and work, and by overcoming the innate urge of all living creatures for their own survival, it was no longer bound to the biological life process. (*The Human Condition* [1958], pp. 36–37)

Clearly, I am unsatisfied with this position. We need to look more closely, for example, at Antigone's role—asking whether her devotion to the inner wasn't somehow courageous in a different way. A central thematic of this book is the question of what it might mean for truth to speak for itself, for us to listen to being, or let women have a voice not borrowed from men. The beginning of this process—and not the end—is the identification of activity within the tragic; that is, we must, as men and women, see what woman's voice has already been. This opens up onto a host of questions which have already been asked and answered by anyone capable of reading and writing in any language. The meaning (value, importance, and possibility of constructive or destructive mutation) of the process of consciousness and history as a whole is what Derrida questions in his confrontation, direct and indirect, with Hegel: différance is itself the productive moment and not the passive site of inscription, play is the disruption of the eschatologies of the public, and dissemination is the subversion of authorial, paternal control. Again and again, it comes back to a question of the roles one may assume within a family and how they are determined.

# i) Antigone is not tragic;
## she works without producing

> *It can be that the right which lay in wait is*
> *not present in its own proper shape to the*
> consciousness *of the doer, but is present only*
> implicitly *in the inner guilt of the resolve and*
> *the action. But the ethical consciousness is more*
> *complete, its guilt more inexcusable, if it knows*
> beforehand *the law and the power which it*
> *opposes, if it takes them to be violence and*
> *wrong, to be ethical merely by accident, and,*
> *like Antigone, knowingly commits the crime.*
> *The accomplished deed completely alters its*
> *point of view; the very performance of it*
> *declares that what is* ethical *must be* actual;
> *for the* realization *of the purpose is the purpose*
> *of the action.*
>
> —*Hegel,* Phenomenology of Spirit

The problem we've been circling, difficult because of the multiple layers from which it unfolds, is the question of the work of the unconscious. Given the generally accepted (and repeatedly enacted) allegorical connections between individual and societal meaning production, we can't be surprised by the quantity of literary and academic productions raising the questions of a woman's place in religion, politics, or culture. That this configuration of sexuality (conceived spatially in terms of roles, or places) becomes questionable in itself—a point too often overlooked—allows us to see that at the very bases of meaning production, at the level we are accustomed to calling unconscious, lies a work which is not unfree (as opposed to Hegel who would have had that work faithfully tied to its place). There, at the level of what, hereafter, we cannot so easily call the unconscious (as opposed to what idea of consciousness, in any case?), we find the possibility for affecting change at a level too often thought to be inviolable.[40] Derrida was already addressing this very problem when he spoke of an excess, or a remains, within différance. This excess, some moment of the overdetermined given, would always be found to exceed the paradigm of consciousness, putting those paradigms themselves in question. But wouldn't this

merely be the expansion of consciousness—
the continuation of the Kantian critical project beyond the limits of reason, down to the
point of making the unconscious accessible
to the text? Perhaps, Antigone opens,
metaphorically, onto a different separation—
one not based on production, either teleological or overdetermined—onto a separation
which affirms meaning within that work
which has never functioned outside of itself
(and we will have to set to the side the question of what complementary realm would be
invoked by this separation). The unconscious
can be criticized, or spoken about, but not
because it fits into the already given system
(or even systems) of reasons for speaking.

The sense of excess is missing in Antigone. She must perform the crucial activity of
consciousness, but not to prove her own
freedom. Instead, she does the work of fate,
the work of the underworld for these absent
gods, in need of human activity to make
their unwritten edicts actual. She testifies to
Polynices' freedom to die (which is clear in
*Oedipus at Colonus*)[41] and to Creon's dependence on an unconscious culture of rites and
festivals to maintain his pragmatic position
of control (which is more clear in Anouilh's
*Antigone*). She doesn't fight for her recognition as free subject but for the recognition of
others. Like her presence to Oedipus between Thebes and Colonus, she must testify
that all is true, by acceding to the voice of
another, to Oedipus, father of the family and
patriarch of the state. Why, then, punish Antigone? The clue, from the point of view of
androcentric culture, is that woman is in an
unspeakable position in the system of exchange, caught between the role of sister
and wife:

40. It seems crucial to question
whether resistance to an immutable law is *sufficient* as a
political contestation of compulsory heterosexuality, where
this resistance is safely restricted to the imaginary and
thereby restrained from entering into the domain of the
symbolic itself. To what extent
is the symbolic unwittingly elevated to an incontestable position precisely through do-
mesticating resistance within
the imaginary? If the symbolic
is structured by the Law of the
Father, then the feminist resistance to the symbolic unwittingly *protects* the father's law
by relegating feminine resistance to the less enduring and
less efficacious domain of the
imaginary. Through this
move, then, feminine resistance is both valorized in its
specificity and reassuringly
disempowered. By accepting
the radical divide between
symbolic and imaginary, the
terms of feminist resistance re-
constitute sexually differenti-
ated and hierarchized "separate spheres." Although
resistance constitutes a temporary escape from the constituting power of the law, it cannot
enter into the dynamic by
which the symbolic reiterates
its power and thereby alter the
structural sexism and homo-
phobia of its sexual demands.
(Butler, *Bodies that Matter*
[1993], p. 106)

41. (Polynices)—don't hold me
back. The road is waiting—
    I must travel down that road,
    doomed by fate

and the curses of my father,
    all his swarming Furies.
But the two of you, god bless
    you on your way
if you carry out my wishes
    once I'm dead . . .
you cannot help me any more
    in life.
Now let me go. (Gently slip-
    ping free of Antigone.)
Goodbye, dear ones.
You'll never look on me again,
    alive.

(Sophocles, *Oedipus at
Colonus* [my ellipsis])

42. This, again, is the point of
intersection between social and
individual theories of meaning
and meaning-production, between the idea of work and the
polemics over who is responsible
for, and who gets paid for, the
work:

> From the side of the analyst
> the analytic procedure, from
> start to finish, is a "work," to
> which corresponds, on the
> part of the analysand, another
> work, the work of gaining in-
> sight whereby he cooperates
> in his own analysis. This work
> in turn reveals a third form of
> work, of which the patient
> was unaware—the mecha-
> nism of his neurosis. These
> three ideas go together to
> form the content of the psy-
> choanalytic concept of tech-
> nique. Why is analysis a
> work? Primarily and essen-
> tially because analysis is a
> struggle against the patient's
> resistances. From this point of
> view the art of interpretation
> is subordinated to the analytic
> technique as soon as the latter
> is defined as the struggle

It is significant in this respect that the
only deities referred to by the chorus
are Dionysus and Eros. As mysterious
nocturnal gods that elude human comprehension and are close to women
and foreign to politics, they condemn
first and foremost the pseudo-religion
of Creon, the Head of State who reduces the divine to the dimensions of
his own poor common sense so as to
saddle it with his own personal hatred
and ambitions. But the two deities also
turn against Antigone, enclosed within
her family *philia* and of her own free
will sworn to Hades, for even through
their link with death, Dionysus and
Eros express the powers of life and renewal. Antigone has been deaf to the
call to detach herself from 'her kin' and
from family *philia* in order to embrace
another *philia*, to accept Eros and, in
her union with a stranger, to become in
her own turn a transmitter of life. ( J.-P.
Vernant, "Tension and Ambiguities in
Greek Tragedy," *Myth and Tragedy in
Ancient Greece*, pp. 41–42)

To labor is to bring form from formless-
ness—like sculpting rock. Freedom is, in the
sense of tragedy, denying that fate had de-
creed the content of man's action; freedom is
embracing activity and its goals. Labor is
alienated, unfree, if the worker does not recognize himself in the products, if he didn't
choose the ends of his work. The extreme
selflessness of Antigone's labor precludes the
time of looking in mirrors, of reflecting on
her 'own' goals (from taking the male perspective).[42] Even those of us with such time,
looking back on this labor, *recognize* the

object, the reason, the end, of her labor in the maintenance of man's prerogative. The difference, the point of subversion, is that she announces the humanity of an individual, the mortality of an individual man, his defeat and not his victory. Recognition, the key concept spanning the history of criticism surrounding tragedy, knows only the self as audience, only the self as the space of producing the truth (and only the male occupies that space by nature). Antigone's work is not *for* herself. She recognizes an other in Polynices, if she even asks that *type* of question at all; she announces, for another audience (neither herself nor Polynices) the meaning of a death that is not merely the conclusion, or end, of life.

against resistances; if there is something to interpret, it is because there is a distortion of the ideas that have become unconscious; but if there is a distortion, it is because a resistance has been opposed to their conscious reproduction. The resistances that lie at the origin of the neurosis are also those obstructing insight and every analytic procedure. Hence the rules of the art of interpretation are themselves part of the art of handling the resistances. (Ricoeur, *Freud and Philosophy* [1961], pp. 407–8)

The work that remains resistant to interpretation, here, is that which produces no resolution. Antigone buries Polynices; she doesn't kill him. She buries him, but doesn't forget. Against Ricoeur, we are looking for a health other than recuperation, otherwise articulated than as mine.

# Death of, exactly, a sister

43. At the crux of modernity, as separated from antiquity, is a reappropriative look at production (which doesn't break the old model of active sperm and passive blood): "By the same token, the true meaning of labor's newly discovered productivity becomes manifest only in Marx's work, where it rests on the equation of productivity with fertility, so that the famous development of mankind's 'productive forces' into a society of an abundance of 'good things' actually obeys no other law and is subject to no other necessity than the aboriginal command, 'Be ye fruitful and multiply,' in which it is as though the voice of nature herself speaks to us" (Arendt, *The Human Condition* [1958], p. 106).

Ismene's survival can't be found odd in this case. Antigone seems to have no doubts about which laws she must be obedient to. Her sister, Ismene, plays the doubled role. She is tempted to follow Antigone's course but opts instead for the literal reproduction of culture, the reproduction of children, the role of wife.[43] Here the distinction between blood and desire, relation by nature or choice, achieves importance. A woman who desires is a woman with a consciousness that is independent of male control. As such her consciousness, her desire, is an alien possibility to men, someone else's possibility, even if kindly disposed, and therefore unfit to perform any role. Hence, the continuing emphasis on woman as object of desire and not as desiring subject, as well as the significance of the father giving away the daughter in marriage—she transfers smoothly from

71

role to role, without any time which is undefined from the standpoint of the male.[44]

When this analogy is extended to include the male world of the public sphere,
we see that to be patriotic—that is, nationalistic—is to embrace the unwritten laws of
the national spirit over the written laws of
the individual ruler. Antigone's death is, perhaps, more closely related to her inability to
delay the decision of allegiance than to the
'bad luck' of her conflicting roles. She would
seem to be a tragic figure in as much as she
chooses the allegiance with death. Polynices
has no choice to make when he chooses to
fulfill the phophecies of his masculine role;
the role is typically laid out for him, articulated in the abstract language of the death
which is tragic because he is young, because
he is living his father's destiny. Antigone's position is more interesting precisely because
her roles are not so abstractly, coldly, and ir-
retrievably determined. Polynices and Etiocles live twinned destinies in the unity of
male striving—they both die in war. Antigone and Ismene live, from structurally the
same position, opposite destinies. The political stance of greatest freedom—and *Antigone* is a political play—is the position of sister. The options available are both
determined roles (and in real life, even
where there is almost never merely an ei-
ther/or, all positions are still more or less determined in their typical articulations,
modes of understanding, and self-conceptions), but the sister, the woman and not the
man, has the political stance of greatest freedom because she stands, hesitates, *before* the
decision, and is not doomed to living out the
abstract role as it was predetermined—like
the man who merely molds himself to the

44. Or, in Hegel's language, justifying the relegation of women
to their prescribed roles:

> Both these relationships [Par-
> ents to children, children to
> parents] are confined within
> the transition and the dispar-
> ity of the sides which are as-
> signed to them. The relation-
> ship in its unmixed form is
> found, however, in that be-
> tween brother and sister.
> They are the same blood
> which has, however, in them
> reached a state of rest and
> equilibrium. Therefore, they
> do not desire one another,
> nor have they given to, or re-
> ceived from, one another this
> independent being-for-self;
> on the contrary, they are free
> individualities in regard to
> each other. Consequently, the
> feminine, in the form of the
> sister, has the highest *intuitive*
> awareness of what is ethical.
> She does not attain to *con-
> sciousness* of it, or to the ob-
> jective existence of it, because
> the law of the Family is an
> implicit, inner essence which
> is not exposed to the daylight
> of consciousness, but remains
> an inner feeling and the di-
> vine element that is exempt
> from an existence in the real
> world. The woman is associ-
> ated with these household
> gods [Penates] and beholds in
> them both her universal sub-
> stance and her particular indi-
> viduality, yet in such a way
> that this relation of her indi-
> viduality to them is at the
> same time not the natural one
> of desire. As a daughter, the
> woman must now see her par-
> ents pass away with a natural

emotion and ethical resignation, for it is only at the cost
of this relationship that she
can achieve that existence of
her own of which she is capable. Thus in the parents, she
does not behold her own
being-for-self in a positive
form. The relationships of
mother and wife, however, are
those of particular individuals,
partly in the form of something natural pertaining to desire, partly in the form of
something negative which sees
in those relationships only
something evanescent and
also, again, the particular individual is for that very reason a
contingent element which can
be replaced by another individual. In the ethical household, it is not a question of
*this* particular husband, *this*
particular child, but simply of
husband and children generally; the relationships of the
woman are based, not on feeling, but on the universal. The
difference between the ethical
life of the woman and that of
the man consists just in this,
that in her vocation as an individual and in her pleasure,
her interest is centred on the
universal and remains alien to
the particularity of desire;
whereas in the husband these
two sides are separated; and
since he possesses as a citizen
the self-conscious power of
universality, he thereby acquires the right of desire and,
at the same time, preserves his
freedom in regard to it.
(Hegel, *Phenomenology of
Spirit* [1807], pp. 274–75)

For the failure of this project,

roles of war offered to him (this, of course,
exactly mirrors Chodorow's comments about
gender roles in modern society).[45] Structurally, then, we see a sister caught between
two roles: Antigone's (as guardian of the unwritten but understood laws of an ethical nation, of nationalism) and of Ismene's (as producer of new life, as life, without concern for
the particularity of the rules enforced). One
must stand in relation to the tradition, but
how the space of that standing in relation is
constructed is the important point: if all relating is between competing intentions, one
either battles to control the implementations
of intentions or is oneself the object of intentions. Perhaps, even, one is always subject to
war, always the object of intentions. But the
'always already' of war need not constrain
the production of the relation to the tradition as a reiteration of war. One can be, for
example, unproductive.[46]

By blood, the duty lies in the relation to
the father and the father's line: this is why
Antigone's role in *Oedipus at Colonus* (as
faithful daughter) is not in conflict with her
role in *Antigone* (as faithful sister to an un-
faithful son)—given, as well, that the duty to
the father had already been delivered. The
character of her faithfulness, however, must
be abstract. In order not to fall into contradiction with herself she must do exactly
what is expected of her roles, without regard
to a self-conscious reappraisal of the value of
these roles (which is part of why Anouilh's
*Antigone* is such an absurd modern—that is,
reflective—character). For her to manifest a
will is to interfere with her ability to bring
into actuality the will of others. She must
take work onto herself in a purely mechanical way, allowing men to be sure of their

course by being sure of the woman's position (as in John Donne's famous metaphor of the two legs of a compass, the man's course being true only if the woman's place is fixed and immutable—"A Valediction: Forbidding Mourning"). Thus, a wife could not perform a sister's task: it is not expected of her; Polynices' wife is only mentioned in passing, as the object of an exchange value, bringing Polynices allies; her role, as wife, would be to produce children to continue the man's line. Once she assumed that role she would better perform her duties by obediently raising the children or, in the case of his death, by bearing the husband's brother's children (same family, clan, or nation—which given Polynices' situation in exile, further explains his wife's absence from the play: he would have to either become a founding patriarch of his adopted nation or return to Thebes in order to have, or participate in, a lineage). A mother belongs to the father's generation and cannot be dispensed to do her son's work: she serves only as a fixed referent of childhood happiness (at least for those of us born in the wake of romanticism). A daughter could never be asked to give up her life, since the possibility of new life is exactly what she represents. Neither would a lover be able to fill the task: love (of this type) is desire—that is, it involves a particularity and occurs in time. As such it is accidental and not essential, free and not bound. As such, it is untrustworthy from the point of view of another accidentally alive human being trying, desperately, to prove his relation to the essential. Antigone makes a particular decision to fulfill the role of sister, but the determinants of that role are essential, are blood.

one might see S. Shepard, *Fool For Love* (1983).

45. "Masculine identification processes stress differentiation from others, the denial of affective relation, and categorical universalistic components of the masculine role. Feminine identification processes are relational, whereas masculine identification processes tend to deny relationship" (Chodorow, *The Reproduction of Mothering* [1978], p. 176).

46. War, of course, is also a certain type of unproductivity. J.-L. Nancy has recently tried to think of the unworking in general as the site of a new philosophy of community, no longer dependent on the idea of the striving individual who works, or wars, in competition with others as other subjects:

> This is why community cannot arise from the domain of *work*. One does not produce it, one experiences or one is constituted by it as the experience of finitude. Community understood as a work or through its works would presuppose that the common being, as such, be objectifiable and producible (in sites, persons, buildings, discourses, institutions, symbols: in short, in subjects). . . . Community necessarily takes place in what Blanchot has called "unworking," referring to that which, before or beyond the work, withdraws from the work, and which, no longer having to do either with production or with completion, encounters inter-

ruption, fragmentation, suspension. Community is made of the interruption of singularities, or of the suspension that singular beings *are.* Community is not the work of singular beings, nor can it claim them as its works, just as communication is not a work or even an operation of singular beings, for community is simply their being—their being suspended upon its limit. Communication is the unworking of work that is social, economic, technical, and institutional. ("The Inoperative Community," in *The Inoperative Community* [1986], p. 31 [my ellipsis])

47. Here, instead of the usual privileging of articulation, I would advocate a thinking of freedom not dependent on previously given determinate articulations. Lingis, for a sophisticated example of the more prevalent approach, sees the role of the other in existential philosophy as an articulation of the possibility of further articulation:

For Heidegger it is the finitude of every authentic project of existing, the fact that every projection of one's existence is a choice, that explains why the other, the authentic other who pursues resolutely the tasks destined singularly to him, concerns me. The fatality of not being able to actualize the thinker, artist, craftsman, lover he was destined to be save by sentencing to death the parent, inventor, virtuoso, visionary he was also destined to become is the way

We recognize, I believe, that the question we face is the same as Sophocles's: How far are we constrained and how far free in the things we feel, believe, and do? Answers have been proffered in myriad fashions, new names have been given, new descriptions offered, but the basic practical problem remains: what laws does one follow, and how does following any law imply freedom? I wish, at this point, to cast a glance forward as well as recoup some of the breadth of the question.

What we have come to call postmodernism—at least in several of its major philosophical manifestations—is dominated by something of a return to romanticism (after the impetus of positivism, indeed of grand narratives in general, had faltered, there was a general search for something other than the positivistic view of technology). My distinction here would never match any time line, if only because a time line assumes that cultural domination is a successful exclusion of other moments (and, after all, romanticism, for one example among many within our culture, never really died). My point, to the extent that I'm working within postmodernism, is to forefront a redefinition of freedom (what I was turning toward with Antigone) which is no longer a reenactment of a man's privilege, of a privilege of public courage and determining activity. Only to the extent that freedom no longer subtends articulation (as ground and goal), no longer relies on articulation for its very possibilities of action (as if articulation were the only space of work),[47] can freedom—and here I intend the full scope of that functioning—escape the reproduction of existence, of the meaning of existence, figured as the move away from life (away from the continuation itself). That is, in the rethinking of freedom we are searching for, we are doubting the instantaneity of the act which describes—we are doubting the ease of the descriptive word, the innocence of speaking. Levinas, I feel, starts us towards rethinking this moment. We find, almost at the beginning of *Totality and Infinity* (1961), the following:[48]

> To die for the invisible—this is metaphysics. This does not mean that desire can dispense with acts. But these acts are neither consumption, nor caress, nor liturgy.
>
> Demented pretension to the invisible, when the acute experience of the human in the twentieth century teaches that the thoughts of men are borne by needs which explain society and history, that hunger and fear can prevail over every human resistance and every freedom! There is no question of doubting this human misery, this dominion the things and the wicked exercise over man, this animality. But to be a man is to know that this is so. Freedom consists in knowing that freedom is in peril. But to know or to be conscious is to have time to avoid and forestall the instant of inhumanity. It is this perpetual postponing of the hour of treason—infinitesimal difference between man and non-man—that implies the disinterestedness of goodness, the desire of the absolutely other or nobility, the dimension of metaphysics. (p. 35)

one knows oneself as one that was born. That is, that was given one's existence, that did not invest oneself with one's potentialities, that cannot convert the passive receptivity for them into an active conceiving and elaborating of them. If, Sartre explained, one were not born, given a being to be, but engendered oneself, one would not have invested oneself with potentialities that one could not actualize, that were not compossible. The other, then, in inscribing upon the course of the world his own authentic itinerary, also sketched out on the substance of things those other destinies he was not able to realize, and he leaves them to me as the goodness of his own life, that is, that which makes authentic existence—another authentic existence—possible. The birth of each deathbound other concerns me as the sole source of the possibilities which make my authentic existence possible. But this also means that in finding, not in the blank abysses of nothingness but in the articulation of the world, the possibility addressed to me, the chance and the task that will make it possible for me to become myself, I am in reality coming to the assistance of the other, I am putting my forces in his place to take up the burden of an existence his own and excessive for him, I am putting myself in his place to answer for his wants and his failings and for his very responsibility.

I substitute myself for him in his dying. (*Deathbound Subjectivity* [1989], pp. 183–84)

This is a powerful and increasingly prevalent interpretation of the meaning of Levinasian obligation and ethics as extending from Heidegger's thinking of finitude. It also, at least here, misses the level at which the other is outside of economy, or the productivity of articulations.

48. In a textual explication we will follow later, we will compare the sense of time and justice in *Totality and Infinity* with the sense of passivity and the Good in *Otherwise than Being* to get a better understanding of how Levinas stands in relation to my theses. Suffice it for now to say that, even in his earliest works, even in those works most dependent on the concept of a feminine space of dwelling, he provides a clue to rethinking the present constellation of sexism in our culture: he provides the space for questioning the freedom of virility.

Levinas does not mention Antigone here—once she has acquired the name, the role, "Antigone," she has decided and committed herself to the inhumanity. His analysis precedes the analysis of artistic production—ethics precedes articulation. She is most free, most conscious, when she is still not yet determined as a sister. She will sacrifice herself to the role she plays, but each moment holds a reserve. Even in her death, she is unshaken in purpose but unwilling to accept the hypocritical position of grandiosity in death. She cannot think she has made Polynices' name hallowed; she has, instead, committed herself to the rights of the silenced. The decision—and we should be clear, it is a total sacrifice either way one decides—to sacrifice one's freedom for the silenced and not for the already voiced, for the weak and not the powerful, is the ethical decision itself. This sacrifice cannot be measured in results, returns, or products. It recognizes the "Prisoner's Dilemma" as absurd exactly because there is no escape to the 'outside' of prison—there is no 'free' world. At best, if we were to try and ground an ethics, we could say that any other comportment towards the ethical question of whose laws to obey—besides the comportment that privileges the silenced over the voiced, the dead over the living—merely reinstitutes the public violence of everyday forgetfulness. To lay claim to a life where one finds a meaningful relation, of any sort, one must understand the ethics of listening before speaking.

It will, therefore, be appropriate—if against expectations—to introduce the doctrine of the Christian Trinity—God, the Father; God, the Son; God, the Holy Spirit—

in order to begin a sketch of the literal meaning of what is itself a figure or set of figures—universalization, objectification, externalization. Hegel's thinking of Christ, and of the progress of the human culminating in a Christian state, have both served as the great (if sometimes caricatured) foes through which postmodernism defines itself. More importantly for me, Christ is the great figure of the Son who enacts, who produces and creates in the name of the Father. God's creative freedom is articulated in Christ's presence. To think, as I propose, the metaphorical breadth of the daughter is not to have refuted, or replaced, the tradition—to be a daughter, instead, is to twist an inheritance, to delay the son's ascendence, and be otherwise than as the fleshly incarnation of divinity.

It seems that the great debates on Christology leading to Augustine's (by no means final) refutation of Manicheanism (which holds that there are two forces in the universe, one Good, one Evil) and Pelagianism (which denies original sin and election of God's chosen) will provide the basis for everything from the aesthetics of Thomas Aquinas to Sartre's analysis of boxing in the *Critique of Dialectical Reason*, or any exemplary individual theory; that is, to be *modeled* on God, on the word of God, on the actual manifestation of God, is to see your destiny, your truth, and your actuality in the physical (historical) presence of Christ. It is to see yourself, as well, as embodied spirit. It would also imply, contrary to the lessons we have been drawing from Antigone, that the truth of the roles assumed supersedes the decision to adopt those roles. Arendt (see note 43) uses the analogy of Christ as externalization to talk of Marx's theory of labor (as does Lukács) and Husserl's not far off the same mark with his theory of empty and filled intentions (the activity of consciousness fulfills the meaning of the presence which has already been given in apperception). Theories of myth and symbol (of intentionality) in Cassirer and W. James are much more clearly modeled on Christianity's self-constituting story.[49] That the Christ story has become a less and less conscious part of our collective and scientific explication points to its strange power of transmutation. And to the urgency of our taking up the task again, from the beginning.

Hegel's ability to identify the narrative of Christ's passion with the general structure of taking up a public stance, with, that is, an articulation of a meaningful community, justified the (military and capitalistic) expansion of a 'Christian' world in his time, with its overt colonizing agenda. In our time, very few of us would still speak of Christianity's mission in Hegel's terms, yet much of the triumphalism of post-cold-war capital has to do with the feeling that something like Hegel's ideal public space is now being implemented, albeit without the express content of Christianity. Our task, here, is to encounter this legacy in its force, as Christian, as the militant ascendence of the Son to

49. The standard version of this history—only standardized since the Reformation if at all—would claim a giant misattribution on my part not to have merely pointed to Plato and Aristotle's complex debates on Ideas and how Augustine used those ideas to reconcile primitive Christianity with philosophical belief. This would be to dramatically underestimate the importance of the Christian (and Jewish) relation to time and eschatology—see below. The two loci of the debate in this century are, to some extent, H. Blumenberg, *The Legitimacy of the Modern Age* (1966) and K. Löwith, *Meaning in History: The Theological Implications of the Philosophy of History* (1949).

the throne, and reimagine our time, in all its brutality and callousness, in its own continual and thoughtless transformation, in its very withdrawal, as somehow opening a space for the daughter who could respond.

Postmodernism, in my view, is no less guilty of having too easily believed itself capable of merely abandoning the great narratives, without having to deal explicitly with the baggage. The excursus that follows is designed to address the way in which both the narrative of Christianity itself and the philosophical notion of what it means to be in a world conditioned by narratives have affected our thinking about meaning, and about leading meaningful lives. Narrativity (and the narrative of Christ's passion, above all) is meant to provide the space within which any particular instantiation of meaning will work. We (sons of God) model ourselves on Christ, himself the instantiation of the eternal. My question, instead, is whether we can think of Christ as the *failure* of an instantiation. Whether we can think of his death as a failure which creates the space within which our finitude can function. Or more: can *not* function. My question, to Christianity and its heirs, is whether one can be (human, mortal, meaningfully alive) without being a follower of some model. This is not to ask whether other religions are excluded by Christian hubris, but to ask about what type of life we think one should lead; is religion, like all life, as with Hegel's Christianity especially, only a process of learning how to function appropriately within the public spaces provided by that religion (learning to be the upright citizen in the Christian state)? Is all participation in the public spaces of our world appropriately constrained to productive activity? With the question of what role women play in our society, with the question of how the workplace (and the exclusions perpetrated by the workplace) is constituted, we return to an old question, an almost religious question about how we may be inside our societies (with/towards others): what are we (allowed/called) to do? With postmodernism, I am attempting to show, the emphasis falls on the way in which this question is asked; the emphasis starts being, itself, a question of the style of our asking.

# Christic and Word

## the Son of the Eternal

*Young man I think I know you—I think this*
*face is the face of the Christ himself,*
*Dead and divine and brother of all, and here*
*again he lies.*

> —Walt Whitman, "A Sight in
> Camp in the Daybreak Gray and Dim"

*A song of the rolling earth, and of words*
*according,*
*Were you thinking that those were the words,*
*those upright lines?*
*those curves, angles, dots?*
*No, those are not the words, the substantial*
*words are in the ground and sea,*
*They are in the air, they are in you . . .*
*The workmanship of souls is by those inaudible*
*words of the earth.*

> —Walt Whitman, "A Song
> of the Rolling Earth"

*This first saying is to be sure but a word. But*
*the word is God.*

> —Emmanuel Levinas,
> "Language and Proximity"

Perhaps the hardest thing to convey through philosophical writing is the relevance of minutia to the whole. Books tend, therefore, either towards the trudging tome or the condescendingly simplified polemic. Here as well, the technocratization of society manifests itself in a dizzying increase in technical jargon—and the increasing distances between discourses. I'd like to say, quickly, that the celebration of this divisiveness overlooks the ethical content of language generally, but that would beg the question of how particular individuals, single letters, or single words, have importance for an entire discourse. The

problem of how to write both seriously and accessibly is a double of the stylistic and formal questions that we have already been asking: How does a particular come to have a name? How does a word come to be more than a single
designating act?

The odd unlocatability of Plato's forms is paradigmatically ambiguous.
Outside of mere appearances? Inside my head (our heads—however that
plural is maintained)? Somewhere there is a universal typology, one which the
actual things of the world more or less approximate. We recognize here immediately the question of how we place ourselves (that is, the things we say) in relation to the roles others expect of us (of our words, and in relation to the
things they say of us). We recognize, as a problem, the relation of a situation to
the articulation of that situation. The Enlightenment brought the question of
forms generally into the realm of language and the individual's representations,
and at least since Hegel, and certainly by the time of the popularization of
Freud's conceptions of the unconscious, we have understood all our processes
of speaking, thinking, and even learning as being essentially preconditioned
by a language with more implications than we are consciously able to name,
much less being able to exert explicit control over.

Meaning came to be more and more a problem of a background and the
things that fill it up; the history of determinations, of other people's determining acts, provided the background for my own determining acts, and the truth
of any particular act could only be measured by its correspondence with some
facet of the background (its matching up with the context from which the naming was generated/derived). One hears, for example, that great writers are the
ones who say something we've always known (at some level), but have never
been able to adequately articulate for ourselves. As readers, we recognize our
own context of determining experiences, reworked, articulated, made poetic—
but the words themselves are really no more than correlates of our own experiences (at least in so far as they speak true). If the fundamental claim of humanism is that man makes the world, he must also understand himself in terms of a
lineage of creators: the truth of our experience as men is that we have created
that which we experience; we are our own audience. The articulation of our
world, at its deepest level, aims at expressing the fundamental fact of our creative power within the world. We come to know ourselves, as the ones who
know, in so far as we can name ourselves as the ones who name. I never exert
control over the situation as an individual, but I can come to understand, and
come to terms with, what it means to belong to the human situation itself.

Constantly in view here as well is the fact that the *structure* of these basic
acts of naming is repeated at ever more complex levels.[50] The self-conception
of the Enlightenment human—the self-made, self-named man, in his various

50. And the reason for writing this section, in terms of whatever unity this book proposes, lies in the possibility of retrieving and questioning these basic acts. Thus, by referring to Christ, I wish to recontextualize our discussion of naming and desire beyond the somewhat constrained modern configuration of feminism vs. patriarchy—only then to rebuild that affiliation from the perspective of a reappropriation. In strictly philosophical metaphors, I'm using Christ as a key word to designate the Hegelian unity of man and God in the speaking consciousness and, against Hegel, as the possibility of a reappropriation and re-working of the process of consciousness itself (thus Christ is a double of Antigone), thereby questioning the facile embrace of a certain conceptual violence which is Hegel's modernism. That is, Christ metaphorizes that humanism which corresponds to the metaphysics of presence while woman, as metaphor (and in other ways), is caught in that trajectory precisely as not really belonging. The ways in which Christ, too, doesn't really fit—or, rather, articulates the possibility of *meaningfully* not fitting—will serve as a bridge between the two metaphors. Our question of Christ, or his question to us, has to do with the failures we have inherited from a Christian trajectory: not with the promise of some triumphant return of God.

51. "This view of man's negative freedom, of a private sphere surrounding him that cannot be entered (first by other individuals

guises—is accepted uncritically as *the* category of success by the vast majority of Western (and Westernized) women and men. As the story is normally told, the West stands alone in world history—at least since the time of the Protestant Reformation—as the land of the individual, striving, energetic, active, man. (Women's role, as we have already seen, is ambiguously passive, active, and plural.) We are accustomed to thinking of the period about four hundred years ago—and the exact date is constantly being debated—as the foundation of all which is distinctively good about Western man and society. We have also, more recently, begun to think of all these features as interconnected. The discourse of incorrigible private realms leads to talk of rights and of the social contract.[51] The critique of the divine right of kings feeds the ethical turn to individual self-responsibility that restructures the legitimation of social hierarchies away from the strict patriarchal lines of medieval societies towards (the myth of) the self-creation of value in and as oneself: the wealthy deserve their wealth because they are its source. We may not be able to name all the causes, all the background elements forming our beliefs, but they all stand, as elements, in potency towards a (set of) judgment(s) with which we can claim to have achieved our own self-determination and self-control (we are said to be trying to learn to name ourselves, to become literally autonomous, and the more we can claim to have already achieved this separation from others' names and laws and customs, the better off we are).

According to this latter story, before 1500 a person fulfilled only the roles offered to her/him at birth by an all-knowing god.

After 1500 each individual, according to his/her individual attributes, was responsible for her/his individual destiny. Of the various determining attributes of election, however, one came consistently to the fore: energy. Man need only be productive to ensure himself wealth (and happiness). Eventually the goals of that activity—increasingly diversified according to the various particular instantiations of the unencroachable private realm—faded in importance and the value of every man was measured merely by the fact of his activity. (There is no such thing, for example, as an industrious thief in the popular imagination; if a man is industrious, he is producing for the good.) The given roles were no longer constraining, but the transformation of one's life into a destiny (the concept of a role in the abstract generalized into the activity of forming roles) became the only measure by which one could call oneself (successfully) human. Paradoxically, man's activity is specifically designed to separate him from the (feminine) crowd at the same time that it raises him to the truth of the essentially human (man's destiny is thus his loneliness, but we all share in this fate). Society is either seen as an evil, something one should minimize in its ill effects on the individual, or as a necessarily lost moment of childlike and natural innocence which only striving men can reappropriate and reform into a private (and sometimes, with truly great men, a public) realm of enjoyment.

The Enlightenment told itself the story of its own inventions as the virility of a world-historical people, of a time of energy and excitement unmatched by the basically feminine (unchangingly passive) time that the East and the Dark Ages languished in.

and eventually by the state) without his consent, becomes the standard view of freedom in the liberal tradition, interlocking neatly with the Cartesian view of the person" (I. Shapiro, *The Evolution of Rights in Liberal Theory* [1986], p. 277).

Social hierarchies stagnated when set in the stone of inherited privilege; the energy and activity of man had no end or reason if not for the individual's self-advancement. The Enlightenment did not argue for the elimination of social roles; it merely translated those roles into processes, into functions of activity (filled by any appropriately energetic individual). The great men who (re)constituted a 'modern community' tried to do such exactly in terms of breaking with past communities; modernity is characterized (individually and societally) by a conception of self based on separation. If the division between passive and active (belonging and alienation) is eliminated (or transformed), then all the theoretical structures of modern Western society will need to be rethought: the legal system based on possessed rights, the political system based on representative men, the family system based on the working father. I do not, in opposition, then propose to eliminate society in a revolutionary thrust (nothing is more based on a blind trust of energetic ejaculation than the theory of a violent revolution justifying itself); I propose to rethink the ground of continuation, and from there approach the possibility of thinking towards real change. That this rethinking would include a turn away from those metaphors specifically said to be 'about' women accords with my sense of history, or of trajectories within history, never being determined in their course because they always depend on the aleatory structures of an audience, on the necessity of being taken up—a Christian woman, for only one of the many pertinent examples, can become such without assuming one of the woman's roles within the church. It is merely a mark of our self-conceptualizations within modernism that those roles seem ever more proscribed by tradition. (This argument, on my part, is possible largely because I don't presume to think that articulations, the way for example one speaks about oneself, exhaust the self; that a woman still cannot become a priest in the Catholic church is a related problem exactly to the extent that the exclusion is justified by the appeal to a particular tradition's view of the self and its appropriate roles.)

It is in this context that I will say something impertinent: Christ is a word. Not to say that he is a word equal to all other words, or that words are somehow metaphysical, but that Christ is a word actually spoken (and already spoken) by someone. Or, more importantly, Christ is a word (already) spoken to someone in particular. Notice I have not said that Christ is a symbol or that God is the externalized qualities of humankind; he does not express a time before or outside of history, but, rather, he is our expressing the expression, our saying, directly and not through God, that words are (at least relatively) transcendent. The word 'Christ' metaphorizes the fact that we speak together. (And this word, again against expectations, would also be available to the non-Christian—there is, in principle, no closure to the set of words, to ethical significations, just as there is no closure within the single utterance addressed to an other; after all, the other may yet respond; after all, Christ has failed to yet return.) My point is that Christ, like all words, is not a symbol: the word says more about those who say it than about the issue to which they refer. Hegel, articulating the very depths of the connection between eurocentrism and modern science, would claim that Christianity was a necessary precondition for self-consciousness. To contest this, we would have to see exactly where the various religions differ on their conceptions of becoming unified in (or by) the word. We would also have to have presumed to have determined the true nature of the relations between culture, knowledge, religion, and social practice. For my more humble purposes, Christ is merely an exemplar of personified divinity or enacted transcendence—he is just a word—but, for those of us born after Nietzsche announced the death of God, such words are everything. Questioning our relation to the Christian religion—or any religion—merely restates the question of the book; rather: any answer to any of the questions of this book would have to include, more or less explicitly, an answer to the question of the religious life (which is not exactly a question of belief)—a question of our relation to the divine. It is the question of our own meaning.[52] To that extent, the divine word is not the truth: it is a first approximation—but not an approaching of the true. Rather, it is an approximation towards, an approaching of, the future. As a word, Christ already encompasses a silence—the possibility of meaning is not determined (or constrained) by this word (as it

52. This is, and should be recognized as, an atheism in the strong philosophical sense; Christ is the god of my tradition and the god which has been used to validate the very idea of tradition within modernism; Christ, as word then, is the possibility of a certain religiosity within my tradition, as it is specifically thought through our relation to language as an inheritance. What I am searching for, within these theories of speech, is the possibility for a new saying, not for rediscovering a lost faith, nor even for finding a new sense to an old word. On the other hand, this way of phrasing my question *of* Christ also precludes any 'scientistic' atheism, the atheism which merely contests the propositional content of beliefs, or insists on the bare existence of every proposition's referent. Further, in not merely excising the words, I'm trying not to foreclose questions about how the specificity of Christian history has affected our historical and philosophical development. Of course, there is no true path that Christianity has deviated from, and so there is no question of simply purifying our self-conception of any Christian taint. Rather, as a first step towards thinking, we need to eschew the willful blindness towards the actual historical development of our thinking—a blindness encouraged by a faith in the unity of the field established by (the reasonability of the unity responding to) the simple (and immediately 'obvious') question of truth (and of a subject's true belief).

would be if there were such a thing as *a* Christian tradition). Rather, and this is what I will be attempting to show at several junctures, such words, by reaching towards a future, make silences possible. The word does not mark the possibility of fulfilling thought, in representing what had lain in wait, hoping to be given voice: such words, approximations of the divine, mark instead the very failure of the intention to simply fulfill the already promised.

"O God, Why hast thou forsaken me?" The question, from the cross, calls *us* (the audience and inheritors of Christ's dying) to take on the power, and the responsibility, of our acts—and yet, from where do acts get their power? From where do we get the power to respond to a dying god? Or, in what amounts to the same question, more generally formed, what (and how) do we understand when we read? And, perhaps most importantly: how, in these questions, do we interpolate (or have we already interpolated) a 'we'?

Tocqueville, commenting on the antihistoricism of the fiercely independent Americans of the first decades of the nineteenth century, said that Americans were all Cartesians without ever having heard Descartes's name. Hegel, writing at the same time, was, descriptively, explaining how a sense of national identity could be established, and, writing normatively, he prescribed, as the truth of being, the self writ large as nation, the identity of nation and self: Hegel explained how it could come to pass that a nation of Hegelians could be so oddly aware and unaware of their own Hegelianism. The mechanism is called (by others) forgetfulness and its expression in this case is our constant longing for childhood innocence—for our immediate and unquestioned sense of belonging to a group. That group itself is defined by its history, the tradition of its self-conceptions. We who were born into a Cartesian state are thus caught in a double bind.

Hegel's task, in the (polemical) story I am telling, is to provide the links between (1) our conception of the human, (2) the history of our conception of the human, (3) the history of the conception of the human as it relates to the divine, and (4) the conception of divinity which lets us understand the concept of the human as basically historical (progressing towards its fulfillment/meaning). The critique I've already been pointing at will circle around the ways in which Hegel's thought remains eurocentric: once at the level where it is presumed that the purpose of being human is found in the creating of the space for the self as individual capable of being autonomous (of naming, and judging, in one's own name) and then again at the level where the act of naming is taken as the appropriate model for all types of activity which can justifiably be called human (that is, at the level where mental activities, or what separates men from animals, are all that can be truly called human).

As a (possible) key to beginning to understand Hegel, begin with the idea that there is one process that repeats itself in many guises: the most basic acts of knowing (including eating), all forms of desire, the creation and appreciation of art, learning or speaking a language, conquering or being conquered by another country or culture, bartering goats, writing treaties, watching T.V., worshipping a divinity, being a divinity. Circles within circles, overlapping other circles. As long as possible, we will not name the process, only enumerate its manifestations—that is, enumerate its articulations. Take as an example, from almost the end of the *Phenomenology*:

> The works of the Muse now lack the power of the Spirit, for the Spirit has gained its certainty of itself from the crushing of gods and men. They have become what they are for us now— beautiful fruit already picked from the tree, which a friendly fate has offered us, as a girl might set the fruit before us. . . . (a gift) which is the inwardizing in us of the Spirit which was still (only) outwardly manifested. (Hegel, *Phenomenology of Spirit* [1807], pp. 455–56. [my ellipsis])

The German '*Geist*' (Spirit) had earlier been translated as 'Mind' and this is an exemplary passage for showing the inadequacy of either translation, or at least some of the complexity of the original German. Spirit is an animating principle. For Hegel, it is animation itself. It is the essence of all things and the concrete existence of all things. It is the concrete life of a nation and its individuals. It is the abstract principle

53. Hegel had, in his articulation of these moments, relied explicitly on the story of a god become human through the aid of a woman:

> Spirit has in it the two sides which are presented above as two converse propositions: one is this, that substance alienates itself from itself and becomes self-consciousness; the other is the converse, that self-consciousness alienates itself from itself and gives itself the nature of a Thing, or makes itself a universal Self. Both sides have in this way encountered each other, and through this encounter their true union has come into being. The externalization [or kenosis] of substance, its growth into self-consciousness, expresses the transition into the opposite, the unconscious transition of *necessity*; in other words, that substance is *in itself* self-consciousness. Conversely, the externalization of self-consciousness expresses this, that it is *in itself* the universal essence, or—since the Self is pure being-for-self which in its opposite communes with itself—that it is just because substance is self-consciousness *for the Self*, that it is Spirit. Of this Spirit, which has abandoned the form of Substance and enters existence in the shape of self-consciousness, it may therefore be said—if we wish to employ relationships derived from natural generation— that it has an *actual* mother

but an *implicit* father. For *actuality* or self-consciousness, and the *in-itself* as substance, are its two moments through whose reciprocal externalization, each becoming the other, Spirit comes into existence as this their unity. (Hegel, *Phenomenology of Spirit* [1807], p. 457)

54. What we are really trying to say is that capitalism, through its process of production, produces an awesome schizophrenic accumulation of energy or charge, against which it brings all its vast powers of repression to bear, but which nonetheless continues to act as capitalism's limit. For capitalism constantly counteracts, constantly inhibits this inherent tendency while at the same time allowing it free rein; it continually seeks to avoid reaching its limit while simultaneously tending toward that limit. Capitalism institutes or restores all sorts of residual and artificial, imaginary, or symbolic territorialities, thereby attempting, as best it can, to recode, to rechannel persons who have been defined in terms of abstract quantities. Everything returns or recurs: States, nations, families. That is what makes the ideology of capitalism "a motley painting of everything that has ever been believed." (Deleuze and Guattari, *Anti-Oedipus* [1972], p. 34)

which orders the concrete life of a nation and its individuals. It is desire as well as that which desires and that which is desired. It provides all answers and undermines the arrogant claim to free questioning. It is matter and form, substance, subject, and consciousness.[53]

Let us return to the girl whom we rob (who gives us) of the fruits of her labor, the child substituted for a once powerful Muse. We find ourselves eating, something we cannot do without in any case, but this time we are eating a delectable fruit. Or rather, it is some sort of remains, a "crushing of gods and men": the Greek Spirit conquering the Trojan Spirit, mercantilism conquering feudalism, industrial capitalism crushing the 'free' workers (after having created them). We are allowed to nibble on any, all, and each of these corpses.[54] Suffice it now—as precondition to our meal—that they are dead.

Perhaps the clue lies with the eating. There are, for example, rules of eating—determined by who eats, how many eat, what is eaten, what utensils are used, and, not least of all, who (as author) has prepared the meal. Eating, internalizing, incorporating, remembering. Hegel starts the *Phenomenology* proper with the process(es) of consciousness. Begin with the here and now of Sense-certainty—the particular, singularity. It is in the nature of time to pass away (here is Hegel's irreducible), for the immediate 'here and now' to become 'then and there'. Time is this passing, but it is also the process of passing from one to the other: nostalgia, sexual or instinctual drives, national patriotisms, even aesthetic taste, all come together as a process of shifting attention, of appropriating, individualizing, naming, movements—enacted by individuals in acts of determining judgments and by nations in the great expressions of their defining projects (usually wars or other monuments).[55] Of ultimate interest for us is that, for Hegel, this casts consciousness in a negative light (indeed, as 'the' negative itself), and also importantly, as it ties into Derrida's reading of Hegel, it turns on an example of the written as such:[56] If I write down the time, the lived immediacy of 1:47 A.M.—if correspondingly I say to myself, "Now it's 1:47 A.M."—when I return to what was once indubitable I find the truth's content is now false: it is 1:48 A.M. Trivial up to this point, we find that preservation (the historicity of consciousness) takes a negative hue: it is lived as the dying of the particular. What is preserved as truth—what lives on—is not '1:47 A.M.' but the abstract universal form 'now is'—a form which allows us to imply the abstract identity of all previous and future times. The playing field is infinite through time and space, but leveled off, constrained by the form of universalization, of appearances understood in terms of the production of meaning, such that the *way* of being will be the same for all possible objects appearing within the field. This conception of time, and time's relation to conscious processes, is still dominant today. For Hegel, language—always a negative universal moment belonging to, or approximating, consciousness—mediates: it is our relation to that which is 'this'. The contemporary critique of the 'metaphysics of presence' rests on an understanding (and often dismissal) of Hegel which is this sim-

55. "Desire is the negating (overcoming) of a present which is the negation (absence) of that which Desire desires. As such, Desire, the first name for the way of Being of human being, is another name for the dialectic founding the identity of Spirit and time; the dialectical structure of Desire outlines a temporal process and opening up of a world. As such, Desire is another name for the 'restlessness of life'; it is 'the portentous power of the negative' underpinning and defining Spirit as the Being of the real" (D. Schmidt, *The Ubiquity of the Finite* [1988], p. 57).

56. Derrida's reading is well represented in "The Pit and the Pyramid: an Introduction to Hegelian Semiology" (1968), in his *Margins of Philosophy*. Hegel himself says,

To the question: "What is Now?" let us answer, e.g. "Now is Night." In order to test the truth of this sense-certainty a simple experiment will suffice. We write down this truth; a truth cannot lose anything by being written down, any more than it can lose anything through our preserving it. If *now, this noon*, we look again at the written truth we shall have to say that it has become stale.

The Now that is Night is *preserved*, i.e. it is treated as what it professes to be, as something that *is*; but it proves itself to be, on the contrary, something that is *not*. The Now does indeed preserve itself, but as something that is *not* Night;

equally, it preserves itself in face of the Day that it now is, as something that also is not Day, in other words, as a *negative* in general. This self-preserving Now is, therefore, not immediate but mediated; for it is determined as a permanent and self-preserving Now *through* the fact that something else, viz. Day and Night, is *not*. As so determined, it is still just as simply Now as before, and in this simplicity is indifferent to what happens in it; just as little as Night and Day are its being, just as much also is it Day and Night; it is not in the least affected by this its other-being. A simple thing of this kind which *is* through negation, which is neither This nor That, a *not-This*, and is with equal indifference This as well as That—such a thing we call a *universal*. So it is in fact the universal that is the true [content] of sense-certainty. (Hegel, *Phenomenology of Spirit* [1807], p. 60)

ple. However, even with the complex additional schemas of twentieth-century philosophy, it remains unclear whether anyone has truly surpassed the sense of language as an opposition to nonlanguage, of thinking as opposed to what is thought about, at least as long as negation remains as the privileged moment of consciousness.[57] Negation is, and this speaks the strange unity of modern thought, the dying of the particular for the greater life of the universal. The move which is so difficult for us to think after Hegel, which stands at the end of metaphysics, is the move which established the formal principle of the privilege of death over life, or, changing the ground of the metaphor, the crucial move after Hegel would be refusing—in our thinking and acting—our murderous fear of death or change; we must[58] begin to think the character of past and future without clutching to the overarching superiority of the 'now' as a moment of vision (of the present, as process, as universal, being the spirit of the universal itself). The key is, instead and with exact parallels to seeing Antigone's activity, understanding the activity, the systems of obligations, that are already implicated in the 'now'. This understanding is not the same as comprehending the tradition, or reviving the intentions of the founders of the tradition: it is questioning, or gaining the space of the question of, the original intentions themselves. To gain a space for thought without merely negating what stands opposed. . . .

But slower. Not only is each particular a tragic apostasy, stepping down from the realm of undivided light, but each universal is the dying-off of the immediate particular

57. Perhaps the first problem—and unfortunately, one that will have to be worked out in other writings—would be asking about what is meant by an opposition in general. Heidegger, more than anyone else, seems to have made this question central to his thinking. For only one (fairly germane) example among numerous possible citations:

> Looking back to the earlier episode, we may now ask: In what way does the dwarf make the interpretation of the imagery, that is, of the gate-way and the two avenues, too easy for himself? Zarathustra indicates the answer when he goes on to command, "Look at the gateway itself—the Moment!" What does that directive mean? The dwarf merely looks at the two paths extending to infinity, and he thinks about them merely in the following way: If both paths run on to infinity ("eternity"), then that is where they meet; and since the circle closes by itself in infinity—far removed from me—all that recurs, in sheer alternation within this system of compensations, does so as a sequence, as a sort of parade passing through the gateway. The dwarf understands nothing of what Zarathustra means when he says—bewilderingly enough—that the two paths "affront one another" in the gateway. But how is that possible, when each thing moves along behind its predecessor, as is manifest with time itself? For in time the not-yet-now becomes the now, and forthwith becomes a no-longer-now, this as a perpetual and-so-on. The two avenues, future and past, do not collide at all, but pursue one another.
>
> And yet a collision does occur here. To be sure, it occurs only to one who does not remain a spectator but who *is himself* the Moment, performing actions directed toward the future and at the same time accepting and affirming the past, by no means letting it drop. Whoever stands in the Moment is turned in two ways: for him past and future *run up against* one another. Whoever stands in the Moment lets what runs counter to itself come to collision, though not to a standstill, by cultivating and sustaining the strife between what is assigned him as a task and what has been given him as his endowment. To see the Moment means to stand in it. But the dwarf keeps to the outside, perches on the periphery. . . . That is what is peculiar to, and hardest to bear in, the doctrine of the eternal return—to wit, that eternity *is* in the Moment, that the Moment is not the fleeting "now," not an instant of time whizzing by a spectator, but the collision of future and past. (Heidegger, "Nietzsche's Fundamental Metaphysical Position in Western Thought: The Doctrine of Eternal Recurrence of the Same" [1937], *Nietzsche*, 2: 56–57 [my ellipsis])

58. The "must" is difficult here: we are being asked to learn (and learn to question) the force of an obligation felt from out of a tradition. The glorification of the "new" in modernism fell back on the security of a single process (life thought in the singularity of its appropriative processes) and finds any attempt to question how life itself (as process, as desire, as goal) is constituted as a moral obligation to be a threat on par with murder; "hell," itself, "is other people." The "must," then, is to be read "under erasure," as the question we are learning to ask: must we respond when we are called? Perhaps not. Perhaps our freedom (and our errancy) lies here. Perhaps, tentatively, a distance from Levinas would also be stated here precisely where freedom takes place.

59. The difficulty of Derrida's work, at least in his early writings, seems tied to his recognition of this duplicity and his attempt to articulate its pervasive grasp on the structures of our experience (and of our articulations) where we least wish to find anything but a unified field. For only one example:

> But if Rousseau could say that "words [voix], not sounds [sons], are written," it is because words are distinguished from sounds exactly by what permits writing—consonants and articulation. The latter replace only themselves. Articulation, which replaces accent, is the origin of languages. Altering [for the worse] through writing is an originary exteriority. It is the origin of language. Rousseau describes it without declaring it. Clandestinely.
>
> A speech without consonantic principle, what for Rousseau would be a speech sheltered from all writing, would not be speech; it would hold itself at the fictive limit of the inarticulate and purely natural cry. Conversely, a speech of pure consonants and pure articulation would become pure writing, algebra, or dead language. The death of speech is therefore the horizon and origin of language. But an origin and a horizon which do not hold themselves at its exterior borders. As always, death, which is neither a present to come nor a present past, shapes the interior of speech, as its trace, its reserve, its interior and exterior

thing in itself. Two deaths are articulated at once, as alternating moments of murder.[59] Many of the fiercest philosophical battles have been fought over the hierarchy of these violences, over the search, or abandonment of the search, for worlds of natural innocence or Utopias of postcritical nonviolence.

There is a gap between knowing and eating, the closing of which is the moment the Hegel excerpt ("like beautiful fruit") points to as the completion of a nation's self-consciousness and takes the form of the simplest, and outside of photosynthesis, the most common, act of violence. It sets the stage and model for all violence to come, of all forgetfulness and drunken revelry taken to be the truth: like Iphigenia's forebears we eat happily of the meat at the table, even though it was once a member of the immediate family. The moment of consumption must be further conceived as desire itself: there is no essential division in Hegel between the decision to eat something and the actual digestion. Eating is oddly paradigmatic because it is both violent—gnashing of teeth, acids of digestion—and satisfying of an obscure—instinctual? biological? learned?—lack. For Hegel, this desire, the motivating force which causes us to eat, to universalize, is the desire for unity, the certainty that such unity is mine by essence and right.[60] The desire for unity is dialectically conditioned by the perception of conflict. Importantly, (1) this unity always happens at the site of an individual stomach; (2) progress itself is defined as the victory of one stomach over another (the food chain; social Darwinism), finally completed in the abstract ideal of representation as digestion; and (3) desire is a term defined only tautologically in terms of activity; only a level of analysis that starts outside of any individual would describe desire as a search for death.

And thus have we eaten. But we are not satiated: we must eat again. Only by this route, says Hegel, do we reach the manifold. The corresponding move in language is illuminating as we find the necessity of multiplication in/as the thing itself (as a dissemination of words).[61] "This salt is a simple Here, and at the same time manifold; it is white and also tart, also cubical in shape, of a specific gravity, etc." (*Phenomenology of Spirit*, p. 68).

It is the magic of the '*Aufhebung*', the superseding which negates and preserves, that when we eat the salt, all of its characteristics —although unnamed—remain; the magic of the language is that when we say 'salt' we also say, albeit in silence, 'white', 'tart', and 'cubical'. Consciousness, as a moment of vision, only works because it is also silently (and violently) appropriative. Of course, we may decide not to eat the salt. Only then does it truly die out, like a pre-Homeric Greek, for the particular is only preserved by being taken out of the flow of time from which it sprang and being reconstituted in a now present consciousness—such is the logic of 'appropriation', that much touted eclecticism of art, religion, and philosophy. Our silent saying of 'white', 'tart', and 'cubical' is still recognizably a negative moment, just like the actual saying of 'salt'. In this way, even the most insignificant of details are susceptible to being drawn from the limited sphere of 'this' into the greater life of the eating individual, which individual also forfeits the narrow confines of 'this' life for a stake in the greater life of a world-historical

différance: as its supplement. (Derrida, *Of Grammatology* [1967], p. 315)

60. And what consciousness will learn from experience in all sense-certainty is, in truth, only what we have seen viz. the This as *universal*, the very opposite of what that assertion affirmed to be universal experience. With this appeal to universal experience we may be permitted to anticipate how the case stands in the practical sphere. In this respect we can tell those who assert the truth and certainty of the reality of sense-objects that they should go back to the most elementary school of wisdom, viz. the ancient Eleusinian Mysteries of Ceres and Bacchus, and that they have still to learn the secret meaning of the eating of bread and the drinking of wine. For he who is initiated into these Mysteries not only comes to doubt the being of sensuous things, but to despair of it; in part he brings about the nothingness of such things himself in his dealings with them, and in part he sees them reduce themselves to nothingness. Even the animals are not shut out from this wisdom but, on the contrary, show themselves to be most profoundly initiated into it; for they do not just stand idly in front of sensuous things as if these possessed intrinsic being, but, despairing of their reality, and completely assured of their nothingness, they fall to without

ceremony and eat them up. And all Nature, like the animals, celebrates these open Mysteries which teach the truth about sensuous things. (Hegel, *Phenomenology of Spirit* [1807], p. 65)

61. Derrida is speaking of Thoth, the Egyptian god of wisdom, learning, and writing, but (perhaps) could have equally been speaking of Christ: "As a substitute capable of doubling for the king, the father, the sun, and the word, distinguished from these only by dint of representing, repeating, and masquerading, Thoth was naturally also capable of totally supplanting them and appropriating all their attributes. He is added as the essential attribute of what he is added to, and from which almost nothing distinguishes him. He differs from speech or divine light only as the revealer from the revealed. Barely" (*Dissemination* [1972], p. 90).

62. To complete our insight into the Notion of this movement it may further be noticed that the differences themselves are exhibited in a twofold difference: once as a difference of *content*, one extreme being the Force reflected into itself, but the other the medium of the "matters"; and again as a difference of *form*, since one solicits and the other is solicited, the former being active and the other passive. According to the difference of content they are distinguished [merely] in principle, or *for us*; but according to the dif-

(national) spirit, which in its turn becomes part of the life of Absolute Spirit (God) itself. In parallel, long after we have eaten the salt, without having paid attention to our eating, we may be able to express things about the salt which had previously been unexpressed. Still we are moving too quickly.

Consciousness requires a third moment (1 = thing, 2 = perception of thing) before it is complete, this third moment itself analyzed into two parts: Force and Understanding. Force is naturally occuring relation; understanding is consciousness of force. It is the simple division (and rejoining) of content and form.[62]

There is an important move here; one that takes Hegel a long way towards the completion of metaphysics as ontology[63]—towards theorizing the unity of God and Being. Imagine two opposites: rising and falling, seen in one dimension. Change your perspective: these two opposites are united in two dimensions as a circle. We can't, however, understand this too quickly. It is slightly different from the example of eating salt. With the salt we had noted a multiplication of qualities which could all be subsumed and incorporated through the one act of eating. No understanding is required to see the relation of the attributes; they exist as singular. It does require, however, that the eating subject be other than what is eaten. Self-consumption is non-sense; it would be coterminous with death. In the same way, you, the understanding subject, must be opposed to the circle you observe. 'You' must be posited as the *subject* observing; you must be given an eye to see with. To see the line as two opposite one-dimensional movements—rising and falling—you must exist in a two-dimensional space outside the line. Correspondingly, to see it as a two-dimensional, unified circle, you must occupy a three-dimensional space outside the plane of the circle. Once you occupy three-dimensional space, the circle is given to you, the viewing eye, immediately, with all of its attributes, like salt. What risks being too easily understood here is the movement of understanding itself—the movement from *life* in two dimensions to *life* in three dimensions. We forget the moment that constitutes the *self* as *eye*. It becomes tempting (and dangerous) at this point to view knowing oneself as essentially the same as any other act of knowing. One uses the technologies of self to constrain and transform the given body into the ideal form: one works out, is disciplined, becomes thin. . . .

And Hegel, as every Marxist should know, founds the dialectic of materialism (albeit topsy-turvy). Each of these systems, idealism and materialism, ground the subject-object dichotomy in the diremption, the negative movement and division, of one organic whole tearing *itself* into a set of parts. The culmination of philosophy is the reunification of the organic whole, the dead soul's joining with God, the proletariat appropriating (his) own labor: the end of alienation. That from which we arose will find its truth in our return to it; the determining context of our meaning will have been determined (known; appropriated).

For Hegel, freedom is not resident in the decision. Rather, freedom is self-consciousness itself; seeing the movement as movement, being the movement as the seeing of movement. Schematically, but true in relation to the way modern philosophy in

ference of form they are independent and in their relation keep themselves separate and opposed to one another. The fact that the extremes, from the standpoint of both these sides, are thus nothing *in themselves*, that these sides in which their different essences were supposed to consist are only vanishing moments, are an immediate transition of each into its opposite, this truth becomes apparent to consciousness in its perception of the movement of Force. But *for us*, as remarked above, something more was apparent, viz. that the differences, *qua differences of content and form*, vanished in themselves; and on the side of form, the essence of the *active, soliciting* or *independent* side, was the same as that which, on the side of content, presented itself as Force driven back into itself; the side which was passive, which was *solicited* or for an *other*, was, from the side of form, the same as that which, from the side of content, presented itself as the universal medium of the many "matters." (Hegel, *Phenomenology of Spirit* [1807], p. 85)

63. It maintains that fixing an interconnection between a being, *on*, and *logos* already represents a decisive (not a random) *answer* to the guiding question of philosophy. This answer, which was of necessity prepared at the start of ancient philosophy, was brought to completion in a

radical way by Hegel. That is, *by really carrying through the answer,* he brought to real completion the task which was implied in ancient philosophy. (Accordingly, *a being as such,* the actual in its genuine and whole reality, is the idea, or the *concept.* The concept, however, is the power of time, i.e., *the pure concept annuls time.* In other words, the problem of *being* is properly conceived only when *time is made to disappear.*) The Hegelian philosophy expresses this disappearance of time by conceiving philosophy as *the* science or as absolute knowledge. (Heidegger, *Hegel's Phenomenology of Spirit* [1930–31], p. 12)

general interprets self-consciousness: (1) The typifications, the words, which we use to name ourselves, including all the things of our world, come from the language which is created by the active spirit of a people's language use. (2) Self-consciousness is knowing yourself as being seen, as if you saw yourself. Seeing yourself from the outside, as if you yourself were some type of product, is the truth of this motion; freedom is knowing yourself as product. Marx says no more than this; Heidegger's innovation in *Being and Time* is to question this appropriative technology, and all the appropriate techniques of logic. If, following the technological understanding of ourselves, consciousness is conceived as an effect of the material—or if material and consciousness of material proceed in a dialectic through material and spiritual history—then the line we spoke of no longer truly has an eye perceiving (or at least no need of that particular eye's work). In some sense, you are the whole line; or rather, the moment of recognition that enables your turn from one dimension to two, from individual to class consciousness, reestablishes the simple unity of being (the whole line; the whole plane; the whole itself) with itself.

Simply imagine yourself to be a line: if another line passes through you it is given immediately as there, and since you are one-dimensional, it is only there and nothing else. A second line is needed (you must live, or experience, life as two lines) to determine the direction the line is being drawn in—whether it rises or falls. A second line and (or, which is) an understanding of relation in time (or, in more Hegelian language, understanding as the mediation of negating preservation: the universal, the sign, which remains after the immediate presence is lost).[64] To understand these two moments, however, one must be both lines, one must live the experience of being crossed and understand the relation of before and after as the life of two lines being crossed—which defines, at the least, a plane, or more properly, life as a plane. Hegel—as well as those who follow in his tracks—is merely understanding time like a line itself, defining the extra dimension of time as the place in which/as which we live. In this determination of time human subjectivity is reduced to its function as opposite, either master or slave, to the material world. It imbues the material with meaning by recognizing itself as material. All things rational, in this sense, correspond to reality; if, however, possibility is higher than actuality, freeplay higher than necessity, then the death of the correspondence theory of truth is the birth of a serious child—one who stands out into life, negotiating the terms of her marriage or her death.

Hegel's understanding of time allows him to disregard the particular observer or particular experiencing subject (reducing the subject to the status of just another being among beings) and speak of a formal, universal, structure of understanding: a structure which is 'is', a structure which being itself follows whether or not an individual actually sees it. My critique here is two-fold. Briefly, flattening past, present, and future into the single identity of the structure 'now'—such that each past was also structured as a now—creates for itself the illusion of progress by effacing the privilege of the now from which we write; it is the facile benevolence of unquestioned humanism. This is worked out further in later sections,

64. "Since the real difference belongs to the extremes, this middle term is only the abstract neutrality, the real possibility of those extremes; it is, as it were, the *theoretical element* of the concrete existence of chemical objects, of their process and its result. In the material world *water* fulfills the function of this medium; in the spiritual world, so far as the analogue of such a relation has a place there, the *sign* in general, and more precisely *language,* is to be regarded as fulfilling that function" (Hegel, *Science of Logic* [1812], p. 729). This is also quoted as an epigraph to Derrida's "The Pit and the Pyramid" (1968), *Margins of Philosophy*, p. 71.

but—as a foreshadowing—my response would be that there is an anarchic time, a time based on the creativity, the efficacy, of the individual (and we will see later how this "individual" is not like the creative "subject" of modernism) and not on the faithfulness of an individual to an exterior model (exterior either as belonging to the context from which the individual arose or as having confronted the individual as some particular thing to be copied).

The second criticism argues against Hegel's conception of the end of activity. Since he argues the strict logic of return, we are said to be active for the sake of activity; we are said to become parents for the sake of having children—not for their sake *as* children, nor for their sake *as* individuals, but for their sake as future bearers of future children. By virtue of the identification of self with nation-self, which slides easily into the identity of the rational animal with Reason (the vacuous international humanity based on a supposedly identical functioning of the eyes of humans), Hegel is able to claim that the end, or goal, of all activity (including patriotic wars, for example) is the return to the origin of that activity. Others call it the will-to-death, or nihilism.

Philosophically, he founds here the capitalist argument that the unregulated energy of every striving subject greedily looking out for personal self-interest will result in the magical creation of a universally happy world, just as Augustine proclaims that all evil returns to God's true path. Driving down the street, every billboard proclaims that the things of the world merely await your personal consumption, your comforting digestion. In a city at night every sign fights for your attention; the net effect is said to be beautiful, glamorous. Or if *you* prefer the wilderness, that's your *choice*. There is no evil to expressing your personal values, no evil to selling whatever the market wants, for all consumption returns to the perfect innocence of eating the dead; to question the *desire* to eat, the system of consumption, is to dispute every *man's right* to happiness. To question that right, without merely eliminating all individual privilege, all specificity, is to question how the field of all possible meaning became reduced to a single form of interaction: appropriation.

Heidegger, in a lecture course on Hegel's *Phenomenology of Spirit* given in 1930–31, gives us the implication of this understanding of "Force and Understanding" as it relates to the problem of how to lead the good life:

> In the simple proposition, a is b, the *is* is stated. But this "is," being [*Sein*], obtains its actual, true, and absolute meaning only as the speculative "is," which is stated in mediation. However, the "simple," one-sided proposition does not by itself reach the speculative form unless the term *is* is given in advance (of) the meaning, not of a one-sided, but of a sublated-sublating unity. This unity as the unity which sublates all dissension, and along with it all

unhappiness, is the absolute as happiness. It unties the entanglement and appeases the conflict. Happiness, entangling, untying, and redeeming—these are determinations which resonate in Hegel's concept of the absolute. What is happy in this sense, what reconciles, is the true being [*Seiendes*]; and it is according to *its* being that all beings are determined in their being.[65] (Heidegger, *Hegel's Phenomenology of Spirit*, p. 98)

Our understanding of how the "is" of predication works obviously has numerous correspondences with the way we conceive the world. To recapitulate, for Hegel, we begin with immediate presence and then our perception of that presence, as moments of a positive particular related to a negative universal. That negative universal, our particular perception, serves as a positive particular for the next negating universal. We find here the sense of a result obtained. Once we (and this may be the actual work of another individual) have learned the unifying logic of the circle (once we learn to live the life of a plane), it becomes an acquired signification, a part of the language we speak; it gives itself (having grown into itself) immediately as a circle—with all of the accompanying implications—just as the salt gives itself immediately as white, cubical, and of a certain specific gravity—just as I give myself immediately as 'I'.[66] With a fulfilling recollection, we may also see that it has always been such (although the consciousness which perceived this is created in the present—the unconscious is an effect of the remember-

65. He continues with one of his clearest explications of his use of the word onto-theo-logy: "*Ontology* is the speculatively conceived and *thus* speculatively grounded interpretation of being, but in such a way that the actual being [*Seindes*] is the absolute *theos*. It is from the being [*Sein*] of the absolute that all beings *and* the *logos* are determined. The speculative interpretation of being is *onto-theo-logy*" (Heidegger, *Hegel's Phenomenology of Spirit* [1930–31], p. 98).

66. Lacan, whom we will be looking at more closely later, provides us with some of the most Hegelian models of the self. For example, from early in his career, he explicates the *Gestalt* nature of the first identifications of self as an infant encounters a mirror:

This jubilant assumption of his specular image by the child at the *infans* stage, still sunk in his motor incapacity and nursling dependence, would seem to exhibit in an exemplary situation the symbolic matrix in which the *I* is precipitated in a primordial form, before it is objectified in the dialectic of identification with the other, and before language restores to it, in the universal, its function as subject.

This form would have to be called the Ideal-I, if we wished to incorporate it into our usual register, in the sense that it will also be the source of secondary identifications, under which term I would place the functions of libidinal normalization. But the important point is that this form situates the agency of the ego, before its social determination, in a fictional direction, which will always remain irreducible for the individual alone, or rather, which will only rejoin the coming-into-being (*le devenir*) of the subject asymptotically, whatever the success of the dialectical syntheses by which he must resolve as *I* his discordance with his own reality.

The fact is that the total form of the body by which the subject anticipates in a mirage the maturation of his power is given to him only as *Gestalt*, that is to say, in an exteriority in which this form is certainly more constituent than constituted, but in which it appears to him above all in a contrasting size (*un relief de stature*) that fixes it and in a symmetry that inverts it, in contrast with the turbulent movements that the subject feels are animating him. Thus, this *Gestalt*—whose pregnancy should be regarded as bound up with the species, though its motor style remains scarcely recognizable—by these two aspects of its appearance, symbolizes the mental permanence of the *I*, at the same time as it prefigures its alienating destination; it is still pregnant with the correspondences that unite the *I* with the statue in which man projects himself, with the phantoms that dominate him, or with the automaton in which, in an ambiguous relation, the world of his own

ing, recollecting consciousness of the anarchic present).

Thinking more carefully about the movement of understanding, however, we cannot pass up the fact that time for Hegel is born of an opposition: the immediate certainty of the line disrupted by the intersection. This strife calls for a unifying peace (such as death or happiness). This peace exists as the articulation, the expression, of the relation.[67] Two facts standing in opposition desire either unification or war (which ends in the unity of peace); naming the unity of the two opponents satisfies their desire (their agitated opposition). This is the power of the word, the sense of saying that the truth will set you free. (Or, with Emily Dickinson, "After great pain / A formal feeling comes"). It is also why it is not incorrect to see force as an activity of the subject: trivially, the production of words, theologically, the production of worlds.

This manifestation, this articulation, however, does not need an Other who brings it into presence; it is self-manifestation as, using the example of the circle above, the unity of being (space) and time:

> What something is, therefore, it is wholly in its externality; its externality is its totality and equally is its unity reflected into itself. Its Appearance is not only reflection-into-an-other but reflection-into-self, and its externality is, therefore, the expression or utterance [*Äusserung*] of what it is in itself; and since its content and form are thus utterly identical, it is, in and for itself, nothing but this, *to express* or *manifest itself*. It is the manifesting of its essence

in such a manner that this essence consists simply and solely in being that which manifests itself. (Hegel, *Science of Logic* [1812], p. 528)[68]

At this stage, as an approximation to thinking the truth of externality as an absolutely given, scientifically available, exterior (as essential givenness, the giving of essences), we are thinking God (and the articulation of God in/for self-consciousness): "Consciousness, then, does not start from *its* inner life, from thought, and unite *within itself* the thought of God with existence; on the contrary, it starts from an existence that is immediately present and recognizes God therein" (Hegel, *Phenomenology of Spirit* [1807], p. 458).

There is much that, descriptively, is unarguable in Hegel. The problem, as briefly as possible and echoing Heidegger's criticism, involves the following points:

(1) By couching description in ever more abstract terms, Hegel effaces the inherent being-questionable of being merely alive. In more traditional words, the distinction between intuition and recognition, or reflection and intuition, ignores the fact of what could be characterized as intuitive decisions (based on evidence which could only be called suggestive), decisions made about, and for the sake of, intuition as the suggestive/evocative (understanding that life is not identical to itself). Hegel assumes that acquired structures of consciousness (when fixed in place by the truth of infinitely iterable Science) can always remain unaltered (for the purposes of future descriptions). Metaphorically, he assumes a silent and faithful sister (or wife).

making tends to find completion." ("The Mirror Stage as Formative of the Function of the I as Revealed in Psychoanalytic Experience" [1949], *Écrits*, pp. 2–3)

67. Georg Lukács is, I think, at least partly right when he tags as the key to Marx's reading of Hegel the category of externalization—*Entäusserung*—in *The Young Hegel* (1938). Under this reading, the truth of the individual is his/her externalized product. Unreified consciousness would be based on consciousness of exchange between humans: a relation unmediated by reified forms of money. Heidegger's reading, which is still a critique, finds the essential moment to lie with the idea of the concept itself (specifically the concept of self-conscious finitude as the cancellation of finitude understood as dependency).

68. This bears a close resemblance to Derrida's formulation of *différance*:

In constituting itself, in dividing itself dynamically, this interval is what might be called *spacing*, the becoming-space of time or the becoming-time of space (*temporization*). And it is this constitution of the present, as an "originary" and irreducibly nonsimple (and therefore, *stricto sensu* nonoriginary) synthesis of marks, or traces of retentions and protentions (to reproduce analogically and provisionally a phenomenological and transcendental language that soon will reveal itself to be inadequate), that I propose to call arch-writing, archi-trace, or *différance*. Which (is) (simutaneously) spacing (and) temporization. (p. 13)

He formulates his relation to Hegel, speaking of how to translate *"differente"* in *"Diese Beziehung ist Gegenwart, als eine differente Beziehung"* ("This relationship is [the] present as a different relationship"):

Writing *"differant"* or *"Différance"* (with an *a*) would have had the advantage of making it possible to translate Hegel at that particular point—which is also an absolutely decisive point in his discourse—without further notes or specifications. And the translation would be, as it always must be, a transformation of one language by another. I contend, of course, that the word différance can also serve other purposes: first, because it marks not only the activity of "originary" difference, but also the temporizing detour of deferral; and above all because *différance* thus written, although maintaining relations of profound affinity with Hegelian discourse (such as it must be read), is also, up to a certain point, unable to break with that discourse (which has no kind of meaning or chance); but it can operate a kind of infinitesimal and radical displacement of it, whose space I attempt to delineate elsewhere but of which it would be difficult to speak briefly here. (Derrida, "Différance" [1968], *Margins of Philosophy*, p. 14)

(2) Hegel characterizes description in terms of description. That is, all things which exist must be capable of being said, must possess a word. Further, these words were determined as possible contents of consciousness in the first instantiation of consciousness—that is, all history is dominated by the initial discovery of the structure of representation (this *discovery* itself being the active acquisition of a previously given language/set of articulations).

(3) Since this structure is figured as a return to the truth of the starting point, as energy only expended for the sake of progress, for the sake of the true appropriation of the initial process/project of being human for the sake of personal (or suprapersonal) enjoyment, Hegel cannot conceive of the gift that does not oblige; he cannot conceive of the child without a father or the father who wants a daughter and not a son (since only the boy can return to the suprapersonal self—the order of the family—as father).

(4) Ethical responsibility is always a late addition to theories of being based on either the representation of the true or on the expression of force (such as Hegel's). Because an initial separation is posited between subject and object (as the Absolute suffers itself to enter into its own concept as the process of alienation and reabsorption), a patchwork ethics is needed to reestablish the duty of the subject. It's interesting in that respect that codified ethical conduct arose first within mercantile societies where personal relations between all the major partners were no longer possible. Accordingly, a search for a better understanding of the ethical obligation which subtended the original

relations is what turned people toward the realm of the family—or to the feminine—as ethical foundation. Hegel turned here but only saw another category
of knowledge and not the relations of obligation. The search for other alternative grounds to ethical relations has seen, correspondingly, a renewed interest
in the aesthetic as well. Hegel said the works of the Muse were no longer alive
for us (for that "us" which now lives in a Christian world)—here we recognize
our destination in a distanced, unethical, and ultimately meaningless existence, regulated by pure abstractions called laws. In this distance between
subjects, all laws must be written (or otherwise committed to the collective
memory).

Hegel began to understand the failures of a life without connection to re-
generating time in/as affective relationships, but failed its implications, when
he said we should merely enjoy the fruit since it is sweet and no trouble to col-
lect. He *starts* to ask, perhaps for the first time, a serious question of the girl,
the servant, and her vision (I am restoring more of the context to the quote
from above):

> The tables of the gods provide no spiritual food and drink, and in his games
> and festivals man no longer recovers the joyful consciousness of his unity
> with the divine. The works of the Muse now lack the power of the Spirit, for
> the Spirit has gained its certainty of itself from the crushing of gods and men.
> They have become what they are for us now—beautiful fruit already picked
> from the tree, which a friendly Fate has offered us, as a girl might set the fruit
> before us. It cannot give us the actual life in which they existed, not the tree
> that bore them, not the earth and the elements which constituted their sub-
> stance, not the climate which gave them their peculiar character, nor the
> cycle of the changing seasons that governed the process of their growth. . . .
> Our active enjoyment of them is therefore not an act of divine worship
> through which our consciousness might come to its perfect truth and fulfill-
> ment; it is an external activity—the wiping-off of some drops of rain or
> specks of dust from these fruits, so to speak—one which erects an intricate
> scaffolding of the dead elements of their outward existence—the language,
> the historical circumstances, etc. in place of the inner elements of the ethical
> life which environed, created, and inspired them. And all this we do, not in
> order to enter into their very life but only to possess an idea of them in our
> imagination. But, just as the girl who offers us the plucked fruits is more than
> the Nature which directly provides them—the Nature diversified into their
> conditions and elements, the tree, air, light, and so on—because she sums all
> this up in a higher mode, in the gleam of her self-conscious eye and in the

gesture with which she offers them, so, too, the Spirit of the Fate that presents us with those works of art is more than the ethical life and the actual world of that nation, for it is the *inwardizing* in us of the Spirit which was still [only] *outwardly* manifested; it is the Spirit of the tragic Fate which gathers all those individual gods and attributes of the [divine] substance into one pantheon, into the Spirit that is itself conscious of itself as Spirit.(*Phenomenology of Spirit* [1807], pp. 455–56 [my ellipsis])

But Hegel fails to ask the question of her difference, his privilege and her servitude, because he makes the assumption that, insofar as she is conscious, she is just like him—or just as he wishes to be, withdrawn, serene, simply (simplistically) happy (would she also consume the fruit in a moment of enjoyment? or of need? or distraction? would she also be content with life within the Christian church?). There are, perhaps, still ways of descriptively comparing individuals—I'm merely questioning the efficacy of assuming the truth of our similarity is the universal fact that we know our death as death,[69] as an absolutely violent infringement on our freedom (the idea that truth occurs when we see ourselves as others see us; when the history of our being determined is comprehended in our own determining act). Our truth is, according to Hegel, that having eaten fruit, we will produce fruit, or rather, for that part of the audience which is not female, a woman may yet offer to share of her fruit. For, in her gesture, she offers us something, she speaks to her audience; in our gesture, we merely take, and then pronounce

69. Of course, my language does not kill anyone. And yet: when I say, "This woman," real death has been announced and is already present in my language; my language means that this person, who is here right now, can be detached from herself, removed from her existence and her presence and suddenly plunged into a nothingness in which there is no existence or presence; my language essentially signifies the possibility of this destruction; it is a constant bold allusion to such an event. My language does not kill anyone. But if this woman were not really capable of dying, if she were not threatened by death at every moment of her life, bound and joined to death by an essential bond, I would not be able to carry out that ideal negation, that deferred assassination, which is what my language is. (Blanchot, "Literature and the Right to Death" [1949], *The Gaze of Orpheus and Other Literary Essays*, pp. 42–43)

judgment on the value of her gifts. And thus, with this question of gifts, we reenter into the question of divinity as well, and divinity as a certain type of death (or crucifixion).

Hegel doesn't see Christ, nor Christianity, as dead in the way that the Muse's works are supposed to be: that is, even where he thinks of the divine and finitude together in the word, Christ is not merely a word for Hegel (because, and Kierkegaard complains of this, we live in 'Christian' nations, because the Bible is still read as the great book of our tradition, Christ is supposedly alive for us, through our being Christian). Christ, for Hegel, is a principle of divinity, of mediation, of externalization, sublimation, and subsumption. Christ is the profound possibility of the word which the earlier religiosity could not understand. Christ was the purpose of speaking in that self-consciousness reached towards the divine self-understanding—but Christ was not merely a word. My purpose, against Hegel's conception of divinity, is to say aloud that Christ is a word—that all the great narrative landmarks (which taken together constitute any tradition) are, in fact, words. That words, perhaps, are other than the leftover fruits of a once living idea (or world).

# Christ as the failure of extension

## (speaking without determination)

*—woman would theoretically be the envelope (which she provides). But she would have no essence or existence, given that she is the potential for essence and existence:* the available place. . . . *If she enveloped herself with what she provides, she could not but necessarily be conceived of as existing. Which, to an extent, is what happens: women's suffering arises also from the fact that man does not conceive that women do not exist. Men have such a great need that women should exist. If men are to be permitted to believe or imagine themselves as self-cause, they need to think that the envelope "belongs" to them. (Particularly following "the end of God" or "the death of God," insofar as God can be determined by an era of history in any way but through the limits to its thinking.) For men to establish this belonging—without the guarantee provided by God—it is imperative that that which provides the envelope should necessarily exist.* Therefore *the maternal-feminine exists necessarily as the cause of the self-cause of man. But not for herself. She has to exist but as an a priori condition (as Kant might say) for the space-time of the masculine subject. A cause that is never unveiled for fear that its identity might split apart and plummet down. She does not have to exist as woman because, as woman, her envelope is always* slightly open *(if man today thinks of himself as God, woman becomes, according to Meister Eckhart, an adverb or a quality of the word of God).*

—Irigaray, "The Envelope"

The unity of intuition and object, thought in Hegel, relies on a new thinking of the role of the human as productive. No longer merely the more or less faithful audience of God's true activity, one produces the forms of one's appearances (and intuitions). The envelope of those productions, however, cannot itself be thought as one of those productions: Kant accordingly had to separate noumenal from phenomenal, the thing in itself from its appearance. Hegel refused this separation in the name of a new thinking of actuality. To think the progress of the actual (the external, the determined, or articulated) as itself the determining milieu, or the envelope, for any particular given time within the progression keeps any individual moment from being free of determination (and thus unintelligible, or irrational) and thus puts the whole within our reach (at least for our species, or our Spirit, or our science) as well. We see the world, and its movement, and "recognize God therein." Such a "recognition," of course, is the trademark of ontotheology: God is understood on the basis of the objects of the world (or by analogy to the way in which we understand objects). God, even if invisible (beyond determination) to the extent that he is the *way* in which things are determined, is made available to man (or is even identical to the rationality of a 'making available to man') through the externalizations/determinations which are his trace/mark in the world.

For the premoderns, humans are put, as objects within one harmonious cosmos, on equal footing with all created objects. To be a creator is to be in a special relation to the created object: I know what a chair is since I am responsible for (or am capable of) making it; God knows what a human is (or is for) since he has made each individual according to his design. If God, as creator of all determinations (as the one who guarantees all essence its rational place), can serve as the envelope within which all our activity is performed, then what we do can be securely judged according to its approximation towards the purposes of God. It was necessary for Hegel's view of the progress of determination that this envelope be understood in terms of a process (a way of fulfilling experience, etc.) and not in terms of singular objects that exist transcendentally, apart from any and all determining activity attributable to mankind (attributable to the work of finite creators).[70] The pretension to being ourselves the masters of our fate reduces our fate (and all the structures of our meaning) to the hubris of our volition. Many appeals to traditional religion are based simply on the certainty one gains (as a believer) of having a meaningful place in life. The moral individual is the one who acted to secure this certainty; one was good in searching to do the good (and, at least ideally, one could even know what this good actually was).

Modernism's certainty, no longer based on the literal space of our upbringing, was less stable than the recourse to a transcendent topology provided by God, and it correspondingly became all the more important that we secure our sense of belonging (of possession, and being possessed). This, following the epigraph from Irigaray, is why man needs woman's existence to be

70. Blumenberg explains the problem Christian philosophers (in this case, Nicholas of Cusa) faced:

> Apart from the Bible, the root of the medieval concept of transcendence is above all Neoplatonic. The conception of transcendence deriving from Platonism can be traced back to a *spatial* schema in which the primary assertion about the Ideas is that they are nothing in or of this world but rather are located outside and apart from it; on the other hand, the biblical "transcendence" of God is more a temporal state of affairs, insofar as God's crucial presence for the world and for man either is an exemplary and comforting past—from the Creation up to the interventions in the history of the Chosen People—or else is still impending as His eschatological becoming present to men, which will put everything in order. The biblical God Himself withholds Himself in His transcendence, so as to make possible faith as the attitude of submission and thus at the same time as the condition of the retraction of His withholding of Himself. This sort of transcendence is thus an intrahistorical reservation; it can be cancelled in eschatology and thus is not "substantial." It can be related only to a process, not to a static system. (*Legitimacy of the Modern Age* [1966], p. 486)

certain (in order to be secure in his knowledge of himself). If the "process," the "productivity" of man, could not be rationally grounded in the structures of our being, then there was nowhere else to turn for meaning within our lives (no static answer, no particular place, would suffice). The envelope had become a process (the process of becoming autonomous men, in a public realm made to measure for a community of such men); but every possible glitch in that process had also thereby become a source of anxiety. What if I am not recognized as autonomous? If I am not allowed to live the life of the landed gentleman (albeit in bourgeois, or urban, imitation)? Then I am nothing but a slave, and better off dead. What if I am not recognized as a desiring subject, as one of those worthy of designating the objects of the world as beautiful or desirable? Then I am no better than a woman. . . . Heidegger, in his critiques of modernity, has seen how far wrong this story has taken us. Our difficulty in 'making sense' of Heidegger, perhaps, has to do precisely with the distance we have traveled along the path of a modern self-conception. My task, in part, will be to think through Heidegger's conception of dwelling, of the importance of our factical situation, without conceptualizing every situation in terms of the dyads (subject/object, container/contained, form/content) we have tended to set up for ourselves. In particular, I want to begin to think of that situation (and here I believe I am following Heidegger) otherwise than as the determining environment which explains what we can be (our moral character being displayed in whether we have energetically appropriated the best of those possibilities).

For Levinas, and this is the clue I will follow from him, the key to thinking the specificity of our situation, without thinking of that situation as mechanistically determinative, lies in thinking of the structures of encountering others, encounters which themselves provide the point of commencement for the encounter with structures, as well as with the objects disclosed within those structures (my somewhat tortured sentence here merely marking how inappropriate a language of structure and content would be within Levinas's thought). Before moving on to Levinas, however, I would like to look a little more closely at modernism's self-conception. Hans Blumenberg's *The Legitimacy of the Modern Age* provides us with an interesting polemic in this regard.

Think of two types of knowledge: (1) the lived immediacy of our own body, and (2) knowledge of the possibility of objects: knowledge of what an object might have been or may become but not a knowledge of what actually is. A Kantian might call it the what and the how of our knowledge, but there are essential reasons for separating premodern religiosity from Kantian transcendental thinking. Blumenberg, using the philosophies of Nicholas of Cusa and Giordano Bruno (the Nolan) as exemplars of an epochal change in our conception of the universe, tries to explain how it became possible to think the unity of these two types of knowledge. For Cusa, before the epochal turn, the first type of knowledge characterizes the finite (or mortal) and the second the infinite (or divine). The impetus which leads to modernism would be found, according to Blumenberg, in Bruno's conception that all possibilities must have been exhausted as

71. Blumenberg explains Bruno's cosmology (and the exclusion of Christ from that cosmos):

In this universe, the Divinity had already fully spent Himself in the Creation. Since He did not and could not hold anything back, vis-à-vis the infinity of worlds, He was left with nothing to make up in relation to any creature in this world. Nothing "supernatural" is possible. Only the infinite cosmos itself can be the phenomenality, can be such a thing as the "embodiment" [*Verleiblichung*] of the Divinity, to think of which as a person—that is, as bound to a definite creature in the world, made actual by a temporal position—is something that the Nolan is no longer able to do. In his thought, the conflicts that were painstakingly concealed or were still "adjusted" in the Cusan's system are fully carried through; alternatives are posed in the triad of theology, cosmology, and anthropology and are decided. (*The Legitimacy of the Modern Age* [1966], p. 551)

72. We have already remarked that the basic determination in the ontological proof of the existence of God is *the sum total of all realities*. It is usually shown, first of all, that this determination is *possible* because it is free from *contradiction*, reality being taken only as reality without any limitation. We remarked that this sum total thus becomes simple indeterminate being, or if the realities are, in fact,

taken as a plurality of determinate beings, into the sum-
total of all negations. More
precisely, when the difference
of reality is taken into account, it develops from difference into opposition, and
from this into contradiction,
so that in the end the sum
total of all realities simply becomes absolute contradiction
within itself. Ordinary—but
not speculative—thinking,
which abhors contradiction,
as nature abhors a vacuum,
rejects this conclusion; for in
considering contradiction, it
stops short at the one-sided
*resolution* of it into *nothing*,
and fails to recognise the positive side of contradiction
where it becomes *absolute activity* and absolute ground.
(Hegel, *Science of Logic*
[1812], p. 442)

73. Although, in that extreme
case, knowing takes on a passive,
almost feminine air. Hegel,
again, constrains the meaning of
the role:

The spiritual being thus exists
first of all for self-consciousness as law which has an *intrinsic* being; the universality
associated with testing the law,
a merely formal, not an *essential* universality, is now behind
us. The law is equally an eternal law which is grounded not
in the will of a particular individual, but is valid in and for
itself; it is the absolute *pure
will of all* which has the form
of immediate being. Also, it is
not a *commandment*, which
only *ought* to be: it *is* and is

God's body extended infinitely—that is, in
an idea of possibility (and of the determinative nature of creation) which allows all
things (and all possibilities of form) to be
deduced from the way bodies are given
(within/as the whole).[71] It is in this sense
that Bruno provides the basis for modern
science, with its watchmaker God. The idea
of extension here is crucial: at the bottom of
his (and modernity's) thinking of actuality
lies a claim about the spatial (present-at-
hand) existence of substance. God is all
things; all things exist in space as beings. If
God has a unity, or has a will, it is only insofar as he is the relatedness of beings in
space[72] (and every so often we see headlines
about physicists or astronomers who've discovered this god).

If we return to the example of a line,
understanding is by virtue of a discontinuity: I 'am' as a line intersected by an alien
point which 'is', which, forcibly, becomes
(is+time) part of me. Remembering that relation is understood through time and time
is understood as merely an extra (or at least
an analogous) dimension of space, we see
that to be all lines in all directions is to be
the omnipresent, omniscient God. To know/
be all possibilities, according to this simplified schema, would merely require a few
more dimensions than being/knowing all
actuality.[73]

Heidegger, without invoking a deity, has
made clear how this conception of knowledge has failed to capture the truth of the
meaning of being. Heidegger leads us to
think about the ground of reality by turning
back to the *way* in which we are, and by
avoiding the presupposition that our being is
properly understood in terms of an actuality,

or a present world, which is itself in need of explanation. "In point of fact, the being that can least of all be conceived as extant, at hand, the Dasein that in each instance we ourselves are, is just that to which all understanding of being-at-hand, actuality, must be traced back" (Heidegger, *The Basic Problems of Phenomenology* [1927], p. 119).

We will be following, throughout the rest of this book, the question of what type of questions Heidegger's turn away from the modern subject leaves us with. The enigma we still have not approached, in terms of Heidegger's contribution to philosophy, is how Dasein, as envelope, provides the transcendence (which conditions/determines) all particular acts of presence, how Dasein has its own history, its own determinations, its own way of being, and yet is neither the substrate (as pure activity) for all determinations nor itself exhausted in its being-determined (the question, then, has to do with the freedom of Dasein, or better, Dasein's being within a freedom not conceived from out of the violence of a singular determining act).

*The Basic Problems of Phenomenology* is a text created on the basis of a lecture course given by Heidegger in 1927. Among the other concerns of this lecture course, Heidegger is dealing with the question of the characterizations of medieval and modern philosophy. Where Blumenburg (defending modernity) saw a completion of Cusa's thinking of the possible in Bruno's thinking of the actual, Heidegger sees a break in the conception of essence and possibility separating modernity from the middle ages. He shifts the problem back to the scholastics and their understanding of the relation of

*valid*; it is the universal "I" of the category, the "I" which is immediately a reality, and the world *is* only this reality. But since this existent law is valid unconditionally, the obedience of self-consciousness is not the serving of a master whose commands were arbitrary, and in which it would not recognize itself. On the contrary, laws are the thoughts of its own absolute consciousness, thoughts which are immediately its *own*. Also, it does not *believe* in them, for although belief does perceive essential being it perceives it as something alien to itself. Ethical *self*-consciousness is *immediately* one with essential being through the *universality* of its *self*; belief, on the other hand, starts from the *individual* consciousness; it is the movement of that consciousness always towards this unity, but without attaining to the presence of its essential being. The above consciousness, on the other hand, has put its merely individual aspect behind it, this mediation is finished and complete, and only because this is so, is this consciousness immediate self-consciousness of the ethical substance. . . . The *relationship* of self-consciousness to them is equally simple and clear. They *are*, and nothing more; this is what constitutes the awareness of its relationship to them. Thus, Sophocles' *Antigone* acknowledges them as the unwritten and infallible law of the gods. (Hegel, *Phenomenology of Spirit* [1807], pp. 260–61 [my ellipsis])

It is of critical importance that if the ethical consciousness is not immediately present, without the work of consciousness, to the individual (and this is the ethical sphere of woman; the role Irigaray, in my epigraph, would give to the envelope), then there would be no sense to obeying the laws; civilization itself would be a mockery.

74. It is not clear to me if this sense of enveloping would be maintained if we followed out the finitude of appearance in terms of its lack of necessary continuity and did not, as *Being and Time* tried to do, reestablish the unity of that envelope in terms of the ontological structure of care. Heidegger, of course, didn't take this unity for granted: the attempt to ground this unity in a transcending (ecstatic) temporality and not in the creative powers of a subject is what (in my eyes) marks the great originality of Heidegger's work. That he continued to insist on the nondetermined character of this unity (or, at least, of its being in some sense a 'whole') grounds a large part of what I would like to explore in my writing. In a lecture course immediately following the publication of *Being and Time*, Heidegger explains (with reference to Kant and Leibniz) why his idea of transcendence excludes the modern conception of the subject (and its corresponding reduction of God to a set of ontotheological determinations):

> For Kant, both concepts, that of identity and of truth, are linked together in the primor-

essence to existence in two theses: (1) Being actual belongs to the essence of God since his essence and existence are the same. This implies, however, that there are no possibilities for God since he already is (see p. 88). The absence of possibilities results, of course, because God is outside of time and possibility can only be understood in terms of time. The problem is how what is eternal mediates itself with the temporal. (2) Created beings aren't equivalent to themselves in their way of being and in the fact of their being. They have their possibilities outside of themselves.

In planning to build a chair, for example, I have at my disposal all possible objects which fit the requirements of sitting. I may have learned that there are certain materials, techniques, aesthetic flourishes, and pragmatic concerns which (in terms of my cultural/practical expectations) bear on the creation of a good chair. The purposes of the chair, however, the reason we call it a chair and recognize it as such, have to do merely with the requirements of sitting and answer to the most general 'appearance' of a 'chair' only in so far as each thing which appears and answers to the purpose of sitting can thus be named a 'chair'. The self-appearance of the form as if, as form, it belonged to some other place besides the one of its particular appearance is, as with Heidegger's critique of Hegel, the destruction of time (the finitude of appearance) in favor of Being (the permanence of the form of appearance/determination/externalization). Once every actual appearance of a chair known to us has disappeared (finite, after all), only the most general meaning associated with these objects remains: a remains which corresponds, oddly enough, with the beginning of the task of building a chair: its purpose, that is, fulfilling the requirements of sitting. True knowledge of the chair can only come from true knowledge of its purpose. This quickly leads to an infinite regression if we begin to question: Why sitting? Why legs? Why people? Why anything at all? The most general question of meaning envelopes all specific ones.[74] For the Scholastics, the essence, the universal, the ultimate purpose of the chair can only be known by the creator who creates himself: God. Likewise, of course, every object (and people included) finds its justification in the eyes of God—in its place on the coordinate planes of a divine mathematics.

Cusa begins to speak of a role for the finite creator within the purposes of human nature—which is why Blumenberg puts him at the epochal threshold. The sense of Cusa's argument resides in the types of knowledge I referred to above. Knowledge as bodily experience, or, equivalently, experience of bodies, requires that knowledge—in infinite time or rather outside of time but still based on the analogy of the number line—be borrowed from always already existent (circumscribed) categories of purposes. Instead of something which is outside of time and occupies all space, God (or whatever secularized name you might want to give to this envelope) is thus conceptualized as the limit (the circumscription of all possibilities) to that which can occur at any particular time given the constraints of what is now (eventually extrapolated back in a causal chain to the time before any 'is'). God is time outside of space. But he is a time which is abstractly equal throughout all time to every particular time—like each point on a number line. As

dial unity of the synthesis of transcendental apperception. [In Kant] identity is traced back, with the help of the truth of judgment, to the condition of the possibility of the execution of every cognitive act. The "I" is that subject whose predicates consist in all representations, everything in any way contributing to knowledge. Only now it becomes fully clear how this concept of knowledge is connected with the idea of what simply is and its being. *Intuitus* and *identitas*, as essential characteristics of truth and knowledge, the "logical" in the broadest sense, are derived from the *simplicitas Dei* as guiding ideal of what, in the genuine sense, is. Because the identity theory of judgment refers back to these metaphysical connections, to the construal of being mentioned, and because all judgment and knowledge is knowledge of beings, we must now also make clear how Leibniz orients the interpretation of being on the same ideal. Even the exemplary being, God, still appears in the light of a definite construal of being as such. (Heidegger, *The Metaphysical Foundations of Logic* [1928], p. 69)

75. Hence, although God could have foreseen many things which He did not foresee and will not foresee and although He foresaw many things which He was able not to foresee, nevertheless nothing can be added to or subtracted from divine foresight. By way of comparison: Human nature is simple and one; if a human being were born who was never even expected to be born, nothing would be added to human nature. Similarly, nothing would be subtracted from human nature if [the human being] were not born—just as nothing [is subtracted] when those who have been born die. This [holds true] because human nature enfolds not only those who exist but also those who do not exist and will not exist, although they could have existed. In like manner, even if what will never occur were to occur, nothing would be added to divine foresight, since it enfolds not only what does occur but also what does not occur but can occur. Therefore, just as in matter many things which will never occur are present as possibilities so, by contrast, whatever things will not occur but can occur: although they are present in God's foresight, they are present not possibly but actually. Nor does it follow herefrom that these things exist actually. (Nicholas of Cusa, *Learned Ignorance* [1440], book 1, chapter 22, p. 77)

the form of time, he is precisely not within the temporal flow of the world. This conception of time, this formal unity, preconditions all appearances, and reduces the multiform functioning of temporality to a single mode of appearing (what Heidegger at first calls the present-at-hand and later, expanding and modifying its application, refers to as the standing reserve).

Still, within this new framework provided by Cusa, it is possible to speak of relative and absolute creators. Out of the possibilities available to God, all things are created. Out of the possiblities of a human, humanity's things are created: God equally provides for the car and for the not-car; that the car exists is to humanity's credit (or debit—but how would you keep score without positing a divine will and/or purpose?); that humanity exists (and makes these decisions) is to God's credit.[75] This is a position that Nicholas of Cusa does not maintain rigorously. Blumenberg gives us the clue: "Thus in the Cusan's early work, providence is already referred to the concept of possibility, so that it would remain unaltered even if something were to happen that in fact will not happen. But that means that the individual cannot find a justification of his existence in the concept of providence" (*The Legitimacy of The Modern Age* [1966], p. 522).

In case it is not clear, we are still talking exactly of the relation of subject to predicate. There is justification for, meaning for, the individual's life (seemingly accidental, like a predicate) insofar as she/he is an immanent moment, a necessary part of the subject's (God's) purpose. The subject is that which we refer to over time as being the substrate, the constant identity behind the predicates which appear in time. The truth of the acorn consists in part of the adult tree it will become, in part of the firewood it ends as; the substance is that which endures as present behind all those appearances.[76] What I am stressing, following Heidegger, is that the basis for understanding the traditional idea of truth relies on a conception of the possible transparency of all the 'facts of the world', a simple identity of (at least the forms of) lines, of life as lines within time, of time as a web of identifiable, precisely locatable, lines. Time, as a philosophical inquiry, is thought to be no more problematic than the postulation of a substrate that endures as present behind all particular appearances; all philosophical questions concerning time would thus be answerable in terms of the model of the geometric representation of space.

Based on the distinction Heidegger drew above for the medievals between actuality and essence (in terms of creator/created) we were able to see that only the creator could know an object which was not immediately given as a personally possessed body (the sense of knowledge being here the sense of possession or owning: you're sure of only the fact that the knower is, not of the facts the body tells you). Heidegger's question has to do with the nature of our creations: Are we small deities, creating personal worlds? Are we audiences of another's creations? Or can creation itself (time itself) be thought before we name the space (objectively determine the possibility) of creating? As far as modernism's response goes, Heidegger finds the question ill formed:

The motive of this primary orientation toward the subject in modern philoso-

76. "The figure of the seed (let us call it thus provisionally) is immediately determined: (1) as the best representation of the spirit's relation to self, (2) as the circular path of a return to self. And in the description of the spirit that returns to itself through its own proper product, after it lost itself there, there is more than a simple rhetorical convenience in giving to the spirit the name father. Likewise, the advent of the Christian Trinity is more than an empiric event in the spirit's history" (Derrida, *Glas* [1974], pp. 27–28).

77. What this heroic individualism would always miss is that the death analysis is prepared for by an analysis of the worldhood of the world, and of the care structure of that world. Heidegger explains the purpose of fundamental ontology in the book he published immediately after *Being and Time*:

Anxiety is that basic disposition which places us before the Nothing. The Being of the being, however, is in general only understandable— and herein lies the profoundest finitude of transcendence— if in the ground of its essence Dasein holds itself into the Nothing. This holding-itself-into-the-Nothing is no arbitrary and occasionally attempted "thinking" of the Nothing, but is rather an event which underlies all instances of finding oneself in the midst of beings which already are, and this event is one which must be elucidated according to its inner possibility in a fundamental-ontological analytic of Dasein. "Anxiety" thus understood, i.e., according to fundamental ontology, completely removes the harmlessness of a categorical structure from "Care." It gives it the peculiar precision necessary for a fundamental existential [*Grundexistenzial*], and so it determines the finitude in Dasein not as a quality which is at hand, but rather as the constant although mostly concealed shimmering of all that exists. (Heidegger, *Kant and the Problem of Metaphysics* [1929], p. 162)

The death analysis motivates the turn towards understanding our complicity in constructing a world; it doesn't posit death as a limit moment within the system of speaking, nor does it see the individual facing death (as in Hegel's analysis of war) as the true creator of value in the world. That is, Heidegger doesn't see our complicity in the production of a world as following the model of a subject's determining judgments about an object.

78.  And perhaps this is where Derrida's thinking of the experience of the impossible is leading. It must answer to the exigencies of a determined social and political milieu, and yet must promise something other than those determinations, must be other than the mere unfolding of a promised content. Derrida's work on Marx makes this clear in relation to messianism: "we will not claim that this messianic eschatology common both to the religions it

phy is the opinion that this being which we ourselves are is given to the knower first and as the only certain thing, that the subject is accessible immediately and with absolute certainty, that it is better known than all objects. In comparison, objects are accessible only by way of a mediation. (*Basic Problems of Phenomenology* [1927], p. 123)

(B)y this turnabout, by this allegedly critical new beginning of philosophy in Descartes, the traditional ontology was taken over. By this allegedly critical new beginning ancient metaphysics became dogmatism, which it had not earlier been in this style; it became a mode of thought that with the aid of traditional ontological concepts seeks to gain a positively ontical knowledge of God, the soul, and nature. (Ibid., p. 124)

Heidegger, in the course of reviewing previous approaches to these questions, then refers to Kant and to a different way of responding to the same dilemma. To begin with, there is a refinement in the meaning of being a mortal (and this refinement is the true point of Heidegger's death analysis—as opposed to a supposed heroic individualism):[77] "*Finitude is being referred necessarily to receptivity, that is, the impossibility of being oneself the creator and producer of another being*" (Ibid., p. 150).

This finitude is our question as ones who question. The receptivity, in Kant, had been tied to our inability to access the thing-in-itself (we have only our appearances with which to philosophize). In Heidegger, the finitude is no longer merely the finitude of appearances, but the necessity of rethinking how one belongs to (is finite within) a situation. If our situation, as philosophers and beings-in-the-world, as inheritors of previous thinking, is not merely determined, this lack of determination must be explained by the way in which our receptivity is thought. The failure of extension to explain our possibilities, the failure of Christ to have maintained his presence, is not thought within Hegel's logic of ever-successful/ever-triumphant progress (nor within any religious thinking which believes in a redemption achieved or achievable). This failure, the withdrawal of Being, provides us with the delay, the time between our birth and our death, which is where our meaning will play itself out— without reference to anything but the failure, the impossibility of the success.[78] What does this imply for our thinking concerning the meaning of creation? This is Heidegger's question itself, and the answer seems best understood in the strange multiplicity of the language of "letting."

> In summary, the result relative to the characteristics of realitas is that they all develop with regard to what is configured in configuring, formed in forming, shaped in shaping, and made in making. Shaping, forming, making all signify a letting-come-here, letting-derive-from. We can characterize all these modes of action by a *basic comportment of the Dasein* which we can concisely call *producing [Herstellen].*[79]
> (Ibid., p. 108)

That is, a production which is attuned to the receptivity of finitude, a letting-come-

criticizes and to the Marxist critique must be simply deconstructed. While it is common to both of them, with the exception of the content [but none of them can accept, of course, this *epokhe* of the content, whereas we hold it here to be essential to the messianic in general, as thinking of the other and of the event to come], it is also the case that its formal structure of promise exceeds them or precedes them. Well, what remains irreducible to any deconstruction, what remains as undeconstructible as the possibility itself of deconstruction is, perhaps, a certain experience of the emancipatory promise; it is perhaps even the formality of a structural messianism, a messianism without religion, even a messianic without messianism, an idea of justice— which we distinguish from law or right and even from human rights—and an idea of democracy—which we distinguish from its current concept and from its determined predicates today [permit me to refer here to "Force of Law" and *The Other Heading*]" *(Specters,* p. 59).

79. The relation of creator to producer is also mirrored (for different methodological purposes) in the relation of Lordship to Bondage (Master to Slave). See Hegel, *Phenomenology of Spirit* (1807), and my "Antigone is not tragic: she works without producing," above. Heidegger is perhaps too concerned at this point with inventing and refining a vocabulary. We point to 'producing' as a term outside capitalistic appropriation but it immediately

falls back into being a technology when it becomes a term in a discourse: better to allow the same word several resonant registers, or to allow the same resonances to several words (as when translating). For example:

*Herstellen*, as with all of the German words formed from *stellen* and used by Heidegger, presents a special problem for the translator. Albert Hofstadter, for one, translates *herstellen* as "produce," above, and as "setting forth" in "Origin of the Work of Art." In that later piece (which Hofstadter had translated earlier), the sentences "Die Erde herstellen heisst: sie ins Offene bringen als das Sichverschliessende. Diese Herstellung der Erde leistet das Werk, in dem es sich selbst in die Erde Zurückstellt," are translated as "To set forth the earth means to bring it into the Open as the self-secluding. This setting forth of the earth is achieved by the work as it sets itself back into the earth" (Heidegger, "Origin of the Work of Art" [1943], *Poetry, Language, Thought*, p. 47). Other possible translations of *herstellen* include: place here, set up, establish, prepare, bring about, create, make, manufacture, or build. *Stellen* itself is to put or place, while the noun *Stelle* is a place, position, site, or spot. Possible translations of *vorstellen* include to signify and *Vorstellung* is often translated by idea or representation (as in Kant). For now, I will have to be satisfied with the evocation, and not the resolution, of these problems for eventually thinking through (and for translating) Heidegger's contribution to thinking.

here instead of a going out to grab. We can think of this straightforwardly in terms of the appropriate word, the correct naming of that which stands opposite: it's calling your best friend by first name, becoming (it is a future-oriented being) familiar with a language, asking for an oddly shaped salt shaker by saying, 'salt'. There is still an activity, a creation, which has yet to be full, specified: it always already exists over and against, as other to the perceiving subject whose task is to appropriate appropriately. With Heidegger, it is again necessary to formulate two critiques of the subject (the complexity of holding both being paradigmatically the complexity of reading Heidegger): (1) the criticism of the individualist, particularist subject who is supposed to possess knowledge and (2) the criticism of the average everyday subject who refuses to accept the responsibility for (which is not the possession of) knowledge. The former category we are currently in a position to explore, but the second requires an understanding of time and resoluteness which is novel to the tradition (at least since the modern turn toward subjectivism) and requires the former critique as a framework. Briefly, to be one with that which is known, in its specificity, is an act of community, of communication as openness to the other. To be the line before you are an eye on the line is to reach into space by being created.

One can also relate these subject critiques to the question of how one lets women speak (or, phrased more neutrally, how it is possible that women speak, and are heard). The question will partly be of how much one shares another's purposes, or if there is, in fact, an obligation to another's purposes—whether one must take on the position of the moral subject in order to fulfill one's obligations. We must question, then, both the ability to say your own productive activity is appropriate and the possibility of criticizing the moral attitude, the appropriateness of the words, of others.[80] Heidegger, with an almost methodological insistence on avoiding the characterization of the creative being in terms of the determinations appropriate to beings, refuses to begin from the obligations which center around an ego as such:

> If the ego is determined by the mode of being of acting and hence is not a thing, then the beginning for philosophy, which starts with the ego, is not an active thing but an active deed.
>
> The question remains, How is this acting itself to be interpreted as a way of being? In reference to Kant the question becomes, Does he not after all fall back again into conceiving this active ego as an end which is in the sense of one extant being among other extant beings? *The interpretation of the ego as a moral person provides us with no really informative disclosure about the mode of being of the ego.* (Ibid., p. 142)

The products of our activity are, in fact, the categories of intuition. By turning to the subject, Kant is showing us that the appearance of one chair-form behind two actual extant chairs does not occur as magic but as the productive act of universalization. The problem is that to turn to the subject as if it were just another object (as if it could provide the substantive presence, or ground, the

80. For the Cusan, the question is not already decided by the fact that in his theory of knowledge he interprets man as creative. For this daring is blunted by the requirement that what man projects must be appropriate to the divine Creation. The question is now posed more radically, and specifically because it seeks in man's status as "created in the image of God" the element of infinitude as well. In the treatise *On Conjectures*, man is designated as *humanus deus* [a human God]: "Human being (*humanitas*) is a unity, and that means that at the same time it is infinity realized in a human manner (*infinitas humaniter contracta*). Now, however, it is the nature of such a unity to unfold beings from itself (*ex se explicare entia*), for it contains in its simplicity a multiplicity of beings. So also man has the capacity (*virtus*) to unfold everything from himself into the circle of the region he inhabits (*omnia ex se explicare intra regionis suae circulum*), to make everything arise from his power at the center (of that circle)(*omnia de potentia centri exercere*)." Here the diagram of circle and center represents the inclusiveness of the relation between creative origin and projected world, the way in which the reality that arises from man refers back to him. "Human being itself alone is the goal of the creative process (*activae creationis*) founded in it. Man does not

go beyond himself (*non pergit extra se*) when he is creative (*dum creat*): rather, in the unfolding of his power, he comes to himself." (Blumenberg, *The Legitimacy of the Modern Age* [1966], p. 533)

81. And further,

This has made the Incarnation a universal, a cosmic event. Nowhere is there talk of the fact that man's sin has compelled God to sacrifice His son. The Creation, not sin, the deficiency of nature, not that of man, presses toward this consequence. But is it already the ultimate consequence? Has the theological furor of the late Middle Ages been successfully reconciled with the will of perplexed man to secure his own right over against transcendence and not himself to come to nothing in the face of an inflated God? The death of Giordano Bruno will be a beacon signaling the failure of this reconciliation. (Blumenberg, *The Legitimacy of the Modern Age* [1966], p. 547)

82. Bruno's conception also replays (and adumbrates) a certain thinking of sex (which we will look at again later):

Language is likewise an institution, as is the celibatory machine, to the extent that it constitutes a closed language and a practice (of reading, not of speaking). The celibatory machine, though, has no need to disclose something hidden. A refusal of the title, "son of,"

endurance across time, regardless of time's specificity and modality) is to forget the situation of knowing, to believe, that is, that the ultimate purpose of knowing (attaining the moral status of being a proper and self-certain subject in the world) is to be found in the production of universals (or judgments). Reviewing my earlier positions, we see that Kant's thinking of the subject must, as with all philosophy which starts with the ego, be faithful—as woman to man, active passivity to active activity—to that (substance) which is antecedent, and which endures outside of time's movements. Further, this production is measured in its appropriateness by its faithfulness to the original (paternal) active activity—that is, a self-caused will—a project beyond ourselves in its form (its law) but not in its obligations (we are where those laws insist). Levinas, among others, accuses even the later Heidegger's use of 'Being' and 'the disclosure of Being' as falling into this paternalism (into an election of some elite, a predestination of the Volk, a hegemony of Spirit, etc.). It is perhaps possible to rescue Heidegger from Levinas with a close reading of his texts but in any case the answer to the criticism is going to have to take the form of explaining freedom of/as creation.

Giordano Bruno adumbrates the importance of the polemics against (and around revised versions of) Christianity in the move to modernism; his refusal to find a place for the Son of God on Earth is, after all (at least according to Blumenberg's account), the issue which caused Bruno to be burned at the stake.[81] The move to modern scientific or technological ways of thinking occurred as a moment of freeing mankind from the goals of a singular creation willed by a singular and arbitrary god—this hatred of the aleatory, in its turn, enslaves humanity to freely working out the determined contents of the actually existent. (All creative activity is dictated by its relation to the already existent.) Thus no one is surprised when Hegel speaks of the unity of knowing and being. Bruno has no place for Christ because he thinks of God as identically Being and being expressive.[82] For Hegel, Christ is the externalization, the expression, the word. So that: (1) Cusa's Christ (as with any mortal), as creative, adds to the world; (2) Bruno's Christ (as with any mortal), as creative, cannot exist, because God in his infinity has already created everything, leaving only the space of observer and unfolder for the mortal mind; and (3) Hegel's Christ (as with any mortal) brings to the actual world, by expressing thoughts, that which was eternally prefigured in the concept of man, but which was under the constraint of a process of development, which he called the progress of spirit or mind. According to modernity, then, man, as he assumes the role of the moral subject, is not a creator but an observer (doomed to a re-creation, merely clarifying or expounding upon the true and original intention). Even the most creative of poets would merely be writing as if from dictation.

I would like—and I think of myself as Heideggerian here—to conceptualize a theory of language, of mortality and divinity, which, with Cusa, sees the possibility and need for creation, for an active involvement with and as the world, and, apart from Cusa, sees that Christ does not exemplify or represent mankind—the world, for one example of the disanalogy, is not trying to crucify us

is the very principle of this construct featuring the Separate, the celibate and readable god. There is nothing hidden because *exteriority* takes its place. The recognition of an absolute *outside* dispenses with the need to introduce *into* the text a concealed/disclosed allusion to an authority that would make it believable. Mysticism presupposed the internal perception by an ego of its exteriority, in other words, it had to quote the other in the text. The celibatory machine keeps the other outside of itself. *Fortgehen ohne Rückschau.* The very exactness of its details (each part is a well arranged item) emphasizes their separation from one another, within systems themselves carefully distinguished. No confusion intervenes to make us forget about difference. The apparatus shines like a blade. It has the cleanliness of a suicide which *makes way* for the world's alterity, with no compensation. Having put an end to the *co-incidatio oppositorum*, and having washed its hands of any "consolation" overcoming difference, the machine's essential characteristic is that it is male. It behaves as such at its place of production. It confesses (or flaunts, whichever you like) its relation to its limit, the limit of being masculine and nothing but. The celibate of the machine, in effect, returns to the fundamental, structuring form of difference—sexuality—and refuses to exercise any masculine power of expressing the feminine in speech [dire la femme]. A cutting refusal, made exactly at the time when the impossibility of becoming, through pain, the writing of an other (feminine) causes the ambitions formerly invested in death to flow back toward the erotic. (M. Certeau, "The Arts of Dying" [1975], *Heterologies Discourse on the Other*, p. 166)

so that we are in need of a powerful redeemer. Instead, Christ exemplifies communication, writing for those beyond us, humanly, as sacrifice—Christ exemplifies the need for us to give up ourselves, our possessions, our selves as possessions. He, perhaps, even exemplifies our need to give up our Christianity, our very sense of belonging to a tradition.

This same transformation of Christ's story could be seen as a priority of contemplation over energy, a privilege of death over life, which Hegel—like the entire modern tradition—cannot conceptualize because for him life remains a reified end in itself. Perhaps I should merely abandon the metaphor of death, but how else can we summarize the meaning of finitude? One could try to reconceptualize the 'life of the mind', the contemplative life that Aristotle valorizes as being above mere life, but that is the exact correlate of transcending earthly death with a heavenly life, earthly contingencies with universal (dead) abstractions. That is, it would not conceptualize a mortality proper to itself. The problem remains that there is a privilege of the dead (of the nonliving, the immortals, the divine, the Other) even within the mind, within the contemplative, which is effaced (covered over, not eliminated) by the arrogant claim that our present life contains the truth of all past and future lives, the claim that the dead are dead *for* us, *for* me, the one who sees (who in this arrogance loses any sense of mortality). The question remains as the criticism of energy conceived of as its own salvation—the belief, for example, that technology will solve all of its own problems. It is, in Derrida's terms, the question of remains, of an unproductive product of activity, of Hegel's bastard child.

Carefully, we need to think Christ's relation to possibility and actuality: he is the mediation of the two irreducibles, of infinite possibility and finite actuality, of desire and possession. He is the mediator between the limited world of human creation (production in Heidegger's sense) and divine creation (which is merely the reason why, ultimately, we do such things as build chairs). This might be easier to see in relation to the oft-repeated heresy of Manicheanism: that God is not all powerful, but one of two (or more) powers.[83] For Manes, there is light and dark, good and evil, spirit and matter. This is closely associated with the reading of a mysogynistic Aristotle which Homans gives (above) and is identifiably the Platonism which Nietzsche is accused (by Heidegger) of (merely) standing on its head.

Further, dualism is intimately related to the question of free will and moral activity. If God is the creator of "the best of all possible worlds," why is there such pain and suffering in the world? The answer—the refutation of Manicheanism—usually revolves around, since at least Augustine, God creating the space for humans to will: they can either will in accordance with God's plan or against it. (The Spirit, God's will, is absolutely prior to the material.) Man's will, however, even as it tries to fight against the Good, eventually falls back into the Good: even the most evil of acts is given in time and God is given, abstractly so that he might hold on to his unity, as the peaceful reconciliation expressed in the death of time.[84] All activity is absorbed back into the good; there is no act which doesn't somehow fit

83. For Marcion, however, it was not primarily a speculative problem, but a religious one. If God were at one and the same time good, all-knowing, and all-powerful, how could he permit the deception and the fall of man? Since this was precisely what he had done, it followed that God could not be possessed of all three of these attributes. For a good tree did not bear bad fruit. The presence of two kinds of fruit bore witness to the existence of two kinds of trees. To account for the difference between salvation and creation and to achieve his "special and principial work," which was "the separation of the law and the gospel," Marcion posited the existence of two gods, "one judicial, harsh, mighty in war; the other mild, placid, and simply good and excellent." The former was the Creator of the world, the God of the Old Testament; the latter was the Father of Jesus Christ, who had descended to earth for the first time in the fifteenth year of the reign of Tiberius Caesar. (J. Pelikan, *The Christian Tradition* [1971], 1: 73–74)

84. "Against any disparagement of the creation of the Creator Augustine insisted that 'being is good simply because it is being [esse qua esse bonum est]'; therefore the sinner was of God insofar as he was a living creature, and not of God insofar as he was a sinner. The grace given to Adam in the state of integrity was the grace of innocence, but not

yet the grace of perfection: innocence was appropriate to the alpha-point of human history, but perfection could only come at the omega-point" (J. Pelikan, *The Christian Tradition* [1971], 1: 299).

85. Thus when Hegel says: "It is more consonant with justice that he who has money should spend it even in luxuries, than that he should give it away to idlers and beggars; for he bestows it on an equal number of persons by so doing, and these must at any rate have worked diligently for it" (*The Philosophy of History* [1831], p. 423), he is affirming man's freedom to become in accordance with the appropriate mode of becoming: production. "[I]t was acknowledged to be more commendable for men to rise from a state of dependence by *activity*, intelligence and industry, and make themselves independent" (Ibid., p. 423). One understands this again as a story of Father and Son. A woman may give birth to an abstractly legitimate son, but he only proves his legitimacy by actively becoming like the father: he deserves the products of activity—always defined by the father—only inasmuch as he is active in accordance with the father's rule. There is, in this formula, no place for gratuitous love, no envelope without its being possessed. All activity only has meaning in relation to its end. When the end is production, and Hegel claims all ends are produced, no nonproductive act has meaning and no thing is not a product.

into God's plan, no act which has not been enveloped in advance.

An abstraction at this level, however, means that no existent creature can claim an essential relation to truth in its specificity. Free will here finds its truth—the limited earthly salvation of a good conscience—only in doing in accordance with what is expected of it. The typifications of the universal—whether inspired by God or created in history—are not merely the easiest way to think but the truth of our thinking, the true way to think. The wise men of every generation, so the saying goes, have said that wisdom resides in acting in accordance with the rules and customs of the generation. This adequation to reality is the materialist conception of truth as expression, of the triumphant word of Christ (merely an expression of God's will) displacing the devil. What, then, are the implications of a Christ who is neither good nor evil—beyond good and evil?

Take, again, the example of a word and duration. Presented with an object, say this pencil, the appropriate name, 'pencil', comes to us from our habituation with/within the language. A moment of productivity is needed to distinguish between all that is merely possible within language and that which has actually come to be—this black mechanical pencil and not a red pen. The productivity is or is not correct (in the sense of adequation of representations) in so far as it reiterates the conventions of the language in such a way as to be understood within the intersubjective community. If Christ is come to fulfill the covenant, he comes as the appropriate word to indicate our election, to show us the way to our salvation; he comes as the positive content of our activity; he exists as God's sign to man that man is the legitimate son, in God's image, who deserves what he inherits, who deserves from grace and not from deed (appropriate deeds are grace, like capitalists rewarded for supporting capitalism, regardless of the consequences for existing individuals forced to live under the abstraction made concrete for the sake of the abstraction).[85]

On the other hand, as exemplar, as the specific word or position of our violence and not the abstraction of our happiness, Christ is doubly important because his death on the cross speaks of the subversion of power through writing, a subversion which continues to operate whether he represents the oppressors or the oppressed—precisely as a subversion of representation. In contrast to such a subversion (or failure of achievement), Christ as the fulfillment of originally prescribed categories gives us the same Hegelian conception of truth based on obedience to the rules of the nation (realized in their transhistorical truth as the rules of reason)—Hegel gives us the forgetfulness of all cruelty, the machinations (and banality) of fascism; it is always knowing the true answer before hearing the question. It is this last Christ in whom we choose (or don't choose) to believe; it is this Christ who is the object of historical verification; it is this Christ whom I would abandon, as having already, and necessarily, betrayed us exactly in announcing that victory was to be gained. The Christ who subverts power, who refuses the ideal of triumph, precedes the act of faith (of articulating a belief, out loud, for others to hear as a testimony, or proof of moral standing) which is con-

86. Giordano Bruno's universe, as the necessary and unreserved discharge of the *potentia absoluta* [absolute power] of God the Creator, occupies the systematic position space that for the Cusan had been occupied by the intratrinitarian generation of a divine Person, the creation of the world, and the clamping together of both in the Incarnation of the Son of God. One can verify this once again in the critical point of differentiation of the two systems, in their attitudes to the Incarnation.

For the Cusan, the Incarnation of the Word was the supplementation and perfection of the Creation, *complementum et quies*, as he says in the sermon *Dies sanctificatus*. Only in this divine self-insertion into the Creation does God's power fully actualize itself (*quiescit potentia in seipsa*). The duality of generation and creation is closed at this juncture and integrated into the unity of God's self-expression. But this presupposes that time, by which an interval is laid between the Creation and Incarnation in the midst of history, is a purely human measure of successiveness, which is imposed on the inner and essential unity of the divine action. The Cusan's theory of time as a category produced from the human spirit accords with this.

Only in the temporal form of human speech is it admissible and necessary to say that the Creation was incomplete and imperfect and contained a reserve of something that was possible for the Divinity before it received its Christological complement. But still more: The Cusan also interpreted this connection teleologically and used it to prove the singularity of the created world, since the uniqueness of the Son of God presupposed the uniqueness of the world into which he could enter and to which he could bring perfection ("*Et ipse quia unus, est unus mundus . . .* "). And still another step: The essential constitution of this world was defined and relieved of contingency by the complement that was provided for it, in that what remained in reserve for perfection determined just what would be capable of this perfection: *"Et propter ipsum omnia, quae in mundo sunt, id sunt quod sut"* [And on account of this, everything that is in the world is what it is].

Just this framework of positions now yields the condition that was to be fulfilled by the Nolan's cosmological speculation. Since for him creation and generation lose their differentiation, since the Creation is already the whole of what could and had to "come forth" from the discharge of *potentia absoluta*, not only the Christological complement but also its teleology, which required the singularity of the world, falls away. The *infiniti mondi* [infinite worlds] fill the scope that had been left open by discon-

sciousness, that is, precedes the question of whether God *is*—ontically—or not.

Of course, such a reading of Christ requires a reading against the modernist narratives concerning the meaning of Christ's appearance, and of his death. Our concern, against that interpretation, is to think the meaning of our life on earth without a constant reference to a lost unity. Blumenberg explains, in summary, the appeal of thinking of salvation as a return to the origin (and as a response to Manicheanism):

> In its historical function, the Christian dogma of the Trinity was, after all, intended as a means of barring the way to dualism, by reducing the impact of the bifurcation of the divinity that the production of the Son brings with it, by means of a third agency that the two cooperate in generating, and binding that bifurcation to the origin, without retracting it or destroying its meaning in terms of salvation. In this way the dogma succeeds in doing what Neo-Platonism had failed in, when it was able to produce everything—in the end, the manifold appearances of the visible world—from the original ground of the One in no other way except by rebellion and apostacy, by loss of being and forgetfulness of the origin, so that the only possible recommendation was to trace the result back to its origin and surrender it, again, in the latter. This metaphysical history of the world as a single turning away of entities from their origin is the root of everything in our tradition that makes the inner decomposition of the divin-

ity a precondition of man's world, which is seen as essentially tempting. (*Work on Myth* [1979], p. 552)[86]

Or, in Hegel's slightly more lyrical language:

The Kingdom of the Father is the consolidated, undistinguished mass, presenting a self-repeating cycle, mere change—like that sovereignty of Chronos engulfing his offspring. The Kingdom of the Son is the manifestation of God merely in a *relation* to secular existence—shining upon it as upon an alien object. The Kingdom of the Spirit is the harmonizing of the antithesis. (*Philosophy of History* [1831], p. 345)

The harmony of secular (temporal) and universal (atemporal in that it has no meaning as time—"mere repetition") existence is the human recognition of Christ, of Christianity, as the word which appropriately describes man's unity of purpose with the Creation. What had looked (to some of us) like a possible opening—a chance for the new creation of gratuitous objects—in the system of an alien creation, what had looked like the chance for the freedom of the individual, was eliminated in the definition of freedom as the fulfilling (and appropriation) of exactly that which earlier had been seen as constraint (freedom is the freedom to impose the law upon oneself). That is, the Father needs the Son to fulfill the purposes that the Father—in his atemporality (omnitemporality)—was unable to give to time by himself. The Son—in his temporality without purpose, fulfilling without object to fulfill—needed the Father.

tinuing the restricting teleological intention of the Cusan's speculation, a scope in which the unreserved logic of absolute omnipotence's complete self-exhaustion could now be discharged as the double infinity of the created world. (Blumenberg, *The Legitimacy of the Modern Age* [1966], pp. 565–66)

87.  This is the reading of Hegel that Derrida gives when he suggests a more rigorous move toward understanding ceaseless differentiation as itself the cause and goal of all things:

Here we are touching upon the point of greatest obscurity, on the very enigma of *différance*, on precisely that which divides its very concept by means of a strange cleavage. We must not hasten to decide. How are we to think *simultaneously*, on the one hand, *différance* as the economic detour which, in the element of the same, always aims at coming back to the pleasure or the presence that have been deferred by (conscious or unconscious) calculation, and, on the other hand, *différance* as the relation to an impossible presence, as expenditure without reserve, as the irreparable loss of presence, the irreversible usage of energy, that is, as the death instinct, and as the entirely other relationship that apparently interrupts every economy? It is evident—and this is the evident itself—that the economical and the noneconomical, the same and the entirely other, etc., cannot be thought *together*. If *différance* is unthinkable in this way, perhaps we should not hasten to make it evident, in the philosophical element of evidentiality which would make short work of dissipating the mirage and illogicalness of *différance* and would do so with the infallibility of calculation that we are well acquainted with, having precisely recognized their place, necessity, and function in the structure of *différance*. Elsewhere, in a reading of Bataille, I have attempted to indicate what might come of a rigorous and, in a new sense, "scientific" *relating* of the "restricted economy" that takes no part in expenditure without reserve, death, opening itself to nonmeaning, etc., to a general economy that *takes into account* the nonreserve, that keeps in reserve the nonreserve, if it can be put thus. I am speaking of a relationship between a *différance* that can make a profit on its investment and a *différance* that misses its profit, the *investiture* of a presence that is pure and without loss here being confused with absolute loss, with death. Through such a relating of a restricted and a general economy the very project of philosophy, under the privileged heading of Hegelianism, is displaced and reinscribed. The *Aufhebung—la relève—*is constrained into writing itself otherwise. Or perhaps simply into writing itself. Or, better, into taking account of its con-

The self-manifestation of all reality is seen here as the productive activity of a working and re-working (which, we should remember, has been cast as a negative moment, a violence or eating) on the part of mortals with the goal of achieving abstract universal peace (the third term of the dialectic): death or endless continuation.[87]

Earlier I had tried to introduce a conception of freedom as the hesitation a daughter feels between the law of the Father and the law of the Son—the woman who is no longer daughter but not yet wife. This freedom can only be actualized in one or another of the prescribed roles, but the moment of freedom lies before the decision, not after. Or, in my reappraisal of Christ's passion, his freedom, his divinity and exemplary humanity, lies in his decision to accept death on the cross and not in his resurrection or transcendence. Note also that freedom does not endure; it has no duration, but, as delay, precedes duration. It is in that sense that freedom belongs to the other: to the precedence of their time. Derrida tells us how this precedence, in its exteriority to time's flow, leads to the critique of modernity itself:

> The structure of delay (*Nachträglichkeit*) in effect forbids that one make of temporalization (temporization) a simple dialectical complication of the living present as an originary and unceasing synthesis—a synthesis constantly directed back on itself, gathered in on itself and gathering—of retentional traces and protentional openings. The alterity of the "unconscious" makes us concerned not with horizons of modified—past or future—presents, but

with a "past" that has never been pre-sent, and which never will be, whose future to come will never be a *production* or a reproduction in the form of presence. Therefore the concept of trace is incompatible with the concept of retention, of the becoming-past of what has been present. One cannot think the trace—and therefore, *différance*—on the basis of the present, or of the presence of the present.

A past that has never been present: this formula is the one that Emmanuel Levinas uses, although certainly in a nonpsychoanalytic way, to qualify the trace and enigma of absolute alterity: the Other. Within these limits, and from this point of view at least, the thought of *différance* implies the entire critique of classical ontology undertaken by Levinas. And the concept of the trace, like that of *différance,* thereby organizes, along the lines of these different traces and differences of traces, in Nietzsche's sense, in Freud's sense, in Levinas' sense—these "names of authors" here being only indices—the network which reassembles and traverses our "era" as the delimitation of the ontology of presence. ("Différance" [1968], *Margins of Philosophy,* p. 21)

I think it is too easy to forget how close the position of différance is to Hegelian categories of relation and difference; we are speaking of the absolutely fundamental categories of thinking, of the thought that thinks itself in the moment of its contact with being—that is, in the moment when it stops being thought.[88]

sumption of writing. ("Dif-férance" [1968], *Margins of Philosophy,* p. 19)

88. First of all, there is a differend between the first addressor and the subject. The subject knows its idiom, space-time, and can only accord referential value to a phrase uttered in this idiom. But it knows, *qua* addressee affected by sensation, *qua* receptivity, that something, some sense, on the side of the other seeks to phrase itself and does not succeed in phrasing itself in the idiom of space-time. This is why sensation is a mode of feeling, that is, a phrase awaiting its expression, a silence touched with emotion. This expectant wait is never gratified, the phrase that does take place is uttered in the language of space-time forms, which the subject "speaks" without knowing if it is the language of the other. This differend is on the scale of the loss of the concept of nature. (Lyotard, *The Differend* [1983], p. 63)

89. But what would be "enough"? Heidegger gives us an early definition of his concept of poetry:

> But even relatively original and creative meanings and the words coined from them are, when articulated, relegated to idle talk. Once articulated, the word belongs to everyone, without a guarantee that its repetition will include original understanding. This possibility of genuinely entering into the discourse nevertheless exists and is documented especially in this, that the discoveredness which is given with a word can be rectified with certain sentences and developed further. Indeed, articulated discourse can help first by grasping possibilities of being for the first time which before were already always experienced implicitly. The discoveredness of Dasein, in particular the disposition of Dasein, can be made manifest by means of words in such a way that certain new possiblities of Dasein's being are set free. Thus discourse, especially *poetry*, can even bring about the release of new possibilities of the being of Dasein. In this way, discourse proves itself positively as a *mode of maturation, a mode of temporalization* of time itself. (*History of the Concept of Time* [1925], p. 27

The debate on Christology had itself never escaped the dichotomy of poetic and literal language, but since the romantics, the relation to Christ has been cast, in various forms, as the central question. Also at this point, we note that the metaphor for war need only be a metaphor: we can speak of exactly the same modes of self-manifestation of articulated truths under the rubric of play. This is, perhaps, still not enough.[89]

# Writing Christ

## saying Christ

*It must further be observed, that in this truth, the relation of man to this truth is also posited. For Spirit makes itself its own [polar] opposite—and is the return from this opposite into itself. Comprehended in pure ideality, that antithetic form of the Spirit is the Son of God; reduced to limited and particular conceptions, it is the World-Nature and Finite Spirit: Finite Spirit itself therefore is posited as a constituent element [Moment] in the Divine Being. Man himself therefore is comprehended in the Idea of God, and this comprehension may be thus expressed— that the unity of Man with God is posited in the Christian Religion. But this unity must not be superficially conceived, as if God were only Man, and Man, without further condition, were God. Man, on the contrary, is God only in so far as he annuls the merely Natural and Limited in his Spirit and elevates himself to God. That is to say, it is obligatory on him who is a partaker of the truth, and knows that he himself is a constituent [Moment] of the Divine Idea, to give up his merely natural being: for the Natural is the Unspiritual. In this Idea of God, then, is to be found also the* Reconciliation *that heals the pain and inward suffering of man. For Suffering itself is henceforth recognized as an instrument necessary for producing the unity of man with God. This implicit unity exists in the first place only for the thinking speculative consciousness; but it must also exist for the sensuous, representative consciousness—it must become an object for the World—it must* appear, *and that in the sensuous form appropriate to Spirit, which is the human.* Christ has appeared—*a Man who is God—God who is Man; and thereby peace and reconciliation have accrued to the World. . . . Moreover the sensuous existence in which Spirit is embodied is only a transitional phase. Christ dies; only as dead, is he exalted to Heaven and sits at the right hand of God; only thus is he Spirit. . . . To the Apostles, Christ as living was not that which he was to them subsequently as the Spirit of the Church, in which he became for them for the first time an object for their truly spiritual consciousness.*

—Hegel, Philosophy of History

The value of Christ's death is not merely, cynically, that his image is more easily manipulable than his actual presence. He must regain his divinity (infinitude) after having been the least (finite). He has marked the place of man's existence as inconsequential—one is, properly speaking, oriented past death, past one's present place. (This is the function of writing in Derrida, and the import of Christ's character as word.) The confusing—and difficult—space for my work lies in the fact that I am not strictly speaking (or at least not merely) arguing against Hegel. Neither do I 'without further condition' identify myself as Derridean, Irigarayan, Levinasian, or Heideggerian. I seek, as Homans said of women, to enter the symbolic order gradually, on my own—human, mortal—terms, as a reader. We need, then, to find the space of a contemplation, of a thinking, which does not rest on the death of the flesh, of the natural, of the specific individual. In other words, I seek an ethics which neither ignores nor accepts the liberal humanist cultural relativism which is my heritage. To do thus, and this is where I will invoke Girard's work, we start with a Christ which is relatively pallatable to the humanist tradition and—without (like Girard) reclaiming some pure, previously hidden, intention (a true God on earth)—reaffirm the possibility of speaking, and of writing, towards another, from the obligation to the ethical itself. However, before entering that course, I want to keep the question of finitude bouncing off the question of the infinite (the sense of the changing characterizations of the infinite—from God, to community, to history, to language, to economy, to Other—is what we will follow in the second section on sisters).

In his essay "The Pit and the Pyramid: Introduction to Hegelian Semiology," Derrida notes that, for Hegel, "(m)emory, the production of signs, is also thought itself" (p. 87). This double moment of retention and production speaks the crux of the sign's position in the economy of time passing, of the death of presence and the resurrection of/as life. For Hegel, there had once been a time when we lived the simple immediacy of being a circle, but we must renounce that immediacy if we are to know our life as a sign, that is if we are to retain the meaning of each moment as a determinate part of having a meaningful life as a whole—which is another way of phrasing the philosophical escape from the mundane through reflection (of grounding the work of reflection in the moment of judgment). We do not experience the divinity of pure presence immediately; we see it, instead, at a distance so that we might recognize presence itself (articulation, externalization, expression) as God. We take the word to be us and the tradition's words to be the true, the possibility of our truth. Knowing, for Hegel, is the ever-distancing movement away from particulars, storing them (as universals) as acquired possessions for future use. Memory relies on repetition—if we cannot in some sense access the past lived immediacy as if it were still present, then the past can have no meaning for us. The sign lives the permanence of what has been lost. My (eventual) critique of this position is directed against the negative characterization of signification itself. Derrida still, perhaps, relies too much on the act of signification, but he understands that signification cannot exist as the mere desire to possess—it includes a moment beyond the economic (and this problem is clearly central to his own most recent work).

Signification, for Derrida, begins to escape the simple schema of 'I speak, I write as the record of having spoken'. Memory itself requires an ideal absence—

an absence Hegel too hastily identified with death/redemption (it is, after all, not the mere absence of a particular living being). Memory marks the fact that we address the absent divine, that we live towards the future, and not the fact that we have been addressed in the past. Iterability is different from repeatability, as Christ crucified differs from Christ alive, in that iterability marks an absence, announces an anticipated absence and seeks an addressee who can respond (which is how it takes part in/as productive passivity as well as how Derrida links the basic structures of signification to desire). It will remain to ask the 'why' of our addressing itself, for if the concept of writing erases the need for a reader, or an audience, then writing would merely be the description, as pure possibility, of nothing other than itself.[90]

> (A)t least this distance, divergence, delay, this deferral [différance] must be capable of being carried to a certain absoluteness of absence if the structure of writing, assuming that writing exists, is to constitute itself. It is at that point that the différance [difference and deferral, trans.] as writing could no longer (be) an (ontological) modification of presence. In order for my "written communication" to retain its function as writing, i.e., its readability, it must remain readable despite the absolute disappearance of any receiver, determined in general. My communication must be repeatable—iterable—in the absolute absence of the receiver or of any empirically determinable collectivity of receivers. Such iterability—(iter, again, probably comes from itara,

90. I can delay a criticism of Derrida on Levinasian grounds (from the claims of the ethical) only to the extent that the structure of delay disrupts (and constitutes) the functioning of writing such that the ethical earns a point of articulation before there comes a point where an ethical rule might have been deduced. Levinas and Derrida are in disagreement exactly here, over the ethics of the excess which writing would articulate after the disappearance of all audiences: my goal is to rethink our description of the possibility of describing—to rethink, with Derrida and Levinas, our obedience to the enveloping deity called technology. The idea of a concept, of an intentional whole only vaguely meant, left as a task to be fulfilled by future generations (this task is thought as the moment of ethics insofar as it is based on the judgment which holds an obligation or a situation to be true or just) is defined (tautologically) as the formal condition of all speech or writing; technology names the particular concept which, socially and philosophically, has best expressed that tautology's self-closure, which would outlaw the very possibility of not fitting within the domain of technology's (or more formally, the concept's) grasp. The question of whether the guiding spirit (the defining concept) of the Enlightenment was liberal humanism or the scientist domination of nature or the reification of the word of the Father (or some other conceptual primogenitor) falls late within the trajectory of questions we are broaching here, questions

which seek to ask of the possibility of fidelity or infidelity to a tradition—a question which, in turn, quickly pushes us to ask of the possibility of a tradition at all.

*other* in Sanskrit, and everything that follows can be read as the working out of the logic that ties repetition to alterity) structures the mark of writing itself, no matter what particular type of writing is involved (whether pictographical, hieroglyphic, ideographic, phonetic, alphabetic, to cite the old categories). A writing that is not structurally readable—iterable—beyond the death of the addressee would not be writing. (Derrida, "Signature Event Context" [1971], *Limited Inc.*, p. 7) (This passage can also be found in *Margins of Philosophy*, p. 315)

Derrida is too often understood merely as a skeptic of language's ability to correctly communicate a unified meaning when he is actually seeking to approach a different moment of signification, one outside of the perfect identity of infinite repetition, of a closed system of possibility, act and actuality—outside of time seen as an infinite, perfectly regulated, number line. Much of Derrida's writing is dedicated to asserting a space of writing, a congruence of writing with death (the point at which the living voice stops) and an approach of writing towards the absolute finitude of writing (its very reliance on the structure of death).

Iterability, as a moment of production, must be seen as a going towards, a breaking with the same in favor of the other (although we must not rush to say—beyond the structure of the delay, of death, or of the trace—what this other is; it is not, for example, either human or divine). Placing the iterability of writing where the originality of the voice was said to have ruled our thinking is, unquestionably, already an ethical move and is thus intimately involved with questions of authentic knowledge and appropriate writing. The ethics of the trace, in Derrida, stem in part from Levinas' theory of signification and expression, and the trace—in its ethical moment—speaks the strange priority (which Derrida wants to establish against Levinas) of the written over the spoken—not merely that every spoken word relies on (an) inscribed previous experience(s) (necessarily polysemenous),[91] but that the writing itself, in its orientation towards absence, breaks the bonds of stagnation (this is a reiteration, and a reworking, of a Hegelian move which privileges death—determination—over life—indetermination):

> If polysemy is infinite, if it cannot be mastered as such, this is thus not because a finite reading or a finite writing remains incapable of exhausting a superabundance of meaning. Not, that is, unless one displaces the philosophical concept of finitude and reconstitutes it according to the law and structure of the text: according as the blank, like the hymen, re-marks itself forever as disappearance, erasure, non-sense. Finitude then becomes infinitude, according to a non-Hegelian identity: through an interruption that suspends the equation between the mark and the meaning, the "blank" marks everything white (this above all): virginity, frigidity, snow, sails, swans' wings, foam, paper, etc., *plus* the blankness that allows for the mark in the first place, guaranteeing its space of reception and production. (Derrida, *Dissemination* [1972], p. 253)

91. This seems to me to be how Derrida is often read, which makes (for example) his *Speech and Phenomena* [1967] trivial (and wrong). It seems more instructive to take his alliance with the Levinasian conception of the trace more seriously—especially where that alliance fights against an understanding of inscription which would merely mimic the idea of the act. That the infinite is marked by this qualitative overdetermination (not merely the very large number of marks which a tradition would encompass) points us away from a deification of acting for its own sake (to paraphrase the hyper-Hegelianism Derrida is accused of).

92. Girard I think is most Hegelian (at least most crafted by the Enlightenment) when he says,

> The Gospel writers are the necessary intermediaries between ourselves and him whom they call Jesus. But in the example of Peter's denial, and in all of its antecedents, their insufficiency becomes a positive quality. It increases the credibility and power of the witness. The failure of the Gospel writers to understand certain things, together with their extreme accuracy in most cases, makes them somewhat passive intermediaries. Through their relative lack of comprehension we cannot help but think that we can attain directly a level of comprehension greater than theirs. We have the impression therefore of a commun-

We are still speaking of a debate with and over Christianity, of the relation of the finite to the divine. For Hegel, the figure of this unity, construed
broadly, is the same as for Augustine: We regain our (infinite) selves in God by
losing our (finite, natural) selves. For Derrida, the completion of this finitude
is infinitely delayed, just as Levinas' conception of human freedom relies on
the deferral of the moment of injustice. This is a variation on the Hegelian
conception of Christ, this time deliberately keeping Christianity from (ever)
claiming its victory. Taking that contestation seriously in terms of the word, I
would now wish to think back towards the ethics of words (spoken and written). Hegel's view of Christ, summarized in the epigraph to this section, announces the achievement of divinity, the defeat of the merely natural, in Man's
reconciliation with God. Hegel knew this to be process, to be a new conception of time; with Derrida, the relation to time is infinitely delayed, never resolved into its moment 'as' merely a relation, as a relating of one towards another. With both Hegel and Derrida, however, there is a violent marking of
this time—a marking which makes freedom (as knowledge or as delay) possible. I want to take seriously, for a moment, before returning to Derrida, the
possibility of yet another relation to time. It is suggested, if not worked out as
such, by Girard's reworking of the figure of Christ: perhaps time is not the violence of marking (or being marked), but is rather the word which refuses
(and thus makes possible our refusal of) the simple violence of determining
words. If time remains to be thought *with* writing, it is only with the writing
which rends the poetic word (itself an announcement of the fact of speaking's
impotence to do other than be written, other than to be its own separating
from itself).

René Girard reworks the basic Hegelian thematics of Christ (he traces it
back to the actual message of Christ to be read behind the weak and distorting
transcriptions of the Apostles)[92] to produce an understanding of the Christian
Passion as the paradigmatic story of peace overcoming violence:

> By maintaining the word of the Father against violence until the end and by
> dying for it, Jesus has crossed the abyss separating mankind from the Father.
> He himself becomes their Paraclete, their protector, and he sends them an-
> other Paraclete who will not cease to work in the world to bring forth the
> truth into light.
>
>     Even if the language astonishes us, even if the author of the text some-
> times seems dizzy before the breadth of vision, we cannot help but recognize
> what we have just been discussing. The Spirit is working in history to reveal
> what Jesus has already revealed, the mechanism of the scapegoat, the genesis
> of all mythology, the nonexistence of all gods of violence. In the language of

the Gospel the Spirit achieves the defeat and condemnation of Satan. (Girard, *The Scapegoat* [1982], pp. 206–7)[93]

It should be clear at this point that to speak of the working, living Spirit we must be speaking of those activities which can be actualized in/through human activity. The Spirit lives within us to the extent that we are convinced of the goals of Christianity (or broadly construed, as with Girard, the goals of nonviolence) and direct all of our productive activity towards bringing acts of oppression to the light of day. Christ as word is rigorously taken to be a process of transcendent nonviolence as meaning and not as Christ the reified, eternally stagnant, *object*. This change in the conception of Christianity denies that truth is an ever-abstracting motion away from particulars: a sense of community is no longer formed through the abstract 'we' left over after expelling a scapegoat; conscience, as consciousness and community, works as Antigone remembers Polynices. With Girard, we must be careful to understand exactly what can and cannot be assented to. For example, even as we are willing to rethink the divinity—the possible nonviolence—inherent in a name (such as Christ), we must ensure that naming itself does not take on a divine aura: the justice, or injustice, of an occurrence does not exhaust the possibilities of time (that is, of the other's future).[94] Here in Girard we must recognize a certain overlap with the Hegelian categories of the self-manifestation of actuality: what is comes to be as a result of a play between texts (although we must be careful of attributing an originary status to the idea of a text in general).

ication without intermediaries. We gain this privilege not through an intrinsically superior intelligence but as the result of two thousand years of a history slowly fashioned by the Gospels themselves. (*The Scapegoat* [1982], p. 163)

93. "Parakleitos in Greek is the exact equivalent of advocate or the Latin ad-vocatus. The Paraclete is called on behalf of the prisoner, the victim, to speak in his place and in his name, to act in his defense. The Paraclete is the universal advocate, the chief defender of all innocent victims, the destroyer of every representation of persecution. He is truly the spirit of truth that dissipates the fog of mythology" (R. Girard, *The Scapegoat* [1982], p. 207). Which is to say that the Spirit is what Nietzsche identifies with the Will-to-truth. Girard, then, seems to have a conception of the true based on the possession of the scientific, technological, attitude.

94. Isn't the I also divested here of its power qua addressor of sense to be no more than the ear of the unpresentable that calls out to it?—No, for this confusion to be possible, it would have to be supposed that the foreign phrase wants to phrase itself through you as its go-between, that it wants something from you because it would like to be itself. Or, that Being (or language) (*die Sage*) has need of man [he cites Heidegger]. But you are nothing but its advent (whether addressee or addres-

0

sor or referent or sense even, or several of these instances together) in the universe presented by the phrase that happens. It wasn't waiting for you. You come when it arrives. The occurrence is not the Lord. The pagans know this and laugh over this edifying confusion. (Lyotard, *The Differend* [1983], p. 116)

Again, Girard is useful in giving us the relationship of writing to Christ. He is using the example of reading a particular text (which, although claiming to be historical, makes the scientifically incredible claim that a community of Jews had caused a plague), but we are not expected to limit our lessons to the text understood as anything less than a world and its history.

> When I exclaim at the end of his text: "The Jews are scapegoats," I am stating something that does not appear in the text and that contradicts the sense intended by the author. The latter is not presenting a distortion from the persecutor's viewpoint but what he believes to be the bare truth. The scapegoat released to us by the text is a scapegoat both in and for the text. The scapegoat that we must disengage from the text for ourselves is the scapegoat of the text. He cannot appear in the text though he controls all its themes; he is never mentioned as such. He cannot become the theme of that text that he shapes. This is not a theme but a mechanism for giving structure. (Girard, *The Scapegoat* [1982], p. 118)

This is a wonderfully abbreviated (since still accurate) synopsis of modernist hermeneutics. Recapping in the more convoluted language of my writing: the truth is the process (the play) and not the product of the process. For this position, peace as the unity of knower and known—as the true revelation of the repressed's voice—is the culmination and end of war. For humanity more generally, and for the history which it interprets and reinterprets, Christ plays the role of scapegoat, suffers the violence of persecution, so that violence itself may be overcome—with the advantages which a history of violence bestowed on us still held firmly in place (are not the fruits of international capitalism, so seemingly sweet, built on countless acts of more or less violent appropriation?). The turn, and this is a recurring issue in the history of Christianity as well, is that if Christ died on the cross for a particular group of elect then he institutionalizes violence, in fact, requires that violence continue in the name of the progression towards the final judgment (a teleology which—as a structuring trope supposedly directing all interpretive activity—makes it impossible to think that the good fruit of modernity could have evolved in any other way besides through capitalism's violences).

As a preliminary marker, and we can do no more, let us call injustice exclusionary enjoyment. The present systems of rights ensure that personal enjoyment is not destroyed by the claims of others—in other words, it codifies exclusionary practices as either justified or unjustified. At a certain level it makes sense—I found the apple, I should get to eat it. When we throw the finding of the apple into the broader networks of concern that a meaningful life entails, instead of separating it from its contexts, we find that a life lived as the accumulation of objects is meaningless. Why were you looking for an apple? Eventually, and this is what modern subjectivism covers up, the only possible reason for collecting the apple was so you could give it away. Analogously, if you are a god, why become human? Simply put, it is to show mortals that true life is directed away from the self, always striving toward the infinite (and the death of god puts the sense of showing, or appearance, itself into question). This striving is what religious feeling has always grappled with. The travesty of modern subjectivism is to reinterpret the infinite as the summation of all objects spread bodily through space—unattainable only in its multiplicity, approximated in personal accumulation.[95]

My complaint with the modern viewpoint, then, would need to be couched not in the adequateness of a representation to what has already happened—as a representable fact—but in its inability to mark the withdrawal of the infinite, to delimit the *failure* of that awaited arrival, as the proper space of our desiring activity (so that we are not merely awaiting some success or another, but thinking the aporetic structure of the failure itself). It will be my task to show that withdrawal as coterminous with the site of both justice and injustice: our world is shaken to its foundations by the facts of our exclusions. Christ cried out on the cross, "O God, Why hast thou forsaken me?" Why can't I forge a world of love? Simply put, according to this story, Christ did not represent the end of history, but the beginning of the historical life of the oppressed.

95. That this life *is* only insofar as it is appropriated for the narrative truth of history itself becomes the truth of Christianity and of Christianity's historical ascendency. Lyotard tells the story in terms of that narrative that taught us to love the narrative event itself: "Love as the principal operator of exemplary narrations and diegeses is the antidote to the principle of exception that limits traditional narratives. The authorization to tell, to listen, and to be told about does not result from a common affiliation with a world of names which are themselves descended from primordial narratives, it results from a commandment of universal attraction, *Love one another*, addressed to all heroes, all narrators, and all narratees" (Lyotard, *The Differend* [1983], p. 159).

To present presentation is to express the identity of the active ego that produces the categories of intuition and the passive ego that sees; it is to see that the subject is an acting and not an accomplished fact. Has God withdrawn from the world? Yes. Otherwise, there is no space for the child. Consciousness, memory, justice, sociality, and writing all depend on a space of creation, on the responsibility of the individual for the future of the world. We do not progress easily toward the coming of Christ—we may fail the task, not just of ensuring ourselves a place in heaven (there is no such exchange), but of giving our children a future at all.

Violence, death. They sometimes seem more to be tropes themselves than signifiers that can be used to explain unclear metaphors. As bluntly as possible: Christ is the internalizing of the written (not the spoken) word—that is, he is the referent of justice as an ethical rule, the guarantee that signifiers outlast their death, the call of the Good, as the call of God, the call to respond to the weak and the dead, to the finitude of others. The crucifixion of Christ has always announced his real death, his community with the finite, his entrance into the society of mortals. Take Christ, in his essence, not to be a person but a principle; he tells us—if nothing else, then this is everything—that every act of oppression is a transgression against the divine (a telling which puts the 'us' of our hearing in question as well). A mortal, a subjectivity, a power: to become a word he must give up what is beyond nameability. The act of oppression inherent in naming is coterminous with what Heidegger criticizes in those dogmatic trajectories of ontotheological metaphysics that reduce

God and the divine to the categories of objects in the world, what Derrida criticizes when speech-act theorists reduce agency to its effects or iterability to reproduction. Christ's subjectivity—as word—writes the space of letting texts speak for themselves, of hearing women speak through the long labors of undocumented darkness—with their own voice.[96] Even then, criticizing a still modern position, it seems to be a male ear which chooses whether or not to listen (and we will return to my problems with this characterization of voice).

To say Christ is internalization itself, or speaks it, is to give precedence to the call of the Law, of his call to help those in need, over the violence of appropriation. God's death serves two purposes here:

(1) It ends the era of symbolic lack—we need not fight for 'our' knowledge competitively as if it were the last piece of bread. His death announces the full presence of all which will come to be—I situate my entire time as after his death. This does not imply—as Bruno thought—that all possibilities in fact exist and humanity is called merely to express one possible manifestation of the eternally prefigured truth (even if truth is not understood as a collection of particular beliefs, the space of truth's occurrence as/within extensive concepts is eternally determined). Rather—and the structure of divinity itself speaks this—God exists, positively, as a word or command, before an individual perceives, or ignores, the command (a command to do something and not a command to merely be something). Christ asks us why violence remains amidst the plenty of existence. Our creative acts are

96. There is betrayal of my anarchic relation with illeity, but also a new relationship with it: it is only thanks to God that, as a subject incomparable with the other, I am approached as an other by the others, that is, "for myself." "Thanks to God" I am another for the others. God is not involved as an alleged interlocutor: the reciprocal relationship binds me to the other man in the trace of transcendence, in illeity. The passing of God, of whom I can speak only by reference to this aid or this grace, is precisely the reverting of the incomparable subject into a member of society. (Levinas, *Otherwise than Being* [1974], p. 158)

Levinas is not speaking of Christ here, but of the relation to God as trace, a relation Derrida has worked out in close relation to the concept of writing.

not directed towards products—durable goods—but towards the lives of others. Under different religions the command exists differently but command is never an economic relation. Simply put, there is no one person who doesn't exist as subjected to command. This fact need not extend into a theory of predestination—the fact of understanding precedes economy, precedes because the divine has been given, as a process of inclusive language, always already. Our task is to begin to think in the face of this given.

As exemplary, Christ shows the truth of sacrifice, the unity of knowing and sacrifice, the absolute giving up of self so that the future might prosper, the unity of the subject and the circle.

> It is not because there exists, among beings, a thinking being structured as I, pursuing ends, that being takes on signification and becomes a world; it is because in the proximity of being is inscribed the trace of an absence, or of the infinite, that there is dereliction, gravity, responsibility, obsession and I. The I, the non-interchangeable par excellence, is, in a world without play, what in a permanent sacrifice substitutes itself for others and transcends the world. But this is the source of speaking, for it is the essence of communication. (Levinas, "Language and Proximity" [1967], *Collected Philosophical Papers*, p. 124)

(2) Christ's death, his mortality, or finitude, and not his mere absence, calls us to create. The 'death of God', as Zarathustra proclaimed, is the call to step into, to create, time. 'God' is not an old man with a white beard but the abstract unity where all find their home. Christ, insofar as he is God's death, the death of abstraction's own unity, is the call to speak, to leave the home, to give up your safety, to sacrifice yourself to the other. But Christ's death doesn't leave an abyss; the words are all there and need not be fought for; are there, but must be taken up, cared for, shepherded; are there, but are not exhausted in their presence/articulation.

What I am trying to show here, and will try to show throughout the rest of this book as well, is that the traditional theories of our relation to the divinity (to meaning), that is to the existence of things as objects which fit into a system, are not wrong relative to the infinite but rather inadequate in their conception of the position of the subject (insofar as they efface the process of that positionality, exactly to the extent that the other's future won't be your own, exactly to the extent that the other's recognition, the other's articulation of an agreement with you, as two in an economy, does not provide the determining milieu, or the meaningful envelope, of your acts). It would be possible—even laudible—to say that our knowledge needs to be recontextualized, but if the whole moral network of signification—of intending your words for another's ears—is not reinstituted in our relation to the divine as a still indeterminate future, then Christ's divinity remains merely the divinity of a sacred goat.

Precisely by being absent he calls the individual to the word, to be capable of the word which the always already absent speaks. To present oneself, the freedom—or time—at one's disposal, as a sacrifice, is to dedicate time to creation. To speak towards another is to reach out into a world without hope of reappropriating your words for your own uses. God said, "Hear me, O Israel." Hearing before hearing—God was already gone—we each answer, to the face which stands where the call seemed to have originated, and we each reply, "Here I am."

> Like someone put under leaden skies that suppress every shadowy corner in me, every residue of mystery, every mental reservation, every "as for me . . . ," and every hardening or relaxing of the plot of things by which escape would be possible, I am a testimony, or a trace, or the glory of the Infinite, breaking the bad silence which harbors Gyges's secrecy. There is extra-verting of a subject's inwardness; the subject becomes visible before becoming a seer! The Infinite is not "in front of" me; I express it, but precisely by giving a sign of the giving of signs, of the "for-the-other" in which I am dis-interested: here I am [me voici]! The accusative [*me* voici!] here is remarkable: here I am, under your eyes, at your service, your obedient servant. In the name of God. But this is without thematization; the sentence in which God gets mixed in with words is not "I believe in God." The religious discourse that precedes all religious discourse is not dialogue. It is the "here I am" said to a neighbor to whom I am given over, by which I announce peace, that is, my responsibility for the other. "Creating language on their lips. . . . Peace, peace to him who is far and to him who is near, says the Eternal" [Isaiah 57:11]. (Levinas, "God and Philosophy" [1975], *Collected Philosophical Papers*, p. 170)

This is, I recognize, very lyrical and high-sounding religious language. It will be the task of the rest of the book to make sense of these passages, with some appropriate amendations and addenda. With that opening, we mark the preliminary closure of a circle.[97]

We are still left with all of our doubts; I am unsure of what to say for Iphigenia, still waiting—is there truly such a thing as an infinite delay?—for the knife to descend to her throat. I would continue this deferral by backtracking, entering where we began: we are playing a certain type of genre, which allows

97. It is also appropriate to mark the differences between Hegel and Levinas on these points. Fortunately, the work has already been done:

> After having spoken of taste, touch, and smell, Hegel again writes, in the *Aesthetics*: "*Sight*, on the other hand, possesses a purely ideal relation to objects by means of light, a material which is at the same time immaterial, and which suffers on its part the objects to continue in their free self-subsistence, making them appear and reappear, but which does not, as the atmosphere or fire does, consume them actively either by imperceptible degrees or patently. Everything, then, is an object of the appetiteless vision [*la vue exempte de désirs*], which, however, in so far as it remains unimpaired in its integrity, merely is disclosed in its form and colour." This neutralization of desire is what makes sight excellent for Hegel. But for Levinas, this neutralization is also, and for the same reasons, the first violence, even though the face is not what it is when the glance is absent. Violence, then, would be the solitude of a mute glance, of a face without speech, *the abstraction* of seeing. According to Levinas *the glance* by itself, contrary to what one may be led to believe, does not *respect* the other. Respect, beyond grasp and contact, beyond touch, smell and taste, can be only as desire, and metaphysical desire does not seek to consume,

us a certain type of gain. Yet the question with Iphigenia, the question of what it might mean for an author to stage an event, to rework an already staged event, is transformed by having been thrown back into the ethical questions one associates with language: who is it who speaks? Who is spoken to? How does writing mark the space within which speech will come to function? How am I called to be present, within the other's view, as responding to them? How does a tradition shape our very possibilities for asking questions (and thus for transforming our world)?

In some sense, only now are we in a position to answer the questions which motivated this long digression. What do universalization, objectification, and externalization mean? Only from a certain type of clarity in these terms can a critique of society based on these terms make sense; that is, only from a clarity in these terms can our overdependence on 'clarity', on the singularity (the 'only in this manner') of truth, be dismantled (and this *is*—or would be—politics, polemics, itself):

(1) Universalization—a movement, a falling away from lived presence to the position of, eventually, peaceful, abstract universality. The motive force is desire as resolution of conflict, as taking all opposites into one, as eating, as death. To universalize is to know from a distance. Further, it is to know, from a distance, what was once your own lived experience (you are the line disrupted by the other line). This knowledge occurs as durability. To form a concept is to entrust the fading present to a durable concept, a concept which in its durability would be repeatable (but not strictly speaking iterable

until we have some theory of externalization and objectification). What is important for our critique of Hegel at this point is the necessity of Christ's death, the necessity of violence (even within the proclamation of love), the necessity of founding a space, the negative character of the universal. We also saw that within this movement, we can save the truth of Christ's death by relating to it as subject and not as a product, as a subjectivity and not a productivity. With Levinas, we see that the essence of thought is not universalization but sacrifice, not appropriation but openness. Universalization, thought, need not be based on internalized scarcity. One can write towards another, reach out beyond death—speak without judging, think without eating.

(2) Objectification—appropriation, eating, taking as an object of your experience, subjecting the salt to your ends. It becomes, as well, the very base of signification as modernity understands it; the illusory full presence to which universalization refers is the complete appropriation of objective experience. It would be meaning exhausted in its utterance, meaning which had arrived, fruit consumed dispassionately, passively, at a distance—offered to us by a girl with a self-conscious gleam in her eye (and we consume her in our gaze as well, for we presume to know what her gesture says, a presumption she may also share), a girl complicitous with our desires. Unhesitant.[98] Universalization, revalued, has the possibility of coming to us, as a word, in a positive moment. We don't give names to the world in a dialectic; the world comes to us with/as names already, in abundance; gifts are always given to others, and cannot be stolen.

as do Hegelian desire or need. This is why Levinas places sound above light. ("Thought is language and is thought in an element analogous to sound and not to light." What does the *analogy* mean here, a difference and a resemblance, a relation between sensible sound and the sound of thought as intelligible speech, between sensibility and signification, the sense and sense? This is a question also posed by Hegel, admiring the word *Sinn*.) (Derrida, "Violence and Metaphysics" [1964], *Writing and Difference*, p. 99)

98. War is not the collision of two substances or two intentions, but an attempt made by one to master the other by surprise, by ambush. War is ambush. It is to take hold of the substance of the other, what is strong and absolute in him, through what is weak in him.

War is looking for the Achilles's heel; it is to envisage the other, the adversary, with logistic's calculations, like an engineer measuring the effort needed to demolish the enemy mass. The other becoming a mass is what describes the relationship of war, and in this it approximates the violence of labor.

In other words, what characterizes violent action, what characterizes tyranny, is that one does not face what the action is being applied to. To put it more precisely: it is that one does not see the face in the other, one sees the other freedom as a force, savage; one identifies the absolute character of the other with his force.

The face, the countenance, is the fact that a reality is opposed to me, opposed not in its manifestations, but as it were in its way of being, ontologically opposed. It is what resists me by its opposition and not what is opposed to me by its resistance. (Levinas, "Freedom and Command" [1953], *Collected Philosophical Papers*, p. 19)

99. Not the play, but the affirmation of the spacing, the experience of the possibility/impossibility of thinking the very ground of our groundlessness (of the turning towards the thinking of our play itself).

The critique of objectification (even of a nondialectical type) would have to rest on the fact that even the best suited of words fails to reach its conclusion (fails to nail down the truth of the signified, once and for all): the address, or destination, of being is constantly postponed. The structure is not the process of play but, and these are only separated by a hair's breadth, the delay[99] (and not the duration). Sacrifice here means that one gives up the protective distance between subject and object; the delay, which is not merely memory but also a directedness, a re-collection, means the sacrifice was a decision and not a destiny, a deciding on (or rather against) destiny.

(3) Externalization—this is the movement of Spirit. It is the guiding rule of articulation, and the central mode of appearance of all objects whatsoever. It claims to be everything and for that reason it is the word most difficult to approach (which is why I was forced into the circuitous route of reworking the metaphor of Christ). To the extent that this writing is atheistic—and a Hegel would have to see it as such—the atheism lies in refusing to believe in the Spirit's *truths* (the atheism lies in seeing within the Spirit a movement other than the disclosure of truth).

Externalization is the mode of appearing of the self-manifestation of God, the production of Christ as the historical completion of an imperfect existence: "the reconciliation that heals the pain and inward suffering of man." The key to this self-manifestation, however, is the activity of human consciousness: "Man, on the contrary, is God only in so far as he annuls the merely

Natural and Limited in his Spirit and elevates himself to God." The objectification of the world is then, for Hegel, the identity of productive activity (conceived as the making durable, universalizing) on the part of men (housework, for example, is not productive) with the self-manifestation or externalization of a divine plan which lies outside of any particular productive activity. It is the blueprint for the mindless machinations of international capitalism, and Marxism's dependence on this category of externalization is (perhaps) the central reason for its failure. Culture is a word which makes sense only as a productive origin of meaning (it is a Christian concept) and it's unclear whether any culture could oppose itself, 'as' culture, to technology's objectifications. The key to our critique is not, then, a turn to some 'other', previously established, position, but would be best seen as the revaluation of the reasons behind our activity (specifically doubting whether all activity is inherently directed towards a taking of positions). This answer will play the length remaining of the book; there is, perhaps, still a sacrifice, not of the general's daughter, but of the self: a sacrifice which is the taking of responsibility at the same time as it renounces the claim to rewards—that is, it (attempts to) answer(s) the complex problem of how Heidegger can maintain critiques both of the subjectivity which is presumed to know and of the subjectivity which flees in the face of the call of conscience.

All of these movements are dependent on some originary cause, some reason for which they move. This may be figured as the unmoved mover God, pushing with or without a goal, or as some form of either increasing entropy or some corresponding tendency to come to an absolute rest. For the tradition, at least since Hegel revived the saying of Heraclitus, war has been the father of everything new. Consciousness exists as the conflict between subject and object, universalizing consciousness exists as the rising and falling, in conflict, asking for their resolution into a circle. History, of any sort, exists under this schema as the conflict of world-historical destinies—the strongest destiny winning in time. Thus Christianity is right because it has displaced all the other socioreligious discourses; it's valid because the judgment of history has shown that it is best able to rule, best able to incorporate and appropriate the new forms of technology. The rise of Protestantism therefore coincides with the economic switch to decentered authority, competitive mercantilism, not because Luther acted at the behest of particular merchants but because the logic of mercantilism, and later industrialism, was best suited to the individual accumulation of goods, the logic of the individual path to salvation. Further, the logic of competition, and exclusion, was the best suited for meeting, and creating, new demands.

At its simplest, this becomes merely a vulgar social Darwinism, but we

100. This is complicated by the fact that Hegel also criticizes representation. The problem with Hegel is that he returns to an idea of the supraindividual based on representation—that is, on his conception of Christ. Towards the end of the *Phenomenology*, Hegel points to the openness of communication, but insists on the return, the return which ensures the interiority, the unity of the structure of representation:

> The self-knowing Spirit knows not only itself but also the negative of itself, or its limit: to know one's limit is to know how to sacrifice oneself. This sacrifice is the externalization in which Spirit displays the process of its becoming Spirit in the form of *free contingent happening*, intuiting its pure Self as Time outside of it, and equally its Being as Space. This last becoming of Spirit, *Nature*, is its living immediate Becoming; Nature, the externalized Spirit, is in its existence nothing but this eternal externalization of its *continuing existence* and the movement which reinstates the *Subject*. (Hegel, *Phenomenology of Spirit* [1807], p. 492)

should think, with Hegel, the ways in which this progress is based on the ability of competitive systems, of wars, to create, to represent, value. The question of what remains after the war, of what may still be promised, as our future, after a war, is the question of thought without representation.[100] That the burden of what comes next rests on the shoulders of the living has always been true, just as there will always be excuses for shirking that burden; as Heidegger says, "we must become capable of the capable word."

Here the relation of the individual to her/his time needs to stand out. Taking for example the canonical piece of literature, it gains its status not by divine fiat but because in the court of final appeal, the judging consciousness (usually of the white male), it is found to represent the truth of that consciousness's experience of the world. Since the individual judging consciousness (the power of universalization) is formed by internalizing the previous representations of truth, there are nationalities, cultural groups of one sort or another, who find their unity in artistic representations, that is, in an *expression* of the national spirit. The mechanism of representation is thus intimately associated with the possibility of the simultaneous workings of externalization, universalization, and objectification. A work is validated (read and revered) by greater numbers of appropriating (objectifying, representing) individuals, as it is more able to articulate the unity of the various genres of discourse each individual has already incorporated as a mode of consciousness. What becomes validated as the most universal structure is finally the thinking individual's representation as consciousness, as experience (humanism becomes international). Accordingly, as we are told repeat-edly, each of us is a writer, living life as the narration of our own stories, expe-riencing life in the preexisting categories of written works. Literary biographies become more interesting—and have long been better sellers—than literary productions (which tend of themselves to be excessively autobiographical). The corresponding move in political representationalism is the embracing of politicians who espouse narrowly self-interested regionalistic, ethnic, or na-tionalistic programs.

The necessary palliative is not a new theory of literary production but of lit-erary reception. The ideal of validated representationalism, of externalized products competing among themselves for the approval of isolated judging con-sciousnesses (unified at one or another level of the universalization of experi-ence) depends on, and results in, the systematic isolation of individuals. Politi-cally, to take an American example, Republican ideals are concentrated into a single statement, externalization, of Republican principle, held to be unified in an individual—say Ronald Reagan. The same is held to be true of, for example, John F. Kennedy for the Democrats. The voter picks the man who best repre-sents her/his internal view of politics—the one who can promise to resolve the perceived external conflicts. Each individual judges separately, but judges by the rules they have internalized. The broadest rule—representation itself—holds the two maxims that the individual is the site of all valuation (and value) and that the universalization, the valuation, occurs as the result of conflict (debates are staged on TV). Decisions of value, reflexively, turn therefore on measures of aggregate self-interest—like nationalism, regionalism, racism, or sexism.

To conceive of Christ as a marker of mortality, as finitude, to see the cruci-fixion (that is representation, as universalization, externalization, and objectifica-tion) as an act of our own cruel violence, is the possibility of displacing the site of valuation away from the *self* (and eliminating the *need* for war in the imaginary one against all).[101] He does not hold value because, like a scapegoat, we killed him; neither does he hold value because he defeated the devil in combat—bibli-cally, after all, his triumph in the desert was merely the withdrawal from the questioning, from the devil's rules of the game, refusing an evil economy. Christ's value is his weakness, his need, his ability to die. Taken representationally, Christ is merely the fulfillment of each individual's desire to transcend the cross. In-stead, taken literally as the god who has died, he defines the possibility of desir-ing in the place of the divine, of answering every, 'God, why hast thou forsaken me?' with a simple 'Here I am; I have remembered'. It is to believe that instead of being the receptors of God's grace, we are the situatedness (the obligation), the creation, of the Good itself; further, we are creators only to the extent that we displace the site of valuation away from ourselves, only to the extent that we cre-

101. Two ways of reading the end of the necessity of war because of finitude present themselves. First is that *finitude* speaks contingency itself:

> Hegelian man is not mortal in his facticity; his death is not a matter of his own most genuine singularity. Rather, his death is a matter of the universal, which establishes itself by surmounting death. As the universal is the eternal life of a people, and as, according to good speculative logic, the latter is as much the start as the result, the death of individuals is in a definitive sense a matter for the state, which demands genuine ethical truth from individuals by sacrificing them in war to the demands of its absolute self-production. The death that is genuinely human and no longer natural is not the death of a person, but an "anonymous" death in the fray of battle. If this reading is accurate, it might help us better understand the insistence with which Hegel rejects social contract theories. The fact is that these theories—even when, like that of Hobbes, they relegate the contract to a single founding moment of the state and remove every negotiable character from it—at least preserve the bond between politics and the domain of finitude. If the state results from a contract, then its alleged necessity is tainted with contingency, and it is more theoretical than apodictic. This reading also helps us better understand

ate for others. The Fall from Eden would be our failure to be either gods (above death and finitude) or men (obedient to a rule of exclusion); it would be Eve's fault (and the essence of the human feminine), for she was not created for her own ends. (And to say something similar in the words of other traditions, of other deities or other myths, might yet be possible—although, as with the professed Christian reading these pages, I would not expect an adherent to recognize his/her beliefs reflected in the saying itself—it would be antithetical to 'belief', no matter which tradition's vocabulary it was phrased in.)

For the moment, we have used the conception of desire as existing in the place of the absent god rather loosely; we can only specify an actual content to this formula within a criticism of the economic conceptions of the formation, and reification, of desires (in the next section). In brief, in politics, it would be voting not for your representative, but voting for/as a commitment to the needs of others. In literature, the value of the reading is turned outward: no longer enjoyment and the externalization of, or assent to, private goods; the meaningfulness of an entire style of life—the closed loop of validating representations of private enjoyment—comes to be questioned by literary anti-representationalism. This book, at this point, has jumped ahead of its argument, but has not thereby lost sight of its purposes.

In summary, we have tried to motivate, with appropriate markers of limitations, the central continuity of western metaphysics as a relation to the produced object which nullifies our relation to the divinity. Heidegger's understanding of time as a poetic articulation (which leads into Levinas's understanding of time as encounter with the Other) provides a counterbalance to this conception of the world as technological object (tekhnē). This points to our need to speak of destination (the destiny of being, the addressee) and articulation (poetry). Derrida stakes his arguments with Heidegger on exactly this point:

> In a word, this is what I am trying to explain to him. *Tekhnē* (and doubtless he would have considered the postal structure and everything that it governs as a *determination* (yes, precisely, your word), a metaphysical and technical determination of the *envoi* or of the destinality (*Geschick*, etc.) of Being; and he would have considered my entire insistence on the posts as a metaphysics corresponding to the technical era that I am describing, the end of a certain post, the dawn of another, etc.); now *tekhnē*, this is the entire—infinitesimal and decisive—*différance, does not arrive*. No more than metaphysics, therefore, and than positionality; always, already it parasites that to which he says it happens, arrives, or that it succeeds in happening to [arrive en arriver]. This infinitesimal nuance chances everything in the relation between metaphysics and its doubles or its others.
>
> *Tekhnē* does not happen to language or to the poem, to *Dichtung* or to the song, understand me: this can mean simultaneously that it does not succeed in touching them, getting into them, it leaves them virgin, not happening to arrive up to them [*n'arrivant pas à arriver jusqu'à eux*],

Hegel's rejection of institutions such as elections and restraints to power. Such institutions assume that it is within finitude itself, within the singular perspective of his project, that the individual is a citizen. They assume as well that the power of the state, however formidable, cannot possibly come full circle and tear itself free of the ground of finitude. (J. Taminiaux, "Hegel and Hobbes" [1982], *Dialectic and Difference*, p. 35)

Second is the more radical displacement of value both away from transcendent historicality and away from a supposed individual choice towards a concern for others that transcends war, that is, the transcendence of time's contingency through universalizing war, since it already sacrifices the self in/as every moment. This is a sacrifice which doesn't ask for the spoils of war, for the eternal recollection of the warrior's name in the collective consciousness.

and yet it has to happen to them like an accident or an event because it inhabits them and occasions them.

In Strasbourg, I had wanted to tell her that I love her all the while being afraid of her seer's lucidity, which is frightening because she sees true (*juste*), but she is mistaken because she is just, like the law. I did not dare say it to her, and moreover we have never been alone together.

The entire history of postal *tekhnē* tends to rivet the destination to identity. To arrive, to happen would be to a subject, to happen to "me." Now a mark, whatever it may be, is coded in order to make an imprint, even if it is a perfume. Henceforth it divides itself, *it is valid several times in one time*: no more unique addressee. This is why, by virtue of this divisibility (the origin of reason, the mad origin of reason and of the principle of identity), *tekhnē* does not happen to language—which is why and what I sing to you. (Derrida, *The Post Card* [1980], p. 192)

What needs to come out at this point is that these words are the remnants of fights gone by: the auto-expression, manifestation of time, is, in all of these, cast as war and violence. I need to be careful here; two positions match without matching. For Derrida (it seems to me), we are still asking of the truth of writing—asking of its answers and not its questions. These answers escape the cruel overdeterminations of progress not because they have confused origins (in which case the Derridean critique would be trivially dismissed), but because they are multiplied in their address, aiming towards a future (unknown) and not toward the reappropriation of some past. What's my criticism of Derrida? Nothing, simply. Unless it seems that the answer to the questions, "Why write?" "Why read?" should precede the declaration that the reading and writing had been found enjoyable (and hasn't Derrida's more recent work on mourning and messianism emphasized just this?). Or, rereading his insistence on the nonarrival of the mark, perhaps we can begin to see that the multiplicity of the audience, the nonsingularity of the addressee, already indicates a certain lack of structure—perhaps, since she has no claim to having been a seer, Eve would have no destination at all (neither achieved nor frustrated) within the structures of technology. Applied to (and against) Girard's Christ, we no longer preference the narrativity itself as the truth—Christ does not remind us to tell stories, not even to speak for the oppressed, but to be as a speaking towards others, away from the proper of your 'own' destiny. Or, mimicking Derrida, we are merely asking: what if Christ were a woman?

In terms of style, it is a question which can never fit into the trajectory of a narrative.

But infinite time is also the putting back into question of the truth it promises.

The dream of a happy eternity, which subsists in man along with his happiness, is not a simple aberration. Truth requires both an infinite time and a time it will be able to seal, a completed time. The completion of time is not death, but messianic time, where the perpetual is converted into eternal. Messianic triumph is the pure triumph; it is secured against the revenge of evil whose return the infinite time does not prohibit. Is this eternity a new structure of time, or an extreme vigilance of the messianic consciousness? The problem exceeds the bounds of this book. (Levinas, *Totality and Infinity* [1961], pp. 284–85)

What is at stake between Heidegger, Derrida, and Levinas here? Perhaps, it is merely a style. None of them is willing to pretend to live outside of history, yet none of them would be bound by the idea of the historical which Hegel left us with. That, stylistically, is the sense of turning towards, and demarcating as words or tropes, the trajectories encapsulated in words like "Christ" or "woman." Just as postmodernism has already announced the historical bounds of man within a framework of the several centuries of the Enlightenment (now, presumably, ending). Its completion has left us at a juncture; we need not return to any other model; we need not say that any existent being is already thinking this way (although this, perhaps, would be possible); we have the chance, have had the chance, to articulate our future. This is fundamentally different from a theory of crisis. Technological thinking has never been so strong; Being's night has never been so dark. Crises only fall at the end of a progression. We stand at the juncture where we may stop thinking of ourselves as the end of all previous history (itself a juncture we obviously have always been facing): we must say that there have been moments which are not us, just as we shall not endure, physically, past our own time, just as endurance is no longer conceived as the refutation of time. This implies, among other things, that openness to time has always been a possibility, indeed has always been the actual condition of thought or forgetting, merely articulated in different fashions. To think the future need not be an openness to Being (rather, it is an openness to that which is not, at least not yet, but perhaps not ever destined to be). An articulation 'for everyone and no one', then, asks us to be particularly conscious, particularly concerned, with whom we will be for, how we will respond, and not merely fanatically paranoid in our insistence that we continue to be.

That this can be said at any moment in history goes without saying—almost as much as saying that we are, at this moment in history, as far from being able to take advantage of the moment as a society as at any other moment. Today's poets will always be judged inefficacious by today's philosophers: they are always looking in opposite directions. Allegorically, philosopher and poet are man and woman, and we are still asking what it might mean to be human without pretending to a genderless abstraction.

# B)    Sisters—part 2

*The epiphany of that which can present itself directly, outwardly and eminently—is visage. The expressing helps the expression here, brings help to itself, signifies, speaks. The revelation of the face is language. The Other is the first intelligible. But the infinite in the face does not appear as a representation. It brings into question my freedom, which is discovered to be murderous and encroaching. But this discovery is not a derivation of self-knowledge; it is heteronomy through and through. In front of the face, I always demand more of myself; the more I respond to it, the more the demands grow. This movement is more fundamental than the freedom of self-representation. Ethical consciousness is not, in effect, a 'particularly commendable' variety of consciousness, but is the contraction, the retreat into oneself, the systole of consciousness without itself.*

—Levinas, "Signature,"
Research in Phenomenology[102]

It is reasonable to ask: Why Sisters? Answer: Because they are a forsaken possibility, a shadowy double of the male, brotherly self; further, they are the object of the other man's desire—our point for controlling others through manipulating the economies of desire, manipulable for us precisely because prohibited to us (as siblings), and in this prohibition, thus constituted as the general object of all male desire, of the generalized male gaze. We (men) are enslaved by the rupturing freedom of our desiring; our gaze is turned towards what we won't allow ourselves to have. To answer the question of sisters, to approach male desire and the male gaze critically, we will have to reconstrue the meaning of language. Instead of free men in exchange forming a society of enlightened self-interest, we must learn to see how the retreat of presence within writing moves consciousness, and its attendant languages, outside of the realm of the self and his interests. We will have to learn in what ways the retreat subverts victory—in what ways "the systole of consciousness without itself" abandons the will-to-power.

This is not a discourse which explodes, opposing the theories of sense and sensibility with the nonsensical. But neither do I speak from the standpoint of rationality, from the surety of meaning. Instead of a voice joined in the certainty of its origin or birth—an 'I' who speaks and knows what he has said, will say—we are joined in the object, like all the discussions so far, as much as we speak of the family and consciousness, of women and words, of the distance between speaking and writing. In that sense, there is no transcendental unity of the object towards which we orient ourselves; instead, one only finds the opening between speaking towards and having spoken (or written), one only finds the distance between the intention to speak and that which is born(e) by/through the speaking. This distance, insofar as it constitutes the possibility of all other distances, is the deferral of a certainty, a refusal to complete: that is, in one sense, it is a deconstruction of the spoken (we no longer believe in its perfect closure, its pure origin and unsullied trajectory from intention to understanding), but in another sense it is the refusal of the *economy* of writing, of the tautological belief that death itself might hold meaning. Our purpose, as an audience of what is being written here, is to speak to, and within, that difference (i.e., we are writing the question of style itself). And if we don't quail before the responsibility of using old words, seemingly dead—like 'object', 'we', 'I', and 'speak'—it's because we know, without demanding certainty or stability, that we are not exhausted in the spoken word: relationships of exchange do not express my species-being; my saying the word 'Christ' does not commit me to a religious doctrine; saying the word 'woman' announces an overflowing presence (obligation), not an essence; writing is not your death, nor any other's.

102. Which reminds me, before we leave Christ completely:

> (the death) of the abstraction of the divine Being. . . . is the painful feeling of the Unhappy Consciousness that God Himself is dead. This hard saying is the expression of innermost simple self-knowledge, the return of consciousness into the depths of the night in which 'I'='I', a night which no longer distinguishes or knows anything outside of it. This feeling is, in fact, the loss of substance and of its appearance over against consciousness; but it is at the same time the pure subjectivity of substance, or the pure certainty of itself which it lacked when it was object, or the immediate, or pure essence. This Knowing is the inbreathing of the Spirit, whereby Substance becomes Subject, by which its abstraction and lifelessness have died, and substance therefore has become actual and simple and universal Self-consciousness. (Hegel, *Phenomenology of Spirit* [1807], pp. 475–76)

The movements have similarities in form, yet with Levinas there is no pure certainty to be gained, no freedom to be invested with truth through sacrifice, only infinite—incomprehensible, inevitable, external, and anarchic—demand.

# i)                    Sisters as token of exchange

Most commonly, one speaks of the exchange of wives, but that misconstrues the relationship: daughters and sisters are exchanged, the taking to wife is incidental to the moment (and in so far as she is alienable, a daughter is most like a sister in this economy). The advantage comes, in such an economy, to the one who gives and not to the one who takes—although in theories of the sale of women and the giving of words, careful attention is given to the rhetoric of joy and gain in reception: consumption runs any economy. Noticeably, this rhetoric is most often employed in terms of the possible reproduction or enrichment of the recipient's line—sons (after accepting a woman into your private life) or, analogously, future poetic creation (after internalizing the canonical works). All production returns to self (aggrandizement, glorification, justification, fortification); all consumption returns to production. In cases of an imbalance in supply and demand, brothers might have to pay someone to take the responsibility for feeding a sister (for the purposes of this story, she is not allowed to feed herself), and poets of difficult works—in an economy based on quick and easy consumption of products—may never find an audience.

Society is based, so the story goes, on the exchange of objects of one sort or another—I hesitate for a moment before calling them products. There is, of course, the assumption that the giver of the object has the right—however construed—to give and the taker has the corresponding right to accept. Consider a certain metaphorical connection of women and words (each paradigmatically *objects*) very seriously; the criticisms of both sides of the analogy can in fact be worked out, if not fully, at least simultaneously.

In the system of marriage used as social exchange, exogamy, we find the excess of the exchange relationship installed as a social value:

> The marriage exchange thus functions as a mechanism serving to mediate between nature and culture, which were originally regarded as separate. By substituting a cultural architectonic for a supernatural primitive one, the alliance creates a second nature over which man has a hold, that is a mediatized nature. (Lévi-Strauss, *The Savage Mind* [1962], p. 128)

Lévi-Strauss elaborates on this mediation in an earlier book:

> As opposed to endogamy and its tendency to set a limit to the group, and then to discriminate within the group, exogamy represents a continuous pull towards a greater cohesion, a more efficacious solidarity, and a more supple articulation. This is because the value of exchange is not simply that of the goods exchanged. Exchange—and consequently the rule of exogamy which expresses it—has in itself a social value. It provides the means of binding men together, and of superimposing upon the natural links of kinship the henceforth artificial links—artificial in the sense that they are removed from chance encounters or the promiscuity of family life—of alliance governed by rule. (Lévi-Strauss, *The Elementary Structures of Kinship* [1947], p. 480)[103]

The excess of the particular woman is found in her ability to tie diverse men to a single rule of relation.[104] We note first of all that rule-governedness is a matter of restraint. People are governed by rules only in so far as in one way or another they are bound to those rules—ultimately, without rules, the state of universal war threatens (and no violences have been more terrible than the violences perpetrated in the name of avoiding a primitive state of nature which never existed: that war is a learned desire is a fact that capitalism cannot abide, a fact which threatens the 'natural' rights of those who would impose their own rules). The loaded terms in Lévi-Strauss's passage here would be the 'natural' links of kinship as opposed to the 'artificial' ties of marriage. The duplicitous bind of being a woman lies precisely here—she is natural as the site of the reproduction of children, the natural bonds of kinship upon which true relations are formed (which is why the unnatural union of Jacosta and Oedipus leads to a war among the male progeny, Etiocles and Polynices); yet, woman—

103. We know today how, in society, a whole distribution of functions in a play of alternation is grounded on this terrain [sexual differentiation]. It is modern structuralism that has brought this out best, by showing that it is at the level of matrimonial alliance, as opposed to natural generation, to biological lineal descent—at the level therefore of the signifier—that the fundamental exchanges take place and it is there that we find once again that the most elementary structures of social functioning are inscribed in the terms of a combinatory. . . . The only thing that I am bringing to the light of day at this point is the remark that, in fact, in history, primitive science has taken root in a mode of thinking which, playing on a combinatory, on such oppositions as those of Yin and Yang, water and fire, hot and cold, make them lead the dance—the word is chosen for its more than metaphorical implications, for their dance is based on dance ritual profoundly motivated by the sexual divisions in society. (Lacan, *The Four Fundamental Concepts of Psycho-Analysis* [1973], pp. 150–51)

104. "Since power is dependent upon women, everything rests upon the love one pretends to have for women, but which in fact is destined to power alone. But how does one tell pretence from reality? Love and politics were thus to become one" (Kristeva, *Tales of Love* [1983], p. 342).

metaphorically—is artificial in so far as she represents an alien project (in this either her own will, or her father's or another man's) or the creation of an affiliation with someone not legally bound by blood (as in the production of illegitimate children, or children with the mother's traits and not the father's). Of course, unallegorically, a woman—every woman, as an individual—must live a separate destiny; even if she merely sits on the other side of the dinner table from the man, sharing as lesser part in everything else he does, she will still have had a different project.

## a)  An excess of meaning; desire exceeds (is the form of) economy

If, for some unknown reason, we were to try to conceive of the basic metaphors of nationalistic, free-market societies from the point of view of the woman, the woman's right to freely choose a husband would merely be the complement of the right of the modern worker (in fact, one step further down the hierarchy) to choose between different but approximately equal—and possibly universally abhorrent—employers. You are free to choose the destiny offered you. Sociality, from this perspective, is the submission of the individual will to the validating will (assuming one enters on favorable terms) of the social group. Exchange, as the social bond, paradigmatically the giving of women or words, acts to keep man from suffering the accidents of fate; even if he dies, he knows that his project continues. To enter into the law of the father is to affirm the rule, the process, of fatherhood. The production of sons only expresses truth in as much as each son also enters into the order of fathering; parenting only extracts man from the contingency of his mortality if the progeny exactly mirror him, if the woman has been a passive and faithful producer of sons. The order of kinship and speech are not merely metaphorically combined here, for the man enters the public realm, gaining the public approval of the 'we'—once his house is set straight—just as he enters the rule of the father, of fathering; both his childhood and his private life will be renounced for their explicit association with the home, that realm dominated by the mother. To become a father is to assume the voice of the Father. The Father, as such, the theory of great men and seminal thinking, rests on/grounds the priority of public over private, the priority in/as the polis which Hegel reinstitutes in his concept of the family. An important example in this light would be Lévi-Strauss's conception of the bonds of sociality and his description of exactly how the exchange of women expresses the structural ties generally:

> In this way, language and exogamy represent two solutions to one and the same fundamental situation. Language has achieved a high degree of perfection, while exogamy has remained approximate and precarious. This disparity, however, is not without its counterpart. The very nature of the linguistic symbol prevented it from remaining for long in the stage which was ended by Babel, when words were still the essential property of each par-

105. Lévi-Strauss is ending a long book. He nods to one rather obvious fact without working it out in terms of any subversive potential, only as one might see a wife as being more valuable (to the man) than just any mere excess word of the language:

> But, to the extent that words have become common property, and their signifying function has supplanted their character as values, language, along with scientific civilization, has helped to impoverish perception and strip it of its affective, aesthetic and magical implications, as well as to schematize thought. Passing from speech to alliance, i.e., to the other field of communication, the situation is reversed. The emergence of symbolic thought must have required that women, like words, should be things that were exchanged. In this new case, indeed, this was the only means of overcoming the contradiction by which the same woman was seen under two incompatible aspects: on the one hand, as the object of personal desire, thus exciting sexual and proprietal instincts; and, on the other, as the subject of the desire of others, and seen as such, i.e., as the means of binding others through alliance with them. But woman could never become just a sign and nothing more, since even in a man's world she is still a person, and since in so far as she is defined as a sign she must be recognized as a generator of signs. In the mat-

rimonial dialogue of men, woman is never purely what is spoken about; for if women in general represent a certain category of signs, destined to a certain kind of communication, each woman preserves a particular value arising from her talent, before and after marriage, for taking her part in a duet. In contrast to words, which have wholly become signs, woman has remained at once a sign and a value. This explains why the relations between the sexes have preserved that affective richness, ardour and mystery which doubtless originally permeated the entire universe of human communications. (Lévi-Strauss, *The Elementary Structures of Kinship* [1947], p. 496)

After all, the 'incompatible aspects' of women pose the problem that must be resolved; man is not looked at, has no aspect, is a value unto himself. One could, of course, remedy this sexism either by working out man's position as sign or by denying that either women or men are viewed. In the former, we risk the commodification of the male body—fashion magazines speak one side of that already existing process—and in the latter, the dangerous denial of sexuality, the willfully closed eyes of prurient manners—as well as the righteous disavowal of the AIDS epidemic—which threatens to force existence into the most abstract of categories.

ticular group: values as much as signs, jealously preserved, reflectively uttered, and exchanged for other words the meaning of which, once revealed, would bind the stranger, as one put oneself in his power by initiating him, [gives] something of oneself and acquires some power over the other. The respective attitudes of two individuals in communication acquire a meaning of which they would otherwise be devoid. (Lévi-Strauss, *The Elementary Structures of Kinship* [1947], p. 496)[105]

What is this excess of meaning? The assurance that the other is bound to your will, your valuations, your self-interest. Society, according to this view, is the result of men binding themselves together through exchange relations. I teach a stranger (or my son) my language, and then I know—and this surety is more or less vague—that he is tied to my way of thinking. I give him a sister and he is bound to support the interests of the family. (That can be, as in our more "contemporary" setting, as broad as "compulsory heterosexuality" in its complicity with capitalism.) Being conscious, having a mind, is being able to plan for (control) the future. Of course, the partners in exchange want as much control as they can bargain for: that is, the assurance that a woman, or language, once achieved (purchased) is his to do with as each man pleases. Thinking of society, language, and economy in this way—and what intellectual today really doesn't?—the revelation that women or words have lives of their own threatens the very foundations of society and self. To hear them speak—outside the bedroom or kitchen, outside seductive phrases and economic commands—is to found society on plenitude and not scarcity, on obligations (which are not contractual) and not exchange relations. Structuralism had been able to account for the fact that meaning didn't arise from the individual's production of an individual meaning—meaning had to arise in a moment of being meaningful within an intersubjective structure of activity. However, to remain at the level of the public articulation of meaning—be it subjective or structural—is to remain oriented by the task of making public (where all obligation is interpreted in terms of the duty to fulfill a promise or comply with an existing structure of rights). Production for the purposes of exchange comes to be the only way of conceptualizing any production (no artwork, for example, is good until it finds an appreciative audience)—and production, as we have just seen in the Christ sections, has already come to stand in for all the modes of our existence, as if the meaningfulness of existence were exhausted in its character as product of human activity.

In order to be as clear as possible about the relation of these differing, structurally similar, systems, we should see the existing economy of exchange as both a political and an individual problem. Here is where the difficulty of writing a metaphor, of commenting on style and the possibility of style, becomes essentially entwined with the difficulty of thinking itself. If we can't use a new language, if we can't speak towards a future poetics, then all speaking and writing fall back into its supposed origins (as a representation, more or less faithful, of a previous thought). My goal is to enact the possibility of speaking without giving in to the facile political belief that all writing must return to its origin: that all truth must reside in the public, in the economy; or that the tradition has already given us everything truly worth saying (and we live either the decadence of our age, or, undeservedly, as children of our more productive fathers, enjoy the fruits of previous works). We begin by sketching the limits of present theories of economy; only later will an alternative view show itself.

Habermas, in an article on Bataille, explains the basic problem of economics after modernism:

> Economics, including political economy and its critique, has until now been pursued under the restricted viewpoint of how scarce resources can be effectively deployed within the energy cycle of the reproduction of social life. Bataille opposes to this particular scarcity-based viewpoint the *general* viewpoint of a *cosmically expanded* energy ecology. On the basis of this change in perspective—which he executes on analogy with the change from the perspective of the microeconomic actor to that of the macroeconomic system—

106. Habermas has a rather un-friendly take on Bataille; much of Habermas's critique relies on his conception of the proper role of language—and the correspond-ing demarcation between poetry and philosophy. I have already begun a polemic against this dis-tinction, and will continue it specifically in terms of Haber-mas—which is why I am begin-ning with his summary of the sit-uation. It should also be clear that I am looking for a theory of communication which is neither teleological—like Habermas's—nor violent—like Bataille's. Habermas adds, concerning Bataille: "The erotic writer can still use language in a poetic way, such that the reader, assaulted by obsenity, gripped by the shock of the unexpected and unimagin-able, is jolted into the ambiva-lence of loathing and pleasure. But philosophy cannot in the same way break out of the uni-verse of language: 'It deploys lan-guage in such a fashion that si-lence never follows. So that the supreme moment necessarily transcends the philosophical problematic.' With this state-ment, however, Bataille under-cuts his own efforts to carry out the radical critique of reason with the tools of theory (Habermas, "Between Eroticism and General Economics: Bataille" [1983], *Philosophical Discourse of Moder-nity*, p. 237).

107. "The prohibition of incest is less a rule prohibiting marriage with the mother, sister or daugh-ter, than a rule obliging the mother, sister, or daughter to be given to others. It is the supreme

the fundamental economic question is inverted: The key problem is no longer the use of scarce resources but the un-selfish expenditure of superfluous re-sources. That is, Bataille proceeds from the biological assumption that the liv-ing organism collects more energy than it uses to reproduce its life. The surplus energy is used for growth. When this comes to a standstill, the unabsorbed surplus of energy has to be spent un-productively—the energy must be lost without gain. This can occur in either a 'glorious' or a 'catastrophic' form. So-ciocultural life also stands under the pressure of surplus energy. ("Between Eroticism and General Economics: Bataille" [1983], *The Philosophical Dis-course of Modernity*, p. 234)[106]

We should pay attention, perhaps, to the microeconomics first, although Hegel has put the distinction between micro and macro in question for all of us, especially Bataille. Bataille's conception of language is based on—as for Freud as well—a restric-tion, a castration.[107] This restriction is re-lated both to the general move of internal-ization we had noted in the story of Christianity and the conception of worlds of meaning coming to be in the self-restriction of the deity—a self-restriction which calls for the absolute emptying of the creative subject (mortal and/or immortal). But we should remember that this restriction is not strictly speaking inside the economy—rather, it is its form. One finds the economy restricted; the economy is oriented by that restriction, by that which enforces the re-striction and towards that which the restriction causes to be desired. Desire runs the economy, but the economy is where the objects of desire are decided upon. Or, perhaps, it is possible to ask about the economy at the level of its instantiation of desire—at the level of the shape it gives to the objects of that economy, as desired (or not); at the level of the "one finds the economy," before it is found to be "restricted."[108]

Bataille is important to me because he is concerned with the placement of the subject in/beyond these economies. In Hegelian terms, and that is the way he sees himself, his theory of language is a theory of diremption—his questions: what can break the stagnation, the closed economy of the already existent? For Levinas, the breakup of the same is achieved in contact with the Other (who is immediately meaningful, who is, for that reason, as a commencing of meaning, the infinite). For Bataille, since he takes the Hegelian Absolute—the unity of self and other—seriously, only the glorious ejaculation without meaning (sexual contact with the abyss: joining self with infinity) can disrupt the monotony of being without time (only the explosive can accomplish the self-diremption of the economy and introduce the temporal as play and violence). For Levinas, this disruption is itself a calling into question, and thus already has a certain meaning. Bataille's theory of language, like political terrorism, trusts more in a reaction than in a plan; like terrorism, it is doomed to the slow movement of appropriation which changes the most shocking moments of the avant-garde into merely banal paragraphs in the encyclopedia of progress, the chronicles of war. At this point, however, we are only trying to learn to speak about what structures an economy.

rule of the gift, and it is clearly this aspect, too often unrecognized, which allows its nature to be understood" (Lévi-Strauss, *The Elementary Structures of Kinship* [1947], p. 481). And:

> And yet there can be no incest prohibition without incestuous desire. But as we know, desire cries out for something else: "It isn't my mother I wanted. It was never her—or even simply a woman. I wanted to know the world, produce it, people it with my creation. I wanted to explore every possible connection, visit every site on earth and leave again." In that case, what analysts label "incestuous desire" must somehow be installed in the subject from without, by society. And how is that "desire" installed? By means, it seems to me, of an indirect prescription, by the fixating of desire on the mystery of Woman (predominantly the sister in this case)—a prescription that merits the name "incest commandment." (K. Theweleit, *Male Fantasies* [1977], 1:376–77)

108. Ending a book on Sartre's work from 1950–1960, R. D. Laing and D. G. Cooper see the historical and political answer to war in the comprehension of scarcity—the macroeconomic counterpart to the Hegelian negative consciousness—as the possibility of transcending the individual viewpoints at war:

> The scandal is not in the simple existence of the other, but

in the violence undergone or threatened in each person's perception of the other as one-too-many through interiorized scarcity. Under the rubric of interiorized scarcity the rationality of the praxis of each is the rationality of violence. Here, violence is not a simple, naive ferocity of man, but the comprehensible reinteriorization of each of the contingent fact of scarcity. Finally, what is the rationality of the comprehension by a *third* of the struggle? Can he realize by his mediation a transcendent and objective unity of positive reciprocities? Here we come to the beginning of our next task, history as such. For history is the totalization of all the practical multiplicities and of their struggles, and the extent of its intelligibility is the dialectical limit of the praxis-process of the different practical structures and the different forms of active multiplicities that between them lie. But that is a story that we can only now perhaps begin to tell. (Laing and Cooper, *Reason and Violence* [1964], p. 176)

My problem with this is twofold: (1) the move of totalization, which necessarily follows on the various economies of scarcity (for consciousness in that it is a necessary facet/precondition of dialectical appropriation, and socially, where it is a contingent fact), represents the truth as totalized and as totalized on the model of the individual's representation; and (2) this theory of meaning

Too quickly, when speaking of language and desire, we enter into the language of passion, of passionate commitment, of passive possession. The opposition between passivity and activity—in traditional terms, the difference between East and West or female and male—becomes an issue for philosophical thought at the level of signification. That is, we are asking whether the speaking subject actively forms ideas and opinions or merely voices already existent, inherited or learned, words within an economy. As everyday humans—and regardless of philosophy—we usually ask these same questions as matters of responsibility (i.e., was having an illicit affair my fault or just me succumbing to human nature—or some other sort of devil?). As philosophers, we too quickly separate the question of responsibility from the question of how we signify. Instead, in order to grasp the full implications of our activity, we need to identify that part of our inherited modes of thinking which is accessible to our activity—that is, which we are responsible for. The question will become— and this is the question of this book— whether we are ultimately responsible even for the very fact of our desire (the fact, at least, that our desire has a shape, an inclination towards an acting, and I would add that there is no "pure" desire, there is no otherwise than inclined). An economy usually designates something in which one participates, but, to a large extent, we now tend to think of that participation as obligatory at some level (one speaks, for example, of the economy of scarcity, or of the economy of violence in language). Although occasionally someone will object against the inclusiveness of an economy (usually on the more or less Kantian grounds of a 'something I know not what' beyond the economy), only with Levinas has a space opened up for thinking the obligation to an other (not to the economy within which the other appears) and only with the trace (as developed somewhat differently in Levinas and Derrida) have we approached thinking of the opening of the economy 'preceding', or 'commencing', the economy itself.

For Bataille, passivity is death—in exactly the way Hegel meant death as the precondition to knowledge and as the dialectical opposite of life. He theorizes the urge to passivity, the active search for death, as the hidden truth, the precondition of Hegel's dialectic—Bataille sees death at every corner and asks us to embrace it. The melding of passive and active here is immediately superior to, because more encompassing than, the language of individual desire seeking individual pleasure. The definition of the subject is shifted from the gross economics of material need and material satisfaction, but there remains lack and satisfaction; Bataille—and this reading follows Hegel's religious philosophy, especially the move from material to spiritual—understands that the satisfaction itself creates the lack, that the creation of lack subtends and defers (indefinitely) satisfaction.[109]

We lose the distinction between passive and active, and this happens as a structural necessity of how the subject is conceived, of how a subject's being is structured methodologically and systematically by the inquiry, when the distinction between the individual and the society is blurred—in the subject's constructions both of desires and of specific obligations. However, to ask the question of

necessarily falls back on the idea of the individual's enjoyment— the representation of truth as the satisfaction of individual desires—as the end toward which all activity strives. That said, I would like to keep something of the approach which emphasizes the necessity of thinking about our situation in its broadest instantiations—in the history of its forms of being-comprehensible. The point, then, would be whether the form of scarcity is not a contingent imposition, from our theories about language, consciousness, and the human, onto the way we think about (and live) our participations within the world. Levinas is interesting here insofar as he sketches the possibility of a different appointment with truth, this time couched in the language of the Talmud: "Let us not forget the seventy languages in which the Torah is read out. The Torah belongs to everyone: everyone is responsible for everyone else. The phrase 'Love your neighbor as yourself' still assumes the prototype of love to be love of oneself. Here, the ethic is one which says: 'Be responsible for the other as you are responsible for yourself.' In this way we avoid the assumption about self-love which is often accepted as the very definition of a person" (Levinas, "The Pact" [1982], *The Levinas Reader*, p. 225). The point is that the subject who would take the position outside of the 'rationality of violence' must also be a situated subject—only to the extent that this site is not primarily concerned with a self could the position of speaking 'outside' of the rationality of violence be attained.

109. It is the constitution of a positive property of loss—from which spring nobility, honor, and rank in a hierarchy—that gives the institution its significant value. The gift must be considered as a loss and thus as a partial destruction, since the desire to destroy is in part transferred onto the recipient. In unconscious forms, such as those described by psychoanalysis, it symbolizes excretion, which itself is linked to death, in conformity with the fundamental connection between anal eroticism and sadism. The excremental symbolism of emblazoned coppers, which on the Northwest Coast are the gift objects *par excellence*, is based on a very rich mythology. In Melanesia, the donor designates as his excrement magnificent gifts, which he deposits at the feet of the rival chief.

The consequences in the realm of acquisition are only the unwanted result—at least to the extent that the drives that govern the operation have remained primitive—of a process oriented in the opposite direction. "The ideal," indicates Mauss, "would be to give a *potlatch* and not have it returned." This ideal is realized in certain forms of destruction to which custom allows no possible response. Moreover, since the yields of *potlatch* are in some ways pledged in advance in a new *potlatch*, the archaic principle

how to demarcate 'individual' from 'social' determinants or results is to be sucked into the question of paternity. To begin the analysis elsewhere, away from the questions of property and rightful heirs, toward ethical habitation within a language, is to escape the narrow circles of scarcity and war. Of course, we don't simply escape our material conditions—we don't choose not to be hungry—but we must see that our material conditions are not the goals of our activities; we can't eat merely in order to eat again: consumption is not its own good.

## b)   On Speaking—Who is it who gives the gift?

What's interesting about Bataille in this context, as Habermas points out, is that he understands that the dynamic of accumulation re-creates—out of its own logic—the scarcity which determines the economy precisely as an economy of scarcity. That is, no privileged presence dominates his sense of economy; there is no moment in which satisfaction is reached precisely because satisfaction of material needs only highlights the emptiness of the material. Against Bataille, the problem remains, in a word, that each act of consumption and expulsion is centered on the individual subject as agent (even when expressing a macroeconomic utility). Because he concentrates too heavily on the individual desiring subject, he loses the sense in which (the content of) desire is—insofar as the individual relates to the larger society—passive. He doesn't see the political content of desire (he speaks only of its form). He can never succeed in reconnecting the individuals to each other—society remains within exchange relations, in the state of one against all (even in the moment of the abyss, in the moment of sexuality). The transcendence of the individual, Bataille sees, is dependent on this brush with the infinity of the other, an encounter which prescribes a going beyond the self and not a privilege for the self.[110] However, as a Hegelian, he cannot see the progression of time as anything but the death of the past, present scarcity created from past consumption; he can't see our desires as anything but the voices of the dead, as the production of a divine death or sacrifice (after all, glorious expenditure is merely the will to die transformed into the will to become a god). That is, he cannot conceive of a meaning outside of the economics of value-production—even if that value is the pure coincidence with producing and thus exceeds every objectification. To escape the sexist construction of the dichotomy of passive and active, to let the passive voice speak, we need to address the matter of these dead voices. "Who is it who speaks?" we ask with many others, but since we were speaking of microeconomics, we ask with a certain Lacan:

> Don't go into a sulk, I am merely referring obliquely to what I am reluctant to cover with the distorting map of clinical medicine.
>
> Namely, the right way to reply to the question, 'Who is speaking?', when it is the subject of the unconscious that is at issue. For this reply cannot come from that subject if he does not know

of wealth is displayed with none of the attenuations that result from the avarice developed at later stages; wealth appears as an acquisition to the extent that power is acquired by a rich man, but it is entirely directed toward loss in the sense that this power is characterized as power to lose. It is only through loss that glory and honor are linked to wealth.

As a game, *potlatch* is the opposite of a principle of conservation: it puts an end to the stability of fortunes as it existed within the totemic economy, where possession was hereditary. An activity of excessive exchange replaced heredity (as source of possession) with a kind of deliriously formed ritual poker. But the players can never retire from the game, their fortunes made; they remain at the mercy of provocation. At no time does a fortune serve to shelter its owner from need. On the contrary, it functionally remains—as does its possessor—at the mercy of a need for limitless loss, which exists endemically in a social group. (Bataille, "The Notion of Expenditure" [1933], *Visions of Excess*, pp. 122–23)

---

110. "Ecstasy is different from receiving sex pleasure, but less different from giving it. I don't give anything. I'm illuminated by an (impersonal) outer joy that seems sure and I intuit it. I'm consumed by this awareness as I'm consumed by a woman when making passionate love.

The 'point' that 'cries out' is similar to an orgasm in human beings, and the idea we have of it is like the idea of a 'pleasure point'—or orgasm—in the throes of sex" (Bataille, *Guilty* [1943, 1961], p. 35).

111. This space of inter/intra will have to be developed later, but we note that it has an implication for the address, the reception of the address:

> For it is clear that the state of nescience in which man remains in relation to his desire is not so much a nescience of what he demands, which may after all be circumscribed, as a nescience as to where he desires. This is what I mean by my formula that the unconscious is '*discours de l' Autre*' (Discourse of the Other), in which the *de* is to be understood in the sense of the Latin *de* (objective determination): *de Alio in oratione* (completed by *tua res agitur*). But we must also add that man's desire is the *desir de l'Autre* (the desire of the Other) in which the *de* provides what grammarians call the 'subjective determination', namely that it is *qua* Other that he desires (which is what provides the true compass of human passion). That is why the question *of* the Other, which comes back to the subject from the place from which he expects an oracular reply in some such form as '*Che vuoi?*', 'What do you want?', is the one that best leads him to the path of his own desire—providing he sets out,

what he is saying, or even if he is speaking, as the entire experience of analysis has taught us.

It follows that the place of the 'inter-said' (*inter-dit*), which is the 'intra-said' (*intra-dit*) of a between two subjects,[111] is the very place in which the transparency of the classical subject is divided and passes through the effects of 'fading' that specify the Freudian subject by its occultation by an ever purer signifier: that these effects lead us to the frontiers at which slips of the tongue and witticisms, in their collusion, become confused, even where elision is so much the more allusive in tracking down presence to its lair, that one is surprised that the *Dasein* hunt hasn't done better out of it. (Lacan, "The Subversion of the Subject and the Dialectic of Desire in the Freudian Unconscious" [1960], *Écrits*, p. 299)

We will be returning to the problem of the subject in Lacan, but for now we need to mark at least the disintegration of the site of the subject (in the saying which occurs between two subjects). Desire, as with the romantics, was seen as the motor force of the appearing of any object (or value) within the world; desire, however, does not belong to the one who speaks (even when he/she expresses that desire as her/his own) but to the structure of language itself. The gift of speaking, like Bataille's example of the potlatch, announces the word's entry into the economy, fulfills the obligation toward the economy, precisely by not being possessed (possession would constitute the purity of the signifier). The location of that economy, as Lacan understands, is not simply exterior to the subject, but it doesn't thereby exist as the subject: the terms of possession (or rather the lack of it) are what substantiate the analogy Lacan makes between the unconscious and language.

Lacan is constantly concerned with the evidence of clinical experience (with the attempt to find an appropriate methodology for approaching the speaking subject as a site of meaning, as the space of occurrence for a language). The primary instance in the standard view of clinical experience is early family life—the child's relation to the social environment, its habituation to the world of meaning. This (stylistic, metaphorical) starting point is—for essential reasons—part of why so much can be said relating Freud and Hegel. The child experiences the initially undifferentiated satisfaction of desire. Then comes birth. Early childhood experiences will mark all the future stages: that is the connection between Freudian recollection, recognition, and Plato's anamnesis—the memory of truths repressed by the pain of birth. Lacan's thinking of evidence—based rigorously on the language of the encounter between analyst and analysand—understands the economic power of language. The moment which constitutes that power as economic, which constitutes the opening of the economy itself, is the moment we need to question in both Bataille and Lacan: perhaps, instead, we will find that there is no such thing as experience, at least of the type which the economics of experiencing subjects is based on.

During the early postdelivery stages, the Mother is the Other for the child with the help of the skills of a partner known as a psychoanalyst, to reformulate it, even without knowing it, as 'What does he want of me?' (Lacan, "The Subversion of the Subject and the Dialectic of Desire in the Freudian Unconscious" [1960], *Écrits*, p. 312) (which means that she assumes the space of the Same). Satisfaction of desires, as with privation, rests with whether she grants their fulfillment. Simply, others feed the child, care for the child's needs, anticipating what those drives are before the child articulates the need. A guesswork is needed on the part of the other (the other must be providing objects which are filled with meaning: food satiates the presumed hunger). One's undifferentiated needs are articulated as particular objects, given by others who cannot satisfy the desire for an abstract feeling (anxiety, hunger), but can give a particular thing, based on their perception of the need (a blanket, food—and, importantly, gender differentiations begin at this stage as we treat the child according to our already socially conditioned guesses about their feelings, instituting an appropriate style in the child). That the duty of mothering need not be, as traditionally conceived, an exclusively feminine role, has in fact extremely important implications for the future of the family, psychoanalysis and philosophy. That this structure of demand and fulfillment extends, in ever more complicated fashions, into/through all stages of life, is the Freudian insight (and, for that reason, to argue against Freud is to argue against the narrative model of meaning at its widest applicability). We should remember, however, that we were speaking of economics:

> The psychoanalytic experience has rediscovered in man the imperative of the Word as the law that has formed him in its image. It manipulates the poetic function of language to give to his desire its symbolic mediation. May that experience enable you to understand at last that it is in the gift of speech that all the reality of its effects resides; for it is by way of this gift that all reality has come to man and it is by his continued act that he maintains it.
>
> If the domain defined by this gift of speech is to be sufficient for your action as also for your knowledge, it will also be sufficient for your devotion. For it offers it a privileged field. (Lacan, "The Function and Field of Speech and Language in Psychoanalysis" [1953], *Écrits*, p. 106)

I wish I could say that, as a result of what has passed before in this book, such a quotation needs no explanation—and doubtless there are those who, for whatever reasons, understand. Whom is this gift given to? How does symbolic mediation constitute the gift of language? How does the gift that man gives come back to him as all reality? Is it the same for a woman? How does this giving constitute a desire, constitute a libidinal economy?

As I have mentioned, Lacan is concerned with psychoanalysis as a practice. This was undoubtedly true for Freud as well but where the founder of psychoanalysis had been concerned with the definition of the subject, of the person who was the object of analysis (the analysand), Lacan is more intimately concerned with the analyst, with the subject who asks of the object that he/she speak (and neither Freud nor Lacan naively theorized an absolute separation). From that questioning, Lacan would establish a "privileged field": a field already coterminous with the evidence available. This seeming circularity is, speaking as a structuralist, the very definition of an economy. Speaking as a Heideggerian, it is the question of finding a method which would be capable of beginning—that is, it is a question that does not take the idea of an economic relation between questions and answers for granted.

If we situate ourselves in the midst of an argument, it's because there's always a risk of being misunderstood. Lacan is commenting on Jung's theory of archetypes when he suddenly turns to criticize Paul Ricoeur's hermeneutic reading of Freud. Hermeneutics presumes that all meaning can belong to a moment of presence (a dream, for example, can be interpreted in terms of its vague pointings towards some now buried, but at some past point definite and clear, lived experience).[112] Lacan doesn't see meaning as dependent on the narrative structures of lived experience (and this is where his critique of the idea of the subject is grounded) but as dependent on the structuring which desire itself offers:

> What we have here is not some scholastic quibble, some small difference of opinion. For what Freud intends to make present in the function of this libido is not some archaic relation, some primitive mode of access of

112. Ricoeur, for his part, says of Lacan's most famous dictum: "We can retain, then, with the reservations just made, the statement that the unconscious is structured like a language; but the word 'like' must receive no less emphasis than the word 'language.' In short, the statement must not be divorced from Benveniste's remark that the Freudian mechanisms are both infra- and supralinguistic. The mechanisms of the unconscious are not so much particular linguistic phenomena as they are paralinguistic distortions of ordinary language" (Ricoeur, *Freud and Philosophy* [1961], p. 404).

thoughts, some world that is there like some shade of an ancient world surviving in ours. The libido is the effective presence, as such, of desire. It is
what now remains to indicate desire—which is not substance, but which is
there at the level of the primary process, and which governs the very mode of
our approach. . . .

I maintain that it is at the level of analysis—if we can take a few more
steps forward—that the nodal point by which the pulsation of the unconscious is linked to actual reality must be revealed. This nodal point is called
desire, and the theoretical elaboration that I have pursued in recent years will
show you, through each stage of clinical experience, how desire is situated in
dependence on demand—which, by being articulated in signifiers, leaves a
metonymic remainder that runs under it, an element that is not indeterminate, which is a condition both absolute and unapprehensible, an element
necessarily lacking, unsatisfied, impossible, misconstrued (*méconnu*), an element that is called desire. (Lacan, *The Four Fundamental Concepts of Psycho-
Analysis* [1973], pp. 153–54, [my ellipsis])

I would like to not lose sight of the unifying concerns of this book. We are,
here with Lacan, involved in the same critique of the history of metaphysics we
followed with Heidegger on Hegel. And, as a Heideggerian (Lacan is not always a Heideggerian), Lacan gives us the same difference relative to time: the
*constitution* of present desires, as such, as constituting a field of desire, is privileged over the individual productive acts that had been said to have determined the given economy of a subject's desiring. One can, from the privileged,
if somewhat imaginary, view from outside of the system, pretend to describe a
causal chain of signifiers which would leave the subject without recourse.
However, the fact that this is a possible undertaking doesn't make it the truth
of psychoanalysis. Self-understanding is not the passive acceptance of an exterior destiny; it constitutes, instead, in the moment of desire, the possibility of
a destiny. One can manipulate the order of desire. Of course, these projects are
entirely reconstrued (although some of the questions remain) if we move into
the ethical retreat within consciousness which counters (seduces? commands
from the heights of destitution? subtends?) the outward grasping of a desire
construed as lust for power. On the surface it can almost seem to be 'a scholas-
tic quibble', but it is a difference of, exactly, the location, the certitude, of the
subject.

Ricoeur sees desire as force:

Taking up the theory of affects in our present reflective language we shall say
this: if desire is the unnameable, it is turned from the very outset toward lan-

guage; it wishes to be expressed; it is in potency to speech. What makes desire the limit concept at the frontier between the organic and the psychical is the fact that desire is both the nonspoken and the wish-to-speak, the unnameable and the potency to speak. (Ricoeur, *Freud and Philosophy* [1961], p. 457)[113]

For Ricoeur, desire itself can do no wrong (only acts, as in acts of interpretation, can be wrong or right); it simply desires (it is the form of mediation, the desire for expression), and by desiring, the facts of the world are uncovered, or brought to language and language's rationality (the narrative structures of lived experience, of a subject's reaching out towards a world). For Ricoeur, as with the tradition of philosophy generally, desire is not the site of meaning (of any type of ethical decision), but a fact to be dealt with, to be interpreted (either rightly or wrongly), to be expressed or repressed, channeled or fought. Lacan sees that hermeneutics conducted from that site would be a discourse of the same (of the subject as, at least potentially, self-present), effacing as contingent facts the only actuality the analyst deals with: the unconscious becomes a subsidiary moment to consciousness, desire becomes a motor force on the way to language, the economy which enables language's production always returns to language's legitimate uses. In the name of process and progress, Ricoeur throws out all the pears and apples while looking for fruit.

I think it is possible to understand Lacan's work here in terms of intersubjectivity and sacrifice, continuity and the opening of an economy of meaning (that is, exactly

113. Desire, however, does not play the pivotal role for Ricoeur that it does for Lacan precisely because understanding, or interpretation, tames the force of desire. The presence of the libido is merely a symptom, or a sign to be interpreted.

So little did Freud reduce the interpretation of meaning to the economics of force that the paper on "The Unconscious" ends with a significant circular movement that takes us back to the starting point, that is, to the deciphering of the unconscious in its "derivatives." This return to the point of departure deserves to be examined for the structure of its argumentation. The topography separated the systems from one another, and the economics completed that separation with the theory that each system has its own peculiar laws (the intrasystemic relations). But the economics also requires that we finally come to consider the intersystemic relations; that is why "The Unconscious" ends not with the "special characteristics of the unconscious system" but with a consideration of the "communication between the systems." Only then will there be a true "recognition" or "assessment" of the unconscious. The communication *between* the systems can only be deciphered, however, in the meaningful architecture of the derivatives: "In brief, it must be said that the *Ucs.* is continued into [*setz sich in*] what are known as derivatives." Freud especially focuses on those derivatives which present both the highly organized features of the conscious system and the characteristics of the unconscious; we are well acquainted with these hybrid formations as the fantasies of both normal and neurotic people and as substitute formations. The composite nature of fantasies assures us that the unconscious must always be deciphered, or diagnosed, in what we called at the end of our previous analysis the "symptom of being conscious." Furthermore, these derivatives of the unconscious, these "intermediaries between the two systems," not only afford access to the unconscious but open the way to *influencing* it—which is what psychoanalytic treatment is based upon.

What is the meaning of this circular movement of the argumentation? This movement would be unintelligible if the economic point of view were to free itself entirely from the interpretation of meaning through meaning. Psychoanalysis never confronts one with bare forces, but always with forces in search of meaning; this link between force and meaning makes instinct a psychical reality, or, more exactly, the limit concept at the frontier between the organic and the psychical. The link between hermeneutics and economics may be stretched as far as possible—and the theory of affects marks the extreme point of that distention in the

the terms at stake in the story of Christ.) This can be seen in his essentially differing view of the role of psychoanalysis. The question will return, repeatedly for the rest of this book, of how one responds to the call to speak, and of how one teaches another to speak—the secret to their answer lying in the unity of the two questions. Lacan is speaking of training (and analyzing) analysts:

> Of course, his demand is deployed on the field of an implicit demand, that for which he is there: the demand to cure him, to reveal him to himself, to introduce him to psychoanalysis, to help him to qualify as an analyst. But, as he knows, this demand can wait. His present demand has nothing to do with this, it is not even his own, for after all it is I who have offered to speak to him. (Only the subject is transitive here.)
>
> In short, I have succeeded in doing what in the field of ordinary commerce one would dearly like to be able to do with such ease: with supply I have created demand. (Lacan, "The Direction of the Treatment and the Principles of its Power" [1958], *Écrits*, p. 254)

The analyst does not explain the subject to himself (or herself); in the act of offering to speak, the analyst creates the analysand—and paradoxically, the analyst (as analysand) speaks by agreeing to listen. The book in your hand is constituted around/with the question of the relation of freedom to necessity. This leads us, unsurprisingly, into the sphere of how we formulate our demands and desires; that is, how free or constrained we are in our choice of the objects we desire for sex, food, art, T.V., presidents—any type of consumable. The story of liberal humanism can be told as the progressive reification of individual opinion (and opinion is progressively commodified around opinion: "I rate her a $7\frac{1}{2}$")—treating opinion as an inalienable possession, even to the extent that we've lost the right to question it, and its relation to possession, as such.[114] No longer centered under a literal monarchy, the public sphere is controlled by the principle of private (that is, exclusive) ownership, abstracted from actual content. Our rights are conceptualized as rights to consumption, our duties as duties to produce.

The move to postmodernity, insofar as there is a general applicability to the name postmodern, is woven around the diverse topics associated with the decentered subject, with the subject no longer identifiable as the locus of certain (certifiable) rights and possessions. We see over and over again that the questions of philosophy are merely questions of how we name ourselves as unified, how we constitute our own identities as individuals and groups. Philosophically, we are accustomed to thinking of some interplay between the tradition of words, the economy of possible expressions as they are already constituted for the individual who chooses to speak, and a demand (or desire) for freedom from the constraints of that economy (a demand which usually is seen as in some way belonging to the economy as well). The decentered subject, and in this I am not following the course of what one usually says about the decentered subject, marks a moment which is not originally given within the economy. The subject's con-

Freudian metapsychology; still the link cannot be broken, for otherwise the economics would cease to belong to a *psycho*analysis. (Ricoeur, *Freud and Philosophy* [1961], pp. 150–51)

114. This latter story is to be found in Habermas, *The Structural Transformation of the Public Sphere*, where he notes, I think correctly: "*The fully developed bourgeois public sphere was based on the fictitious identity of the two roles assumed by the privatized individuals who came together to form a public: the role of property owners and the role of human beings pure and simple*" (p. 56). This adumbrates (negatively) Habermas's larger project. "The theory of communicative action seeks to find the form of a truly free critical speech—one unencumbered with ideologies and leading to a society where people exist in a type of 'unity', a 'nonreified communicative everyday practice'" (*The Theory of Communicative Action* [1981], 2:398). "The theory of communicative action aims at the moment of unconditionality that, with criticizable validity claims, is built into the conditions of processes of consensus formation" (ibid., p. 399). Importantly, and to his credit, Habermas realizes that there is no necessity to the growth of freedom: a moment in history will come with a choice, an opportunity we may miss:

The theory of modernity that I have here sketched in broad strokes permits us to recognize the following: In modern societies there is such an expansion of the scope of contingency for interaction loosed from normative contexts that the inner logic of communicative action 'becomes practically true' in the deinstitutionalized forms of intercourse of the familial private sphere as well as in a public sphere stamped by the mass media. At the same time, the systemic imperatives of autonomous subsystems penetrate into the lifeworld and, through monetarization and bureaucratization, force an assimilation of communicative action to formally organized domains of action—even in areas where the action-coordinating mechanism of reaching understanding is functionally necessary. It may be that this provocative threat, this challenge that places the symbolic structures of the lifeworld as a whole in question, can account for why they have become accessible to us. (Ibid., p. 403)

115. Lacan, for his part, doesn't miss the problem of the supposed punctuality of perception or understanding (although we may yet question some of his conclusions). He draws the conclusions in terms of the formation of a subject:

> I am taking the structure at the level of the subject here, and it reflects something that is already to be found in the natural relation that the eye inscribes with regard to light. I am not simply that punctiform being located at the geometral point from which

stitution of itself, as Lacan notes, comes from the Other. But to take that constitution, as many theorists do, as a productive activity of the Other (or of an economy of otherness) is to miss the critique of punctuality (of the now as a universally valid interpretational site) which we followed with Heidegger's critique of Hegel.[115]

What we are asking here is really a question of methodology, of how to approach establishing a field for our questioning. This eventually includes the 'question of the question', the problem of establishing that any questioning, as an activity, can act as a gateway to the answers we seek (this is not a trivial problem, it reduplicates all the questions of freedom and necessity on the field which precedes our explicit questions about freedom and necessity). To establish a field, like entering into a symbolic order, requires something gradual. It cannot be a series of sure, punctually certain steps toward a goal (either teleologically hinted at or completely uncertain). Each movement must also escape the simplicity, or the security, of positing essences. No movement is individual. I will be delaying any answers, precisely because I am deferring the moment of actually phrasing the question. The seeming strangeness of appropriating overburdened words from a tradition without either marking their distance from a canonical reading or my acceptance of some particular interpretation enacts (as a style of deferral) the same entrance I cannot simply act out for myself: this book, as possibly read, as the object of multiple possible readings, is the identity which cannot be presupposed. It wants to be read, it wills its finitude, its death, its being taken up by others who cannot be named in advance. This book, more than its author, enacts the field which is the decentered, postmodern subject.

I will ask this self-same question again when we speak of social ontologies and the creation of the self under the section "Mothers"—the possibility of an iteration is what must be accentuated against the logic of secure judgments. For now, we are asked merely to remember that all of these various constitutions of identity are predicated on a relation of male subjects (at one or two steps removed—relating to mothers or wives) directed towards women (objects and satisfiers of need). I have been trying to ask of the methodology employed in Lacan's turn away from the interpreting (modern) subject, in his turn towards a certain field of reflections, of demands and desires originating outside of the self, organized in an economy of reflections.[116] We will return to Lacan's formulations later, but for now I want to mark certain hesitations on my part. My purpose is to establish the possibility of questioning the space of our questioning itself. Lacan already placed desire, the presence of which defines the field of inquiry for psychoanalysis, within the confrontation with a lack (or a possible castration). That this has to do, essentially, with the possibilities of speaking, with the possibilities of asserting an identity, would stem from Lacan's conceptualization of the meaning of death[117] (and is what we will be doubting in so far as it presumes to know the meaning, or structure, of that death).

> Whether it is the drive, the partial drive, that orientates him to it, or whether the partial drive alone is the

the perspective is grasped. No doubt, in the depths of my eye, the picture is painted. The picture, certainly, is in my eye. But I am not in the picture. That which is light looks at me, and by means of that light in the depths of my eye, something is painted—something that is not simply a constructed relation, the object on which the philosopher lingers—but something that is an impression, the shimmering of a surface that is not, in advance, situated for me in its distance. This is something that introduces what was elided in the geometral relation—the depth of field, with all its ambiguity and variability, which is in no way mastered by me. It is rather it that grasps me, solicits me at every moment, and makes of the landscape something other than a landscape, something other than what I have called the picture. (Lacan, *The Four Fundamental Concepts of Psycho-Analysis* [1973], p. 96)

116. "A principle which can be simply stated: that castration cannot be deduced from development alone, since it presupposes the subjectivity of the Other as the place of its law. The otherness of sex is denatured by this alienation. Man here acts as the relay whereby the woman becomes this Other for herself as she is this Other for him" (Lacan, "Guiding Remarks for a Congress on Feminine Sexuality" [1958], *Feminine Sexuality*, p. 93).

117. Which isn't so far off of

Bataille's, in spite of the literary concerns of the latter: "The illusion of completeness which I'm (humanly) aware of in the body of a woman with her clothes on: as soon as she's even partly undressed, her animal nature becomes visible and (while I'm watching) hands me over to my own incompleteness. . . . The more perfect, the more isolated or confined to ourselves we are. But the wound of incompleteness opens me up. Through what could be called incompleteness or animal nakedness or the wound, the different separate beings communicate, acquiring life by losing it in communication with each other" (Bataille, *Guilty* [1943, 1961], p. 27).

representative in the psyche of the consequences of sexuality, this is a sign that sexuality is represented in the psyche by a relation of the subject that is deduced from something other than sexuality itself. Sexuality is established in the field of the subject by a way that is that of lack.

Two lacks overlap here. The first emerges from the central defect around which the dialectic of the advent of the subject to his own being in the relation to the Other turns—by the fact that the subject depends on the signifier and that the signifier is first of all in the field of the Other. This lack takes up the other lack, which is the real, earlier lack, to be situated at the advent of the living being, that is to say, at sexed reproduction. The real lack is what the living being loses, that part of himself *qua* living being, in reproducing himself through the way of sex. This lack is real because it relates to something real, namely, that the living being, by being subject to sex, has fallen under the blow of individual death. (Lacan, *The Four Fundamental Concepts of Psycho-Analysis* [1973], pp. 204–5)

There is a strange unity to the metaphor of the circle—itself a metaphor of unity. Paradigmatically, the center is that part of a circle which is both part of the shape—after all, without a center, firmly fixed, a circle never completes itself—and outside of the shape; there is no point on the actually drawn circle that you can designate as the center. This metaphor was used in politics to speak of the monarch and in religion to speak of Christ.[118] The same metaphor also expresses the relation of the public man's role to the private woman's. It is interesting that a perfect circle implies that the fixed foot of the compass, doing all the important work, nevertheless does not leave a mark— "the hand that rocks the cradle rules the world" (which always means there's a boy in the basket) or the idea that leaders merely express the will of the people (the president's mind is the blank slate on which public opinion scribbles its headlines). Only by leaving the family realm, by gaining a distance on the ethics of the private sphere, can man—and it is always man here—see that the actuality of ethical life must be made by a break with the empty universal codes of family life (although, of course, the man is bound to return to exactly that same family life himself in the guise of the Father). Only by positing the absolute value of the inscribed circle (the written laws, or the public discourse) over the nonenduring work of the foot of the compass (immediate moral feeling or private contemplation and reception) can man ensure the stability of the circle. Likewise, the glorification of family values finds its justification in the production of good citizens, and must orient itself exclusively towards this end if it is to be called a 'good' family.

The rejection of metaphysics I wish to formulate bases itself on a different relation to the objects and subjects of the world than the necessarily negative moment of "scientific" epistemology (or of an equally negative literature/aesthetics of desire). In this way, many postmodern theories of the subject, including Lacan's, still suffer under a metaphysics of war, of fundamental conflict be-

118. "Man's freedom is entirely inscribed within the constituting triangle of the renunciation that he imposes on the desire of the other by the menace of death for the enjoyment of the fruits of his serfdom—of the consented-to sacrifice of his life for the reasons that give to human life its measure—and of the suicidal renunciation of the vanquished partner, depriving of his victory the master whom he abandons to his inhuman solitude" (Lacan, "The Function and Field of Speech and Language in Psychoanalysis" [1953], *Écrits*, p. 104).

119. If he eats, drinks, lives somewhere, reproduces himself, it is because the system requires his self-production in order to reproduce itself: it needs men. If it could function with slaves, there would be no 'free' workers. If it could function with asexual mechanical robots, there would be no sexual reproduction. If the system could function without feeding its workers, there would be no bread. It is in this sense that we are all, in the framework of this system, survivors. Not even the instinct of self-preservation is fundamental: it is a social tolerance or a social imperative. When the system requires it, it cancels this instinct and people get excited about dying (for a sublime cause, evidently). We do not wish to say that 'the individual is a product of society' at all. For, as it is currently understood, this culturalist platitude only masks the much more radical truth that, in its totalitarian logic, a system of productivist growth (capitalist, but not exclusively) can only produce and reproduce men—even in their deepest determinations: in their liberty, in their needs, in their very unconscious—as productive forces. The system can only produce and reproduce individuals as elements of the system. It cannot tolerate exceptions. (Baudrillard, "The Ideological Genesis of Needs" [1969], *For a Critique of the Political Economy of the Sign*, p. 86)

tween competing subjects. However, there is something positive here to be taken from Lacan as well. Perhaps in that sense, then, the point is not a "rejection" of metaphysics, but a reformulation of the dyads within which our opposition to metaphysics has thrown us. That is, one can perhaps think of the relation to language as other than a relation. One accedes to language, not as one accedes to a regime of power, nor as one learns to deal with the world, but as one becomes part of the world. To learn a language is not to learn the proper way of opposing oneself to the things in the world, nor even to learn how one is also one of the things of the world, but to learn how a world is other than an environment—to learn how a poetry is other than a science.

How, then, do we maintain speech, words, language, without a theory of the acquisition of language, without seeing the word as a possession of the individual which is then doled out in acts of reciprocal exchange, like money to other members of the economy?[119] (And is it merely coincidence that the formulation of property rights, the defense of a hierarchy of the possession of capital, coincided with the concomitant defense of knowledge on the parts of abstractly equally autonomous and equally separate literate individuals?) How then can we say of the center of the circle, as Cusa said of God, that it is not-other than the circle? Can we learn, against modern epistemology, to think of the 'how' of creation without privileging the thing produced as if it had been the exclusive end and purpose, exhausting all the potentiality, of the creative mode of existence itself?

Perhaps our answer lies with rephrasing

the problem of subjectivity and desire. The constancy of my desires cannot constitute a unity to the extent that they cannot be fulfilled, to the extent that I was not the origin of those desires and therefore cannot be the site of their completion. But presence in general cannot serve as an encompassing unity either (as we have already seen). I cannot find my desires fulfilled merely by claiming my allegiance (or identity) with those fathers who at first controlled, and possessed, the desired object. My point, stylistically, allegorically, is that this is equally true of the word as marker of a power to name (to bring to conscious presence as a moment in the narrative of 'my' meaning) and of the desire for love that a woman's presence (sister, mother, wife) is supposed to fulfill.

> Demand in itself bears on something other than the satisfactions it calls for. It is demand of a presence or of an absence—which is what is manifested in the primordial relation to the mother, pregnant with that Other to be situated *within* the needs that it can satisfy. Demand constitutes the Other as already possessing the 'privilege' of satisfying needs, that is to say, the power of depriving them of that alone by which they are satisfied. This privilege of the Other thus outlines the radical form of the gift of that which the Other does not have, namely, its love.
>
> In this way, demand annuls (*aufhebt*) the particularity of everything that can be granted by transmuting it into a proof of love, and the very satisfaction that it obtains for need are reduced (*sich erniedrigt*) to the level of being no more than the crushing of the demand for love (all of which is perfectly apparent in the psychology of child-rearing, to which our analyst-nurses are so attached).[120] It is necessary, then, that the particularity thus abolished should reappear *beyond* demand. It does, in fact, reappear there, but preserving the structure contained in the unconditional element of the demand for love. By a reversal that is not simply a negation of the negation, the power of pure loss emerges from the residue of an obliteration. For the unconditional element of demand, desire substitutes the 'absolute' condition: this condition unties the knot of that element in the proof of love that is resistant to the satisfaction of a need. Thus desire is neither the appetite for satisfaction, nor the demand for love, but the difference that results from the subtraction of the first from the second, the phenomenon of their splitting (*Spaltung*). (Lacan, "The Signification of the Phallus" [1958], *Écrits*, pp. 286–87)

Or rather, from their *addition*. Like fruit, a particular is immediately a universal; an apple is a fruit, a gift of love. But, and here the question must be preliminary for it doesn't yet have a ground from which it can be asked: Why

120. "But love's element is infinitude, inexhaustibility, immeasurability. If you will to keep your love, then, by the help of the debt's infinitude, imprisoned in freedom and life, you must take care that it continually remains in its element; otherwise, it droops and dies—not after a time, for it dies at once—which itself is a sign of its perfection, that it can only live in its infinitude" (Kierkegaard, *Works of Love* [1847], p. 176), and

> *Worldly wisdom thinks that love is a relationship between man and man. Christianity teaches that love is a relationship between: man-God-man, that is, that God is the middle term.* However beautiful the love-relationship has been between two or more people, however complete all their enjoyment and all their bliss in mutual devotion and affection have been for them, even if all men have praised their relationship—if God and the relationship to God have been left out, then, Christianly understood, this has not been love but a mutual and enchanting illusion of love. *For to love God is to love oneself in truth; to help another human being to love God is to love another man; to be helped by another human being to love God is to be loved.* (Ibid., pp. 112–13)

121. [The proletariat] cannot abolish the conditions of its own life without abolishing *all* the inhuman conditions of life of society today which are summed up in its own situation. Not in vain does it go

must love be the complement of desire, other than the desire, instead of being given as desire itself? Why must the play of presence and absence be a source of anxiety, an anxiety which, seemingly, anchors desire to a single economy? We already began to approach something of an answer when we reworked the Christian narrative concerning the presence of divinity, and the functioning of that presence. A further answering will have to wait for later, although the problem of seduction, in the next subsection, is nothing but the question of where to find the cause of desire. The key to those answers lies, over the longer course of this book, with the contact one can have with the universal, with the infinite as source of meaning: that is, as Levinas teaches us, the other comes as an overflowing desire. (Is this a metaphysical claim? Is it merely descriptive? Or somehow both?)

With the question of economies, we are dealing with the heart of the structuralist and poststructuralist projects. The historical grounds of this movement stand with the Western left-wing reappropriation of materialism—often but not always Marxist—as a means of criticizing the functioning of capitalism. For any person trying to make such a critique in a present-day democracy, the first priority is to explain the nature of 'false consciousness'. How is it that the masses fail to recognize their own interests?[121] Why do the poor consistently vote for the interests of the rich? In Marx, it seems as though there is an object—man's consciousness, his species-being—which is overlaid with false contents. This is complicated by the fact that Marx understood consciousness itself to be, I think correctly, a process—the relation of man to

man—and not the product of that relation.[122] The element (the real component) of
that relation, for Marx, is still the product of
man's activity—and we can say basically the
same thing for all structuralists (and poststructuralists), even if they have put the
meaning of "man" into question. Take for example, not completely accidentally:

Today consumption—if this term has a
meaning other than that given it by
vulgar economics—defines precisely
*the stage where the commodity is immedi-
ately produced as a sign, as sign value,
and where signs (culture) are produced as
commodities.* (Baudrillard, "Towards a
Critique of the Political Economy of the
Sign" [1972], *For a Critique of the Political Economy of the Sign,* p. 191)

Thus, in the "fetishist" theory of consumption, in the view of marketing
strategists as well as of consumers, objects are given and received everywhere
as force dispensers (happiness, health,
security, prestige, etc.). This magical
substance having been spread about so
liberally, one forgets that what we are
dealing with first is signs: a generalized
code of signs, a totally arbitrary code of
differences, *and that it is on this basis,
and not at all on account of their use values or their innate "virtues," that objects
exercise their fascination.* (Baudrillard,
"Fetishism and Ideology" [1970], *For a
Critique of the Political Economy of the
Sign,* p. 91)[123]

To stay a brief moment here, we find
that by concentrating on the system and

through the stern steeling
school of *labour.* The question is not what this or that
proletarian, or even the whole
of the proletariat at the moment *considers* its aim. The
question is *what the proletariat is,* and what, consequent on that *being,* it will be
compelled to do. Its aim and
historical action is irrevocably
and obviously demonstrated
in its own life situation as
well as in the whole organization of bourgeois society
today. (Marx and Engels,
*Holy Family* [1845],
pp. 52–54)

122. Marx is merely shifting the
place of that production; the
production of a need for sociality, as originary of consciousness, the reification of the economic, underpins the very
possibility of science and of the
community of men. Interestingly, he sees this as a problem
of externalization, of economy,
and of *language:* "Language is as
old as consciousness, language *is*
practical consciousness that exists also for other men, and for
that reason alone it really exists
for me personally as well; language, like consciousness, only
arises from the need, the necessity, of intercourse with other
men. (Marx and Engels, *The
German Ideology* [1846], p. 51).

123. "The triangular structure,
crucial to Lacan's conception, is
not the simple psychological triangle of love and rivalry, but a
socio-symbolic structural positioning of the child in a complex
constellation of alliance (family,

elementary social cell) in which the combination of desire and a Law prohibiting desire is regulated, through a linguistic structure of exchange, into a repetitive process of replacement—of substitution—of symbolic objects (substitutes) of desire" (Felman, *Jacques Lacan and the Adventure of Insight* [1987], p. 104).

124. "All the repressive and reductive strategies of power systems are already present in the internal logic of the sign, as well as those of exchange value and political economy. Only total revolution, theoretical and practical, can restore the symbolic in the demise of the sign and of value. Even signs must burn" (Baudrillard, "Towards a Critique of the Political Economy of the Sign" [1972], *For a Critique of the Political Economy of the Sign*, p. 163).

forgetting the products we find the freedom to criticize the whole. With this insight Marx was able to speak of the government working for capitalist interests even when particular capitalists, for particular reasons, might have fought particular laws. The structures which define class interest are broader than the structures which determine particular interest. Marx doesn't argue against self-interest; he argues against the way that self-interest gets defined in terms of isolated selves. For capitalism, the formula is simply to create an individual who identifies himself as the owner of goods— first, in reality, the small and large business owners who formed the bourgeoisie and needed a mode of accessing their diverse power base to their advantage and later, as a false consciousness, the individual worker who saw (and perhaps still sees) her/himself as trading with the capitalist on a fair market (exchanging labor-time for money). The abstractions of capitalism form a self-perpetuating sign system where people gladly sacrifice themselves to the symbolic, (frequently) forsaking any efficacious work on actual material conditions. Although I find this type of critique useful, I question the assumption that groups can merely recognize their true interests, their true relatedness. Further, this recognition would seem to be hampered by the conception of self-interest inherent in class interest—a selfishness and not a communality. Marx never escapes—no one ever *escapes*—the realm of abstractions, of signs.[124] What is at stake here, and already has been throughout the discussion on Lacan as well, is the proper methodological ground for establishing a field of and for questioning. That this must be the same field which structures the economy of the sign is Lacan's basic insight; that desire is not cast into its shape because of the family, but because of the structures of society in general, is Baudrillard's insight; that this field itself isn't anything so static as an economy or a space (as the metaphor of a field might imply) is what I am seeking to demonstrate through the warping trajectories of reappropriating traditional categories of thinking about meaning (such as woman, Christ, or word).

Habermas identifies the Enlightenment—the modern project—with the systemic, structural change that shifted the power base from the vertical hierarchies of medieval city-states, fiefdoms, papacies, and kingships, where all power derived from a central authority, passed down to agents of the central authority, toward the Enlightenment's horizontal hierarchies of mercantilism, where actors presumed to act in their own name, where no individual authority could center the circle, but where the pure abstract function of centering remained. By identifying themselves with an abstract center—the principle of property—they could do away with the literal center of a literal ruler. This abstraction, according to Habermas, has no brakes and continues unabated (to capitalism's chagrin) in its humanitarian guise, until every human being has been endowed with these basic rights of property (of being a subject in possession of rights). The completion of the modernist project, Habermas's step beyond Marx, is realizing, as a society, that this exchange does not occur in the guise of money but as the speech-act (which you might have been able to construe from Marx's idea of free relations among men). Free consensus formation—freedom from false consciousness and freedom from literal constraints—would then create a government that genuinely reflected the will of the people.

There are two criticisms to be made here: (1) on the microeconomic level, this theory can never return from the sphere of typification and signs (the assumption being that typification is, in fact, the true), and relatedly (2) on the macroeconomic level, it still constitutes a society based on exchange where all ethical rules would also be derived from exchange (although a deeper, foundational, level of exchange, in communicative practice, is identified). Here I am pointing to a problem other than the opposition between negative and positive rights or rights and powers: For Habermas, as for many other similar thinkers about language, there is literally no space to conceptualize that which is not exchangeable. They assume (as a regulative ideal) that people know what they want, why they want it, and can express these desires accurately (and without contradiction). Exchange relations are conditioned by the metaphysics of presence, just as Science is based on the metaphysics of description: Marx failed to see this when he claimed to have turned Hegelian idealism on its head.[125]

125. When, in the name of our fear of all things one cannot touch (of all "metaphysical" propositions which cannot be immediately cashed out) we curtail the field of our discussions, we then foreclose the possibility of the question of justice, of how our call toward others should precede (and be held above) the demand that everything be here and present. Derrida, in responding to Blanchot's reading of Marx, lays it out:

> Let us translate into this language of Blanchot the hypothesis we are venturing to put forward here: opened with Marx's signature as a question, but also as a promise or an appeal, the spectrality whose "logic" we are going to analyze will have been covered over ("filling in a void," as Blanchot says, there where the void "ought rather to be increasingly emptied out") by Marx's *ontological* response. The response of Marx himself for whom the ghost must be nothing, nothing period (non-being, non-effectivity, non-life) or nothing imaginary, even if this nothing takes on a body, a certain body, that we will approach later. But also the response of his "Marxist" successors wherever they have drawn, practically, concretely, in a terribly effective, massive, and immediate fashion, its political consequences (at the cost of millions and millions of supplementary ghosts who will keep on protesting in us; Marx had his ghosts, we have ours, but memories no longer

Structuralism merely validates the view of society as an exchange relationship—ethics in such a society is the ethics of fair exchange and could never, for example, provide direct space for the rights of the woman to be exchanged in marriage (except by giving her 'possession' of her own right to be sold into a particular kind of domestic life). This is not, however, merely a feminist critique (or, feminism is not merely an economic critique). All of us are in the same position, conceived structurally; we live our own lives as stereotypes of ourselves. For Habermas, the theory of communicative action rescues man from the abstract logic of self-perpetuating institutions, but he cannot conceptualize escape from the abstract logic of the subject as individualized site. Further, for modernism, there is no conceivable value to a nonproductive life and no production which cannot be immediately translated into consumption.

Speech-act theory, after all, translates the very act of communication into the relation of producer and consumer (even as the analytic emphasis rests on the relation and neither of the two moments). This institutionalized, all-encompassing logic of production and consumption is the closed loop which, for example, makes both being a teacher and being a student so noxious—students are presented (force fed) consumables in school (nicely divided chunks of easily digested and disconnected material oriented towards their future productiveness) which they see only as products which are themselves later exchangeable for other consumables (in the form of better-paying jobs). If individual people are then further excluded from these structures—

last in line for consumables because of the structural determinants of race, gender, or both, for example—then the reasons for participating in these economies (which can offer no personal return) become personally dubious.

The microeconomic criticism can also be expressed through the case of man's relation to woman, to the passive other. Remember that, for Lacan, the basis of the sign is not money but the phallus.[126]

> Perhaps it should not be forgotten that the organ that assumes this signifying function takes on the value of a fetish. But the result for the woman remains that an experience of love, which, as such, deprives her ideally of that which the object gives, and a desire which finds its signifier in this object, converge on the same object. That is why one can observe that a lack in the satisfaction proper to sexual need, in other words, frigidity, is relatively well tolerated in women, whereas the *Verdrängung* (repression) inherent in desire is less present in women than in men. . . .
>
> One might add here that male homosexuality, in accordance with the phallic mark that constitutes desire, is constituted on the side of desire, while female homosexuality, on the other hand, as observation shows, is orientated on a disappointment that reinforces the side of the demand for love. (Lacan, "The Signification of the Phallus" [1958], *Écrits*, p. 290)

It does not make sense to say that there is no ethical (or political) stance here. I am

recognize such borders; by definition, they pass through walls, these *revenants*, day and night, they trick consciousness and skip generations).

Needless to spell it out here, therefore, still less to insist on it too heavily: it is not a taste for the void or for destruction that leads anyone to recognize the right of this necessity to "empty out" increasingly and to deconstruct the philosophical responses that consist in *totalizing*, in filling in the space of the question or in denying its possibility, in fleeing from the very thing it will have allowed one to glimpse. On the contrary, it is a matter there of an ethical and political imperative, an appeal as unconditional as the appeal of thinking from which it is not separated. It is a matter of the injunction itself—if there is one. (Derrida, *Specters of Marx* [1993], p. 30)

126. "With a knowledge that would out-measure the most self-respecting dogmatic or credulous philosopher, woman knows that castration does not take place. This formula however, must be manipulated with great prudence. Inasmuch as its undecidable mark, a non-mark even, indicates that area where castration is no longer determinable, it describes a margin whose very consequences are incalculable" (Derrida, *Spurs* [1978], p. 63).

unconvinced by an ethics which is based on exchange, unswayed by an argument that finds the subject only in men. Lacan for his part, is also expecting more (although he seems fatally flawed in his ethics by his inability to conceive of the parallels between the analyst's desire and the lesbian's). Lacan is giving us a clue about the meaning of presence, the gift of speaking:

> Nonetheless, it may be objected, the analyst gives his presence, but I believe that this presence is first of all simply the implication of his listening, and that this listening is simply the condition of speech. Furthermore why does the technique require that he should be so discreet if, in fact, this is not the case? It is only later that his presence will be felt.
>
> Anyway, the most acute feeling of his presence is bound up with a moment when the subject can only remain silent, that is to say, when he even recoils before the shadow of demand.
>
> Thus the analyst is he who supports the demand, not, as has been said, to frustrate the subject, but in order to allow the signifiers in which his frustration is bound up to reappear. (Lacan, "The Direction of the Treatment and the Principles of its Power" [1958], *Écrits*, p. 255)

Which again is pointing to the difference between Freud read as a way of mediating exchange between unconscious and conscious and speaking of the analyst as the site of a production of a given discourse. This attitude of silence, the 'I am here' which responds to and supports a demand (is the space of language's appearance), is an ethical beginning (the commencement of economy and not a function of/within economy). It falls back on itself again in strange ways as Lacan is often concerned with the 'what' of the discourse, especially in his discussion of the phallus; (although admittedly the phallus exists in the mode of always absent, it thus represents the functioning of the economy and not its commencement). I will, for the moment, let both these issues—microeconomics and macroeconomics—resolve back into the question of the Mother, into the paradox of being borne by another, of starting as a child, and then return to the question of sisters, outside, or without, the exchange relation.

For political economies, and we've already seen how this is justified, the figure of the economy, as with the figure of the mother, is that which (as a system of metaphors) cannot be questioned:

> We cannot mistrust our mother tongue (limiting cases such as mystical experience and creative linguistic innovation aside). For it is through the medium of consensus formation in ordinary language that cultural transmission and socialization as well as social integration come about, in the course of which

communicative action is always embedded in lifeworld contexts. By contrast, the monetary medium functions in such a way that interaction is detached from these contexts. And it is this uncoupling that makes it necessary to *re-couple the medium back to the lifeworld*. This recoupling takes the form of legally defining exchange relations through property and contract. (Habermas, *The Theory of Communicative Action* [1981], 2:266)

As I trust is clear, this entire book is an effort to mistrust—systematically and specifically through questioning the sense of a lifeworld, of a public world made up of acts of interpretation—the mother tongue. The sister, as a potential mother, as one whose trustworthiness is not yet certain, constitutes the figure of our doubt. The model of 'exchange' which a sister is supposed to fulfill at the most primitive level (and which is supposedly repeated at ever more complex levels) is what we will question at every level. In a sense, we may find that our mother tongue was indeed beginning to say something other than what we had trusted she would say. Against Habermas, the point is not to find a more 'true' foundation for the functioning of the economy (of sociality seen in its exchange relations), but to understand how we are drawn into the fields of such functionings.

That would be the sense of an indefinition within the horizon of possibility, the possibility of a space of presence which is not played out as an economy of lack and satisfaction, but which makes accessible the play itself (and, as we will see with Levinas, understands an ethical moment as the commencement of this play). Perhaps, before even Lacan's analysis of the sign, there is a moment where the Other institutes desire as a presence instead of an anxiety in the face of our finitude. Lyotard, without giving us a definitive answer, sketches a metaphorical connection (one which we will follow later, under a different section heading):

A baby must see its MOTHER's face as a landscape. Not because its mouth, fingers, and gaze move over it as it blindly grasps and sucks, smiles, cries and whimpers. Nor because it is 'in symbiosis' with her, as the saying goes. Too much activity on the one hand, too much connivance on the other. We should assume, rather, that the face is indescribable for the baby. It will have forgotten it, because it will not have been inscribed. If there is an element of the 'too' involved, it is because there is too much of a mark, rather too much support. The first act is the 'deferred action' Freud tried to elaborate. But he was too much of a psychologist. This mother is a mother who is a timbre 'before' it sounds, who is there before the coordinates of sound, before destiny. (Lyotard, "Scapeland," *The Lyotard Reader* [1989)], pp. 217–18)

## c)     Politics inside (and outside) the Economies (and Aesthetics) of Self and Other

Freud is often considered to have made an argument for a species of determinism. There is no real freedom, only the brutally inscribed experiences of our childhoods, working themselves out and through for the rest of our lives. Ricoeur is taking Freud and asking (among other things), in what sense is Freud's discourse still open to the philosophical question of subjective freedom? For Ricoeur, the answer is that one actively takes Freudian principles (as tools) to grasp onto the unconscious, decode its secrets, and give conscious discourse the 'free' realm of decisions based on the more or less transparent determinants of our past. Lacan, on the contrary, to the extent that he speaks of freedom at all, is talking about the free space provided by the difference—the difference of two almost synonymous positions—the difference between the demand for love and the appetite for satisfaction. The subject becomes radically decentered; in other words, and pushing on/against Lacan's systematic interpretation, time becomes anarchic. No room remains to speak of the freedom of the subject because Lacan has not theorized that passivity philosophically from the standpoint of time. Neither Ricoeur nor Lacan think through the methodological problems surrounding the subject without construing the 'field' of the subject's appearance (or meaningfulness) in terms of a spatial metaphor which structures the tradition (the preexisting economy of meanings) and its possibilities. That move is what we will use Levinas for (later in this writing). We next turn, however, to the question of the general criticism of economic thinking. Lacan is still naming the place of our desire—which naming on his part, and as he understands, philosophically depends on a freedom (on that which does not, and cannot, take place—if anything, but this would still be an approximation, it gives time). My criticism of him, which I will not pursue in detail, would merely be to doubt that the child is originally situated in an economic relation with those around her/him.

Taking seriously this freedom to name, and therefore control, our desires, taking as a real possibility our taking responsibility for our desires, we can speak of the problems with the supposed punctuality of the freedom to name—we can abandon the liberal humanist impulse towards reifying freedom in terms of the instantaneity of a rupture—but still see that an impulse worth following remains: simply, we will say that the quest for knowledge within the context of our intersubjective development is not exhausted by, in fact does not even begin with, the knowledge of the self (individual or collective). Consider, for example, the most political of all questions: What commodities shall I buy? Marx thought that the stage of alienated objects within the world (reification as a process of commodification) could be bypassed by establishing a direct relation between those (other) humans who (also) produce (as producers)—resulting in no alienation from the respective products of their labors. It is unclear in what sense they would still go through a childhood: whether, for instance, that childhood development would still have to rehash all of history on a personal level (as Hegel would have it)—each child living a moment of alienation (an apprenticeship in violence) before any reconciliation (or any unity) becomes possible.

This relation of human to human is not first available without a perceived relation (which is the actual state) of freedom relative to the objects of consumption (and here we deliberately expand the discourse to include all objects of desire as such and we would further deny any concept of freedom which didn't include the questioning of language itself). Achieving irony vis-à-vis the particular objects, a person gains the freedom to pick what reasons will be decisive in the choice of a commodity, choosing the choice of choosing. Why be a vegetarian? Better to ask: why eat at all? Contemplation will also find the issue complex—the reasons involved will necessarily be different in an expensive Californian (vegetarian) restaurant than in an orthodox (vegetarian) Hindu household. The dependence of these decision rules on the contexts in which the questions appear does not imply that there was no contemplative position assumed by the potential consumer (that is, it doesn't imply that context determines the decision); it does mean that the act of thinking does not posit itself as the goal of the thought (that is, it's not a Hegelian theory of self-consciousness, which seeks its unconditioned ground in its freedom of/as contemplation).

Is freedom an activity—a passivity? An active passivity, for freedom is the hesitation, the delay before deciding which says, 'this is a decision: as such it has consequences—which (or how many) of those consequences am I willing to accept?' The names one chooses will still be determined, but one enters into this slavery with the humanity of the decision held in reserve, held up as its condition. The hesitation which makes possible this entry with a reserve is the deferral which makes any meaning possible—it falls on us to make clear why that deferral is, as the instantiation of time itself, more important than the violence which follows on its heels. For Heidegger, all reality comes as an answer to the question of what is at stake. For a Hegelian, this question returns to itself as the process of questioning.[127] The question of art and freedom will be taken up under the next subsection. For now, we should speak of, politically, where we are, where we might want to go.

In fine, what we can keep as the schematic difference between the political question, as we have been able to formulate it so far, and the individual,

127. Bataille, here, is Hegelian: "If to the question 'What is there?' human existence answers in any other way than 'Myself and night, that is, infinite questioning,' it makes itself subordinate to the answer, that is, to nature. In other words, man is explained from the fact of nature and thereby renounces autonomy. The explanation of human existence that starts with the given (any roll of the dice substituted for any other) is inevitable but empty insofar as it answers infinite questioning: to formulate this emptiness is at the same time to realize the autonomous power of infinite questioning" (Bataille, *Guilty* [1943, 1961] p. 133).

128. The idea that an actor can develop motivational orientations vis-à-vis other situation elements—be they opponents, means, or conditions—already exhibits this *reification of transmissable cultural contents.* Of course, an actor can upon occasion also behave reflectively toward his cultural tradition; he can, so to speak, turn around and make ideas, values, or expressive symbols the object of analysis, positively or negatively cathect them as objectified, evaluate them in the light of corresponding standards, and so on. But this does not hold for the normal case in which someone acting communicatively makes use of his cultural tradition in a performative attitude. (Habermas, *The Theory of Communicative Action* [1981], 2:219–20)

microeconomic, question is the difference in the approach to freedom. Freedom, politically, economically, can only be found in the regulated rules of commerce; it is the freedom to produce. Even if we object to the commercialization of our freedom, it remains to be seen if politics in general can escape the realm of economic thinking. Freedom held individually is the ability to stop and question before there is a self—to question the mother language at a level at which Habermas would not want to doubt it.[128] Deliberately, we stop short of saying that the subject can then take the newly found acquisition—the product of this basic interrogation—to the polls. This would obviously be very rarely true in a democracy which never provides more than two viable candidates (both vying for the center)—consensus formation itself needs to be rethought.

Achieving the questioning of one's deepest being, the product of irony in Kierkegaard's sense, requires an understanding of nothingness, of the night. Heidegger would say, enigmatically, that the night has never been so dark, nor the opportunity for thought so pressing. Again, there is a danger of misunderstanding and we find ourselves in the midst of an argument. Structurally, this is the argument of postmodernity: what is the role of aesthetics in life? And how would aesthetics instantiate freedom? Habermas, a modernist, answers that aesthetics is the most valorized of things but, like a housewife, it is unable to understand the harsh realities of the political world, unable to enact freedom in the real world (aesthetes are deluded by an illusory freedom). Habermas, likewise, accuses Derrida of ignoring a fundamental division in the uses of language.[129]

Sometimes, the moderns claim, language looks to (essential) truth and sometimes to sociality (typified truths); sometimes it breaks with traditions and sometimes it connects with traditions. For Habermas, the normal functioning is the one that establishes connections between fundamentally separate individuals; normal functioning reasserts the validity of tradition. Since, in markedly Hegelian fashion, the signs which establish connections are the signs we seek to connect with (and, as signs, are validated as connections because we seek them), the truth of our social-political formations is ultimately determined as the truth of sociality as exchange (this time signs and not money or durable goods)—sociality is coterminous with the public sphere, the proper sphere of all values. In other words, by everyone expressing their desires, determined as desires inherited from the mother tongue, the truth of desiring as a desire for sociality is expressed (although fundamentally conservative—expressed and directed in terms of the existing interests of a class or people or the actual essence of historical, human species-being). Immediately we see that all social relations are again formulated as economic—I love because I wish love in return, I give in order to make the other obliged to me. The end result is that, like Hegel, Habermas is unable to question the subject's desire as desire; he can only ceaselessly ratify it. Like Hegel, he is unable to implicate his own privileges—as professional sociologist, philosopher, and thinker—in the order of society as a whole: he merely views it and, at his most political, asks others to share his view.

It may not, at first glance, be apparent

129. In the end, the analysis leads to a confirmation of the thesis it would like to refute. To the degree that the poetic, world-disclosing function of language gains primacy and structuring force, language escapes the structural constraints and communicative functions of everyday life. The space of fiction that is opened up when linguistic forms of expression become reflexive results from suspending illocutionary binding forces and those idealizations that make possible a use of language oriented toward mutual understanding—and hence make possible a coordination of plans of action that operates via the intersubjective recognition of criticizable validity claims. One can read Derrida's debate with Austin also as a denial of this independently structured domain of everyday communicative practice; it corresponds to the denial of an autonomous realm of fiction. (Habermas, "On Leveling the Genre Distinction between Philosophy and Literature" [1983], *The Philosophical Discourse of Modernity*, p. 204)

Derrida neglects the potential for negation inherent in the validity basis of action oriented toward reaching understanding; he permits the capacity to solve problems to disappear behind the world-creating capacity of language; the former capacity is possessed by language as the medium through which those acting communicatively get involved in relations to the world whenever they agree with one another about something in the objective world, in their common social world, or in the subjective worlds to which each has privileged access. (Ibid., p. 205)

130. A different model for the mediation of the universal and the individual is provided by the *higher-level intersubjectivity of an uncoerced formation of will* within a communication community existing under constraints toward cooperation: In the universality of an uncoerced consensus arrived at among free and equal persons, individuals retain a court of appeal that can be called upon even against particular forms of institutional concretization of the common will. As we have seen, in Hegel's youthful writings the option of explicating the ethical totality as a communicative reason embodied in intersubjective life-contexts was still open. Along this line, a democratic self-organization of society could have taken the place of the monarchical apparatus of the state. By way of contrast, the logic of a subject conceiving itself makes the institutionalism of a strong state necessary. (Habermas, "Hegel's Concept of Modernity" [1983], *The Philosophical Discourse of Modernity*, p. 40)

I am well aware of the fact that it sounds like Habermas is involved in the same critique of the sub-

exactly how much this division of art and politics is in fact a political stance on Habermas's side. Simply put, an emphasis on the material reality of given situations always serves the conservative principles of the existing interpretation. Materialism always assumes—either as personified singly in a monarchy, united as in a self-recognizing class, or as rigorously structured as in the principle of consensus formation (sociality) itself—a perceiving consciousness which judges the validity claims of the individuals in conflict.[130] On the other hand, an emphasis on the aesthetics of the representation of reality always returns to question—or rather to give the reader the space to question—the specificity of the entire world view implicated in the representation (it in fact questions the explanatory utility of a world view). In other words, because aesthetics is better able to implicate individual representations within the structural whole (as opposed to Habermas's idea of agency which assumes a consciousness which is aware of the structural whole and can then decide on the validity or truth of individual representations), aesthetics can claim to be the political champion of the individual without being individualist—aesthetics sees an apple, a pear and a tomato and formulates the question of fruit; the structures of eating assume in advance that one is always eating (the fruit being accidental). In this sense, the aesthetic and the ethical meld; the space of aesthetic being is the retreat into ethical consciousness.

This difference between the universal and the particular, the difference of subject and object, is exactly what Hegel was trying to eliminate: that is, he was trying to stop the differentiation of art and politics. Yet for Hegel (and Habermas), this meant the subjugation of art to politics, of time to being, art remaining only as the beautiful fruit, the corpse, of previous social-political configurations (or even our current configuration, but only in so far as it has *already* been articulated). He destroys the dyad of subject and object by placing them in war (dialectics) and declaring one the winner—having, of course, gained all the positive attributes of the loser as spoils in war. (And this is the sense in which Hegel can both claim to be against representation—as derivative of politics—and be so susceptible to the criticism of representation—since his conception of politics remains representative, dependent on the agency of a unifying consciousness.)

The question would remain as to whether an art that creates political positions is possible, or whether art may any longer be both connected and efficacious and not merely trivially free—trivial in the sense of not being able to implicate its freedom for/in a concrete nexus of individuals. This is not to be confused with art that comments on politics. Neither is art merely a different way of looking at the same object.[131] Habermas wants to keep the idea (and ideal) of a developing, learning, humanity which will eventually come to know itself while instituting, while institutionalizing, the split between universal and particular which is, itself, the violence of metaphysics: the priority of the world of exchange over the world of silence. This silence, of course, cannot be expressed directly. However, we can speak *of* it. It is not the 'worm at the heart of being', at least not that merely—it is rather the pro-

ject I am speaking of. The difference finds itself in not taking the subject as determined by its structural position as an absolute—that is, my criticism of the subject rests on the initial possibility of criticizing the mother tongue, on a priority of art over politics, or rather, adumbrating my future position, the dissolution of the traditional political sphere of mass movements manipulated by political leaders. By emphasizing the question of the will's expression (and the formation of consensus), Habermas leaves the supposedly universal structure of the will (in the way a subject's thought pushes towards its expression in the public realm) beyond all possible question (or intervention). Habermas is merely articulating a further guise of selfish nationalism (human internationalism) and agreeing to preexisting (and politically loaded) definitions of the human and reason.

131. In discussing Weber's sociology of religion in the next chapter, I shall attempt to make the development of religious worldviews comprehensible from the aspect of a development of formal world-concepts, that is, as a learning process. In doing so I shall be making tacit use of a concept of learning that Piaget expounded for the ontogenesis of structures of consciousness. As is well known, Piaget distinguishes among stages of cognitive development that are characterized not in terms of new contents but in terms of structurally

described levels of learning ability. It might be a matter of something similar in the case of the emergence of new structures of worldviews. The caesurae between the mythical, religious-metaphysical, and modern modes of thought are characterized by changes in the system of basic concepts. With the transition to a new stage the interpretations of the superseded stage are, no matter what their content, *categorially devalued*. It is not this or that reason, but the *kind* of reason, which is no longer convincing. A devaluation of the explanatory and justificatory potentials of entire traditions took place in the great civilizations with the dissolution of mythological-narrative figures of thought, in the modern age with the dissolution of religious, cosmological, and metaphysical figures of thought. The *devaluative shifts* appear to be connected with socio-evolutionary transitions to new levels of learning, with which the conditions of possible learning processes in the dimensions of objectivating thought, moral-practical insight, and aesthetic-expressive capacity are altered. (Habermas, *The Theory of Communicative Action* [1981], 1:67–68).

132. To be sure, the confusion of nature and culture by no means signifies only a conceptual blending of the objective and social worlds, but also a—by our lights—deficient

found heaviness which is each particular thing before it is named *and* (and what a difficult 'and') the possibility of a meaningful life as a whole. Habermas criticizes Derrida for not keeping science and magic separated. Derrida would be, according to this story, regressing to some primitive mode of thinking—and some correspondingly primitive and mystical mode of politics.[132] Perhaps the mystical element of the most basic moment of experience is precisely what art calls us to think through, albeit without too quickly jumping to a dogmatic conception of a divine substrate for our finite experiences.

The point we have to emphasize is that there is no separation between nature and culture, between unified relations and artifice, no self (writ small or large) immediately present and merely in need of explication or recognition. Further, we cannot say that free interchange of expressible ideas will necessarily safeguard the fundaments of what is good about life nor that it can produce a community where all members see their values reflected in the higher sphere.[133] There will always be hierarchical decisions buried in the way one speaks. The decision to speak always commits one to a slavery and to a set of obligations which are broader than merely a commitment to the individual subject to whom the subject submits (like company loyalty in a company town). Economic thinking—broader than but including the functionalist reason that Habermas criticizes—cannot allow the space of freedom; it has no way of conceptualizing a decision on the part of the individual, only the decision that the average speaker—as determined by the social scientist—would make. Derrida has often been criticized for not having a political stand. Nothing could be more true, but not in the sense of the abrogation of responsibilities which it is often assumed to be. To question the entire category of the political is to begin to question the mother tongue, the inherited violences. This is, for example, the political implication of Derrida's work with educational reform, as well as the sense of his invocation of violence as always necessary for founding the law.[134]

He refuses a politics which can be codified as true in advance because of a claim to universality, to a 'we' which each 'I' more or less approximates. The politics of deconstruction is a politics of freedom, of time. For Derrida, however, the risk remains that he never leaves the aesthetic, that—in his choice of metaphors, his quest for (or against) the metaphors of self-knowledge— he merely reinstitutes the privilege of self (and presence to self) as the space of that knowledge.[135] Here we find a well-known choice between two strategies:

> Taking into account these effects of the system, one has nothing, from the inside where "we are," but the choice between two strategies:
>
> a. To attempt an exit and a deconstruction without changing terrain, by repeating what is implicit in the founding concepts and the original problematic, by using against the edifice the instruments or stones available in the house, that is, equally, in language. Here, one risks ceaselessly confirming, consolidating, *relifting* (*relever*), at an always more certain depth, that which one allegedly deconstructs. The continuous process of making explicit,

differentiation between *language and world*; that is, between speech as the medium of communication and that about which understanding can be reached in linguistic communication. In the totalizing mode of thought of mythical worldviews, it is apparently difficult to draw with sufficient precision the familiar (to us) semiotic distinctions between the sign-substratum of a linguistic expression, its semantic content, and the referent to which a speaker can refer with its help. The magical relation between names and designated objects, the concretistic relation between the meaning of expressions and the states-of-affairs represented give evidence of systematic confusion between *internal connections of meaning* and *external connections of objects*. Internal relations obtain between symbolic expressions, external relations between entities that appear in the world. In this sense the logical relation between ground and consequence is internal, the causal relation between cause and effect is external (symbolic *versus* physical causation). (Habermas, *The Theory of Communicative Action* [1981], 1:49)

133. "The 'we' of the *Phenomenology of the Mind* presents itself in vain as the knowledge of what the naive consciousness, embedded in its history and in the determinations of its figures, does not yet know; the 'we' remains

natural and vulgar because it conceives the *passage* from one figure to the next and the *truth* of this passage only as the circulation of meaning and value" (Derrida, "From Restricted to General Economy" [1967], *Writing and Difference*, p. 275).

134.  G. Ulmer, *Applied Grammatology* (1985), includes an overview of Derrida's commitment to reforming institutions of education and his interest in legal thought can be found in "Force of Law: 'The Mystical Foundation of Authority,'" trans. M. Quaintance, *Deconstruction and the Possibility of Justice*, ed. Cornell et al. (Routledge: New York, 1992).

135.  A risk Derrida is not unaware of. Early on he speaks of Heidegger as on a similar ground:

> It remains that Being, which is nothing, is not a being, cannot be said, cannot say itself, except in the ontic metaphor. And the choice of one or another group of metaphors is necessarily significant. It is within a metaphorical insistence, then, that the interpretation of the meaning of Being is produced. And if Heidegger has radically deconstructed the domination of metaphysics by the *present*, he has done so in order to lead us to think the presence of the present. But the thinking of this presence can only metaphorize, by means of a profound necessity from which one cannot simply decide to escape, the language

moving toward an opening, risks sinking into the autism of the closure.

> b. To decide to change terrain, in a discontinuous and irruptive fashion, by brutally placing oneself outside, and by affirming an absolute break with difference. Without mentioning all the other forms of *trompe-l'oeil* perspective in which such a displacement can be caught, thereby inhabiting more naively and more strictly than ever the inside one declares one has deserted, the simple practice of language ceaselessly reinstates the new terrain on the oldest ground. (Derrida, "The Ends of Man" [1968], *Margins of Philosophy*, p. 135)

For Derrida there is still a place where agency occurs—that is, the space of the page, the (trace of the) activity of the writer. One can't complain that there is no political in Derrida because he shows precisely that the old metaphor of the political (representation/expression) is fundamentally flawed. (Allegorically, and too frequently in practice, the position of the woman, the other, is unspeakable politically.) Where Habermas was privileging the male realm of the political as the site of that agency which determines the validity of representations (originating, like a child, from the private, feminine, world), Derrida is privileging the space of the production of a text over the reception of the text (and privileging such a space over any naive view of the text's simple production, as if it had no need of the field of its being-produced, that is of its writing, and of its character precisely as written). Allegorically, he claims to find a feminine voice but it might be more appropriate to say merely that he has located an agency in the individual writer as anarchic site and not in the structural determinants considered to be behind that writer. The feminine voice, to follow the allegory more closely, would always only be a reader (and individual writers have been individual readers as well). My point would be that politics lies in the political reading and not in the political writing— which is to say I am and am not advocating a Derridean politics. A different tactic is needed.

If I were to try and summarize this strategy, from what we have seen of economics of/as society, I would have to choose to reiterate the position of consciousness that's been developing more or less successfully since the beginning of this book: the ethical stance of a consciousness oriented towards the future, the possibility of ethical consciousness in general, lies in the deferral and displacement of decision which seeks to phrase the urgency of that decision in its deepest instantiation, in its instantiation as a type of desire (as an economy of desire). In the urgency of this thinking, one finds the decision phrased in terms of an ethics, of a way of living towards others, and not in terms of one's self-interest, nor in terms of one's self-expression (or productivity). In this urgency, one accepts, and thinks through, the human consequence of life beyond the simple self-satisfaction of humanism. It thus, and here we are more tenuous, would call for building a society no longer predicated on the always ruthless command from capitalism—from closing the commons to Africa's slavers—that humanity produce, that production be for the benefit of some self.

that it deconstructs. (Derrida, "The Ends of Man" [1968], *Margins of Philosophy*, p. 131)

## ii)             Consider the sister, Dorothy Wordsworth

*For our purposes here, what is important is not just Dorothy Wordsworth's own project to retain for nature the status of an equal, both in her rhetoric and as a theme, but most especially her practicing this project as a part of reading and literalizing or enacting her brother's words. While she would write this way in any case, she also puts her texts at the service of his compelling demand, letting his texts appropriate hers for the completion of their own design (in much the same way that I have suggested maternity is usurped by patrilineal intentions, both historically and, as we shall see in later chapters, textually). And yet, because she enacts his words so much more faithfully than he does himself, she covertly transforms this passive female duty back into her own project, which is, implicitly and intermittently, critical of William's apocalyptic tendencies. Showing him that meaning can take place when both signifier and referent are present, she speaks for the literal nature that is most often silent within his texts. Literalizing his words and being with the literal and speaking a literal language are, as we saw in chapter 1, aspects of the same female history, even though in this case no pointed references to mother- or daughterhood appear: literalization reproduces the literal language of daughterhood, of the mother's continued presence, and to be a woman of any age is always to be in danger of objectification.*

—M. Homans, Bearing the Word

$T$he history of artistic creation has too often been understood as the human fight to transcend natural bounds. The transcendence attributed to art thus becomes something banal on the level of your person living forever in the body of your work. An equally long history has spoken of the transcendence involved in the reception of a piece of art. Against these traditions, we stop short of the conception of transcendence as the overcoming of natural constraint. The failure of the philosophical project of separating universal from particular itself points away from this conception of artistic production—as Derrida and Heidegger show repeatedly. Transcendence, in a certain sense, must be toward the world; the possibility of a 'toward', however—a 'toward' which wouldn't merely be a pointing toward, or a talking about—is what any theory of judging by a subject about a world is going to miss. Transcending must be as a world.

In some sense, the problem of transcendence is what makes the question of literalization interesting for us here. Nature, the literal, needs no transcendence if it merely is (or merely is for us); similarly, to literalize, as a verb, would be nonsensical (nature already is literal). The natural scientist has no need of a sublime or transcending encounter with the world (Sade's heroes, in the same vein, never experience even their own death as anything besides another opportunity for pleasure—a pleasure taken in minute, scientific, description). But once the arrogance of the detached stance of description comes under scrutiny (it is, after all, a formal prejudice to believe in description), we see that some work must be done to say that a particular belongs to a universal (thus the basis of the Kantian aesthetic project). This work, the subsumption proper to judgment, can be taken into account from various methodological approaches. For some, it would appear that the work has already occurred with the language itself; for others, who do not begin with language but who begin with the judgments that form language, the possibility of that work must either belong (as a faculty) to the subject, or must be won by the subject. This latter position, that the possibility of the judgment doesn't originally belong either to the subject or to the language, but is won in a confrontation between the two, characterizes much of the romantic thinking on the matter (and my project is to think along these lines without allowing the violence of a victory of one over the other, not even of the self-assertion that gives the unity of the self privilege over anarchy, not even the self-assertion, or self-affirmation, of knowing yourself to be the one who is asking). Literalization, as opposed to subsumption, is not a judgment (and is not coterminous with the determination, the instantaneity, of the judgment). In that sense, it would not partake in the dichotomy between subject and object; it is not a talking about: transcendence is already announced in the literal itself.[136] Time is, as has long been held, freedom; this freedom, however, does not belong either to the subject who judges or to the economy which allows subjects to be within it. Time exists in being given (nature is transcended toward when, as in a certain literalizing,

136. I am not following Homans here, at least not strictly, although I feel that the suggestion arises with her usage. For Homans, at the broadest level, the literalization comes from women who are unwilling to take up subject-positions of opposition, yet wish to assert something of (not about) the matter at hand. Similarly, my discussion of literalization enacted what I have in mind with literalization in that it took Hegel's formal idea of fulfillment (which is a kind of literalization satisfied with self-reference) and showed how that act of fulfillment depended on a moment other than the self, or its concept. To that extent, it contradicts that which it literalizes, appropriating the metaphor against its own self-conception.

137. This refusal of the moment of decision, the deferral of the instantaneity of the judgment supposedly originating in a subject speaking about a world, is what Derrida points to in *Given Time* as the "necessity of a certain narrative"—indeed the necessity of a poetics of giving in/through literature instead of in and through determinate judgments. Derrida is commenting on Mauss's *The Gift*, and on the question: "What force is there in the given thing that causes its recipient to pay it back?"

> One can translate as follows: The gift is not a gift, the gift only gives to the extent it *gives time*. The difference between a gift and every other operation of pure and simple exchange is that the gift gives time. *There where there is gift,*

one ceases to speak about, describe, or judge and begins to, for lack of a better word, dwell).

In part, and this mirrors the problem of writing, we are already (and have already been) engaged in a dispute which we haven't yet made public. There are contours, surfaces, already available (and there is no completion to those surfaces). For example, the contours I've been able to give to the question of time have only obliquely referenced the space between Heidegger and Levinas. One might want to say that their intersection (they are in contention with each other, but largely creatures of the same tradition) bears fruit for later thinkers; this is descriptively possible, as one might say that a Derrida had come from that intersection, but it is a description whose possibility depends on a distinction between the one describing and the 'Derrida' described. This is how literalization differs from bearing (or being the recipient of) fruit; when a metaphor is literalized, no third person perspective is taken, no judgment is passed about a supposedly exterior object. Instead, the narrative itself is taken on as a question—as a question of what rhythms it supports, what structures it institutes, what style it asks us to enact as its readers/recipients.[137] A story is not a narrative because it has a plot, but because it calls for a plotting, a literalizing, a responding that moves in time with the story, the song, or the poem.

For example, as readers of their works, we see that Levinas and Heidegger do and do not agree. The contours of their agreements and their disagreements form a space (and I'm not sure in what sense that space would be other than time). One does not

appropriate that space as if it were a daughter being offered in marriage (as if time were
one's own to deploy). One lives that space
by literalizing that space—by reading into,
or toward, or as that time/space (literalization is the search for a word that doesn't betray the reading). One must become a
daughter. Such a literalization, as we will be
following out later, depends on the giving of
that conceptual space, in/as time, and not
just as the possibility of time.[138] We will ap-
prove, in a limited sense, of the idea that the
economy precedes the possibility of the
economy—that is, that its givenness 'as' and
the possibility of that givenness are disclosed under regimes of questioning with
fundamentally different orientations: the
question which might unify these opposed
regimes would be based on a particular response to the question of how the freedom
of constitution arises (that freedom, in its
turn, arises from the given economy itself).
Freedom, however, as a subjective attribute,
is the only way to explain the difference between a world of isolated contents and
meaningful living (meaningful living constitutes the possibility of a life filled with contents). I have tried to present this possibility
of time, stylistically, in various ways: the
skewed appropriation of traditional metaphors, the underexplained notes, the long
citations, the frequent moves between discourses, all come together as one might read
the tradition itself, without adhering to the
strict disciplinary lines of today's academic
training, if one were looking for meaning,
for a rhythm, and not just content, in words.

Perhaps, to better access the problem of
the literalization of a thought, we should
embark on a discussion of the (opposing)

*there is time.* What it gives, the
gift, is time, but this gift of
time is also a demand of time.
The thing must not be resti-
tuted *immediately and right
away.* There must be time, it
must last, there must be waiting—without forgetting [*l'at-
tente—sans oubli*]. It demands
time, the thing, but it demands a delimited time, neither an instant nor an infinite
time, but a time determined
by a term, in other words, a
rhythm, a cadence. The thing
is not *in* time; it is or it has
time, or rather it demands to
have, to give, or to take
time—and time as rhythm, a
rhythm that does not befall a
homogenous time but that
structures it originarily. . . .
That is one of the reasons this
thing of the gift will be linked
to the—internal—necessity of
a certain narrative [*récit*] or of
a certain poetics of narrative.
(Derrida, *Given Time: I.
Counterfeit Money* [1991],
p. 41 [my ellipsis; Mauss is
quoted, in a slightly larger
context, on the same page])

138. Saying this already reenacts
the distinction Levinas wants to
make between himself and Heidegger. One problem with merely
referencing Levinas's reading,
however, is that (to my eye, at
least) it isn't particularly fair to
Heidegger's work (this infidelity,
too, has something to do with
the difference between literalization and subsumption/appropria-
tion). Levinas says, in an early
work:

The concept which appears to
preside over the Heideggerian

interpretation of human existence is that of existence conceived as ecstasy—which is only possible as an ecstasy *toward the end*. It consequently situates the tragic element in existence in this finitude and in the nothingness in to which man is thrown insofar as he exists. Anxiety, a comprehension of nothingness, is a comprehension of Being only inasmuch as Being itself is determined by nothingness. A being without anxiety would be an infinite being—but that concept is self-contradictory. The dialectic of being and nothingness continues to dominate Heideggerian ontology where evil is always a defect, that is deficiency, lack of being: nothingness.

We shall try to contest the idea that evil is defect. Does Being contain no other vice than its limitation and nothingness? Is not anxiety over Being—horror of Being—just as primal as anxiety over death? Is not the fear of Being just as originary as the fear for Being? It is perhaps even more so, for the former may account for the latter. Are not Being and nothingness, which, in Heidegger's philosophy are equivalent or coordinated, not rather phases of a more general state of existence, which is nowise constituted by nothingness? We shall call it the fact that *there is*. In it subjective existence, which existential philosophy takes as its point of departure, and the objective existence of the old realism merge. It is

concept of the sublime. The sublime is the aesthetic complement to the sister (insofar as she belongs to a man). Where the exchange of women had founded intersubjective economies, the encounter with the sublime founded the individual's 'personal' economies of desire, imagination, and creativity. It's a little harder to economize on the sublime across various individuals (some may not see a mountain landscape as anything but a potential rock quarry), but that fact merely points to the differences in approach (method, style) that are possible when approaching the question of meaning. By starting methodologically with an individual who (or an individual moment, such as a judgment, which) creates entire worlds, the question of a meaningful, intersubjectively valid, nature becomes difficult (and probably, for that very reason, nature is taken to be a sublime moment for the individual); on the other hand, if we start with an idea of nature (such as the 'nature of exchange'), then an art which is anything other than commentary on nature is virtually impossible.

In relation to the sublime we find that William Wordsworth occupies a somewhat ambiguous position in literary history. It has been argued that the move to modernity in literature was accomplished in the sixteenth and seventeenth centuries as a simultaneous turning inside and out.[139] The story (and here is the rise of the novel) is endowed with a new specificity; no longer inhabited by broadly inclusive and undifferentiated characters ("Man," "Death," "Virtue"), it actually gives the audience the position of irony. That is, because they see the ways that the characters on stage both embody an allegorical commentary on the human condition generally and also live a specifically human set of constraints, the audience is able to see every life as belonging to a set of transcendent concerns (humanity, or for the moderns, the project of becoming truly human) and as being, as individuals, subject to aleatory (and ultimately unimportant, since in some way 'unmeaningful', or 'merely' individual) constraints. One can see these constraints—nature—as elements that mankind has overcome—or, more paradigmatically, more in line with the metaphors, that which man overcomes by the force of a rupturing with the period of childhood innocence (a time protected by a mother's presence), to later come back into a full (and mastering) relation with nature as (incestuous) wife. It is of historical interest that this movement transpired without renouncing the older literary purpose of displaying the exemplary moral individual. The genius of modernity was to have convinced each individual, man and woman, to take on a metaphorically determined role as if it were a destiny—and, in the same instance, in the choosing of a role instead of a life, to break with the conditions of life, as if life itself were only a period of bondage, and as if freedom consisted in the very refusal of life.

Most poignantly, we see this conjunction of metaphors at work in the rise of the importance of authorship and the idea that the moral act *per se* is to express the human. Lear on the Heath is stripped of all but his humanity; Shakespeare's greatness comes in showing what is left. W. Wordsworth belongs firmly to the tradition of the all-conquering mind at the same time that he argues for (glorifies) a sublime nature (the

because the *there is* has such a complete hold on us that we cannot take nothingness and death lightly, and we tremble before them. (Levinas, *Existence and Existents*, pp. 19–20)

In later works, in the essential turn which motivates my stylistic approach, Levinas will approach the 'there is' without merely reversing the categories of anxiety: rather, he will attempt to remove the presumption of the neuter from Being. Such a removal would have to be an addition; the metaphors of *Totality and Infinity*, it seems to me, enact the addition beyond the simple 'there is' of a subject's encounter with a world, enact philosophy as a question of style (even though we are not thereby committed to Levinas's conclusions).

139. Speaking of *Don Quixote,* a fiction often given standing as the first modern novel: "*For the first time the individual case is more than an individual case; the story of an individual bears a supraindividual significance.* Through the fortunes of a single person, or the picture of an individual situation, the chivalric romance points to the general condition of man. In short, the narrative has become *symbolic*" (E. Kahler, *The Inward Turn of Narrative* [1957], p. 49). Our task, and I think there is a strong current of recent literature pointing toward the same problem, is to think literalization without imagining the exemplary individual. Literalization, unlike individualization, is not simply the opposite of the universal— much less its content.

sublime is a spark for the imagination). One would have to argue that this is perfectly consistent with his appropriation of folk rhythms, of ballad forms, while he emphasized nontraditional conceptions of subjective agency—of the creative power of the mind. W. Wordsworth is making the everyday sublime (or at least possibly, poetically, so). This encounter with the sublime frees one from the everyday interpretation of the things of the world; the individual is given the ironic distance with which to view (him)self. The question, for me, would be whether this type of art can actually reach the ironic displacement it claims to if it doesn't explicitly question the structure of representation—the very idea of the exemplary individual. Homans's argument, briefly, is that D. Wordsworth's literalization accomplishes that questioning (even begins an answer), without having to (philosophically) phrase the question. The question as it is given in (not phrased about) literature is really only a marker of what kinds of questions are being asked by my writing: that is, methodologically, do we take ourselves to be the objects of an economy called language, determined by that economy and only free inasmuch as we win within the rules of that economy, or (and this is equally a methodological question, a question of access) are we only free when we have escaped that economy, refusing to play life as if it were merely a game? (Here, in the metaphorical field of brothers and sisters, we see reiterated Antigone and Polynices, playing against and within an economy of violence.)

Dorothy Wordsworth has, until very recently, been represented as merely a mediocre reader of her brother. There has been some acknowledgment of the ways in which she was used by him, but little serious attention to the idea that her contributions couldn't have been as easily provided by any female. Homans implies that she had seduced her brother to her own purposes, but seduction is always the strangest of games—one wins in seduction by giving the other person what he or she wanted, sometimes in the enviable position Lacan described, of "with supply, creating demand," but even then, an odd freedom at best. As I hope is clear, deciding on the characterization of D. Wordsworth's activity (or, perhaps, the refusal to describe it) would depend on the methodological question of freedom; my goal, by complicating the metaphors of sisters within these theories, is to forefront the problem of approaching that question.

For the romantics, nature is that from which you must separate in order to return later as master. This separation is usually violent—like the Oedipal crisis for little boys—and requires the work of the man in order to recapture what was lost. This 'work' takes the form of poetry—the making of symbols, metaphors, allegories, words that speak the unity (the marriage) of man and nature.[140] Man enters thus as the husband, the metaphors speak his order, his

dominations: he loves his wife, she even surprises and delights him, but she does what
he says (her seduction of him consisting in
making him order her to do what she
wanted to do anyway).

A key to postmodernism's growth since
Nietzsche (and especially through Foucault)
is the argument that the work of literalization might be specific enough to undermine
any claim to (or even the need for) a formal
analysis of the work of consciousness. If this
is true, the modern (and structuralist) understanding of exchange (of women, money,
time, etc.) would founder on the inability to
formalize the rules of exchange. I would
have to either marry my twin (and a woman
would never be twin enough for a man) or
constrain (or at least believe in the constraint of) a woman (all women?) to a certain type of functioning. In terms of the
metaphors surrounding the activities of philosophizing, thinking, or creating, we here
touch on the problem of technology: technology works (we see its successes), but it
carries an ideology of control that exceeds
any particular need for control. Sexism, for
our privileged example, is buried in the way
we conceive of the world itself, is part of our
thinking about thinking. One does not
merely stop being a sexist when one returns
home from work, no matter how much we
love our partners.

A poem—art—which does not circulate, which does not validate, which cannot
be appropriated, is sublime. Art, it is said,
gives us our world (or, at least, our ways of
interpreting our world). This giving which is
not exchange is what is at stake in postromantic (which is for the moment synonymous with postmodern) conceptions of

140. And in a complexity (for
my text) that I can only gesture
at, the romantics are here 'literalizing' or enacting (and in that
sense opposed to) Kant's idea of
the sublime and its instituting relationship to the possibility of apperceptive unities (based by them
on a strong reading of the power
of the imagination).

141. So that, even within a
friendly reading, Heidegger becomes something of a believer in
the reified subject: "Because authentic temporality involves a decision and a project that an individual Dasein can make only for
itself and by itself, it is never in
the first instance shared or public.
It is, instead, the temporality of
Dasein as vereinzelt—that is, as
single and individuated and thus
prior to and independent of the
structures of world-time. It is this
individual Dasein that is the true
bearer of authentic temporality;
and from this it seems to follow
that this individual Dasein must
also be the ground of world-time"
(C. Olafson, *Heidegger and the
Philosophy of Mind* [1987], p. 96).
Instead, I would say that time in
Heidegger, as with Husserl, is not
punctual or individuated by
virtue of its appearance within an
internal structure. The decision
character inherent to a project is
not like a positing judgment
which would institute a rule;
rather, as with our participation
in time in general, it is the growing awareness of one's own (always already enacted) participation in the structuring of (which
transcends as) the world.

142. The punctuality of the
event is, for example, explicitly

language. The romantics valorize poetry *won* through the productive activity of great men (geniuses expressing the *Zeitgeist*); Heidegger speaks of poetry as the foundation of the very possibility of the everyday world (the end of genius and of a certain *Geist*). Heidegger approaches the end of a genre of art criticism (an end not taken up) by not appealing to the conjunction of art, nature, the sublime, and the beautiful in his "Origin of the Work of Art." For, with Heidegger, art no longer gives itself as an occurrence—it is not destined to be phrased (as even Lyotard's theory of the sublime would have it) or communicated, or overcome. Art would neither be abyss nor redemption of the abyss. It is not the fruit (of the past) which we take (from some young girl) and eat, but, if anything, our giving of time (or, in Heidegger's language, our shepherding of being) which itself bears fruit (and the fruit itself stops being the central methodological question; the strange 'giving' that is time becomes itself the object of our questioning).

Why? Or, rather, How? Because of a change in methodology, a change that affects how we, as philosophers, readers, or just people, approach the meaningful. It is true—to some extent—that Heidegger is still ensconced in the problems of *Being and Time* (and of authentic temporality) throughout his career—this problem is his debt to phenomenology as a possibility (not yet a method). The key to our entry into this question is the 'not yet' which must already be a method (this being essential to the trajectory of my writing here). Authentic temporality sought to begin from a conception of meaning which was not punctual; however, the possibility of that authenticity was grounded in a confrontation with death (and an aesthetics dependent on the death analysis would probably have referenced the sublime nature of death).[141] The methodological problem, the possibility of approaching the question, moves away from this model of confrontation as early as the Kant book (although the move is somewhat halting) and in his late work temporality is no longer authentic (owned by the individual), but rather, time is thought from out of its event (*Ereignis*). This 'event' is too often interpreted as determining (as a punctual judgment, or appropriation, or at least as an instituting of a 'phrase regimen').[142] Rather, and this is the trail we're following, with art there is no moment of vision, no interpretive framework offered and decided upon, precisely because the time of art isn't dependent on its reception (it depends, rather, on its giving). In this way, it's a problem of approach (of method in a loose sense, but of a method which encompasses the possibility of any meaning at all and not just philosophical discourse) because it asks us where (or how) time (or meaning) is to be found. To say that art expresses something for me (or for any audience) would only be possible from within the methodological presuppositions of a thinking which limits art to its moment within an economy of signs (a given past, or a future constrained to being only a certain combination of past elements).

With this question in mind, it is interesting that 'sublime' is exactly that category which expresses the strange set of unities that constitute the romantic language.[143] We note, first, that the iteration of many of the formal moves we saw with Hegel (notably the quasi-biological elimination or overcoming of pain as the model for meaning), although the sense of time is different (the assumption of an individual starting point—whole communities do not face the sublime moment together) gives us an idea of original/originating time which is essentially individual; exchange, methodologically posterior to the existence of the productive subjects, is made up of individual acts which conform to a model—the essence, as determined by the telos of each act, is communal, but the method remains 'centered' in the subject.[144] What is important for my work here is the move from an encounter with the indescribable towards a particular type of universality which holds for all universals: the most minimal occurrence of presence.

> *Delight*, or the negative pleasure which in contradictory, almost neurotic fashion, characterizes the feeling of the sublime, arises from the removal of the threat of pain. Certain 'objects' and certain 'sensations' are pregnant with a threat to our self-preservation, and Burke refers to that threat as *terror*: shadows, solitude, silence, and the approach of death may be 'terrible' in that they announce that the gaze, the other, language or life will soon be extin-

what Heidegger won't let Fink use to explicate Heraclitus's lightning strike at the beginning of their *Heraclitus Seminar*. One would have to enter into the possible readings of Heidegger's other metaphorical approaches (forest paths, dwelling, even ecstasis) to see in what ways the time of a gifting of Being was nonpunctual, even nondetermining.

143. *Is it happening?* The question can be modulated in any tone. But the mark of the question is "now," *now* like the feeling that nothing might happen: the nothingness now. Between the seventeenth and eighteenth centuries in Europe this contradictory feeling—pleasure and pain, joy and anxiety, exaltation and depression—was christened or re-christened by the name of the *sublime*. It is around this name that the destiny of classical poetics was hazarded and lost; it is in this name that aesthetics asserted its critical rights over art, and that romanticism, in other words, modernity, triumphed. (Lyotard, "The Sublime and the Avant-Garde" [1984], *The Lyotard Reader*, pp. 198–99)

144. And here we could locate Kant's insistence on the teleological in nature. Lyotard, I think correctly, even places the teleology within the methodology which bounces between ideas and judgments, between universals and the individuals which enact, or literalize, them:

> The judge remedies the absence of a universal tribunal,

of a final judgment before which the regimes of knowledge and of freedom can be, if not reconciled (for they will never be reconciled), then at least put into perspective, ordered, and finalized according to their difference. This supplementation is so evidently on the order of a reconciliation between phrases themselves, and not between their referents, that it must be attributed to nature rather than to the world in the Kantian sense. Nature is the object of the Idea of objective purposiveness, and this is in turn called for by reflective judgment in its attempts to account for the singular existences that the lawfulness of a 'mechanically' determined world does not explain. But inversely, if the activity of precise discernment (*Genauigkeit*)—or, in other words, the attention paid to *différends* that is at work in criticism—could assume this function of supplementation through the objective purposiveness of a certain nature, then that activity or attention would itself be a means used by nature to achieve its own final purpose. This purpose must be accomplished by man because he is the only being in the world that is not entirely conditioned. (Lyotard, "Judiciousness in Dispute, or Kant after Marx" [1985], *The Lyotard Reader*, p. 339)

The key, for Lyotard's own work, is taking that purpose to be an injunction to pay attention to the *différends*, to engage in an ever-intensifying critical endeavor, and

guished. One feels that it is possible that soon nothing more will take place. What is sublime is the feeling that something will happen, despite everything, within this threatening void, that something will take 'place' and will announce that everything is not over. That place is mere 'here', the most minimal occurrence. (Lyotard, "Newman: The Instant," *The Lyotard Reader* [1989], p. 245)[145]

Art, *especially* at its most terrifying, would still be a reassurance. Art would take the frightening darkness of night and say, 'still, even the darkness can be represented'. Man's freedom to represent will yet survive each annihilation of man's bodily existence. The 'here' is taken back into the possibilities of the one who confronts the meaningless; time and meaning, for the romantics, are thought in the resolution of the confrontation. Famously, for Rilke in the *Duino Elegies*, "Every Angel is terrifying." And for the romantics, that power of representation, receiving the terrible message which is an angel, is the still ambiguous victory of man over nature, the proof that angels were sent as messages (or messengers) to/for man. Although sociality is usually conceived as more than just reassurance (some nod to the theories of the economic is usually given), the institution of the mere 'here' in sublime art speaks effectively to the space between the individual and the universal—because it speaks the form of giving/receiving meaning in general but from the perspective of the individual encounter. The sublime grants a type of literalization to the metaphor as such that structuralism cannot offer (because of structuralism's orientation towards the abstraction). The various overlays of meaning, as meaningful, partake equally in the human project of giving meaning: the approaching god is not literally a rock, but rather the other way around (and a reference to time is also included: the rock *becomes* as god).

Structuralists (and all other realists), insofar as they are postromantic, would want to claim that it is absurd to speak of an individual expressing private tropes for nature and thereby literally changing a rock into an approaching god (as W. Wordsworth had done). For them, the individual will always remain the mere intersection of certain complexities in past structural formations, an intersection which is ultimately determined by the form appropriate to intersecting in general but which will be initially determined through the particular formal properties associated with each of the intersecting 'complexities'—and, importantly, this contour would be accessible to the observing social scientist. (Many poststructuralists are merely pointing to the inability of a single structure—or, sometimes, of a single 'language game'—to fully specify the individual found at the crossroads. The argument is purely methodological; it is circumscribed by the simple question of what the scientist can know beyond doubt.) The rock has certain structural significations, as unthinking object of nature; and the approaching god has certain structural significations, as the anthropomorphism of the greek gods, and/or the apocalyptic figure of the second coming of Christ (and, of course, many more determinants on both the sides of god and rock). The poetry of a Wordsworth is, then, determined by structures—more or less

not merely (as it is usually taken) as an injunction to describe the world (to appropriate it for the ends of man's narratives, turning the world beyond into our natural world). For Lyotard, a close reading of the Kantian sublime would disclose the antitechnological work of criticism.

145. "Here then is an account of the sublime feeling: a very big, very powerful object threatens to deprive the soul of any 'it happens', strikes it with 'astonishment' (at lower intensities the soul is seized with admiration, veneration, respect). The soul is thus dumb, immobilized, as good as dead. Art, by distancing this menace, procures a pleasure of relief, of delight. Thanks to art, the soul is returned to the agitated zone between life and death, and this agitation is its health and its life" (Lyotard, "The Sublime and the Avant-Garde" [1984], *The Lyotard Reader*, p. 205). This agitation must be lived, for Lyotard, in the différend, in the confrontation between two phrases in abeyance, both waiting for the time in which to be phrased (to be taken into consciousness or given voice); the genre as such rules all possible phrase genres, time is thought in the human confrontation with meaning (which already exists in some definite mode). That is, against Lyotard, the idea of a phrase regimen still depends, methodologically, on the structure of finitude which Heidegger is trying to rethink without the moment of confrontation giving it its structure as confrontational (dwelling isn't

confrontational of itself, and strife—which is a key element in Heidegger's late thinking—is not lived as the confrontation of different modes of dwelling).

determinable of themselves without reference to either Dorothy or William—that lie in the past: for example, the psychoanalytic reading that relates the absent god to an absent father or the materialist reading that sees both significations as determined by modes of production that reify (formalize, universalize) the private character of production. The case would have to be made (and I'm not entering into that particular argument, or its attending style, here) that any theory of judgment (economic or sublime) would eventually (for reasons of the method implied in the structure of judging, especially its determining sense) fall into a more or less punctual, initially private, conception of the production of meaning, even when that production becomes meaningful 'in the visible world'. (Of course, it's true that if we are going to speak of a literalization, or of a project, or of meaning at all, there must be some access to the production of that meaning; the problem is the method of that access.)

There is undoubtedly a truth to the sense in which structural determinants can describe movements in art, history, or individual lives, but they fail to explain the origins of these phenomena unless they can somehow speak to the way in which decisions between systems—all with claims to validity—can be made. I face, after all, the decision to write, the decision of what to write about, the way in which I wish to write. In truth, all of these questions fall back onto the questions of freedom in reading. The sublime explains the giving of this freedom, without ignoring the precedence of the economy, by explaining the punctual break with the economy which makes the individual possible as individual. The importance of this break is what Lyotard sees. Seduction, on the other hand, at least metaphorically, will explain the nonpunctual possibility of this break. Seduction explains the gradual accession to the realm of the symbolic—and the manipulation of those symbols. More polemically: seduction is a concern with appearances which doesn't forget the audience which is being seduced. A concern which refuses to valorize the break, the instantaneity of freedom, as its own good, seduction moves toward the other without forgetting what constitutes the style of its motion.

For the reader, as a structuralist or an economist, a book can be described in terms of its predecessors, but this explanation fails to see the ethical stand at the base of ontology—at the base of that which is—the ethical stand which does not privilege presence abstractly but does see the fact that there is a reason the reader reads (that consciousness is not merely, not even primarily, descriptive). Such an ontology duplicates exactly the position of an Agamemnon who must decide between competing, and equally heinous, claims. The sin comes when he gives up his humanity with his decision—almost cheerfully embracing the sacrifice of his daughter—effacing the fact that it was a human decision with human consequences. The same is true when we buy any product for personal consumption, committing resources to individual enjoyment instead of to another's good. This is the advantage of a theory of the sublime: if we encounter our own need for the voice, for the reassurance of a naming in the dark, then we can see the moral imperative of speaking to others. The problem comes when this speaking, the judgment which gives a present situation its name, is interpreted as the very form of life itself. With such a formal judgment equated with life's processes, and thus determining the time (the now) that is appropriate to life, we are left only with a single possibility of meaning in life—the possibility of articulating a public space (and one should not discard the public in the name of some reified private space—that opposition itself is what we are trying to avoid in approaching the problem of meaning through a certain literalization of a set of more or less traditional, and traditionally abstract, metaphors).

The point of living is not 'life'—we are not compelled to find meaning in a self-description which fits (in the moment of intuition, or judgment, we usually call meaning) into any given set of previous categories. Living is not dependent on a previously structured life.[146] To defer the time of description in favor of the time not yet owned (not even destined for ownership) is to approach meaning in the other—the method of questioning is not merely the question of what is at stake (or what is happening) precisely because the questioning is not directed toward the past (no matter how recent; the present, since Hegel, has been a species of the past) but toward the future, toward a

146. Is not the inescapable fate in which being immediately includes the statement of being's *other* not due to the hold the *said* has over the *saying*, to the *oracle* in which the said is immobilized? Then would not the bankruptcy of transcendence be but that of a theology that thematizes the *transcending* in the logos, assigns a term to the passing of transcendence, congeals it into a "world behind the scenes," and installs what it says in war and in matter, which are the inevitable modalities of the fate woven by being in its interest?

It is not that the essence qua persistence in essence, qua *conatus* and interest, would be reducible to a word-play. Saying is not a game. Antecedent to the verbal signs it conjugates, to the linguistic systems and the semantic glimmerings, a foreword preceding languages, it is the proximity of one to the other, the commitment of an approach, the one for the other, the very signifyingness of signification. (Levinas, *Otherwise than Being* [1974], p. 5)

time 'without me'. The sense of approaching 'the other', then, lies in abandoning the claim to your own time, living in the time which is other than you. Not transcending nature, in your own name, not living the unity of your life as given (as a possibility) in your confrontation with either the sublime or death, but transcending out of yourself, abandoning the pretense of names and the unities they would denote. Literalization, then, is a project lived under another's auspices—which is why the literal, or the natural, must be the subject of seduction (we are here trying to approach the difficult 'toward' of a transcendence which doesn't escape, or merely speak about, its time).

We are chasing a possibility called the other, the question we are asking now is still the methodological question of how to approach approaching. Seduction, in its metaphorical resonances, complicates this question because beyond my interpretations, or my constructions, seduction implies that the true agency lies elsewhere. Seduction, since it isn't (exhausted in) my activity, cannot be the punctuality of judgment (cannot even cause, in any reliable fashion, the true judgment to arise as my, or as any one individual's, possibility), can't even be the merest of instantaneous occurrences of presence that a sublime might be said to institute. Irony, as a complement to seduction, asks again of the one who asks, and of the possibility of that asking (it is still directed toward the self when one ironically confronts art; only in the step toward marriage, toward the woman, or the human insofar as she is not in the economy, is the irony directed away from the self, and toward the other). Irony is a comportment, not an act, although it is a comportment proper to a world whose appearance is essentially seductive (without essential truth; neither good nor evil). No unity can be instituted, no naked truth revealed, from the encounter with seduction, but an ironic displacement may result which refuses the economy, deferring the question of sex (or rape) in order to phrase the question of clothing.

## a)    Irony/Clothing/Seduction

> *Perhaps signs are not destined to enter into fixed oppositions for meaningful ends, that being only their present destination. Their actual destiny is perhaps quite different: to seduce each other and, thereby, seduce us. If such is the case, an entirely different logic would lie behind their secret circulation. Can one imagine a theory that would treat the signs in terms of their seductive attraction, rather than their contrasts and oppositions? Which would break with the specular nature of the sign and encumbrance of the referent? And in which the terms would play amongst themselves within the framework of an enigmatic duel and an inexorable reversibility?*
> —Baudrillard, Seduction

The ironic position of modernity would be something like the moment which precedes doubt (although, admittedly, neither precedes the mere fact of an economy of given things—both arise, in more or less contingent fashion, *from* that givenness precisely as an *approach toward* that givenness). Descartes demonstrates a lack of irony when he boldly moves to question each thing in its turn, certain of the self that questions. Irony is the questioning of self and thus the moment of freedom—"freedom is knowing that your freedom is at stake." The ironic moment is the hesitation which sees that no concrete thing (nor even the form of a thing) is the content and truth of the self. This moment sees the human's advantage over the rock in the use (or creation) of something only equivocally called freedom. Poetry, art broadly speaking, seen from the side of the creator, is the time when the difference between production and creation becomes clear, and the call to creation is answered. This call emanates from an economy; the answer will even be reintegrated into the economy; the asking's destiny, however, is not in the answer, is not in the continual reintegration that defines an economy.

I have my eye on two Wordsworths, but my point of access, my point of control, will be a discourse surrounding and originating in Kant. I cannot write ironically since writing is always a moment of production, always posterior to creation. The possibility of freedom lies in your creative reading—the reader's encounter with the book is the creation of time. Here we find the difficulty of thinking time; its possibility lies after its creation (you must have read before executing a reading; you must be given the time you create). This difficulty re-plays the methodological problem of thinking (or thinking without) the sub-ject and (his) transcendence (towards or from an economy, a tradition, or a habit). Kierkegaard explains the difference between irony and doubt:

> Hence when irony gets wind of the fact that there must be something con-cealed behind the phenomenon other than what is contained in the phenom-enon, this is merely what irony has always been so keen about telling every-body, namely, that the subject feels free, and so the phenomenon never acquires any reality for the subject. The movement is the direct opposite. With doubt the subject constantly seeks to penetrate the object, and his mis-fortune consists in the fact that the object constantly eludes him. With irony, on the other hand, the subject is always seeking to get outside the object, and this he attains by becoming conscious at every moment that the object has no reality. With doubt the subject is witness to a war of conquest in which every phenomenon is destroyed, because the essence always resides behind the phenomenon. But with irony the subject constantly retires from the field and proceeds to talk every phenomenon out of its reality in order to save himself, that is, in order to preserve himself in his negative independence of every-thing. (Kierkegaard, *The Concept of Irony* [1841], p. 274)

To what extent can we identify irony with freedom? Only to the extent, I would argue, that we can separate a question from the economy of its produc-tion. That question need not be the self—the self is only the content of one of the questions that might constitute a separation. For most of the tradition, since the content of an answer is what their methodology has always presup-posed as an end, the unity of an asking, the self, as this unity—a unity capable of receiving and interpreting a corresponding, objective, unity—would be the only possible carrier of irony, its only possible subject. Kierkegaard's religious subjection to the absurd points away from this coherent interpretation of irony, although most of his commentators have tried to construe the inwardness, or irony, of the subject, as redemptive of that unity insofar as they assume that it must lie at the base of meaning. Further, Kierkegaard's understanding of the relationship between humans (exemplified in the two moments, seduction and marriage) points away from the unifying agency of the sublime (or the encounter with the single, absolutely exterior occurrence).

Without too much attention to Kierkegaard's 'own' view, I would like to literalize his metaphorical use of woman, especially in terms of a seduction—precisely because it doesn't involve the 'taking' which might imply that a unified subject (the husband, the couple, or the form of coupling) lies at the base of any possible meaning.

First, it is always important to note, no matter how varied the issues may appear to be, we always stand within narrowly circumscribed questions. It is for religious reasons that "Kierkegaard" (always a pseudonym) leads his life—thus does he constitute his personal search for meaning. The search for meaning is the search for the religious and the meaning of the search is religious (religion literalizes the search). What can we, who did not create our own world, do in the face of its injustice? What do we do after a god has died? My point, before we get to the question of a seduction, or rather as an entry into that question, is that god's death already appeals to the weight of his presence (Christ's crucifixion, for example, seduces us towards faith); our confrontation with death, mine or the other's, does not mark the negative as the site of desire (as seduction's overdetermined play of affirmations, of masks and costumes, proves). Our first task is to ask of the separation from an economy that, as a distancing and not a breaking or rupturing, is no longer a subject's escape from his conditions.

Sartre comments on (and begins by quoting) Jean Genet:

> "I kept moving forward among the same flowers, among the same faces, but I sensed, from a kind of uneasiness that was coming over me, that something was happening to me. The scents and colors were not transformed, yet it seemed to me that they were becoming more essentially themselves. I mean that they were beginning to exist for me with their own existence, with less and less the aid of a support: the flowers. Beauty too was becoming detached from the faces. Every child who passed tried to hold it back, but it ran off. Finally it remained alone, the faces and flowers had disappeared. . . . Strange hell of Beauty." Strange hell, indeed: Beauty does not fill, it hollows; it is the frightening face of Negativity. (Sartre, *Saint Genet* [1952], p. 378)[147]

The problem comes to the fore immediately when we juxtapose this position with Kierkegaard's. Negativity—in Sartre—works as a moment of exchange between subject and object. It can be a product of doubt, an issuance from an encounter with the uncanny. Kierkegaard is speaking to the same moment and pronouncing the withdrawal from exchange, the moment before one

147. Derrida, for example, wouldn't see this 'strange hell' as a negation, approaching instead, the trace, the very possibility of an inscription, before (and not the negation which comes after) symbolization, metaphor, or meaning: "Thus the flower (which equals castration, phallus, and so on) 'signifies'—again!—at least overlaps virginity in general, the vagina, the clitoris, 'feminine sexuality,' matrilinear genealogy, the mother's *seing*, the integral *seing*, that is, the Immaculate Conception. That is why flowers no longer have anything symbolic about them. 'They symbolized nothing.'" (Derrida, *Glas* [1974], p. 47).

148. Baudrillard, for one:

> Is this to be seduction's destiny? Or can we oppose this involutional fate, and lay a wager on *seduction as destiny*? Production as destiny, or seduction as destiny? Against the deep structures and their truth, appearances and their destiny? Be that as it may, we are living today in non-sense, and if simulation is its disenchanted form, seduction is its enchanted form. Anatomy is not destiny, nor is politics: seduction is destiny. It is what remains of a magical, fateful world, a risky, vertiginous and predestined world; it is what is quietly effective in a visibly efficient and stolid world. The world is naked, the king is naked, and things are clear. All of production, and truth itself, are directed towards disclosure, the unbearable "truth" of sex being but the

commits oneself to a course. Faced with too much, Kierkegaard still knows that productive power rests elsewhere. Faced with everything, Sartre says productive agency rests with the subject—as negating—who can never get enough. For Sartre, you are infinitely free but there is no (or rather, there is only a vanishing moment of) choice because the freedom isn't actual until after you're committed to the course. Kierkegaard understands that the commitment is irrational (other than rational; other than self-productive) but sees that energy is *separable* from commitment and from success—one may fail the task; one may do wrong. This idea of commitment is central to the entire edifice of existentialism but is subsumed under the rubric of predetermined actions in most structuralist thought. The distastefulness of having to embrace this absolute predetermination, perhaps, partly explains the recent turn toward theories of seduction.[148] If irony throws the subject back on the self, doubt places all objects, including the self, under erasure.

Kierkegaard, since he doesn't doubt, does not begin with objects from which Beauty can be detached, but with agencies to which a separate living can be ascribed:

> As soon as desire awakens or, more correctly, in and with its awakening, desire and the object are separated; now desire breathes freely and soundly, whereas before it could not draw its breath because of that which was desired. When desire has not awakened, that which is desired fascinates and captivates—indeed, almost causes anxiety. The desire must have air, must

find escape; this occurs through their being separated. That which is desired shyly flees, bashful as a woman, and the separation occurs; that which is desired vanishes *et apparet sublimis* [and is seen aloft] or in any case outside desire. (Kierkegaard, *Either/Or* [1843], 1:76)

What attracts me to the juxtaposition of these two quotations, at least initially, is how similar they appear to be. In a mime of this similarity, an enactment of that space, we subtract the quotations from their context in order to ask a slightly different question. 'Negativity', or at least its 'frightening face', acts as a sublime in Sartre, but as a sublime which doesn't depend on the activity of the unified self who views from afar (it stands opposed, like nature in itself). Similarly, in Kierkegaard's example, the 'desired', which rather literally can take on the proportion of the sublime 'aloft', escapes the economy (of subjective presencing) within which it had first appeared. The difference I would want to emphasize is in terms of the metaphors. The beauty which detaches from faces runs, in terms of the style of the metaphor, exactly contrary to the trajectory of an abstraction called 'the desired' as it assumes the form of a (bashful) woman. The woman here is not the token of a type; she is the other subjectivity which executes the withdrawal; as agent (outside desire, outside the subject's domain) she shows the one who chases the irony of the chase. The key, however, is that she too was born of the economy: born as the site from which the economy is inconceivable (because, unlike Beauty, she exceeds her expressions within the economy to the extent that she literally has other possibilities

most recent consequence. Luckily, at bottom, there is nothing to it. And seduction still holds, in the face of truth, a most sibylline response, which is that "perhaps we wish to uncover the truth because it is so hard to imagine it naked." (Baudrillard, *Seduction* [1979], pp. 180–81 [with which he concludes the book])

149. Derrida explains his appropriation of Heidegger in terms of
the inconceivability of the naked:

—Well, if, along with the
frame and the column, clothing is for Kant an example of
a *parergon*, in its aesthetic representation, and if then what
is proper to representation is
the "nude," then where shall
we classify certain "old shoes
with laces"? Do they not have
as the "principal" subject this
time *the parergon*, all by itself,
with all the consequences that
follow from that? A *parergon*
without *ergon*? a "pure" supplement? An article of clothing as a "naked" supplement
to the "naked"? A supplement
with nothing to supplement,
calling, on the contrary, for
what it supplements, to be its
own supplement? How would
the shoes relate to the "naked"
thing, to the "nude" and the
"remainder" we've just been
talking about? And yet, in another sense, we just said that
they were "naked," we saw
them quite naked. Is it by
chance that the vestimentary
"metaphor" comes so easily to
Heidegger, when he wants to
think of the thing "pure and
simple"? 'This "naked" (*bloss*)
does however mean the stripping (*Entblössung*) of the
character of usefulness (*Dien-
lichkeit*) and of being made.
The naked thing (*blosse Ding*)
is a sort of product (*Zeug*) but
a product divested (*entkleidete*)
of its being-as-a-product.
Being-thing then consists in
what still remains. But this remainder (*Rest*) is not properly
determined in itself. It

that do not belong to her present form; she
literalizes possibilities, and futures, other
than mine, not meant to be mine).

This becomes a question of clothes, of
externalities, of a presentation which is no
longer 'for' the self. For the purposes of descriptive science, we can abstract from any
particular perception insofar as it partakes of
a closed set of possible perceptions—allegorically, there are a finite (though large)
number of different clothes that a woman
may wear, the naked body still being essentially the same.[149] Doubt sees that there
must be a naked thing; irony finds the
power resident in the effects, in the clothes
and not the nudity, in the seduction and not
the fucking. (And our task, in later sections,
will be to also ask even of the necessity of
this power, or of that questioning, including
that which begins from seduction, which
references only power.) This has profound
implications for our possible methods for
approaching questioning itself. We deny the
object its reality not because we believe ourselves to be the origin of all reality, but (side-
stepping the question) because we believe
that the self is something other than the site
of reality's appearances. Reality (the true) is
not the point of the subject's existence (and
religiosity isn't reducible to its appearances,
or its confessions of belief). Methodologically, a theory of seduction already denies
any solipsistic starting point since it finds
the power beyond the subject, yet it asks no
questions which naively subtract the subject
from the appearances. Our problem, again
as a methodological problem, is to ask with
whom seduction gains its effects (that is,
with the seducer or the seduced). The maintenance of the ideal priority of seduction

over any actually achieved completion rests on a strange complicity between seducer and seduced: they must agree on the supremacy of the moment over any exterior goals—they must forge an agreement concerning contraception, the completeness of the moment itself, the denial of reproduction, or the refusal of a future beyond the given bodies:

> A spirit, an apparition, is reproduction;[150] this is the secret implicit in the coming again. But Don Juan is capable of everything, can withstand everything, except the reproduction of life, precisely because he is immediate, sensate life, of which spirit is the negation. (Kierkegaard, *Either/Or* [1843], 1: 113)

Don Juan, the seducer, does not represent the completion of Kierkegaard's thought, nor even the simple dialectical opposition to Hegel's familial model. Rather, the seducer metaphorizes a way of phrasing the question of the external and the desire for the external. In another metaphorical register, asking the same question, we ask why God would become a man, or why an individual's thoughts would become words. Our answer, in large part, is that thoughts are not other than words, insofar as they exist, yet reach beyond words, when (as in seduction) someone else may yet say something different. The indetermination of the other's future is the methodological problem which leads Kierkegaard to his faith and the absurdity of its leaps. Our attempts here, since we are not committed to the ideal of meaningful self-fulfillment that Kierkegaard still followed, lead toward finding meaning

remains doubtful (*Es bleibt fraglich*) whether it is along the road (*auf dem Wege*) of a subtraction of all product-like characteristics (*alles Zeughaften*) that the being-thing of the thing comes in general to appear. A subtraction (of the being-product) will not restitute the "remainder" to us as a "naked" thing. The remainder is not a naked thing. We have to "think" the remainder otherwise. (Derrida, *The Truth in Painting* [1978], p. 302)

"It symbolizes nothing"—the remainder is not the negation a subject would wield against an object, but a trace, an affirmation, or a giving, which was not of the order of the economic. The metaphoric use of a word (such as 'woman') would depend on the possibility of a remainder (of an 'originary' affirmation) which was other than the stripping away of the literal significations.

150. The translators footnote Hegel at this point:

> The simple identity of the universal subjectivity of the Notion with itself, the sentient creature—which in the sphere of spirit is the ego—is sensibility; if an other is brought into contact with it, it transforms this directly into itself. The particularity, which in sensibility is at first only ideally posited, receives its due in irritability, where the activity of the subject consists in repelling the other with which it is in relation. Irritability is also sensation,

subjectivity, but in the form of relation. But whereas sensibility is only this negative relationship to the other, reproduction is this infinite negativity of transforming what is outside me into myself, and myself into externality. Only then is universality real and not abstract—developed sensibility. Reproduction passes through sensibility and irritability and absorbs them; it is thus derived, posited universality which, however, as self-producing, is at the same time concrete singularity. It is reproduction which is first the whole—the immediate unity-with-self in which the whole has at the same time entered into relationship with itself. (Hegel, *Philosophy of Nature*, p. 358)

151. A word cannot be separated from meaning. But there is first the materiality of the sound that fills it, by which it can be reduced to sensation and musicality such as we have defined it: it is capable of having rhythm, rhyme, meter, alliteration, etc. And a word detaches itself from its objective meaning and reverts to the element of the sensible in still another way inasmuch as it is attached to a multiplicity of meanings, through the ambiguity that may affect it due to its proximity with other words. It then functions as the very movement of *signifying*. Behind the signification of a poem which thought penetrates, thought also loses itself in the musicality of a

in the approaching itself, an approaching which is only characterized as absurd because it is neither mine nor the world's—because it is the future not yet given, yet already spoken toward, or invoked.

So why speak of the erotic at all? Simply, it's because time (in any of its modes) does not exist abstractly as negation, but as the always filled (sensuous) moments of a time which has been "destined" to have meaning—importantly, not one which has the particular meaning, or particular content, already decided, but a time which is open to the meaning, which allows a set of resonances beyond that which can be named—which is why music is the perfect expression of seduction and poetry the language of the ethical, of proscriptions, of the meaning of music, the importance of the music.[151] Music depends on a time of unfolding which may even escape the reference to the space of its production. The materiality of Christ enables him to mediate between the finite and the infinite; if he had been only a sound, he would have been purely finite, without meaning, yet all the more (the occasion for the approach of the) divine. The importance of music is that the term "sensuous existence" must be taken as a transitive, an active, verb which designates the particular moment of a particular constitution as a continual becoming.

Don Juan is something of a caricature of Hegel in Kierkegaard, although, as we saw with the quotation above, he is also Hegel's opposite. Seduction stands opposed to reproduction, refuses the family as paradigm, the child as purpose. But Hegel, too, is a seducer to the extent that he privileges an idea (and the progress of an idea) over the sensuous given. In that sense, seduction stands against the content of an individual event—seduction cannot encounter love in the individual.[152] In terms of our longer trajectories, seduction would be something of a bid to replace the idea of the sublime (or the religious) without resorting to the solipsism which makes every encounter with the sublime into an individuating event. One's sister, a human in general, cannot be taken as sublime unless she seduces the viewer (that is, unless she transcends the mere objectivity of a token within an economy). This enormously complicates the simple model of Don Juan as a seducer who operates as he wishes (or of Hegel as a father who has children who resemble him). When we withdraw, methodologically, from the male perspective, it becomes difficult to think of a sublime encounter with the other at all: as we saw with Antigone, the woman is doing 'work' here as well (albeit, not productive). Neither the moment of completion in the ejaculation nor the fateful glance of the seduction constitute the privileged moment from which meaning could be said to originate. This indeterminism doesn't lie in the fact that there has never been an original moment (has anyone really claimed there was such a moment?) but because the seduction is the work of another (and this equally for sexual relations and for the manipulation of advertisements). Since that work isn't reducible to its intention, with its desire for completion (as we saw with Derrida, but which reaches a different category of deferral when read metaphorically in terms of a sister's appropriations),[153] we have no formal access point to the meaning of that work. The ethical question, which a

poem, which has nothing to do with objects and perhaps varies solely in function of what thought sets aside, what it liberates itself from. Modern poetry, in breaking with classical prosody, has nowise given up the musicality of verse, but has sought it at a greater depth. (Levinas, *Existence and Existents* [1940–45], p. 54)

152. When one reflects on Greek love, it is according to its concept essentially faithful simply because it is psychical; and it is something accidental in the particular individual that he loves many; and with regard to the many he loves, it is again accidental every time he loves a new one; when he loves one, he is not thinking of the next one. Don Juan, however, is a downright seducer. His love is sensuous, not psychical, and according to its concept, sensuous love is not faithful, but totally faithless; it loves not one but all—that is, it seduces all. It is indeed only in the moment, but considered in its concept, that moment is the sum of moments, and so we have the seducer. (Kierkegaard, *Either/Or* [1843], 1:94)

Baudrillard's approach to seduction rests exactly on the lack of reference within the form of encounter which is made possible by a self-seduction of signs. One may try to reinstate the moment of reference, but only at the cost of abandoning the coherence of the system (thus Kierkegaard's leaps). Or one may abandon the search for a reference (as with Baudrillard). The either/or of this dichotomy seems to rest on the poverty of the metaphor—or rather the method of its interpretation—since the opposite of seduction need not be rape: another alternative to seduction is being seduced. For Kierkegaard and Baudrillard, by virtue of their starting points, one can only be seduced by virtue of those categories which already belong to your constitution (advertisements play off of previous advertisements that had themselves already constituted the possibility of a desire, etc.). What remains for us, with a different thinking of the advent of exteriority (what Levinas thematizes in the face), is to think the immediacy of expression without the (self-)reference to the economy.

153. Derrida often refers to questions of the sister within his texts, defending her from naive appropriations, usually. However, the deferral I wish to accent here stems not from the lack of a virgin space called the sister, but from the positive possibility of a future which is neither virgin nor whore (neither mine nor the other man's): a space which would be transformed, gradually and anarchically, through her literalizations.

seducer cannot ask without abandoning the abstractions proper to the activity of seduction, avoids this aporia since it doesn't ask about the self (or my owned structures of meaning): the ethical reaches out to be another's creation, to live another's meaning. We will have to follow this more thoroughly later.

Seduction in Baudrillard becomes a bid for greater control, a gamble where everything is regained because the bet has been unreserved. The seducer's relation to the circle of meaning is thus ontological and not ethical. He sees the negative of the object, the ironic move beyond the immediate individual existence of the particular circle as the move which acquires the truth of the circle as a universal, followed by the addition of the particular determined content (the father's son) as a permanent, reproducible acquisition—thus the Hegelian reading. The move that denies ethics is the initial separation of knowing. The aesthetic validity of marriage lies in reproduction, not in the sense of producing children—although that allegory is what Levinas uses under the rubric of fecundity—but in the iterability of the sociality of the two. This sociality—and not an abstract desire of masculine for feminine—is the ground of the ethical as erotic, of the face as the exterior face of being (the third institutes a different kind of ethical question). People commonly credit childbearing with the end of selfishness; you can no longer live solely for personal enjoyment; others depend on you. Yet, of course, many of the most selfish, irrational, and even cruel acts have been performed in the name of looking out for the children—for just one example, the various cruelties inflicted on

HIV-positive children trying to attend school, but it might be even better to look at the basic spending decisions of (and justifications built around) a 'typical' first-world family as it excludes children from other families. The Immigration and Naturalization Service, for example, is said to be 'protecting our children' in its often cruel 'policing' of our border with Mexico. Given such serious reservations, we still need to follow the allegories of woman and family to see more precisely where they break down.

Ethics resolves into the question of the Mother (my next major section). This occurs on two fronts: (1) (for political reasons) the mother (as typified) is presumed to love her children without regard for her own projects (or any sense of the child's worth as a particular human being), and (2) (psychologically and ethically) the mother represents the bare fact that, before you, the active agent and (male) subject of philosophy, there was still something, even if indeterminate and undefined. Interestingly, the second point contradicts the first since it suggests a connectedness of projects which would make the idea that anyone merely gives up her (or his) own project nonsensical (precisely because projects are not individuated; giving up a project in favor of another's is all one ever does; the question concerns, simply, how abstract that other is). The mother, according to the second metaphor (and against the first), initiates the child into the realm of ethics not because she represents the continuation of the universal, unconscious laws of society, but because she obliges the child to be. Further, because she wills within a contextualized whole, the obligation that the child inherits also rests within a context. Or, more allegorically, the child of a mother has been given life in its plenitude (its obligations and already existent hierarchies) and is not even allowed to steal it.[154] I hope we've already approached abandoning the first model of ethics (regarding women), although I recognize that we are not in a position to fully appreciate the subtlety of the second thinking of obligation. In the section devoted to mothers we will be examining more carefully the sense of an obligation which precedes the subject, but our first task is to complete the question of sisters.

I started by emphasizing a sister's metaphorical alliance with the idea of an economy that rules the possibilities of meaning. It seemed to me that as a controlling point in the economies of desire the sister carries a strong disruptive sense of (at least possible) infidelity (a seduction of me or of someone else). Literalization, I had hoped, caught a little of this sense of an unregulated reproduction of meaning without digressing into one of the various conceptions of time as an instantaneous occurrence (without being, for example, a violent counterthrust). Exteriority is related to the work of others, we may say along with Hegel and Marx, but (contrary to their thinking) exteriority is not explicable in terms of the self-interested (albeit endlessly multiplied) intentions

154. Sartre's virtue here being that he sees the problem of method resident within the question of freedom: if we are going to speak of freedom, it must include the question of for whom the freedom can be used.

And so with Genet: he keeps going; if he stops for a moment, he will remember that he is dead. . . . He dedicates himself to life; he enters it as one enters orders. . . . In any case, the die is cast. Genet is a thief, the girls will be deflowered. Since they are unable to escape the future in store for them, all they can do is refuse to *undergo* it. Sentenced to death, they demand the right to give the order to fire that will kill them. Since men's contempt is inevitable, it must be provoked. A newcomer who does not know who I am is friendly to me. There is no time to lose. Any minute now people are going to start nudging him and putting him on guard against me. I've got to steal his watch or his money right away in order to disappoint his friendly feeling for me, so that he will learn *from me* that I'm a monster. This eagerness to discourage reciprocity will be called sneakiness, treachery. *We* know that it is *dignity*. (Sartre, *Saint Genet*, pp. 56–58)

Unfortunately, no dignity will accrue to Genet, since

(b)efore even dreaming of rebelling, he has already granted them the essential: that he is a thief and that theft is disgraceful. After that,

that supposedly caused the work to be done. Why? Because literalization is not self-interested work. Presence, the process of bringing the literal to its minimal appearance, is not oriented in its completion (its being spoken), but in its being spoken toward. To literalize, in the sense of our metaphors, must involve a seduction oriented toward the literal, because it must have always been a possibility inherent to the woman who was supposed to be bearing the children. The gradualness of the process of literalization, prior to taking on any specific project, is what we need to think through before leaving the question of sisters in order to take up the question of mothers.

## b)   Obligation or event

*Here there is a kind of question, let us still call it historical, whose conception, formation, gestation, and labor we are only catching a glimpse of today. I employ these words, I admit, with a glance toward the operations of childbearing—but also with a glance towards those who, in a society from which I do not exclude myself, turn their eyes away when faced by the as yet unnamable which is proclaiming itself and which can do so, as is necessary whenever a birth is in the offing, only under the species of the nonspecies, in the formless, mute, infant, and terrifying form of monstrosity.*

—*Derrida, "Structure, Sign, and Play,"*
Writing and Difference

There yet remains the question of politics. Sartre spends a lot of time after World

War II working on the assertion that existentialism and Marxism are complementary. This is true for Sartre because of his belief in the efficacy of the Hegelian dialectic—the determinate negation as founding principle of both self and society (insofar as both are externalities). His turn toward Marx, however, is mediated by a strong methodological doubt: one must begin with the moment of determination as an individual's (or, as he calls it in his *Critique of Dialectical Reason*, a totalization). The individual vanishes into this moment (is nothing besides this moment) as the determinations come into being through the determining (or totalizing) act. To that extent, Sartre has taken a certain thinking of the world (and its meaning-structures) to an extreme by positioning freedom (the faculty of determination) at the methodological base of his analyses. The methodological complaint I would bring against Sartre in this context stems from Levinas's questioning of freedom: that is, as we have seen in the discussion of economies, the proper methodological access to the economy comes from the deferral of participation, the gradualness of entry (both of which question the freedom that makes the economy possible; the questioning, which is where the immediacy lies, is more important than the possibility of questioning; the ethics precedes the ontology). In other words, even if, ontologically, the situation, or event, is determined from the exercise of a freedom, the priority of freedom (in terms of the method of approaching these questions) can only arise from a schema which finds meaning to be its own end, which finds the situation, and the description of the situation, to be sufficient

his revolt is doomed to impotence and his most heinous crimes will merely justify the prison cell which they are preparing for him. Let him pillage, let him kill, he will provoke only one comment from his judges. "I predicted as much." Does he steal more often than he would have if he had not been converted? Even that is not certain. He was condemned to theft, he would have stolen out of fear, out of resentment, out of confusion, out of bewilderment, out of need. Only one thing has changed, the inner meaning of his pilfering. (Ibid., p. 58) as questions. The Levinasian question of the other, at several levels, contests the self-sufficiency of the type of questioning which is satisfied with an answer (a determination of the moment 'as' meaningful). The question may emerge from the economy of thoughts (meanings, representations); it need not be destined for an answering that replays that economy. Our task, then, is to think through a type of anarchy which is not merely the disconnectedness of moments in time (each totality, like a monad, existing unto itself), but which thinks through the breaks in the economy, through the necessity of those breaks. This necessity, as I've been trying to develop it, comes from a structure of time which denies the instantaneity of the judgment, or of the determination—not because there are too many terms to resolve with our calculus, but because the future does not belong to me any more than the present is my representation. The face is the external, is the origin of meaning; this fact, taken methodologically, leads us away from the very question of meaning (and of who owns the meaning).

Once we have come to doubt that the formation of the self is correctly described (we are doubting the efficacy of pure description) as an economic relation within a society, once we have questioned representation as a model of consciousness, once we have doubted that the natural voice of the people finds expression (comes to consciousness) through their chosen representative and becomes the truth of government (or literature), then the need to think all levels of social formation over again becomes apparent. We do not abandon description, we merely find that description has its place only by virtue of a previous possibility of questioning which the tradition has systematically ignored: a questioning which Levinas suggestively calls ethics.

In brief, and recapitulating my earlier sections, the Hegelian assumption insofar as politics is concerned is that energy leads to truth (since the truth is the form this energy takes, as negation). This truth is not known as truth until it is recognized in a universalizing moment. Marx is perfectly Hegelian when he expects the proletariat to recognize their common oppression and rise up as a class. The belief of a certain Marxism was that the elimination of the material conditions of oppression would concomitantly eliminate all other oppressions. The mistake, it seems, is that one thus criticizes material forms of oppression (not having access to the products of a consumer-oriented society) and not the violence implicit in negation as representation (the alienation of the thinking subject from the concrete nexus, the responsibility, of knowing).

Internationally, we can no longer think of the grand opposition between Marxism and Capitalism (never a tidy division, after all, even before the demise of the Soviet Union): both have proven to be technological, bureaucratic monsters beyond the control of humanity (beyond those subjects which they had created and called human). We are left, generally, with the political apparatus of the Enlightenment—the nationalism (which is the immediate end of all the theories of recognition of self and community) of the modern state. We can say that this apparatus itself belongs most broadly to the history of will-to-truth as will-to-power. To know something is tantamount to controlling it; exteriority is necessary for knowledge; all aspects of life, as exteriorities, fall under the ever-broadening grasp of the public sphere (whether that sphere wears the name tag of a government or of a multinational corporation is only relevant to the limited extent that these institutions are in competition).

Further, the apparatus that creates itself as a knowing subject—say a bureaucracy—determines, transforms, and creates its object (like any subject that grasps an object). Thus the assumption that there is a legal redress for every ill creates a judicial system that further enforces the belief in legal recourse. That this permeates every strata of U.S. society, far beyond the actual courtroom, is much commented on, but it would be more appropriate (because of a yet greater scope) to point to how our epistemological assumptions are reflected in the judicial system. In the courtroom, two antagonistic claimants—both in possession of certain rights, now in conflict as rights, submit their claim to an external authority. In fine, it is based on a theory of conflict—and it is based on the myth (or regulative ideal) that the judge can escape the circle of knowing in a moment of disinterest, discarding all previously acquired prejudice. Epistemologically, we believe every enigma can be solved if we fight vigorously enough to push ourselves out of the circle where the truth resides. The broadening view (and capitalism is still expanding) which conceives of every member of society as more or less in conflict with every other, possessors of contradictory rights to scarce resources, leads to the legalistic thinking of isolated individuals at war with society, unwilling to help others, unable to see any reason to help someone who has nothing to offer in return.

Heidegger's politics, at least where I would want to expand on them, lie in his rejection of this model of knowledge. Heidegger used the word Dasein, a common German word for that which is, for existence, in *Being and Time* at the places where one expected to see a reference to the knowing (or judging) subject. It is the difference I have been pointing to, allegorically, between being a circle and apprehending a circle. His analysis is descriptive. To see a circle from the outside would merely be to belong to a larger circle; instead, confronting our finitude, we should face the task of thinking the apparatus of the circle itself. A first approximation of Heidegger's criticism of Hegelianism is found in the fact that there is no absolute outside of the circle, outside of time, from which one identifies an absolute center, a goal or a purpose.[155] The lack of an absolute center is, eventually, what forces Heidegger to rethink Dasein in

155. "That which transcends is, of course, *Dasein*; but what it transcends is not some sort of partition between subject and object. It is rather, Heidegger claims, entities as such. This may make it sound as though Heidegger were replacing an epistemological concept of transcendence by a theological, rather than an ontological, alternative, but that is not the case. For what lies beyond entities is not God, but the world; and Heidegger says that it is toward the world that *Dasein* transcends entities" (F. Olafson, *Heidegger and the Philosophy of Mind* [1987], p. 68).

156. This is part of what I was already pointing to earlier, but more explicitly, and as an important example, Baudrillard wants to oppose the idea of a rule to that of a law. The law would be that which establishes a line of transgression, while the rule would only belong to a game. One could merely quit the game, and the rules would not indicate the repressed existence of any hidden discourse or depth since all the rules would be known as such. See esp. Baudrillard, *Seduction* [1979], pp. 131–32. The indeterminism of meaning, however, does not stem from the rule's lack of a destination, nor even from the overdetermination of too many destinations. The indeterminism arises, repeatedly, from the breaks in the system which are constituted by others' intrusions against the system's smooth operation. (Philosophically, methodologically, we are asking: Why would one militate for a new rule?) The break may

terms of the abundant and not of the determinate negation (or, more broadly, not in terms of the process of production).

My purpose in writing here is largely to demarcate the type of postmodernism (the urgency of leaving a modern trajectory of thought) that Heidegger's rethinking of the methodological problems of approaching meaning implies (by my reading, both Levinas and Derrida are taking up this methodological clue—and I again apologize for abusing a word like 'method' in a context where it obviously can only serve as a very clumsy marker for an only vaguely delimited type of question). It is very different from a celebration of diversity in the name of multiplicities of worlds or cultures. It refuses the question of culture. As postmodern, I believe, it would also doubt the efficacy of moves (like Baudrillard's) which would merely doubt the telos of meaning without questioning the circularity (and the constant reinstitution of the circularity) of meaning's self-referentiality.[156] One may recognize the necessity of a circle without embracing its circularity; one may question why one is there (inside) at all.

There is still the question of politics. A postmodernism need not retire from the field of politics merely because it denies the transcendent importance of the political question. Levinas's ethical questioning, in fact, calls for a rethinking of the political from ethical grounds. In a similar fashion, Heidegger's work on technology, far from being antitechnological, delimits technology's control in the name of a new (poetic) approach to Being (one which is no longer controlled by meaning's descriptive telos).

Some recent commentators have tended

to reduce Heidegger to holding a slightly modified Hegelian position. By this analogy, Hegel's variation on Kant (taking subject-centered structural determinants of presencing activity—as in Kant—and showing how these structural determinants rely in fact on a previous present determined by the supra-subjective constellation of being) is echoed in Heidegger's turn from Husserl. The difference, for these commentators, is that where Hegel's conception of historical progress allowed him to make a political critique of existing conditions, Heidegger's conception of an anarchic time, events separated from an originary (historical) institution, disables any possible political critique.[157] This reading of Heidegger is anything but glib, but I wonder if it is still relying on a separation between the ethical and political (traditionally, the individual subject's determining structures and the larger societal or linguistic structures which determine the individual's structures) that Heidegger himself doesn't necessarily make. In brief, if the political is inseparable from the ethical, and the ethical is more than the rule-governed behavior of duties and rights, then the discussion of the structures of an event are political discussions. Likewise, if the particular is inseparable from the universal, if the apple is fruit, then the discussion of the particular is—directly—the discussion of the universal.

Levinas complains, of all of Heidegger's work, regardless of periodization, that it represents an ontology, a description of what is, and not an ethics. He wants to say that there is a fundamental difference between the obligation to be and the resoluteness of Dasein. A decision on the ethical character of resoluteness as a category would require a

find itself articulated as either law or rule, may be reabsorbed into the system or discarded, but the break was never intended to be the system (or part of it): the other is the origin of meaning only as the point wherein meaning can no longer find its own justification. To that extent, his descriptive explanation of the signs' indeterminacy (their mutual seductions) must be interpreted as the result of an ethical problematic (as with Levinas) and not as the result of a choice of regimes (between various rules or games, for example).

157.  For example:

A certain disinterest in mankind's future is evident not only in this conception of place, but also in the conception of time required for understanding today's context as potentially anarchic. An anarchic economy would be one in which thinking and acting espouse the fluctuations in the modalities of presencing. It would be an economy in which the only standard for everything doable is the event of mutual appropriation among entities. It follows that the temporality of that event is no longer to be understood—can no longer be understood—from man's viewpoint. As a place, Ereignis is as irreducible to epochal stamps (Heidegger's second period) as it is to man's projected world (first period). As time, it is irreducible to aletheiological history (second period) as it is to ecstatic temporality (first period). If "destiny" is to designate no more than the epochal determination by retrospective categories—if, in other words, destiny is eschatological—then the event itself has neither history nor destiny. It is "a-historical (ungeschichtlich), or better, without destiny (geschicklos)." Not that the event is atemporal: its temporality is the coming-about of any constellation of thing and world. In such coming-about the preeminence of the future that characterizes ecstatic time as well as aletheiological-historical time is preserved (event as advent). But it is obvious that this originary coming-about of any relation between thing and world differs from the original coming-about of an age just as the 'soundless' play 'without consequences' differs from any inaugural founding deed. These are but two ways of stating the temporal difference between the event as condition and all economies as the conditioned. When Heidegger envisages an 'entry into the event', i.e., a post-modern economy whose only time structure is the originary, he trusts that the event could become our sole temporal condition, one without principial overdeterminations. The crisis he tries to think is not, then, a founding one. Today's destinal break is rather a disseminating crisis. In this sense, the temporality of the event puts an end to the effort to know and decide what the principles of the

close textual analysis and decide only where the note should properly point to its father. Instead, let us note that an ethics preceding ontology—from which ontology is founded—is the issue I have been referring to as the extended/extending moment of freedom: the woman who is not yet married, but no longer a daughter. There may be a hesitation but a commitment is still required; it is impossible not to be. This is far removed from the claim that all ethics must be added on to a political system as the rules for regulating exchange—ethics is decided without recourse to a theory of rights, prior to any theory of rights, always questioning the existing configuration of rights. Levinas is arguing for the priority of an ethical question; he, like Heidegger, is working from within the circle of meaning, but, explicitly against Heidegger's death analysis—Levinas is reaching towards the passivity of meaning, and the structure of that passivity as an obligation:

> The impossibility of escaping God, the adventure of Jonas, indicates that God is at least here not a value among values. (I pronounce the word God without suppressing the intermediaries that lead me to this word, and, if I can say so, the anarchy of his entry into discourse, just as phenomenology states concepts without ever destroying the scaffoldings that permit one to climb up to them.) The impossibility of escaping God lies in the depths of myself as a self, as an absolute passivity. This passivity is not only the possibility of death in being, the possibility of impossibility. It is an impossibility prior

to that possibility, the impossibility of slipping away, absolute susceptibility, gravity without any frivolity. It is the birth of a meaning in the obtuseness of being, of a "being able to die" subject to sacrifice. (Levinas, *Otherwise than Being* [1974], p. 128)

Here we have an alternative to those theories of transcendence which had been blind to the question itself. We aren't saying that all of us already are a (as yet unthematized) whole, transcendence being merely the (nostalgic) attempt to reunify (thematize) what was once entire. Further, we don't have a mere repetition of Heidegger's conception of facticity or of thrownness, nor of his worldhood analysis. However, to measure the originality of this conception, it might serve us to compare it with Heidegger's essentially methodological turn against Cartesianism. With that turn, we are asking how to approach knowledge of being without first presupposing a definition of being derived from our presumptions about objects in the world. Heidegger showed that the structure of finitude inherent in knowledge more accurately opened up our questioning about knowledge—specifically because it accessed the essential necessity of asking about the role of time. Levinas, too, is asking of time, especially in *Otherwise than Being*, which it seems has a more profound approach to the problem of passivity (which is only broached in *Totality and Infinity*). Yet, instead of turning to an idea of originary time, as division 2 of *Being and Time* had done, Levinas is asking us from where the very question of an origin, and the seeking after an origin, might emerge—and how

forthcoming human world on earth should be. (R. Schürmann, *Heidegger on Being and Acting: From Principles to Anarchy* [1982], p. 273)

Something quite convincing is at work here. The difference I would want to accentuate, which I have been trying to mark through the stylistic devices of metaphor and deferral, is the possibility of avoiding the traditional priority of the question of meaning. The question of the meaning of Being, in Heidegger's "first period," would already be, as a methodological treatise, the first step away from the traditional questions of meaning: i.e., what is it? what is it worth? to whom does it belong? It would be, in that sense, against the spirit of Heidegger's work to think of an event as an event of meaning (however temporary). That is, the relation between thing and world is not the question to be asked in the wake of Heidegger—even if that determination will come as a result of an advent, the motivating question has to do with the character of dwelling and not with the things involved in a dwelling.

158. It would be the question of a new concept of passivity, of a passivity more radical than that of an effect in a causal series, on the hither side of consciousness and knowing, but also on the hither side of the inertia of things which rest on themselves as substances and oppose their nature, a material cause, to all activity. This passivity would refer to the *reverse side* of being, prior to the ontological plane in which being is posited as *nature*; it would refer to the antecedence, without any outside yet, of creation, the meta-physical antecedence. . . . But when we see man being born again out of the inanity of man-as-principle, the inanity of principles, out of the putting into question of freedom understood as an origin and the present, when we seek subjectivity in radical passivity, do we not deliver ourselves over to fatality or to determination, which are the very abolition of a subject? That would be the case if the alternative free/non-free were ultimate, and if subjectivity consisted in stopping at the ultimate or at the original. But it is on just this that our inquiry bears. (Levinas, "Humanism and An-Archy" [1968], *Collected Philosophical Papers*, p. 132)

He continues: "The subject does not stand out from being a freedom that would render it master of things, but by a preoriginary susceptibility, more ancient than the origin, a susceptibility provoked in the subject without

such a questioning might come to have a fundamentally temporalizing hold on us.[158] The answer turns out to be no space, or rather, an externality in general, a commencement (a time) which is always moving toward another's future, toward speaking to, and for, another. (Heidegger's Dasein in *Being and Time* is always living into the future, as well, but projecting that future as potentially one's own. That is, such a structure duplicates the privilege of possibility understood as possession and not as expression.)

The necessity of speaking of a face, the most well-known thematic arising from Levinas's work, fades behind the greater thinking of time which lies behind his conception of obligation and passivity. One does not choose to take, or not take, another as a face, as one might choose to not take the time to experience an ocean as sublime. The face is not a species of the sublime encounter (and this contests the most common reading of Levinas). The difference, simply put, is that the time is not invested with meaning by virtue of the face: no subject is goaded into providing meaning because of an encounter with an alien, precisely for the reason that the face does not appear within the structure of an encounter as we traditionally understand that type of event—that is, in the terms of a visual metaphor, as a chancing upon something unexpected. The face, and this is clear in all of his works, is the origin of exteriority, the possibility of exteriority, and not a category (no matter how privileged) within the world of constituted presence (neither of prefigured possibilities nor of given actualities). Does that mean that there are, in some metaphysical sense, multitudes of faces that exist without worlds, outside of all context? Not at all: the time of the questioning, as a method, will find its ground only in the structures of obligation (of the time of that passivity), but this doesn't imply that some subject capable of obligating us has existed outside of the structures of existence. Rather, it merely points to the fact that the existing structures do not exhaust the possibilities of those who come facing us within our economies of words—metaphysics is a relation with the future (which is never solely or fundamentally mine). In one of the central articles leading from *Totality and Infinity* to *Otherwise than Being*, Levinas explains the difference between his thinking of ethics and a traditional thought of recognizing one's obligations within an economy (and then marks the political moment of that same analysis):

> Language, contact, is the obsession of an I "beset" by the others. Obsession is responsibility. But the responsibility characteristic of obsession does not derive from a freedom, for otherwise obsession would be only a becoming conscious. It would be the case of an I obsessed by a fault committed in full freedom, and we would recognize in it the thinking subject, in its splendid isolation, taking up intentional attitudes with regard to beings. Responsibility as an obsession is proximity; like kinship, it is a bond prior to every chosen bond. Language is fraternity, and thus a responsibility for the other, and hence a responsibility for what I have not committed, for the pain and the fault of others. At the antipodes of play, freedom not involving responsibilities,

the provocation ever becoming present or becoming a logos presenting itself to assumption or to refusal and situating itself in the bipolar field of values" (pp. 133–34). Although I will be following this out a bit later, at this point I would want to say that I agree more with the grounds of the question than with the phrasing of the answer: to find a susceptibility before freedom indeed depends on a thinking outside of naming, but the language of a preoriginary (from which he begins to speak of a fundamental humanism and of God) again would resonate with a thinking of the past, and of a repetition of the past, which I feel underestimates the importance of the methodological turn away from freedom. That is, the inescapability of the other, the other by whom I am obsessed, is not due to the strangeness of the other's humanity (its inability to be phrased now) but due to the future within which that strangeness will call. My feeling is that this phrasing would not be foreign to Levinas's thought, although accentuated differently, and that, at the very least, it comes from a type of questioning which is Levinasian.

159. And again, we are trying to make some methodological distinctions between various "postmodern" approaches to these questions. Lacan's discourse of the Other, despite some descriptive similarities, arises from opposed conceptions of the meaning of passivity and time. Grange is speaking of Lacan:

> *Logos*, on the other hand, never lets spirit (*thumos*) fixate itself; never—so to speak—lets it down. Lacan tells us why: "We can say that it is in the chain of the signifier that the meaning 'insists' but that none of its elements 'consists' in the signification of which it is at the moment capable" (*Écrits*, p. 153). In other words, the peculiar property of language is that meaning rolls through it. There is never a place upon which meaning permanently settles. Contrary to desire, which drives *thumos* downward into a place (*epi/thumia*), *logos* (language) drives *thumos* beyond itself, stretching the meaning of its being. Language, therefore, breathes life into spirit and turns it upwards from the corpse of desire whose bloated visage Leontius's speech rightly condemns.

Finally, we must ask about the tension between *thumos* and *logos*. Why is it that spirit, though it naturally aligns itself with *logos*, does not always heed its call? The answer would seem to be in the mirror stage, where the ego, assuming its alienating identity, also takes up fear as its basic posture. To defend proximity is a responsibility that does not refer to my freedom. It is the state of a creature in a world without play, in the *gravity* which is perhaps the first coming of meaning to being *beyond* its stupid "that's the way it is." It is the state of being a hostage. (Levinas, Language and Proximity" [1967], *Collected Philosophical Papers*, p. 123)

Whether we speak of rules or laws, we speak of obligation. Whether we speak of desires or destinies, we speak of obligation.[159] It has become customary to deplore the violences of language, to try, instead, to say the space of 'being open' to the new and unexpected, to somehow signify the silent. The various courts of the world say merely that everyone with something to say may say it (they stand ready to hear)—which would be, in fact, its own kind of progress and not to be taken or discarded lightly—but, politically, before celebrating everyone's equality in their human vocation as speakers of a language, we still need to ask what type of violences are yet committed in the name of the voice.[160] Can we claim merely not to name? Do we renounce the obligation to speak? By no means. Rather, take the obligations as obligation, as imposed by the Other, the Other's rules, the Other's laws. This is essentially different from Kant's claim that with moral judgment, on the part of each individual, the members of a society achieve their freedom by giving themselves the law. The human mind is not the site of that decision. Rather, language speaks the obligation by already existing as a foreign power.

The history of modernity can be told as the turn to inward responsibility. An essential

predicate of this move was the epistemological view that equated universalization with
the negating activity of man. By placing this
negating activity within man's scope, all the
movements of history, all the machinations of
time which seem to transcend the individual
manifestations, become of a kind with, and
centered around, man's present understanding. Certainty of knowledge, of the male gaze,
as Descartes understood, is thus certainty of
man's position in the world.

The methodological turn away from
Descartes implied in Heidegger's *Being and
Time* works differently from, for example,
Ryle's in *The Concept of Mind*, precisely to the
extent that Heidegger's turn is immediately
oriented toward providing a more fundamental domain of questioning and not toward a more coherent answering (based on
excluding certain types of questioning). In
my view, Levinas's approach to language and
obligation radicalizes Heidegger's methodological openness to new types of questions:
the structure of obligation itself becomes the
basis for all other types of questioning—a
transformation which makes explicit, for the
first time, the possibility of a questioning
that is not dependent on the structures of
freedom.

Such a questioning is (philosophically)
new—yet, by hypothesis, has always existed
at the base of any questioning. Like any theory of exteriority, Levinas's depends on language's ability (through metaphorization) to
approach (or literalize) what is being talked
about. To refer to the other as another's face,
or as a woman seducing a man, or as a nature forming a mind, already depends on a
freedom that would have had to have belonged to the author. The constant failures

its own being, however misunderstood, the ego focuses
upon its desires and with all
the insistent clamor of the
child seeks a fixed point as the
fulfillment of its own emptiness. The conclusion should
be obvious: the ego can never
be the center of meaning nor
can its incessant cries ever be
satisfied. When does genuine
meaning arise? When cries are
converted into language and
the process of education
begun. (J. Grange, "Lacan's
Other and the Factions of
Plato's Soul," *Question of the
Other* [1989], p. 170)

Although this aspect isn't obvious, we are still working with a
methodological question: "when
cries are converted into language"
names an individual's appropriation of language—his/her entry
into the orders of meaning
thought of as control. That
power arises as the individual's
interpretation of a confrontation
wherein the rules of the game are
already set (one is expected to
win through an exercise of freedom, such as choosing a different
game, elevating desire to a
winnable sphere). Levinas, instead, gives us the space to question that power because he
doesn't begin methodologically
with either the economy or the
individual, but with a structure
of dwelling better specified as
obligation. Only thus can we escape the simplistic question of
who owns the power, approaching the possibility of phrasing a
question (begun in contact with
the other) which would call for a
restructuring of power itself.

160. And Derrida, more than any other, has taught us how to ask this question in terms of time:

[Speech] does not fall into the exteriority of space, into what one calls the world, which is nothing but the outside of speech. Within so-called 'living' speech, the spatial exteriority of the signifier seems absolutely reduced. It is in the context of this possibility that one must pose the problem of the cry—of that which one has always excluded, pushing it into the area of animality or of madness, like the myth of the inarticulate cry—and the problem of speech (voice) within the history of life.

Conversation is, then, a communication between two absolute origins that, if one may venture the formula, auto-affect reciprocally, repeating as immediate echo the auto-affection produced by the other. Immediacy is here the myth of consciousness. Speech and the consciousness of speech—that is to say consciousness simply as self-presence—are the phenomenon of an auto-affection lived as suppression of différance. That *phenomenon*, that presumed suppression of différance, that lived reduction of the opacity of the signifier, are the origin of what is called presence. That which is not subjected to the process of différance is *present*. The present is that from which we believe we are able to think time, effacing the inverse necessity: to think the present from time as différance. (Derrida, *Of Grammatology* [1967], p. 166)

of voice, the intrusions of others' claims not to be spoken about (and determined by my schematisms in advance of their saying), literalizes the failures of any singular project. Our task, our new possibility, with Levinas's approach to the foundation of meaning, is to think the necessity of (and liberation inherent in) this failure.

The critique of modernity as anthropocentrism, or androcentrism, is this simple—it is merely a criticism of being too certain, a criticism of arrogance. Thus the call to end our egomania is, when radically phrased, coterminous with ending our claim to be the site of negating universalization. Referring again to Dorothy Wordsworth:

If nature is here doing the melting, then she can show her brother and her friend that nature can do what they credit only to the human imagination. Nature is the active agency in these passages, while the human heart is the field on which nature acts. . . . To say that she erases entirely the traces of her own creative act would be to suggest incorrectly that her mode is merely covert symbolism; she makes us doubt that there ever was a creative act. No rhetorical term fully conveys the insubordination of these free parallels between human and natural, in which there is no order of hierarchy. Her parallels have meaning only if nature has as full a value as the human experience, and it can have that full value only if it is not portrayed as subordinate to the human. (Homans, *Bearing the Word* [1986], pp. 53–54)

Language has a twofold relation as gift here: it protects the rights of nature, gives an appropriate name to nature and to those who would want the names of nature. It also, paradoxically, reinstitutes the anarchic laws of nature (the law that there is growth and decay) as superior to the hierarchical laws of man; it nullifies at the same time as it reinstitutes the escape from finitude. Dorothy Wordsworth fails as a feminist (writing in her private journals, contesting a brother's domination, effecting no individual's liberation). She succeeds in literalizing that failure, in giving a new possibility of a contestation exactly here, with Homans, as she provides the text which can literalize (and be literalized) yet again. She has seduced her better known brother by writing on her own— albeit without claiming that the writing (or its truth) had, or could, set her free. Further, however, she would have literalized a difference even had no writing survived (and we are not going to reproduce any of it here). This would be the failure that history can never recoup: the life that wasn't historical (or historically significant). Of course, the finitude of life may have more to do with that failure (and by whose lights is it a failure?) than with the demand that one get busy and change the world before time has run out. Again, and as a question which broaches the very methods inherent in writing, and in writing artistically or philosophically, we ask about the meaning of life—or more, whether the question of life's possible meaningfulness has not led us astray precisely by reducing all of our thinking concerning life to the moment of its possible articulation within a meaningful structure (within the poetics created by some great writer or another within the tradition).

# iii)    The paradigmatic sister, Antigone

*I spit on your idea of life—that life that must go on, come what may.*

—*Anouilh*, Antigone

A viewer of a recent high school performance of Anouilh's *Antigone* complained to me that—besides being a boring play where nothing happened—it was inappropriate to teach adolescents that there are things worth dying for: soon teenage members of the audience would be killing themselves because they had broken up with their boyfriends (he made the assumption it would be a slightly hysterical girl). This seems to me to be a fundamentally misguided approach to both suicide and life (and to the art which treats of them). The growing number of suicides seems far more closely related to a larger problem than any proliferation of bad (or self-destructive) role models could account for[161]—that is, the general malaise of being asked to live a life that is no more or less worthwhile than any other (while the question of worth is more and more

161. One hesitates to generalize around an event so varied in its specific articulations—yet, through a certain metaphorization, or generalization, one approaches what makes suicide a question (and leaves aside the various ways in which it becomes an answer).

241

narrowly phrased around material goods). The position of irony questions the
value of life itself—a question which doubt never poses, or can only pose as a
universal question. A question of this sort must assume the possibility of a very
particular negative answer: my life may not be *worth* it. And because, trivially,
the decision of worth lies outside the purview of the individual when decided
economically, the question put to the individual is all the more harrowing
(who could be so bold as to claim their life was more valuable than any other?).
However, to treat adolescents—as we in fact tend to treat all age groups—as incapable of hearing the answer, or more aptly, incapable of bearing the question,
is to deny them access both to a potentially worthwhile life and to a sense of
the value of their own life. More, it is to accept the regime of exchange—of
judgments of value—as the appropriate field for phrasing the question of how
life should be led. We need new ways of asking about our lives (and, perhaps
primarily, we need ways of asking which do not wield the possessive pronoun
naively); we need a question of life as a whole, and a question that asks in what
terms life is to be valued or not. We need to see how the question of value is essential but not originary.

At this point, more or less haltingly, we should take up the questions of art
again. If we take on role models, after having seen a performance (and all the
world would be a stage according to this understanding of types and imita-
tions), we are projecting ourselves into an identity. Our current approach to
the question of personal identity, in the wake of Lacan, is to think of an act of
identification (or an act of language) that names the identity. This need not assume a space outside of the circle, some metaphysically privileged position of
authority (like the traditional analyst's), but it does assume that the privileged
time of apprehension is the now within which an utterance is phrased. This
has the advantage of being amicable to the way we currently tend to explain
ourselves when we act (and to a prevalent model of scientific explanation). My
argument will involve something of a shift in emphasis, as seen from the level
of our descriptions, although that shift speaks from a different methodological
approach to time.

First, there is the matter of interpreting a play:

> The nature of the recognition is, however, somewhat differently conceived, in
> Freud's discussion of the Oedipus as validating psychoanalytic theory and in
> Lacan's discussion of the Oedipus as illuminating psychoanalytic practice. In
> Freud's analysis, Oedipus recognizes his desire (incest, parricide) as unwit-
> tingly fulfilled, whereas Sophocles' reader recognizes in himself the same de-
> sire, as repressed. The recognition is thus constative, or cognitive. In Lacan's
> different emphasis, however, the psychoanalytic recognition is radically tied

162. Felman goes on to quote Lacan: "To bring the subject to recognize and to name his desire, this is the nature of the efficacious action of analysis. But it is not a question of recognizing something that would have already been there—a given—ready to be captured. In naming it, the subject creates, gives rise to something new, makes something new present in the world" (from Lacan, *Le Séminaire, livre 2* [translated as *The Seminar of Jacques Lacan: Book 2*]).

163. And, I think, Deleuze and Guattarri would be right to see the logical culmination of these structures in a replay of a family drama, albeit always reperformed on different terrains:

> We are all little colonies and it is Oedipus that colonizes us. When the family ceases to be a unit of production and reproduction, when the conjunction again finds in the family the meaning of a simple unit of consumption, it is father-mother that we consume. In the aggregate of departure there is the boss, the foreman, the priest, the tax collector, the cop, the soldier, the worker, all the machines and territorialities, all the social images of our society; but in the aggregate of destination, in the end, there is no longer anyone but daddy, mommy, and me, the despotic sign inherited by daddy, the residual territoriality assumed by mommy, and the divided, split, castrated ego. (Deleuze, and Guattari, *Anti-Oedipus* [1972], p. 265)

up with language, with the subject's analytic speech act, and as such its value is less cognitive than performative: it is itself essentially a speech act, whose symbolic action *modifies* the subject's history rather than cerebrally observing or recording it at last correctly. (S. Felman, *Jacques Lacan and the Adventure of Insight* [1987], pp. 130–31)[162]

Why, when literalizing a play, do we think of the production in terms of a culminating moment (or series of culminations)? Because, I would answer, we tend to look at time as a variation of space (like a number line, infinitely divisible) within which production happens. This view of time sometimes comes from the subject metaphysics which reduces all productions to moments of an individual's freedom, but can also come from a scientistic view of nature that reduces all possible situations to a collection of objects (all objects being, in turn, decomposable).

Lacan himself has already taught us to see this production as a production in the site of the other's desire. Unfortunately, his interpretation of that desire, like his use of Oedipus, rests on a structure of identification which would doom the subject to a repetition of that structure (even though what we think of as the content of those identifications would radically change).[163] At stake here is the dual meaning of a play—a play of significations, or their performance on a stage—as positions are literalized, given human forms, and acted out. We should not think of the identification process as other than entering the circle of understanding. Lacan is not guilty of a subject metaphysics, but he is unable to give us the ground from which to question the structures within which we are caught up.

In any act of viewing, and we should recognize the paradigmatic importance of the idea of sight implied here, we are necessarily caught within a hermeneutic circle which defines (for us, as viewers) the meaning of each object viewed. For a certain strain of postmodernism (inspired by Lacan in large part), the central recognition of postmodernism is the anarchic production (which is not merely a relativism) at the base of meaning. That production occurs at the site of the subject; or, rather, as the coming into being of the subject. Thus, when watching a play, if it is to be meaningful, I must transcend the artificial distances (between my past idea of myself and the play I am watching) by enacting an identification (or some species of partial identification). It would be possible to see this identification as a parallel to Levinas's moment of substitution—of obsession, or being hostage to the other. However, Levinas's approach to the ethical opens up the domain of obsession to a question where Lacan sees the other as a type of answer (as providing the form for any possible answering, thus restricting answering in general to a certain type of production). We could ask, to begin with, what it might mean for a woman to identify with a male on stage, or for a man to identify with a woman (Antigone is a tempting character for all of us), but such plays of identity would not escape the structure instituted by the question of identity. A structure which is still basically enacted as abstraction and control in the realm of the abstract.[164] Perhaps it would be possible to think the act of

My question, of psychoanalysis and of art, has to do with the necessity of the structure of our reading of the play. Why, after all, do we take Oedipus to be the hero (the one we identify with)? Why can't we learn the lesson of the play without enacting the identities of the play? Philosophically, a turn towards the ethics of the face would be a turn away from identification; personal identity (or its maintenance) would not be an unchanging structure, a crosscultural demand we all feel, but would be instituted only at the space, or in the time, of a future contact. Do we stop being ourselves? Perhaps. That possibility is all I would want to establish.

164. But on Lacan's reading [of the Fort/da] much more is at stake. This act of primal speech represents "the games of occultation which Freud, in a flash of genius revealed to us so that we might recognize in them that the moment in which desire becomes human is also that in which the child is born into language" (*Écrits*, 103). What occultation? the magic of language, which allows for presence in absence and absence in presence by constituting a realm of significance within which the human subject can play. Inducted into this realm by owning its speech, the child submits to the demands of culture, renounces its instinctual gratification, and seeks satisfaction through the expression of its desires rather than the actual winning of its

wants. (J. Grange, "Lacan's Other and the Factions of Plato's Soul," *Question of the Other* [1989], p. 163)

watching a play while remaining attuned to the structures which make vision possible (structures like susceptibility, finitude, and imagination, but also, more importantly, a general structure of commencing into a new relationship, undefined by the abstractions, and the visions, which had captured the past).

In terms of a conversation, we need to recognize philosophically (as has long been recognized in polite conversation) that we don't mean merely what we say: that is, if I say nature, I'm not (necessarily) more or less consciously repeating a previous conception of nature (such as the romantics's). I simply may not be (I am probably not) referencing a view as it is commonly held (I am not talking about what one believes, even when I speak as 'the one'). Still, I should be allowed to use the words one uses; ethics (and everyday polite conversation) lies in allowing others to speak past their conceptions (no matter how complicated their conceptions) and reach toward . . . well, the future. In a conversation, as Levinas points out, "I come facing," I come to the conversation ready to say more than what I've already said (which orientation toward the future Levinas uses to justify his preference for the spoken over the written), but also ready to listen.

> To not be an autochthonous being, to be torn up from culture, law, horizon, context, by reason of an absence which is the very presence of infinity, finding itself in the null site of a trace, is not to take on a certain number of attributes that might figure in a passport; it is to come facing, to manifest oneself by undoing one's manifestation. Such is the

face, as we have said, the point at which an epiphany becomes a proximity.
(Levinas, "Language and Proximity" [1967], *Collected Philosophical Papers*,
p. 121)

Transcendence, as it might be expressed in art, takes on a different meaning
when already caught up in a thinking of the face. All of a sudden, and for the
first time philosophically, we are found to be already obliged to produce the
interruptions ourselves. We are not the (sufficient) audience of our own art; we
don't play the character for our own aggrandizement—nor for any other's—
because we play, as we undo our own manifestations, for the sake of a future
which isn't merely a new combination of my manifestations:

> The future for which such an action acts must from the first be posited
> as indifferent to my death. A work which is different from play and from
> computations, is being-for-beyond-my-death. Patience does not consist in
> the agent betraying his generosity by giving himself the time of a personal im-
> mortality. To renounce being the contemporary of the triumph of one's work
> is to envisage this triumph in a *time without me*, to aim at this world below
> without me, to aim at a time beyond the horizon of my time, in an eschatol-
> ogy without hope for oneself, or in a liberation from my time.
>
> To be *for* a time that would be without me, *for* a time after my time, over
> and beyond the celebrated "being for death," is not an ordinary thought
> which is extrapolating from my own duration; it is the passage to the time of
> the other. Should what makes such a passage possible be called *eternity*? In
> any case the possibility of sacrifice which goes to the limit of this passage dis-
> covers the non-inoffensive nature of this extrapolation: to be for death in
> order to be for that which is after me. (Levinas, "Meaning and Sense" [1972],
> *Collected Philosophical Papers*, p. 92)

And, as we have already seen, no character better lives that refusal of the self
(and its literalization as a destiny) than Antigone.

What, finally, is my disagreement with Lacan? Simply, he misses Antigone
in his economy of death. Antigone, like Oedipus, more so than Oedipus, has
been traversed by 'a speech which comes from elsewhere'. The attempt to define one's own destiny is vain, for it always seeks to operate below the level of
speech, below the level of the subject. Antigone, alone, knows and embraces
this (such are the gods of the underworld). She functions, allegorically, as the
relation to (the active appropriation of) memory in its 'passivity'. Instead of
being the forgetfulness of a life which seeks to ignore the unwritten laws, she
alone sees these laws are in fact written across the particular space of the par-

165. "This is a goodness in peace, which is also the exercise of a freedom, and in which the *I* frees itself from its 'return to self,' from its auto-affirmation, from its egotism of a being persevering in its being, *to answer for the other*, precisely to defend the rights of the other man. Non-indifference and goodness of responsibility: these are not neutral, midway between love and hostility. They must be conceived on the basis of the meeting, in which the *wish for peace*—or goodness—is the first language" ("The Rights of Man and the Rights of the Other," *Outside the Subject*, pp. 124–25). The question for us here, as with Antigone, is to ask whose definition of rights is going to be accepted. Levinas, I think rather unconvincingly, would refer to the authority of God (p. 117) and institute a fraternity of reciprocal (and therefore just) life (p. 125). This would be to interpret rights in terms of the past, and not in terms of the future (where a discourse of rights would maintain its derivative status, would remain open to question).

ticular dead. She does not identify with death, nor with the tragic, yet lives past the life where only death and tragedy were offered her. All that is left for her, in terms of the roles, is the choice of what project to follow. Refusing the violence of that economy, she nominates to eternity the name of an individual: Polynices. She says, for him, that his life was seen by others, his name exists. Thus she literalizes her brother's project (to attain immortality) without entering into the economy of war within which the project began (and towards which it was destined to return). The relation to the divine calls us to think of those we help, those we hurt, and those we omit. Every word we say, after all, traverses the dead space of an alien body, an Iphigenia or a Polynices, the space of our own odd conglomeration of carbon, water, and DNA. Antigone is a political text because it calls one outside oneself without nostalgia for return; it calls the speaker to speak for the future of the vanquished, not the victor, to speak without hope of return, without the comfort of a fulfillable role.[165]

The case for Antigone is simple enough: It requires merely that a reading of the play take Antigone as the heroine and not Creon (or Polynices) as the hero. Further, although we can speak of Oedipus as the absent figure who actually shapes the plot of the play, Antigone, alone, takes responsibility for its meaning (which is to say that, if we look, we see things from her point of view, but not *as* her; we live in the meaningful and not in her interpretation as itself a structure of meanings; Polynices is already a name spoken without hope of an audience or destination that would resolve the name into a reference). As allegory, Antigone's self-sacrifice is a structure and not an exemplar. Antigone sees that her words, actions, thoughts, her entire life, will serve some other's purposes. She chooses the ends she will serve; not reflexively, out of an ethical immediacy which cannot separate child from child—which loves all children immediately because of their role as *my* children—but consciously renaming individuals with the names they already bore. Behind all the attributes of a Polynices, an anxious child stood. Polynices, like Etiocles, lived a destiny written outside of him—a destiny in the face of which he could not see his own unity, his own destiny. But only because he believes in the logic of war does he feel anxiety over the loss of this unity which he is incapable of seeing; the tragedy lies in believing in the necessity (the logic) of war. Antigone, for the first time in Polynices' burial rites, has given voice to this unity, has pronounced the destiny, without succumbing to the logic of war, without pronouncing that name as a victory over other attempts to speak. In that sense, she literalizes a language which is neither command nor obedience—the destiny closes with her speaking, opening towards a future speaking which will not be subject to the destination of her articulations: others will say the name differently—her articulation was never available as public (the rites were performed in secret), yet they leave the trace of a name (or, perhaps, of a naming).

This is no Utopia (although it is in fact no place). It is not pleasant and no one was saved. But hers was a life lived outside itself; she knew all her possible roles to be determined, knew that there was no redemption in the assumption of a role. She chose to play the poet; she nominated the place of the vanquished to the history of being (and failed—after all, it is her name we remember best). Like Christ, she is speaking, structurally, the very process of transcending memory, a memory which allows, creates, a place for the divine. Unlike the Hegelian interpretation of Christ, however, she speaks a memory oriented towards its transcendence in the future of another's time. She literalizes the destiny of words offered—not as her identity, but as her humanity. (And the content of the concept 'humanity' will be a central question for us.)

On a more contemporary level, we could criticize the recent move by the United States to glorify the American war dead in Vietnam. There is no attempt to remember the event; everything is done, instead, to reappropriate the war dead to the grand American project. In return for accepting their deaths as unavoidable moments in the complicated machinations of world history (the question of the justice of that war is consciously not asked, the patriotism of fighting itself being glorified as a virtue) they are elevated in the collective mind to a sort of immortality coterminous with the grandiosity of our national pretensions.[166] By co-opting their deaths to our feelings of national immortality, we lose the position of knowledge and freedom relative to the processes of

166. Antigone, then, refuses the grandiosity of this death precisely where she refuses to identify herself with all the future articulations of death, with the structures that demand that all life be judged, from a point of view outside the individual, in terms of the value of each life's encounter with death—so that all life would be meaningful only in its absorption into the universal life, and projects, of the nation.

war. Which is not to say that war is always avoidable (or, rather, often we find that we are not the ones, especially as individuals, in position to choose), but that our conceptions of experience, and of war, lead us to think of the grandiosity of war, and not of the individual who is at stake in a war. War demands that its importance be recognized: ignoring a war, announcing an alternative to war in general, becomes impossible exactly to the extent that, as a society, we believe in war (just as a king was only such by virtue of a collective complicity in obedience, albeit sometimes violently enforced; just as a king claimed for himself a divine status and construed all opposition as an attempt at capturing the throne, and never as a contestation of the logic of monarchy itself). We must learn to see (no single atrocity can give us a Gestalt in these terms) that in war, as in less institutionalized forms of interpersonal violence, people are victimized by forces which have transgressed, interrupted, their individual lives, projects, and enjoyments. A process out of control only because we choose to forget—willfully, narcissistically, and repeatedly—that enjoyment extracts its price, that our prosperity had been built at the expense of others, that our future plans for prosperity continue to exclude others—that our lives are not closed totalities.

I am actually not very convinced by this account of violence, although I'm not sure what alternatives offer themselves in the terms of violence itself (outside of an ideological elimination of the individual's perception of violence in the name of transpersonal forces which could be judged 'just' in spite of their machinations). The problem, briefly, is that our current understandings of violence treat the individual's continuity as inviolable—or rather, it treats the violation of that continuity as an evil—and the justice of a transpersonal 'force' could only be established in terms of a greater continuity (a historical progression, a natural right, or a divine origin). Here we have a rudimentary form of the question of justice and violence as expressed in terms of competing individual claims: If one person's continuity has been bought at the price of another's continued oppression, is there not a legitimate call to violence on the part of the second? The meaning of continuity, or the idea that the meaning resides in continuity, is what I will question in the next section (on mothers). My purpose will be, explicitly, to change the grounds from which we ask about violence and/or the person as the site of a 'claim' to justice. The meaning that comes from exchange, from the conception of individuals which posits the necessity of both their participation in and separation from the economy, is what I've been questioning throughout this section (on sisters). I have been using a set of Levinasian ideas to approach the problems of meaning, as a critique of the more customary accounts, but I have also been avoiding a certain (mostly stylistic) aspect of his answers.

Briefly phrased, Levinas charts his course from the ethical questions that precede ontology to the political questions that follow after ontology (or the refusal of a certain moment of ontology) in terms of an almost Kantian respect for, and concomitant distance from, the other.[167] Here I'm referring to his humanism, but also to his sense of tradition and religion (all of which devolve from his more original ethi-

167. This would not lead to the Habermasian brand of Kantianism since the public sphere would not gain its shape from the fact that everyone shared an orientation towards mutual understanding. Instead, in the refusal to disrupt previous continuities (the refusal of violence), Levinas would preclude anything like 'redistributive justice' (an oxymoron of sorts, after all, at least within capitalism). One answers that the return of skepticism, at the end of *Otherwise than Being*, would institute a continual criticism, a questioning that would never be complete. With this, one avoids the reification of previous continuities (as Kantianism is often accused of); one starts each questioning from its own saying. Skepticism, obviously, gives us a certain type of politics, but does it not also stop short of prescribing redress for historical wrongs? My feeling is that in its orientation toward the future we can find the resources for continually new definitions of justice (as an example, land reform is proving to be a type of redistributive justice which cannot address all the complaints of the modern third world, increasingly urbanized, oppressed—the model of rights as property doesn't make sense on an individual level; instead, such rights are made to the measure, through recent judicial interventions, of international companies, even as these rights had been derived from no longer existent farm economies: the trick, for us, is to think beyond the *tradition* of justice). However, the meaning of proximity, too, must come under (metaphorical)

scrutiny. In Levinas, especially in *Totality and Infinity*, it is based on a thinking of the son in paternity. The metaphors have already switched by the time of his later writings, but my project is to think this switch in terms of the daughter (and not in terms of the order of the third, a conception too immediately abstract), in terms of a very specific metaphorical disjunction. My point in using Levinas, then, relies on the methodological space of questioning opened up to us by his differentiation between the saying and the said, between skepticism and its refutation in philosophy:

> The periodic rebirth of skepticism and its invincible and evanescent force to be sure does not permit us to confer any privilege on its said over against the implicit presuppositions of its saying. But that the contradiction that opposes one to the other does not strangle the speaker, also recalls the fault which, upon the critical examination of this returner, shows itself in the totality of representation, in the universal simultaneity that knowledge requires qua reason. It recalls the breakup of the unity of the transcendental apperception, without which one could not *otherwise than be*. (Levinas, *Otherwise than Being* [1974], p. 171)

Our question: is it possible, or desirable, to live the saying before (regardless of, without anxiety for) the said?

cal questions). At this stage, we can only point in a preliminary fashion, but something of that questioning will carry through into the next sections of this book.

Levinas is greatly respectful of Buber's contribution to the development of dialogical thought, but marks a distance from Buber's conception of both meaning and of the religious in an encounter. This distance will weigh heavily on what you might call Levinas's politics exactly where Buber had imagined the divinity of the neighbor, and not the divinity of the call to responsibility that is seen in the face of the neighbor:

> God is personal insofar as He brings about interpersonal relations between myself and my neighbors. He signifies from the face of the other person, with a significance not articulated as the relation of signifier to signified, but as order signified to me. The coming to mind of God is always linked, in my analyses, to the responsibility for the other person and all religious affectivity signifies in its concreteness a relation to others; the fear of God is concretely my fear for my neighbor. (Levinas, "Apropos of Buber: Some Notes" [1982], *Outside the Subject*, pp. 45–46)

I include this here, partly, to show what God is not for Levinas. We are speaking, really, only of the slim order of passivity that I spoke of earlier. Not much of an order to contest, nor is it clear how any order could be more open to future questioning, less restricted to a single dogmatic religious credo. In other places, Levinas refers to the absolute priority of rights (not specified in a

list, but human) and Derrida has recently, to the chagrin of some of his followers, asserted that perhaps a certain idea of justice lies below (beyond) deconstruction's activity. I would not want to take either claim too literally. One too
quickly devolves into a mutual respect that depends on a previous idea of humanity, and identity, which reifies existing situations as if they constituted justice by virtue of their existence (even if I am rich by virtue of my grandfather's
injustice, it would be unjust to take that wealth away from me since I have
never done anything wrong myself). Clearly neither Levinas nor Derrida
would say this, but, equally, neither is giving us the immediate resources to answer the problem in some other way. If justice and individuation occur on different planes of being, then they will always give birth to tragic situations
(someone will suffer injustice; time itself is injustice, or violence). On my reading of their methodological importance, Levinas, and to a slightly different extent Derrida, have opened up the possibility of the questioning that would ask
both questions (of justice and the individual) at once, from their ground in the
future-related saying of ethics, and yet both have fallen back into a position of
distance and separation. Both have fallen into an aesthetics that waits for revelation, or for the sublime, having outlined the possibility, and character, of its
approach.

And here, as well, I am only marking a distance in accentuation, in metaphors and style. I am not refuting Levinas's thinking of justice, merely suggesting that it lies better with his thinking of the future, and of the time of the
other as a future, than in his thinking of order and tradition. Derrida's metaphors, famously, are less oriented by the call of order. But they continue to resonate with a violence that rests on the 'plane of Being' (in terms of our metaphors, in a violence against the mother). Between Derrida and Levinas, other
books will need to be written. This book, already at a late stage, will try to nav-
igate something of an answer (provisionally, as an echo of the question at work
in their writings) in terms of the metaphors already at work, in terms of the
broader social and philosophical movements which this metaphorization, or
literalization, opens onto.

By the lights of a Creon, or a Hegel, freedom, truth, is the identification of
the individual self with the voices that traverse the individual. For them, there
are no human decisions, only political ones—embraced without reserve. They
could see that an inherited privilege can be rightfully taken away by the state
in an act of violence since that violence belonged to a regime of truth (and the
individual should see, and agree with, that larger truth). For Antigone, there
are political decisions, but they only belong to this time. Human decisions escape the blind inertia of international war and ask, with gravity and somber
irony; Who are the individuals being forgotten? To live for the future is not to

fight for new monuments, but to reach out towards a new memory (one not yet written, one never destined to be written in the collective memory as such). Levinas's conception of God as an 'order', as the order of goodness that precedes justice, reaches towards this question, makes this question possible, but determines the answer in terms of the order at first given (that is, at the level of politics, an abstract equality is respected between individuals under a common law). At the level of listening to what the other's fragility announces (a passivity in the face of the other), one understands fairly intuitively what to do. At the level of the political, at the level where two parties claim a justice or a right in the name of their side, it is less clear what can be said. (I am unsure, for example, how sexism across various cultures might be addressed except by reference to a human essence, such as freedom, instituted by God, since one cannot usually revive, or even reference, a previous order of nonsexism. Proximity, as a structure, would say nothing about the separation of sexual spheres, nor the valuation of those spheres—although it says something about how one would respond to an individual who, for his/her own reasons, felt an injustice to have occurred here.) If we no more believe in the destiny of the other than in the destiny of the self, then Levinas's God no more helps us than one of Baudrillard's rules; Levinas himself argues that all humans share in certain originary rights:

> These rights are, in a sense, *a priori*: independent of any power that would be the original share of each human being in the blind distribution of nature's energy and society's influence, but also independent of the merits the human individual may have acquired by his or her efforts and even virtues. Prior to all entitlement: to all tradition, all jurisprudence, all granting of privileges, awards or titles, all consecration by a will abusively claiming the name of reason. Or is it perhaps the case that its *a priori* may signify an ineluctable authority, older and higher than the one already split into will and reason and that imposes itself by an alternance of violence and truth; the authority that is, perhaps—but before all theology—*in* the respect for the rights of man itself, God's original coming to the mind of man. (Levinas, "The Rights of Man and the Rights of the Other," *Outside the Subject*, pp. 116–17)

To jump ahead to the end of my work, I will try to mark a different thinking of this religiosity, around the metaphorical figure of the daughter. The point I will try to bring out, albeit sketchily, is the alternative to such an idea of order in passivity.

Finally, and as a question I am continually asking myself in this book about my practice as a writer, as a question that encircles our questions of justice, is it possible for the novel—or the epic poem or the tragic play—to write for or of the transgressed without translating their story into another genre, another set of violent typifications? In other words, can one write a book where the individuals, in their infinity, their divinity, as *other* subjects, as other futures, remain larger than the story itself? The self-conception of the modern novelist can only be thought in terms of analogies to God. The author creates a closed world that contains, in miniature, the expression of the world from which the author comes.

Perhaps only in certain of the late modernist projects—noticeably Gertrude Stein's series of portraits and lives (as well as some of the minimalist experiments more recently performed by other authors)—are the distances between reader, author, and subject rigorously maintained, or rather, never instituted (thus never in need of transcendence). Her characters do not lead universal or exemplary lives; there is no remnant of a universal, immortal experience that validates their activity and decisions. She shows us beings, no longer exactly human, who are completely traversed, transgressed, and inscribed by discourses not their own. Yet, like her character Ida, not anxious for the loss of an owned personal identity (it would always have been merely an imagined loss, after all, if one had even taken the time to imagine it). Perhaps Levinas's flip on Heidegger—anxiety in the face of the other instead of in the face of one's own death—should instead move toward a different type of failure, a destiny of failing (of questions never being fully phrased, much less answered), a loss of anxiety over the self's and the other's destinations, with a little concern for the possibilities of the journey. With Stein (unfortunately, I cannot approach this fully in my present writing) perhaps a different model of meaning in life, a different distance between value and life, will eventually grant its own politics, open onto a politics we haven't yet approached, no longer determined in advance by its possible fulfillment in the productive activity of universal, abstract life.

# C )                    M O T H E R S

*Your name was something laid*
*There also against diminishment*
*And I said it to tear the firmament freshly*
*When words turn against their truths*
*Like traitors.*

      —*Ann Lauterbach, "Revenant,"* Clamor

Within the metaphorizations we have been approaching, the name of the mother most often invokes either the linguistic, cultural, or passive spiritual background of our existences, or the material (also passive background) which we (subjects) actively form in order to live within (or as) a culture or language. This distinction of spiritual and material is often contested by those who would place the primary signification of the mother with enveloping matter, or with the body thought in its powers, and I will be following the unifying trajectory of that contestation for the purposes of displaying a possibility other than either of the traditional approaches (both of which are based on the faithful passivity of the feminine). Much of the preceding division was devoted to criticizing the idea of a determining culture, structure, or language. Instead, we found that an idea of time that is not reduced to a single instant, to a moment that culminates previous positionalities, opens up our thinking of personal identity to a different structuring impulse (what Levinas calls obligation to the other; what, therefore, cannot be simply thought under the rubric of the personal). To think this obligation as itself not carrying a structure (without merely duplicating the 'hither' side of the master/slave dialectic, without being merely the slave), requires approaching the future as never to be possessed (and, of course, the refusal of possession is already otherwise than the tradition's definition of a person). That is, beyond thinking of the subject as always borrowing the structures of presence from whatever 'other' happens to be around, we must think through the possibility of approaching the future unarmed, without the safety of a structure; we must think the possibility of a question other than meaning—a nonquestion designated as an obligation for reasons of shorthand—a question other than meaning in that it does not will even its own identity, does not will to be present at the culminating moment called meaning.

Iphigenia, the very archetype of a woman sacrificed to the structures of meaning, could be *described* as obligated to the meaning structures of her father. The cruelty of the situation can be ameliorated, as Nussbaum suggested, by working out the father's appropriate response to that cruelty. Iphigenia, of course, remains bound. Antigone exercises a greater freedom of motion, is the subject of her activity, but again one is tempted to read her death spatially—as the definition of a certain meaning within a certain culture. A meaning we are invited to take up or discard according to our pleasure. Instead, I have been suggesting we also have the possibility of approaching these problems without the methodologies of control (of a man's public activity, forming matter, etc.). The key to this approach, perhaps, is rethinking the meaning of presence outside of the paradigms of distinctness and clarity. This is the methodological force behind the invocation of poetry and metaphor—an antimethodology that prohibits the arrogance of presuming to know even the form of what you will have done before you do it. Instead, one is never sure that any 'event' is over, never knows what will count as 'having happened'.

For example, not completely at random, Woolf's *To the Lighthouse* enacts a gendered contradiction, a difference in approach between women and men, a difference characterized exactly in terms of what is to be approached. There are no simple dichotomies in Woolf's work, but there is a polemic against a particular mode of appropriative knowledge (the father figure of the book is a philosopher).

Already, with Woolf, we are speaking of artistic representations of a lived experience, but what we are finding is a certain refusal to describe—as such, in terms of the history of art, it is an approach to writing that refuses the traditional conception of representation (and, in a less direct way, the usual sense of a 'lived experience'). Unsurprisingly, this difference between representational and nonrepresentational art speaks to what Homans was positing as the difference between women's writing and men's. As with women's entry into the symbolic order, Homans wants to speak of gradual transitions, of no distinct boundaries between bodies and spirit, of a thoughtful, concerned humanity. She literalizes that difference, with reference to Woolf's novel, in terms of an artistic approach to absence and death:

168. The "subtler way," of course, constitutes the difference which makes it precisely not a representation—nor simply an experience. Woolf is speaking of Lily:

> To be on a level with ordinary experience, to feel simply that's a chair, that's a table, and yet at the same time, It's a miracle, it's an ecstasy. The problem might be solved after all. Ah, but what had happened? Some wave of white went over the window pane. The air must have stirred some flounce in the room. Her heart leapt at her and seized her and tortured her. "Mrs. Ramsay! Mrs. Ramsay!" she cried, feeling the old horror come back—to want and want and not to have. Could she inflict that still? And then, quietly, as if she refrained, that too became part of ordinary experience, was on a level with the chair, with the table. Mrs. Ramsay—it was part of her perfect goodness—sat there quite simply, in the chair, flicked her needles to and fro, knitted her reddish-brown stocking, cast her shadow on the step. There she sat.
>
> And as if she had something she must share, yet could hardly leave her easel, so full her mind was of what she was thinking, of what she was seeing, Lily went past Mr. Carmicheal holding her brush to the edge of the lawn. Where was that boat now? And Mr. Ramsay? She wanted him. (*To The Lighthouse* [1927], p. 300)

That Lily, in contrast to Mr. Ramsay, experiences Mrs. Ramsay's loss with such particularity and as a physical sensation exemplifies the difference we have hypothesized between a daughter's and a son's relation to the mother: Lily wants to reproduce her, and wants to reproduce a relation to a present body, while Mr. Ramsay wants to replace or represent her.

This difference leads us to expect that Lily's art would seek not to represent but rather to reproduce Mrs. Ramsay. But Lily's paintings are as different from Cam's reproduction of her mother's nonrepresentational words as they are from the Raphael madonnas that Mr. Bankes has in mind. The shapes on Lily's canvas do not represent Mrs. Ramsay in any conventional sense, but they do represent the shapes of light and shadow made by Mrs. Ramsay's body. Quite possibly, Woolf wants us to see that Lily's painting is representational, if only in a subtler way than Raphael's. (Homans, *Bearing the Word* [1986], p. 284)[168]

I included the note here, in part, to demonstrate the distance between Homans's commentary and the text. That is, only to enact the necessity of the distance that Homans herself is pointing to between description and what Woolf is calling 'ordinary experience' (and we are sure that she doesn't mean what the philosophers mean by experience: even if she is pointing at the same moments, it is not the thematization of those moments which interests us, but their ordinariness, their ecstasy and simplicity). Still, what is subtler about Lily's representation? This should give us a clue to the whole problematic, for it replays in miniature the history of artistic representation in the twentieth century. The earlier ideal of representation had been to as completely as possible displace the essence of the object of the painting into a separate realm—the representational realm of either art or mind, a realm controlled by the knowing subject—with the guiding ideal of thereby maintaining, or reproducing as possessed, all the economic effects of the true object. Control, within this thinking, depends on a spatialization, on an ability to say, 'within this thinking'. An art that creates something new, that names its desire only in and by enacting it, does not depend on the 'within' of a spatializing schema exactly at the point where what is given to be thought is not the nature of the desired thing but the very structuring/coming into event of the desiring itself. Meaning is born of an encounter with/as time—neither as a schema's coming to be within time nor as a thing's coming to be determined within a schema.

The man who knows his representations to be the center of a spatially extended world (or a nodal point within a certain world view), either by analogy with God's representations or through belonging to universally true structures of representation (some 'us' that thinks the same way), to be a (or the) center of an economy, the place where validity is decided, knows that the truth of another person resides in a catalogue of her effects (because there is no other space besides causes and effects where the truth might find its measure). And because these catalogues have always hidden hierarchies of repression, it is easy to spend time (it is in fact worthwhile to spend time) arguing with the catalogue instead of thinking outside of catalogues and lists (one argues against the canon in general, but insists, at least, on a greater inclusiveness). Many apologists for abstract art would hold that abstraction is a better (more inwardly valid) representationalism, more able to hold together the various truths of effects: when Monet uses certain color combinations, in short brush strokes close together, he is not discovering a combination of colors no one else has seen, but creating the visual pop of a bright summer's day in ways that a true representation of color, without the reproduction of an all-surrounding, bright summer sun, cannot duplicate. He represents the subjective experience and not the objective reality. If such a story is possible with Monet, it still seems to sell short what separates the art from the day (precisely as it misses the separation, the differing purposes, of the two)—when we reach into examples less obviously representational, like Lily's, we stretch the everyday sense of representation past recognition. But do not abandon it. That is, Mrs. Ramsay is not forgotten, but literalized—not according to her description, not even according to her emotional effects, but toward a new transcendence, toward a

humanity which is not already listed, not destined to be listed, in the encyclopedia of human names. This literalization is, of course, further enacted by
Woolf herself, as the names of fiction do not reduplicate any 'real' beyond the
work—but don't, because of that separation, then have 'nothing to do' with
the world.

What Woolf is pointing to is a difference in the modes of approach, and
not, as we too quickly assume, a difference in the objects approached. And
that difference in modalities is what in turn points to our earlier problems with
questions like culture, or the mother as the site of a culture (and what Homans
further points to is the question of the maternal body, as art and as presence,
both of which themes I will deal with more fully below). If, with Lyotard, we
take the mother to be a "timbre before it sounds," we should also take culture
to be such a nonrepresentational nonmoment. Culture should not be taken as
a preexisting architecture, a meaningful whole, within which one comes to
being as an individual who in turn represents that culture: rather, one is looking toward a possibility, let's call it justice for now, which that culture's individuals will have found amiable (and which may yet come to question the ease of
adding a possessive apostrophe to the word "culture"). That is, not a possibility that lies latent, pure, and ready for appropriation, but a latency that will
only find itself to have been latent (and multiply so) in the future of its sayings
(like a book that will have been read, that asks to be read again), a latency that,
for now, awaits no meaning. Which is to say, the meaning must come from a
method of approaching meaning, and not be assumed to rest in the 'thing' approached.[169] To understand the idea of a culture without contents also suggests taking the body as such: gravity is not a force to be discarded, not even
an effect or collection of effects, but a field within which something happens;
the body, the temporal possibility of space, is that which precedes the rules
that gravity will impose, but which will be nothing other than the negotiation
of/with those rules before they become spatial—the body is the encounter
with gravity exactly where one thinks through the encounter and not the articulation of the meaning of the encounter.

This is the ethical insistence of refusing possession—an ethics which will
not ignore the constititution of laws, which wills to question the grounds of
questioning.[170] Or rather, as with Lily's approach to the loss of Mrs. Ramsay, it
asks us for the simplicity of not-taking (which is not the unity of drunken forgetfulness)—a simplicity which would be, perhaps, the unity of a question and
an answer before we anxiously separate the two (that is, not a pure unity, untouched by determination, but a question already in the asking and an answer
already approaching). One would have to ask (this book is asking) of the nonrepresentational possibilities of metaphors and of words more generally. If the

words already promise a destiny, is it not only insofar as they are more or less representational? If, as opposed to Heidegger, the moment of meaning lies with an ever-escaping other (an infinite face invoking the future), then perhaps a destiny or destination no longer makes sense (in which case it wouldn't be clear that multiplying destinies was the only alternative to traditional metaphysics). Perhaps security in your mother's (or lovers') arms is not what you are looking for—or, at least, is no more than a conclusion of our searching, and cannot give us insight into the structuring powers of that striving itself.

As with the concluding questions of the previous section, we are here with the metaphors of mothers asking of an affirmation that might precede all questioning, a structuring orientation 'toward . . . ' before any question 'about'. That this affirmation is not 'pure', as a mother is sometimes said to be pure, iterates our characterization of art: one does not act as if Mrs. Ramsay never was; does not paint as if life had never been touched from the 'outside'; but moves toward, approaches that exteriority, not yet saying anything more than a 'yes, you may sit here, be here'.[171] As an affirmation, it bridges the difference between a spatial conception and a temporal conception of the mother. One does not return home, one merely affirms the possibility of letting home come to be.

We are perhaps not yet ready to ask the question of this home as other than a question of the freedom to invite the other, however. We have, it seems, only succeeded in thinking the affirmation of the healthy body, borrowing a thought of Nietzsche's.

169. "However, in existence, man does not proceed from some inside to some outside; rather, the nature of *Existenz* is outstanding standing-within the essential sunderance of the clearing of beings. Neither in the creation mentioned before nor in the willing mentioned now do we think of the performance or act of a subject striving toward himself as his self-set goal. Willing is the sober resolution of that existential self-transcendence which exposes itself to the openness of beings as it is set into the work" (Heidegger, "The Origin of the Work of Art" [1935], *Poetry Language Thought*, p. 67).

170. And here we should see various uses of the term ethical, even within readings of Levinas (who will further clarify, as we will see, the priority of ethics over phenomenality—and over the 'ethics' of a merely respectful comportment which would depend on phenomenality—in *Otherwise than Being*). Derrida is commenting on the work up through *Totality and Infinity*:

The importance of the [Husserlian] concept of horizon lies precisely in its inability to *make* any constitutive act *into* an object, and in that it opens the work of objectification to infinity. In phenomenology there is never a constitution of horizons, but horizons of constitution. That the infinity of the Husserlian horizon has the form of an indefinite opening, and that it offers itself without any possible end to the negativity of constitution (of the work of objectification)—does this not certainly keep it from all totalization, from the illusion of the immediate presence of a plenitudinous infinity in which the other suddenly becomes unfindable? If a consciousness of infinite inadequation to the infinite (and even to the finite) distinguishes a body of thought careful to respect exteriority, it is difficult to see how Levinas can depart from Husserl, on this point at least. Is not intentionality respect itself? The eternal irreducibility of the other to the same, but of the other *appearing as* other for the same? For without the phenomenon of other as other no respect would be possible. The phenomenon of respect supposes the respect of phenomenality. And ethics, phenomenology. In this sense, phenomenology is respect itself, the development and becoming-language of respect itself. (Derrida, "Violence and Metaphysics" [1963], *Writing and Difference*, p. 121)

171. And here aesthetics is experience, or that which makes experience inhabitable: "(T)he simple 'factum est' is to be held forth into the Open by the work: namely this, that unconcealedness of what is has happened here, and that as this happening it happens here for the first time; or, that such a work *is* at all rather than is not. The thrust that the work as this work is, and the uninterruptedness of this plain thrust, constitute the steadfastness of the work's self-subsistence. Precisely

Metaphorically, we are still like the men at a café who would feel free to sit down at the table of a woman sitting alone, or invite her to sit with us if she were standing, but who don't know what the hesitation that precedes the invitation might entail—or what it might imply about the economy of men and women in cafés (the economies of seductions, friendships, and segregations). One here thinks of the affirmation that is a hesitation and not yet a determination. To think liberation as other than the right to sit wherever you please is to turn toward obligation (this is what I've already tried to show). To think obligation as other than the duty to allow someone to sit wherever they please is what we have not yet phrased, although I think the gradualness of entry, the temporal delay of thought, is what will best reach toward our becoming capable of the future where such an obligation could be phrased. Such gradations of time are what a nonrepresentational art (perhaps all art) is striving to represent, why it takes more than one viewing to take it in, to begin to have the vague feeling of having understood (which is why the sublime does not correctly characterize such art: the sublime happens, in the instant, in the presence of its audience, and need only happen once). Such art strives to represent the striving itself, as it moves toward . . . (not even, properly speaking, moving toward a representation), and does not thus represent the singularity of a failed attempt at representation (as a theory of the sublime could still imply).

And here, too, we mark a difficult distance from Levinas. Explicitly, and repeatedly, Levinas declares himself to be a humanist, declares obligation to be the nature of being human, declares the obligation to be, in its turn, toward the other human as such (a humanism instituted, and guarded, by God, it is true, and not by other humans). Perhaps we should say that we are looking at two readings of Levinas, by Levinas, in terms of the face (the exteriority of the other as human) and the body (the exterior as given): the first takes humanity to be other than its essence, outside the economy of conceptualizations within which it is produced as a concept, but precisely as absent, as the goal of the economy's machinations (even when unfulfilled). Thus Levinas can say that obligation is the essence of communication. The second reading, also drawn from Levinas himself, sees that obligation as constantly in the future, and as constantly not mine. This is a reading of the body, of what one could think of as the field of meaning thought in its literalizing, in its gradual accumulation, and not in its enactment. It is, after all, from the body and its enjoyments that we begin to question our freedom (in the face of the other). This doesn't represent a periodization in Levinas's thought, but a problematic that was always there, albeit differently accented.

However, doubting the compatibility of these approaches, if I and another are both found to be human (to possess that type of body), if I know, in whatever vague sense, what it means to be human, and I act for another 'as' another human, then I know the future for which I act to be mine 'as' human (and, against Levinas, this is true even where the only essential marker of the human is the refusal of possession and the incessant recommencement of giving, precisely where the 'giving', always in expression, is always a

where the artist and the process and the circumstances of the genesis of the work remain unknown, this thrust, this '*that* it is' of createdness, emerges into view most purely from the work" (Heidegger, "The Origin of the Work of Art" [1935], *Poetry Language Thought*, p. 65).

giving to other humans). These two readings of exteriority and possibility would seem to be contradictory at the point where one tried to follow them out into practice (and isn't this what Derrida's "Violence and Metaphysics" already sees in 1964). That is, if the structures of taking 'as' and being given 'as' only belong to human language and the articulations made possible only in terms of the enactments of that language, then the new thinking of possibility I am pointing to would be destined to a continual recapturing within that 'human' language and its (formally closed) possibilities of articulation. My task, then, is to question to what extent we are left with a humanism interpreted in terms of determining articulations.

Levinas, however, and even more explicitly in the works that come after Derrida's article, hangs on to the humanism inherent in his project, although he also reworks it. For reasons I will try to briefly replay, Levinas sees an essential connection between the body, language, and the face (in terms of the possible metaphorizations of justice between/as humans). These problems, of bodies and humans, will take us to the end of this section on mothers.

# i) Structuring time: from indefinite to definite

Second: *in the logic of this procedure, "reliability" is the first or ultimate condition of concrete possibility of any* reattachment: *of the product to its usefulness, to its use, to its subject whether wearer or borne, to its belonging in* general. *These reattachments are attached to* Verlässlichkeit, *to this preoriginary gift* [don] *or abandon—*

*—to* THE-MOTHER *then, or from* THE-MOTHER, *and the two shoes are—*

*—how can you go past what is said with these words without thinking first, in its approach,* Verlässlichkeit? *Then don't be in such a hurry to recognize schemas that are too useful. Don't play utilities.*

—*Derrida, "Restitutions,"*
Truth in Painting

With a question of metaphors, when the question is also approaching the problem of a region other than the speakable, we are necessarily also speaking of a methodology (and not just of a rhetorical device). Levinas's arguments against the neuter, which carry the weight of his criticism of Heidegger, have to do with equating the 'neuter' with a metaphorization of being in terms of the 'it'—Heidegger himself has, of course, taught us this critique within phenomenology, yet Levinas feels that Heidegger has not gone far enough. In Hegel there was a certain necessity of metaphorization. The goal of perfect self-comprehension, of Science, structured itself in terms of the increasingly determined explication (bringing to self-consciousness) of that which had initially only been indeterminate Being (which, as indeterminate, would be equivalent to nothingness). The concept of determination itself serves as the goal of all particular determinations, each determination being, in turn, a granting of form to indeterminate matter—an execution of the indeterminate.

By characterizing the indeterminate as neuter, one avoids any assignment of an ethical value to the motor of history (one would not question the mere fact, or already existing form, of desire; or, phrased more in line with Nietzsche, and a little more radically, all becoming is innocent). Heidegger refuses to think of determination as the purpose of determination (such are the forest paths of his later work), but since he concurrently refuses to assign the ethical weight to determination (the necessity to the metaphorization) that Levinas's humanism calls for, he can't make any ethical judgments about history. To complain of this failure to appropriately value the ethical is to (unfairly) read Heidegger's work as a variation of Hegel's—at least insofar as it thinks of time—but it thus also reveals the basically Hegelian conception of temporality (albeit turned around) and of metaphor (or conceptuality) that Levinas himself held at the time of *Totality and Infinity*. Although I will only have the space to sketch out this position, my point is that *Totality and Infinity* has not understood the 'methodological' problem of time as profoundly as *Otherwise than Being*. Levinas's changing critique of Heidegger, I believe, makes this difference clear. In *Totality and Infinity*, after clarifying the sense in which he feels Heidegger's emphasis on freedom sacrifices the other insofar as she/he is as an existing being, Levinas extends his critique to the metaphorizations of Heidegger's later works:

> The "egoism" of ontology is maintained even when, denouncing Socratic philosophy as already forgetful of Being and already on the way to the notion of the "subject" and technological power, Heidegger finds in Presocratism thought as obedience to the truth of Being. This obedience would be accomplished in existing as builder and cultivator, effecting the unity of the site which sustains space. In bringing together presence on the earth and under the firmament of the heavens, the waiting for the gods and the company of mortals in the presence to the things—which is to build and to cultivate—Heidegger, with the whole of Western history, takes the relation with the Other as enacted in the destiny of sedentary peoples, the possessors and builders of the earth. Possession is preeminently the form in which the other becomes the same, by becoming mine. In denouncing the sovereignty of the technological powers of man Heidegger exalts the pre-technological powers of possession. His analyses do not start with the thing-object, to be sure, but they bear the mark of the great landscapes to which the things refer. Ontology becomes ontology of nature, impersonal fecundity, faceless generous mother, matrix of particular beings, inexhaustible matter for things. (Levinas, *Totality and Infinity* [1960], p. 46)

What I wish to bring out in this quote is the modality of the argument. To defend Heidegger (and one would feel compelled to do such if involved in a reading of Heidegger), the lost subtlety of the metaphors, in particular, that the sedentary does not imply the possessive, would have to be reinvoked (we would, for example, and with our epigraph, turn toward a reliability and a letting-be). However, to Levinas's credit, such subtleties are not what lie at stake here. The choice of the metaphors, the poetic freedom of metaphorization (which, of course, is not the disconnected 'freedom' of caprice), that which Heidegger himself taught us to see as primary, is exactly what Levinas contests in his use of the face. The generosity of the mother, in that post-Heideggerian thinking where ontology and approach (or language) are not so neatly divided, is the generosity of a metaphor—Levinas's criticism could be rephrased as the demand for a face, the demand that we respect the necessity of the face, that face which gives every metaphorization (and every ontology) its purpose (and, for that—since metaphors only exist as a projection toward . . .—it is the face that even gives possibility). That is, if the face is a metaphor, it literalizes that instant in which the metaphor stands for the very failure of metaphor in general, for the necessity of the nonmetaphor (which is why the face is said to be the immediate). The freedom of metaphorization, the conceptualization, according to Levinas, is justified (or shown to be injust) in the face.

Why speak against the freedom of the metaphor? Or, even more, for the necessity of a particular set of metaphors (in this case, humanist ones)? Is there some exigency of the real world (say, an Auschwitz taken as ethical atrocity) that demands a new metaphorization, or even an end to metaphorization? Simply, no; Levinas is not invoking a pure time before atrocity, not denouncing a failure of a community that could be said to have already existed; he is *invoking* an eschatology of peace, an ideal of reconciliation (an ideal which is no longer, as with Hegel, death). But he is conscious of the strange and disruptive temporality needed for understanding the power and the force of this invocation of peace. In a fundamental sense, again, the basic interpretation of time is a modified Hegelianism. The very concept of meaning (now found in the ethical relation to the other and not in the domination/determination of the other) controls the choice of metaphors (instead of scientific/descriptive metaphors descending from an ideal of vision and comprehension, one finds the set of metaphors appropriate to an ethical humanism).[172] We would not thus subordinate the face to the 'concept' of the human, but we would still think in terms of a progression of an economy through time in a basically Hegelian model—only, with Levinas, the condition for the possibility of this economy is thought in the encounter with the face and not from out of the economy itself. Against Levinas, on a path that Levinas teaches us, our

172. Early on, Derrida conceived of both Heidegger and Levinas in terms of a certain necessary violence (called writing in his other works). The necessity of this violence is what I would like to contest here, especially as that necessity is thought as the necessity of determination. The key to my argument has to do with avoiding the dichotomies between violence and continuity, that is to rethink time as other than a violence perpetrated against previous spatial (positional) configurations. Derrida's famous summation of the difference between Levinas and Heidegger in "Violence and Metaphysics" would be relatively fair to the spirit of Levinas's *Totality and Infinity*, which is fundamentally organized around the problem of violence in conceptualizations, and not as fair to Heidegger's work insofar as Heidegger was seeking to avoid conceptualization and not to merely find a nonviolent conceptualization (as Levinas's characterization of Heidegger implies). Derrida's main thrust, indeed, was that Heidegger's Being is not a concept (as Levinas's critique assumes) and therefore the violence of Being's historical progression would be nonethical, and nonconceptual ("Violence and Metaphysics," p. 148). It would still be, however, as the series of displacements of time called history, violent. Since Levinas places the concept "on the plane of Being," the violence of historical progression (of time passing in any sense) would be a violence of a concept against the infinite (the face) which doesn't of itself fit

task will be, eventually, to think carefully *against* this very model of making possible and fulfilling the possible in the actual.

The criticism of Heidegger at this point in *Totality and Infinity* is less subtle than the one in *Otherwise than Being*, but I think it's worth following through on several themes from the earlier work, especially, in terms of our questions, concerning the "faceless generous mother" that ontology is said to be. That which makes the mother "faceless" is the subordination of the human other to the freedom of metaphorization—insofar as freedom is a generative ideal, said to avoid any reference to any actual givenness by a particular other. Heidegger, supposedly, thinks that the "truth of Being" is the freedom of ecstatic transcendence, i.e., that the trajectory of time is controlled by its destiny in some truth/abstraction/metaphorization (such as the concept of temporal ecstases) which doesn't refer to the other's immediacy as expressive. Heidegger's preference for the sedentary, for the continuance of man in (and his shepherding of) the truth, would commit a violence towards the other because it demands that all truth be measured by its duration (within Being), by its return to its origin in ecstatic time (freedom of/as a grasping or comprehension of the other). We would have to agree, I think, that there is a problem with the metaphor of dwelling, but I think we might also find, within the multiplication of metaphors, a self-consciousness relative to language, an escape from the necessity of any one type of metaphorization—which is merely to say, a little closer to Heidegger, that dwelling is not freedom, that the freedom of metaphorization is not my freedom as author, as self-originating cause of time, nor my freedom as my destiny (as if I belonged to that freedom); but merely to say, as a problem of method for thought in general, that metaphorizations (mine or others') occur in time, that one dwells or questions within a time designated by its dwelling (a self-reference which I had hoped to approach in the metaphor of literalization).[173] That time itself is subject, in turn, to metaphorization is what necessitates our methodological move away from presence (or even the play of absence and presence) and toward literalization: thus one thinks the gradations of time's coming without simply pretending to stand outside of time.

As opposed to the metaphor of dwelling, Levinas puts forth the idea of fecundity; opposed to the metaphor of possession, he offers the freedom of pardon. Fecundity, as the metaphor implies, is the capacity to have offspring, to engender new beings. Bruno's God, for example, is not fecund (has no room for a Christ), because his ontology assumes an already closed perfection of form (like a faceless, impersonal, nature, always repeating the same). But fecundity also implies a certain debt of the new toward the past, a certain guilt incurred through changing the order of meaning. Pardon will rename the work of reconciliation that Hegel had thought of as a death. We will return to these metaphors more carefully later, but I want to begin by marking a certain congruence here in Levinas's thinking of time and the model of a gradual entry into the economy, a literalization of the inherited tasks such that (and oriented by the necessity that) we can be at peace with them.

The discontinuous time of fecundity

inside of any concept. (And time would be derivative of a concept called violence—or, more properly, of the conceptual pair violence/nonviolence.) For Derrida, what does not fit (the positive infinity called God, or the remains of his passing) gives form to time 'as' violence, as the movement from indeterminate Being towards determinate Being (i.e., the conception of time rests on a spatial teleology, an economy of exteriority, borrowed from Hegel). The differing characterizations of that which remains 'after' the determination is what tracks the (considerable) development of Derrida's work (increasingly distant from what I'm calling the Hegelian formulation).

173. For Heidegger's part, invoking a nobility 'higher' than our customary turn towards humanism, he has the Teacher in "Conversation on a Country Path" (1944–45) say, "(T)he nature of man is released to that-which-regions and used by it accordingly, for this reason alone—that man of himself has no power over truth and it remains independent of him. Truth's nature can come forth independently of man only because the nature of man (as releasement to that-which-regions) is used by that-which-regions in regioning both with respect to man and to sustain determining. Evidently, truth's independence *from* man is a relation *to* human nature, a relation which rests on the regioning of human nature into that-which-regions" (Heidegger, *Discourse on Thinking* [1959], p. 84).

makes possible an absolute youth and recommencement, while leaving the recommencement a relation with the recommenced past in a free return to that past (free with a freedom other than that of memory), and in free interpretation and free choice, in an existence as entirely pardoned. This recommencement of the instant, this triumph of the time of fecundity over the becoming of the mortal and aging being, is a pardon, the very work of time. (Levinas, *Totality and Infinity* [1961], p. 282)

Eventually, in terms of what I've already said about time, we would have to look carefully at the ways in which the instant here is overly privileged (and the ways in which it stems from his thinking of paternity and not maternity). The sense in which a pardon might be the work of time is what interests us first—especially as it does not interpret time to be anxious to complete the act of pardoning. For a pardon is a type of affirmation that issues from one human toward another (neither the grace of a god nor the mere acceptance of a natural fact). Pardon is a freedom that is not performed in one's own name, that does not ensure that the gift of pardoning will be repaid. As he makes clear in the following pages, Levinas is really playing off of Nietzsche's idea of active forgetting, of the innocence of becoming, yet emphasizing that unlike the forgetting which "nullifies the relations with the past," "pardon conserves the past pardoned in the purified present." We are given the present from which to think, not in the I that knows its freedom to be becoming, but in the 'I' that knows that its own 'I' is constantly losing its definition in the indefinition of fecundity and future. This 'I', "the least sedentary, the most graceful being, the being most launched toward the future, produces the irreparable," which will, in turn, be in need of reparation, of pardon.

Pardon, as a moment of phenomenological description, is the bridge between the methodological necessity of continuity, of the I's unique being the same, being responsible as the same, and the continuous ruptures that the face represents within that continuity (ceaselessly displacing the site of meaning away from the individual who is hostage to those other sites, who, unique in responsibility, is the only access point to a sense of justice for the world in general). The Kantian apperceptive unity, the transcendental 'I' of philosophy insofar as it is separated from the body of its occurrence, must dissolve for a future configuration of unity to take place. But if that unity is to have historical meaning, the previous unity must also have its place within the new configuration. The pardon preserves the sense of that previous *unity*, forgiving the violences that were perpetrated in its name, and those that were perpetrated as the dismantling of its unity.

Although it would doubtlessly surprise some readers of Levinas, at this

point he is leaning toward a phenomenological approach to meaning—and, methodologically, a solipsism (of sorts). This accords
well with his thinking of time, as we will see,
even though something of that thinking
changes with *Otherwise than Being* (my thesis
being that the change in Levinas also has to
do with the same problems within phenomenology's method of approach that I am seeking to address). In terms of a method, why
would we think of pardoning the 'I', the one
launched toward the future? Simply, because
the 'I' is the site of meaning, and meaning is
always a violence, always a separation from
your simple enjoyment of the material (is always at the site of an encounter with, and
comprehension of, another human's expression). For that, I obviously don't mean an 'I'
alone in the world, in some type of extreme
metaphysical solipsism; instead, I am pointing to a methodological solipsism that can
understand meaning only as an individual's
conceiving. That individual's conception is
no longer thought of as a grasping, but as a
fecundity, as a transcending toward a future—one is only capable of meaning in the
face of the other, in the face of the other as
the site of meaning, yet one finds oneself
hostage to the other: one cannot approach
that meaning as the master, as the source of
the meaningful; one only approaches the
meaning through the self held hostage by
the other.[174] The dissolution is not the
other's, but mine (which is why I am responsible for the other's meaning; only through
my fecundity, through my dissolution, can I
grant the other the space of my pardon). One
is tempted to say that the face causes the dissolution, but (as the "passivity more passive
than any passivity" of Levinas's later work

174. The metaphor of the
hostage properly belongs to later
works, where the methodological
move is more carefully thought
through in terms of the meaning
of time and the type of constitution that a transcendental ego
was involved in (although *Totality and Infinity* also clearly owes a
debt to this method).

175. In any case then, within
myself, within the limits of
my transcendentally reduced
pure conscious life, I *experience* the world (including others)—and, according to its experiential sense, *not* as (so to
speak) my *private* synthetic
formation but as other than
mine alone [*mir fremde*], as an
*intersubjective* world, actually
there for everyone, accessible
in respect of its Objects to
everyone. And yet each has
his experiences, his appearances and appearance-unities,
his world-phenomenon;
whereas the experienced world
exists in itself, over against all
experiencing subjects and
their world-phenomena.
What is the explanation of
this? Imperturbably I must
hold fast to the insight that
every sense that any existent
whatever has or can have for
me—in respect of its "what"
and its "it exists and actually
is"—is a sense *in* and *arising
from* my intentional life, becoming clarified and uncovered for me in consequence of
my life's constitutive syntheses, in systems of harmonious
verification. (Husserl, *Cartesian Meditations* [1929],
p. 91)

For his part, Levinas:

> *My* substitution—it is as *my own* that substitution for the neighbor is produced. The Mind is a multiplicity of individuals. It is in me—in me and not in another, in me and not in an individuation of the concept Ego—that communication opens. It is I who am integrally or absolutely ego, and the absolute is my business. No one can substitute himself for me, who substitutes myself for all. Or, if one means to remain with the hierarchy of formal logic—genus, species, individual—it is in the course of the individuation of the ego in me that is realized the elevation in which the ego is for the neighbor, summoned to answer for him. (*Otherwise than Being* [1974], p. 127)

176. "We now ask, How is *the whole of this structure*, of being-in-the-world, *founded in temporality?* Being-in-the-*world* belongs to the basic constitution of the being that is in each case mine, that at each time I *myself* am. Self and world belong together; they belong to the unity of the constitution of the Dasein and, with equal originality, they determine the 'subject'. In other words, the being that we ourselves in each case are, the Dasein, is the *transcendent*" (Heidegger, *Basic Problems of Phenomenology* [1927], p. 298). And, "The overstepping as such, or that whose mode of being must be defined precisely by this overstepping, properly understood, is the Dasein" (p. 299).

more clearly shows) the responsibility for that dissolution does not arise from anything other than the structure of the unicity, of the infinity (of the human, or the condition of humanity) itself. The question we will be posing to Levinas, is whether that unicity also implies a continuity, a self-definition in terms of the one who has the originary right to dissolution and pardon, a continuity that loads his ethics down with a conservative traditionalism or at least with an individualism inappropriate for thinking through the types of structural oppressions that characterize our times.

In terms of Levinas's analyses, the method proceeds from the individual encounter with time, finding, as Husserl found of other subjectivities in the *Cartesian Meditations*, that the other is already present within that time,[175] indeed—beyond Husserl—as that which gives the possibility (as 'impossible' limit) that structures time. This brings us to the difference which I think leads to the different accentuations of Levinas's two major works. In *Totality and Infinity* (1961), contact with the face is the structure of meaning (of the immediacy of having meaning—those meanings then being accessible to desedimentations of sense, etc.). This is fundamentally a deepening of the Husserlian concentration on intention as both object and method of philosophy. That he metaphorizes this in a way which explicitly contradicts the scientific vocabulary of Husserl has to do with a number of issues surrounding the neuter and issuing in the claim that ethics precedes both ontology and intentionality. At this point, however, I merely want to mark the fact that this takes the center of Husserlian phenomenology to be the structure of intentionality. The face of the other undergirds the possibility of intentionality—it is a prior, and not an opposed, structuring (although this fact has numerous effects on the later analyses).

This simultaneous critique and appropriation evolved from Levinas's early study of Husserl, and especially from his understanding of thematization (the criticism of which Heidegger's *Being and Time* had already brought to bear against intentional analyses in the name of Dasein's kind of transcendence).[176] Unfortunately, Levinas's understanding of that critique misses the mark—especially insofar as it concerns the other subjectivities of the world—to the extent that it fails to see the full importance of the transcendental ego in the constitutive work of meaning, in the course of a time which is not self-combative.[177] The unicity of the ego, already invoked in *Totality and Infinity*, has the flavor of a responsibility for the moment of contact—the face calls for a judgment, a decision, a justice. The unicity in *Otherwise than Being*, like Husserl's transcendental ego, has stopped being the instituting of a just site: instead, as the very possibility of unicity, of identity in meaning, it is the structure of a time that can come to be either in a site or as continuously errant (although there remains a necessity to the metaphorization of the opposition of motion and rest).[178] He will metaphorize this new thinking of unicity explicitly in terms of the maternal and from that metaphor we will be trying to accentuate the possibilities of new births in time.

I will later take up the discussion of unicity, with which Levinas justifies his humanism, in terms of the body (a discussion

177. Rather, he seems to feel, insofar as the ego exists as the intentional—"*Intentionality is what makes up the very subjectivity of subjects*" (Levinas, *The Theory of Intuition in Husserl's Phenomenology* [1930], p. 41)—that the structures of transcendence, or of transcending, as understood in the interchange between subjects, fully explain the time (the economy of transcendences) as it relates to the individual transcendence. Part of the change in his thinking, which we will not have the space to consider here, would be his introduction of the idea of a trace (beginning in 1963), which, by my understanding, better conceptualizes the participation of others within the economy, or rather, the unicity, of the same.

178. In summary, then, Levinas is trying to better think through the meaning of Infinity, of the separation and connection of the ego from/as the conceptual economy:

> It will then be necessary to show that the exception of the "other than being," beyond not-being, signifies subjectivity or humanity, the *oneself* which repels the annexations by essence. The ego is an incomparable unicity; it is outside of the community of genus and form, and does not find any rest in itself either, unquiet, not coinciding with itself. The outside of itself, the difference from oneself of this unicity is non-indifference itself, and the extraordinary recurrence of the pronominal or the reflexive,

the *self* (*se*)—which no longer surprises us because it enters into the current flow of language in which things show *themselves*, suitcases fold and ideas are understood (les choses *se* montrent, les bagages *se* plient et les idées *se* comprennent). A unicity that has no site, without the ideal identity a being derives from the kerygma that identifies the innumerable aspects of its manifestation, without the identity of the ego that coincides with itself, a unicity withdrawing from essence— such is man. (*Otherwise than Being*, p. 8)

He then goes on to identify Plato's One, "Husserl's pure Ego, transcendent in immanence," and Nietzsche's poetic writing as philosophical examples of this unicity in withdrawal, of this turn towards the human.

179. The will is free to assume this responsibility in whatever sense it likes; it is not free to refuse this responsibility itself; it is not free to ignore the meaningful world into which the face of the Other has introduced it. *In the welcoming of the face the will opens to reason.* Language is not limited to the maieutic awakening of thoughts common to beings. It does not accelerate the inward maturation of a reason common to all; it teaches and introduces the new into a thought. The introduction of the new into a thought, the idea of infinity, is the very work of reason. The absolutely new is the Other.

which will point to more marked contrasts between Levinas's two approaches), but for now I want to explore further the type of time he is invoking throughout *Totality and Infinity*. As Derrida points out in "Violence and Metaphysics" [1963], this sense of time, insofar as it is related to an eschatology, can be phrased "in the form of a question to Hegel, in whom this adventure is thought and recapitulated" (*Writing and Difference*, p. 149). Levinas's later sense of time, less an eschatology than an archeology, would not exist as "a question to Hegel." (And, further, would not be organized by the same problem of violence in/as time; Heidegger's sense of time, I would hazard, does not really issue from this Hegelian problematic at all, even in its earliest formulations).

We noted earlier that determination serves as an organizing telos for Hegel. The determination called justice in *Totality and Infinity* serves a similar purpose except that it explicitly refuses the Hegelian placement of the telos beyond the activity (the time) itself. In each contact with the other, the rational is enacted in its immediacy as nonviolence because the form of meaning and the purpose of meaning coincide in the moment of contact.[179]

Fecundity grants us the indeterminate (explains the possibility of the ego's self-dissolution), but the meaning of time, the eschatology of meaning, always structures that indeterminacy as a movement towards determinacy; that is, contact with the other calls us forth to speak, calls us forth into the diachrony of rupture and response:

> If time does not make moments of mathematical time, indifferent to one

another, succeed one another, it does not accomplish Bergson's *continuous duration* either. The Bergsonian conception of time explains why it is necessary to wait "for the sugar to melt": time no longer expresses the unintelligible dispersion of the unity of being, wholly contained in the first cause, in an apparent and phantasmal series of causes and effects; time adds something new to being, something absolutely new. But the newness of springtimes that flower in the instant (which, in good logic, is like the prior one) is already heavy with all the springtimes lived through. The profound work of time delivers from this past, in a subject that breaks with his father. Time is the non-definitiveness of the definitive, an ever recommencing alterity of the accomplished—the "ever" of this recommencement. The work of time goes beyond the suspension of the definitive which the continuity of duration makes possible. There must be a rupture of continuity, and continuation across this rupture. The essential in time consists in being a drama, a multiplicity of acts where the following act resolves the prior one. (*Totality and Infinity*, pp. 283–84)

The rational is not opposed to the experienced; absolute experience, the experience of what is in no way a priori, is reason itself. In discovering, as correlative of experience, the Other, him who, being in himself essentially, can speak, and nowise sets himself up as an object, the *novelty* contributed by experience is reconciled with the ancient Socratic exigency of a mind nothing can force, an exigency Leibniz again answers to in refusing the monads windows. The ethical presence is both other and imposes itself without violence. As the activity of reason commences with speech, the subject does not abdicate his unicity, but confirms his separation. He does not enter into his own discourse to disappear in it; it remains an apology. The passage to the rational is not a dis-individuation precisely because it is language, that is, a response to the being who in a face speaks to the subject and tolerates only a personal response, that is, an ethical act. (*Totality and Infinity*, pp. 218–19)

Obviously, the distance between Hegel and Levinas here is constituted by a reversal of priorities. Where Hegel's conception of time had concentrated on the achieved definition that closes time (that correctly articulates the form of time), and an exterior violence had always been needed to reopen time, Levinas accentuates the renewal of time in the pardon (the opposite of violence) which always recommences as "the non-definitiveness of the definitive." We will take this up again, but I would like now to mark a doubt about this conception of time exactly where we expect to find the mother, the one who (in a transgenerational slippage of metaphors that Levinas might yet oppose) "separates the father from the son," in fecundity. Levinas continues where we left off:

> Being is no longer produced at one blow, irremissibly present. Reality is what it is, but will be once again, another time freely resumed and pardoned. Infinite being is produced as times, that is, in several times across the dead time that separates the father from the son. It is not the finitude of being that constitutes the essence of time, as Heidegger thinks, but its infinity. The death sentence does not approach as an end of being, but as an unknown, which as such suspends power. The constitution of the interval that liberates being from the limitation of fate calls for death. The nothingness of the interval—a dead time—is the production of infinity. (*Totality and Infinity*, p. 284)

And in this doubt I will be trying to separate the thinking of discontinuity inspired by a Hegelian thinking of time, but more aware of the moment of alterity,[180] from a thinking of time which accentuates a passivity and a hesitation, a time which no longer seeks its death—nor its rejuvenation: such a time would have to give itself to you, the audience of its articulation, the object of its

180. Taking up again with Levinas: "Resurrection constitutes the principal event of time. There is therefore no continuity in being. Time is discontinuous; one instant does not come out of another without interruption, by an ecstasy. In continuation the instant meets its death, and resuscitates; death and resurrection constitute time. But such a formal structure presupposes the relation of the I with the Other and, at its basis, fecundity across the discontinuous which constitutes time" (*Totality and Infinity*, p. 284).

metaphors. Unity and violence will no longer generate the conceptual schemas that would either embrace or rebuke one or the other: one transcends toward the other by (infinitely, incessantly) undoing one's own unity, but one does not thereby reference the purity of a time or an intention. Unity is not a concept, not an ideality, but merely, as Levinas comes more and more to understand, shorthand for the methodological (metaphorical) aporia occasioned by the realization that your own transcendence only has meaning (can only come to be phrased) in (incessant) contact, or proximity, with the (infinitely) other.[181]

What we are trying to open onto, following Levinas through his work after *Totality and Infinity*, is that time which does not demand a dead time, a material other, an indeterminateness of matter (or of the mother), pure in its latency, in order to think the unity of meaning (and we should not underestimate to what extent such an opening would not be 'meaningful', would not reference a tradition of meaningful words). This is the point where a metaphor—as an open problem, a self-consciously questionable freedom of/for metaphorization—is ethically more responsive than intentional descriptions. For you can bet a metaphor, place it at stake in an affirmation without claiming its clarity, its purity, or its reduction to nothingness; you play a metaphor without giving up the ironic distance which knows it was, after all, just a metaphor; in the bet, you don't declare the necessity of the metaphor, nor even the 'necessity' of metaphorization (since the metaphor occurs within, as a responding to, time and does not simply create meaning of its own accord). Here the criticism I am

181. And, of course, the distance between proximity and confrontation is what lies at stake. Proximity would be, as briefly as possible, a contact which does not feel the anxiety of contact, the need to determine, precisely because, in proximity, the other is as a unity (not as the embodiment of a concept called unity), is as that which isn't in need of my determining activity: "Consciousness consists in thematizing across a multiplicity, and in thus manifesting being by proclaiming its unity and its identity. But language as a contact touches the neighbor in his non-ideal unity. Hence we can say that the neighbor does not show, does not manifest, himself. He lacks the horizon of multiplicity in which his identity could be proclaimed, maintained, thematized, and thus revealed. But he lacks what he has no need of. The neighbor is precisely what has a meaning *immediately*, before one ascribes one to him" (Levinas, "Language and Proximity" [1967], *Collected Philosophical Papers*, p. 119).

trying to develop of a time conceived as a trajectory from indetermination to determination (no matter how often recommenced in indeterminism) finds its justification in the problem I first attempted to phrase at the end of the section on sisters.

At that point, I tried to question the purity of an affirmation, of a justice, which could supposedly universally mediate our conflicting (political) claims. The critique of that purity arises from an unwillingness to grant any regulative pride of place outside of the given economy of conceptualizations (one wants to know what, exactly, God is, or at least what he wants, before assenting to his command). That is, if we are to speak of a humanism, we should admit that we are all children of the same (humane) tradition (a Mother, since we are speaking of that part of the tradition which the rest of the tradition takes as its very matter and support) and say "European humanism," "twentieth-century humanism," "Christian humanism," or otherwise mark the incongruity between the ideal (or purely human) and its origin (within a historical or spatial context). The problem is not as simple as it may at first seem, and Levinas's response changes somewhat during the '60s. For all of Levinas's work, the fundamental ideal which structures each human as an infinite other comes from the respect for the other, from "God's original coming to the mind of man"—that which characterizes that coming, however, stops being the instantaneity of contact with the immediate (which, as immediate, has to efface the in-between, declaring it a 'dead time', in order to remove the structure from any taint of a specific context—it is determined as, instead, the universal, and dead, structure of having context), and starts being the patience, or passivity, of a proximity (which no longer relies on surpassing the context, on resolving the indeterminate within the context, turning instead, to speak to the context in its indetermination, as a possibility—only thus do we truly become responsible for the freedom of the other).

The respect for the other, as we earlier noted, takes the very minimal content of a rejection of violence towards others, a respect for their right to self-determination/self-continuity. At the time of *Totality and Infinity*, this respect is justified by the meaning of contact. At the time of *Otherwise than Being*, this respect is justified by the structures of proximity. At first, the differences here would seem trivial, but it will be my purpose, working out this distinction throughout the course of this entire section, to accentuate a certain thinking of time which questions what we mean by respect. If it means no more than the right to hold a constant reserve, to avoid any violence, then it can have no positive contribution to our lives (only a restricting of violences against existing unities). Rather, and with Levinas, we should think through the transcendence itself, the being already part of the economy (which is better thought in proximity than in contact).[182] It is that thinking which will enable us to phrase a question of that whole itself (and not merely work within the whole as it is presently configured).

It would be reductive to think of Levinas's thinking of justice, at any point in his writing, as merely a eurocentric determination of the person (as bearer of rights), but his work would still seem to point to a certain necessary contamination of the mother (a certain debt to a particular tradition), a propensity towards respect instilled by the mother in her children, separating this mother from the generous faceless mother of ontology (as well as thereby suggesting that mothers might have different, perhaps culturally specific, faces). After all, and for the most obvious example here, there are genetic differences between a human and a tree—literally traits inherited from previous generations. Further, as racism seems to prove, we *learn* to love or hate certain traits in faces. Are we then to separate good from bad contaminations, love from hate? If the mother instills, for an obvious example, incestuous desire (and consequently love is always mixed with familial competition and a subject's self-loathing), if the mother is the site of anxiousness or even psychosis, if such anxiety is found to be at the very root of our culture, or even our bodies, are we going to have some ground from which to expunge the impure in the name of the just and righteous impurity? Can our anxiety over anxiety rid us of anxiety?

Mohandas Gandhi posed the same questions within his political—practice, passive or nonviolent resistance?—and the failures and successes of that practice are particularly interesting within our present

182. "The ontological language which *Totality and Infinity* maintains in order to exclude the purely psychological significance of the proposed analyses is hereafter avoided. And the analyses themselves refer not to the *experience* in which a subject always thematizes what he himself equals, but to the *transcendence* in which he is responsible for that which his intentions do not encompass" (Levinas, "Signature" [1963, 1975], *Research in Phenomenology* [1978], 8:189).

183. However, we should not construe Levinas as a believer in this practice. Rather, and one would have to look at this reasoning in depth, in his conception of the human as such, he counts on the force of the external law to maintain even our own adherence to the good: "Here then is our conclusion at this point: we must impose commands on ourselves in order to be free. But it must be an exterior command, not simply a rational law, not a categorical imperative, which is defenseless against tyranny; it must be an exterior law, a written law, armed with force against tyranny. Such are commands as the political condition for freedom" (Levinas, "Freedom and Command" [1953], *Collected Philosophical Papers*, p. 17). In this way, at least in part, Levinas avoids the type of individualism which keeps Gandhi's political program from having deeper structural ramifications, although one would have to ask of Gandhi if nonviolence, as a practice, also came 'from outside', as a command or law.

questions of purity, pardon, and justice.[183] Explaining the failure of passive resistance as a political movement in South Africa, Gandhi references the problem of a context and of a conscience that must have the time to grow:

> We fought to keep the theory of the British Constitution in tact so that practice may some day approach the theory as near as possible. . . . passive resistance . . . is at present inapplicable, its application being confined to grievances which are generally felt in a community and are known to hurt its self-respect or conscience. . . . Our grievances . . . may any day advance to that stage. . . . Till then, only the ordinary remedies of petition, etc., can be and are at present being applied. (Letter of 1915, quoted in E. Erikson, *Gandhi's Truth* [1969], pp. 216–17)

At this level of sophistication, Gandhi's work would constitute only a particularly striking example of the dependence of contemporary politics on the idea of the public, on political demonstrations, and on a general consensus on basic principles. A nonviolent protest would solely fulfill the purpose of elevating the individual protesters to the privileged position of the 'human', a bearer of rights, and would demonstrate (to the community which holds the power) that those rights were being violated (although it doesn't necessarily demonstrate how since there is a displacement of a long-standing grievance into a single instance of exemplary injustice: one wants to get arrested, or beaten up, in order to make the papers, in order to demonstrate the depth of one's indignation). The bases of society are not questioned, and the original promise of communality and justice (as supposedly expressed in the constitution) is all that anyone seeks. Usually, given the vagaries of constitutional hermeneutics, what is eventually invoked is the idea of a human right, or set of rights, that everyone is entitled to 'under the constitution'. As is often pointed out, a revolution in the ownership of the means of production will not occur as a result of nonviolent protests of this sort (although we would have to work through the various examples in the former communist countries). Or, rather more close to the point, such a revolution could not occur without a previous (and generally accepted) change in the conception of human rights such that a different type of control of the means of production was construed as a basic right (and this could perhaps occur in some realms, even in the U.S., such as insurance, health care, housing, or banking).

Even when the successes are spectacular, as in India's Independence Movement or in the United States's Civil Rights Movement, one tends to be dissatisfied with some of the results. True, the nontrivial extension of abstract legal rights in the U.S. has profoundly changed the way daily life is conducted, but the continuation of entrenched concrete manifestations of racism has been both horrific and politically daunting. In the same vein, India won the right to self-determination, but only at the cost of the split with Pakistan (since self-determination was taken to imply a certain religious role in terms of how a culture determines itself) and contemporary inhabitants of the subcontinent continue to be among the world's most victimized. Further, and more difficult to pinpoint as a transgression of any individual's rights, the self-determined governments of the ex-colonies of the world are all at the mercy of the International Monetary Fund and the various less formal coalitions of capital, both inside and out of their own countries, which are serving to bring the world under one single logic of production and expropiation. This logic already raises the ideal of individual human rights as its own banner, and would be difficult to contest in any straightforward way by appealing to the ideal of human rights that we already carry with us from out of our capitalist dominated tradition—more insidiously, in the terms of this tradition, it seems that international capital is always fully justified in advance of any activity, since it merely innocently desires its due profits (and an injustice could be declared only *after* the damages were accrued).

Gandhi, however, was appealing to a tradition of nonviolence in India which did not arise from the European discourse on rights, or respect for the human as such. We should, perhaps, not even talk about this non-European idea of nonviolence as a tradition—since the ideal of nonviolence rather explicitly opposes itself to the concept of a history. That is, the way in which we conceive of cultural transmission (over the dead body of a mother, the intentions of a father pass to the son) fits perfectly well with the (Occidental) idea of rights implied in our conception of the person. On the other hand, the Gandhian idea of nonviolence, and of the religious transcendence which accrues to pure nonviolence, is explicitly not fulfilled in the person who wishes for some type of fulfillment (of self-interest).

That is, in terms of the metaphors of this section, our conception of tradition, as with our corresponding conception of rights, leads us to phrase a dichotomy between originator and recipient (father and son, government and citizen) which demands that the mother be impure (have been possessed, and transformed, by the father). When Derrida proclaims that there is no outside the text, he is merely noting that, within this economy of violence in/as meaning, there can be no pure mother (and therefore no pure son, etc.). My point with Gandhi, and trying to stretch the sense of these basically religious metaphors to reach toward Levinas's reconceptions of his philosophical task, is that the purity he refers to is the purity of a withdrawal, and not the purity of an intention: the contamination of the mother becomes a nonquestion, a question incapable of creating anxiety (the motor force of tradition in the Western sense) precisely because one never *intended* anything to pass across that body, precisely because tradition, the transmission of truth, is no longer *the* question, no longer the source, and destiny, of all anxiety.

Some years, and some significant successes, after the just cited letter, Gandhi is replying to a doubter within the ranks, a man who says that Satyagraha[184] depends on the "[i]mplicit belief that the sight of suffering on the part of multitudes of people will melt the heart of the aggressor and induce him to desist from his course of violence." His reply is exemplary of his feeling for the force of faith, or truth, in swaying people's minds. He agrees that this assumption would have to be true:

> I have argued from the analogy of what we do in families or even clans. The humankind is one big family. And if the love expressed is intense enough it must apply to all mankind. If individuals have succeeded even with savages, why should not a group of individuals succeed with a group, say, of savages? If we can succeed with the English, surely it is merely an extension of faith to believe that we are likely to succeed with less cultured or less liberally-minded nations. I hold that if we succeed with the English, with unadulterated nonviolent effort, we must succeed with the others, which is the same thing as saying that if we achieve freedom with non-violence, we shall defend it also with the same weapon. If we have not achieved that faith our non-

violence is a mere expedient, it is alloy, not pure gold. (Gandhi, *Non-violent Resistance*, pp. 362–63)

In light of the deliberate, and sometimes even horrifyingly well-publicized, genocides of our times, such a claim must seem a little more than dangerously naive. At the very least, one feels some need to appeal to limited contexts within which such publicity and concomitant indignation would work (well-cultured, or well-mothered, nations). But perhaps the real point is, again, the freedom of metaphorization which is possible politically—a freedom which, at its extreme, puts in doubt our sense for the differences between civilized and savage. It is still possible to *describe* all of what Gandhi accomplished as "mere expedient," as yet another technique available within the political. But that was not his own goal. Rather, he sought to make the political realm subject to a certain purity which was not public, a purity which was not the purity of a mother who would transmit the intention of the British Constitution to all humans, but the purity of a withdrawal from violence, of a withdrawal from the necessity of a historical discourse about violence, and to thus allow us to rethink the bases upon which we believe politics, and all human relations, to be founded.[185]

If the human is constituted as that which is capable of peace, if the essence of humanity is that capacity, then one should be able to appeal to the desire to be human. One doesn't decide, according to Gandhi's model, on the basis of self-interest, or of interest at all, but on the basis of a definition, of a conception of nonviolence as truth. He

184. "Satyagraha differs from Passive Resistance as the North Pole from the South. The latter has been conceived as a weapon of the weak and does not exclude the use of physical force or violence for the purpose of gaining one's end, whereas the former has been conceived as a weapon of the strongest and excludes the use of violence in any shape or form. . . . Its root meaning is holding on to truth, hence truth-force. I have also called it Love-force or Soul-force" (Gandhi, extract from a statement to the Hunter Committee, *Non-violent Resistance*, p. 6).

185. True, he argues from "analogy" with the family, but that doesn't imply that the family structure is what he would reproduce: the freedom to find in the family something other than patriarchal domination is the freedom which makes a true politics possible (as it is the freedom which makes a family's life a negotiated complex of meanings, no matter how traditional or liberated)—because it is what makes possible the questioning (both thematized and unthematized) of the most basic structures of our being and of our being-together, because it makes the approach (both thematized and unthematized) towards the future possible.

186. Responding to the question, "But is not the Other also responsible in my regard?" Levinas says: "Perhaps, but that is *his* affair. One of the fundamental themes of *Totality and Infinity* about which we have not yet spoken is that the intersubjective relation is a non-symmetrical relation. In this sense, I am responsible for the Other without waiting for reciprocity, were I to die for it. Reciprocity is *his* affair" (*Ethics and Infinity* [1982], p. 98). Yet Levinas, unlike Gandhi, does not trust in the other with the blindness of a faith, or the passivity of a renunciation of the world: "I have previously said elsewhere—I do not like mentioning it for it should be completed by other considerations—that I am responsible for the persecutions that I undergo. But only me! My 'close relations' or 'my people' are already the others and, for them, I demand justice" (ibid., p. 99).

thus makes the break with the simplistic appeal to a particular granting of rights (the British Constitution) and even with the mere appeal to conscience which invokes the rights of the transgressed (they are not rights possessed by any specific person, but only a general potentiality within humanity, a potentiality that the oppressor should want to fulfill for him/herself exactly insofar as the oppressor, too, should want to withdraw from the economy of violence—in this sense, the oppressed plays a trump card against the oppressor and operates from the absolute solidity, the strength, of withdrawal, merely offering to teach the oppressor the same solidity as found within such an infinite withdrawal).[186] One fatal flaw, it would seem, is that Gandhi didn't foresee the metaphorical uses of Hegel's separation of family and state. He didn't see that the public realm where value and truth are adjudicated could become the neuter being which no longer needed to reference, as end or source, any particular human face. He didn't see that the truth itself lay with violence. In that light, the claim to nonviolence seems only to invoke a nostalgia for lost community, and is easily dismissed in the name of pragmatism and progress.

Of course, all this was already true when Gandhi was writing; he himself had already seen exactly this. What worked so well for Gandhi—albeit not quite well enough—was his ability to make the metaphor new, to apply it to a new realm (it is the opposite of nostalgia to wish for the end of war, if war is all there has ever been). Gandhi does not appeal to the truth of human nature as we have inherited it (Hegel appeals to that humanity); Gandhi invokes the possibility of a different human nature, one which is not anxious over the purity of the tradition, which is capable of a new literalization of the public.[187] That he feels that this human nature has already manifested itself in the family, and in the clan, perhaps proves that he had a sensitive eye for what was only half-visible, or maybe that he was blind to the power relations and violences inside existing families. Perhaps, taking up the political problems left by Gandhi's generation and their heirs, what we need to see is where the polemical force of his resistance to the political—his political resistance against inhumanity—arose as a new metaphorization of the world (and of the meaning of the human) and not just as a repetition of some particular tradition, some culturally lived truth, or any other preexisting thing. Or more, as a metaphorization that demanded that the power of metaphorization constantly, and exclusively, be invoked only in its withdrawal from violence and from the violence of the public realm of agonistics. Perhaps, for our time, humanism is no longer the metaphor which lets us think through the problem of postcolonial oppressions; we have the freedom, however, to begin again, to rethink humanism, or otherwise than humanism, exactly in our ability to separate ourselves from the economy that has formed us. Should we call that a freedom? We would have to take some time, within some context, to think through the metaphor to the literalization. In any case, it would not be won in a miraculous withdrawal, executed once, and for all time, but would be the extension of a hesitation, always asking what we were just saying, what was just said.

187. And Gandhi's famous eclecticism, choosing among various (opposed) traditions, merely marks that lack of anxiety which separates him from the good (modernist) philosopher, anxious to tell the one true story of election.

In that hesitant spirit, then, we should also think of Gandhi's body, and the ways in which it was the object of a control, of purifications and desires. As well as being the site of his humanity. The extent to which the body as the site of a self-control reinstitutes a trajectory from indetermination to determination (and this would be hard to show for Gandhi, since he doesn't have a theory of the communal body founding communal time) will provide us with the problematic of the following subsection—insofar as Levinas will try to eliminate exactly that conception of time, of trajectories, no matter how brief, which structure time as a making determinate (which is to say that determinations do still occur; they just aren't the reason for the occurrence), and insofar as he will try to think that indeterminism in terms of something called a body.

*The ego is not in itself like matter which,
perfectly espoused by its form, is what it is; it
is in itself like one is in one's skin, that is,
already tight, ill at ease in one's own skin. It is
as though the identity of matter resting in
itself concealed a dimension in which a
retreat to the hither side of immediate
consciousness were possible, concealed a
materiality more material than all matter—a
materiality such that irritability,
susceptibility or exposedness to wounds and
outrage characterizes its passivity, more
passive still than the passivity of effects.
Maternity in the complete being "for the
other" which characterizes it, which is the
very signifyingness of signification, is the
ultimate sense of this vulnerability. This
hither side of identity is not reducible to the
for-itself, where, beyond its immediate
identity, being recognizes itself in its
difference. We have to formulate what the
irremissibility and, in the etymological sense
of the term, the anguish of this in-itself of the
oneself are. This anguish is not the existential
"being-for-death," but the constriction of an
"entry inwards," or the "hither side" of all
extension. It is not a flight into the void, but
a movement into fullness, the anguish of
contraction and breakup.*

—*Levinas*, Otherwise than Being

I have already briefly noted that Levinas's appropriation of phenomenology
went from an original accentuation of the problem of intentionality (rethinking its conditioning ground in the encounter with the other) toward a deeper
understanding of the way in which intentionality was already dependent on
the structures (especially the unicity) of the transcendental ego (a fact which
invokes the need for a correspondingly changed conception of time and of our
understanding of what 'conditions' possibility itself). Such a distinction will

188. And, in my terms, we would have to ask in what ways a book—a fiction, a play, or a collection of notes, epigraphs, and narratives—might literalize unicity in such a way as to help us think through (and perhaps modify the sense of thinking *through*) the unique body with which the phenomenologist's method begins.

not suffice to mark some sort of 'turn' in his thought; rather, it is a matter of metaphorization, of an almost stylistic accentuation. By my reading, this difference is best read in light of Husserl's use of the body in *Ideas II*, and, more directly, Merleau-Ponty's appropriation of Husserl's (then still unpublished) work. The body, insofar as we can use a word so burdened with significations, would be a metaphorization of unicity (or a literalization since his idea of unicity itself can only be grasped as something through this metaphor).[188] The body, to play off of our earlier questions, would be the affirmation that allows all metaphorizations, the bet that registers our participation in the economy of exterior things. It would also be, as the only possibility of that engagement, the proof of our existence as hostage, as not merely individual subjects free to choose our positions within the world (it would justify the necessity of a metaphorization of existence in the terms of the human and the human's expressivity).

The body is no longer, as it still was in *Totality and Infinity*, simply part of the economy (or even the very trope of the economy). Rather, and this methodologically pertains to the move of phenomenology toward a thinking of the transcendental ego, the body (before it is thematized) provides the affirmation which makes an 'I think,' an apperceiving ego, possible. Levinas thematizes this possibility in terms of a saying that precedes the said. This difference in tense is crucial to the exposition of *Otherwise than Being* and is brought up within the context of a certain appropriation of phenomenology (beyond the thematization of objects, toward the thinking of the possibility of that thematization, beyond the conditions of possibility, toward the movement of responding to the impossible, a response which is an infinite passivity). The distinction also arises from a disagreement with Merleau-Ponty over the meaning of time in the phenomenology of the body; that is, for Levinas, the thematizations of phenomenology depend on the saying (prior to all time and all constituted flesh).[189] The saying will be called upon to do some of the work previously assigned to fecundity and pardon, but we begin by tracing its roots back to a change in his thinking about the body. In "Meaning and Sense" [1972], Levinas summarizes his understanding of Merleau-Ponty's thinking of the body:

> The cultural action does not express a preexisting thought, but Being, to which, as incarnate, it belongs already. *Meaning cannot be inventoried in the inwardness of a thought.* Thought itself is inserted in culture through the verbal gesture of the body which precedes it and goes beyond it. The objective culture to which, through the verbal creation, it adds something new, illuminates and guides it.
>
> It is then clear that the language through which meaning is produced in being is a language spoken by incarnate minds. The incarnation of thought is not an accident that would have occurred to it and would have complicated its task by diverting the straightforward movement with which it aims at an object. The body is the fact that thought is immersed in the world that it thinks and, consequently, expresses

189. The hither side, the preliminary, which the pre-originary saying animates, refuses the present and manifestation, or lends itself to the said, to the ancillary indiscretion of the abusive language that divulges or profanes the unsayable. But it lets itself be reduced, without effacing the unsaying in the ambiguity or the enigma of the transcendent, in which the breathless spirit retains a fading echo.

But one can go back to this signification of the saying, this responsibility and substitution, only from the said and from the question: 'What is it about . . . ?', a question already within the said in which everything shows itself. One can go back to it through reduction only out of what shows itself, that is, the essence and the thematized eon, of which alone there is a manifestation. But in it the questioning look is only the impossible synchronization of the unassemblable, Merleau-Ponty's fundamental historicity, which the diachrony of proximity has already escaped. (*Otherwise than Being*, pp. 44–45)

this world while it thinks it. The corporeal gesture is not a nervous discharge, but a celebration of the world, a poetry. (Levinas, *Collected Philosophical Papers*, pp. 81–82)

The poetic metaphor is both appropriate and compelling here, for all the reasons that make it inappropriate and tedious to think of poetry as merely representative. The body, after all, is nothing other than itself, has no time other than its own (as we would like to affirm of art as well). Which is to say, with Levinas, that in Merleau-Ponty's concept of the flesh, of the body before it is thematized (before one speaks of my body or your body), we find situated all the temporalities (habitualities, judgments, anticipations, retentions, sedimentations, apperceptions, harmonious verifications, etc.) which make possible the Husserlian analyses of sense.[190] Which is to reiterate that we are asking a question of method, of how to approach the question of meaning. What we are faced with, it would seem, are two ways of interpreting the Husserlian transcendental ego. Merleau-Ponty, in the received reading, sees the possibility of a 'Gestalt' (although Husserl explicitly refused this word) which would find all the meanings sedimented *in* the world simultaneously organized *as* a world. The transcendental ego would be this Gestalt, but not as an observation concerning the world as much as somehow being the world in its configuration (and not some thing operating, like a machine, to produce results). But the apprehension would always be individual, and the sense of the individual's connection with his/her history would be

190. The original incarnation of thought, which cannot be expressed in terms of objectification, and which Husserl may have still been suggesting in *Ideen I*, with the term "apperception," is prior, in Merleau-Ponty's view, to the taking up of any theoretical or practical position. An *Urdoxa*: a synthesis prior to all syntheses, "older" than the theses to which one might want to try to reduce it by setting out from a reasonable will or an intellectual activity of the postulated *I think*, and making a synthesis between *res extensa* and *res cogitans*.
Flesh. Flesh, which is called my body [*corps propre*], flesh which appears also as a body among bodies, but which, in those circumstances, is no longer approached in its concreteness, nor on its own terms. (Levinas, "On Intersubjectivity: Notes on Merleau-Ponty" [1983], *Outside the Subject*, p. 97)

fulfilled in the apprehension (as a determination, or articulation, of the world). Such a thinking of time finds its telos in determination—and also finds its methodology confused with its metaphysics (mistakes the structure of intentionality for the ego itself). The transcendental ego, uncovered by the Husserlian reduction, is not itself given in the reduction, or rather, is only given as that which gives us the possibility of that reduction (this is the sense of Levinas's insistence on thinking through the "saying" in *Otherwise than Being* as a methodological necessity). The structures of the transcendental ego (the inherited structures of education, habit, culture, etc., and the physical structures of vision, hearing, touching, habitualities of movement, etc.) are not the ego itself. For that reason, and again in terms of maternity, Levinas puts the psyche—the "maternal," "latent in intentionality" (*Otherwise than Being*, p. 71)—before the thematizing ego.

What we are looking for is a thinking of transcendence that does not erase the time from which the transcendence must gain its sense. Merleau-Ponty's thinking of flesh, and of the historical sedimentations of meaning to be discovered in the accumulation of "cultural gestures" within the flesh, depends on an apprehension, or determination, that occurs in the moment (which has become a said). Levinas does not deny this moment, but sees a priority within the saying, an activity (more passive than any passivity) of the maternal, which is no longer "dead time." This is a difficult priority, and it has two parts: as an argument against Merleau-Ponty's "anti-Platonism," against his refusal to separate the Good from Being, and as an argument for the methodological necessity of thinking through the ethical, thinking through the importance of incarnation, and of the gestation of a future implied in the metaphor of maternity. First, and on a methodological plane, the fact that transcendence is "enacted in the said" does not imply that the said is identical to that transcend*ing* (nor is it even the possibility of that transcendence, as testified to by the one-for-the-other of signification, which must arise from the time, from the maternal, which allows the other to be without being thematized):

> The meaning of perception, hunger, sensation, etc. as notions signifies through the correlation of terms in the simultaneity of a linguistic system. It has to be distinguished from the signifyingness of the-one-for-the-other, the psyche that animates perception, hunger and sensation. Here animation is not a metaphor, but, if we can put it thus, a designation of the irreducible paradox of intelligibility: the other in the same, the trope of the for-the-other in its antecedent inflexion. This signification in its very signifyingness, outside of every system, before any correlation, is an accord or peace between planes which, as soon as they are thematized, make an irreparable cleavage,

191. And here we look to his well-known insistence on the originary force of the spoken word (as opposed to Derrida's sense of writing as supplemental, as not determined by the structures of speaking). One speaks to the other as also transcendent, as also beyond the said which would make ontology inhuman (and without a face) if the ontological were taken to be sufficient as a mode of producing meaning in itself:

> The entity that appears *identical* in the light of time *is* its essence in the *already said*. The phenomenon itself is a phenomenology. It is not that a discourse, coming from one knows not where, arbitrarily arranges the phases of temporality into a "this as that." The very exposition of Being, its manifestation, essence qua essence and entities qua entities, are spoken. It is only in the said, in the *epos* of saying, that the diachrony of time is synchronized into a time that is recallable, and becomes a theme. The *epos* is not added to the identical entities it exposes; it exposes them as identities illuminated by a memorable temporality. The identical with respect to which temporality comes to be analyzed as a divergency making possible the rediscoveries of an act of consciousness (as though the identical were independent of time, and "then" becomes a flowing) has meaning only through the kerygma of the said, in which temporality which illuminates resounds

like vowels in a dieresis, maintaining a hiatus without elision. They then mark two Cartesian orders, the body and the soul, which have no common space where they can touch, and no logical *topos* where they can form a whole. Yet they are in accord prior to thematization, in an accord, a chord, which is possible only as an arpeggio. (*Otherwise than Being* [1974], p. 70)

An arpeggio is a playing of the notes of a chord in rapid succession, as is often done with a harp, instead of being struck all at once, as we usually think of chords being performed. Here again, as is frequently the case with Levinas, we find metaphors denying their position as metaphors; we are not to understand "animation" as, for example, the fingers of the harpist touching the strings (or similarly extend the conceit); the metaphor would already be a thematization, a simultaneity of planes, a single topos— which is of course to reduce a metaphor to its representational function, to its ability to carry meaning (perhaps more subtly, but still a determining function) from one subject to another, still as a 'said'. To contest, as I would like to do, that there is another possibility of metaphors, a transcendence enacted through metaphorization which is other than thematization, would be to contest the very structures of humanism that Levinas articulates throughout his work.[191] That contestation, on my part, only adumbrated for now, already constitutes the motivation behind this work. At this point, with our examination of his humanism, we are trying to get at the methodology opened up in Levinas's thinking of time and body.

We had at first noted that this thinking is separated from Merleau-Ponty's by the conception of time—what Levinas had metaphorized as the succession of an arpeggio instead of the simultaneity, or Gestalt, of ten fingers striking in unison. In Levinas's earlier work, exteriority had been founded in a specular conception of time, as a play between freedom and obligation, indetermination and determination, my possessions and yours.[192] In the later works, time is still defined as a diachrony, even as a similar play of positions, but the space within which that time plays itself out is no longer determinative of time itself; that is, that space, as the space of the encounter with the other, is not just the possibility of responding either justly or injustly. In the early work, infinity is a production of the dead time, the interval from which infinite times, from which fecundities, might arise. In the later works, there is a growing recognition that the play of thematizations does not reach the true bases of the human precisely because a face does not approach an ego from out of nowhere, or from out of the economy as productive (as regulated by some conceptual schema), but from out of the concrete ego, the unique body held hostage, itself. A prior structure, which he identifies as the body in its susceptibility to others, in its anxiety at its own inability to sustain its incarnation as an identity, must be thought as the meaning of the human. That is, where the earlier work found infinite Desire in the face of the other, occasioned by the other's demand that "thou shalt not kill," where it found a metaphysics based in that Desire, *Otherwise than Being* finds the affirmation of the body, the animation, the non-indifference of the body

for the "listening eye" in the verb *to be*. And it is for that that man is a being of truth, belonging to no other genus of being. *But is the power to say in man, however strictly correlative to the said its function may be, in the service of being?* If man were only a saying correlative with the logos, subjectivity could as well be understood as a function or as an argument of being. But the signification of saying goes beyond the said. It is not ontology that raises up the speaking subject; it is the signifyingness of saying going beyond essence that can justify the exposedness of being, ontology. (Levinas, *Otherwise than Being* [1974], pp. 37–38)

192.   Thus, in 1954, the relation of an ego to the totality is defined in the interplay between opposing freedoms and the face is manifested directly within the economy of things:

The simultaneity of participation and non-participation is an existence which moves between guilt and innocence, between ascendency over others, the betrayal of oneself, and the return to oneself. This relationship of an individual with the totality which thought is, in which the ego takes account of what is not itself and yet is not dissolved into it, presupposes that the totality is manifested as a face in which a being confronts me. This relationship of both participation and separation which marks the advent of, and the a priori proper to, thought, in which the bonds between the parts are constituted only by the freedom of the parts, is a society, is beings that speak, that face one another. Thought begins with the possibility of conceiving a freedom external to my own. Conceiving of a freedom external to my own is the first thought. It marks my very presence in the world. The world of perception manifests a face: Things affect us as *possessed* by the other. . . . Things qua things derive their first independence from the fact that they do not belong to me; and they do not belong to me because I am in relationship with those men from whom they come. Then the relationship of the ego with the totality is a relationship with human beings whose faces I recognize. Before them I am guilty or innocent. The condition that is necessary for there to be thought is a conscience. (Levinas, "The Ego and the Totality" [1954], *Collected Philosophical Papers*, pp. 28–29 [my ellipsis])

towards itself in its unique unthematized accord. One no longer falls under the obligation of the other, one comes to sensibility because of "the passivity of the for-the-other in vulnerability, which refers to maternity, which signification signifies." This maternity, this metaphor for our obligation, is signification, and it will give birth to the justice, in the respect toward the very showing of intentionality, which makes Husserl's (and Merleau-Ponty's) analyses possible:

> The modification of the sensibility into intentionality is motivated by the very signification of sensing as a for-the-other. One can show the latent birth of justice in signification. Justice, which must become a synchronic consciousness of being, is present in a theme in which the intentionality of consciousness itself shows itself. (*Otherwise than Being* [1974], p. 71)

But, in the thinking which identifies the transcendental ego with its description, in its said, we would constitute a system that would forget the very structure (the psyche, the maternity) which made the constitution possible. Justice, then, cannot be mere respect for the articulated truth of a situation; it must refer past its said, and the simultaneity of an organized whole: "One forgets justice, in which this simultaneity is aroused. Justice refers to a psyche, not, to be sure, as a thematization, but as the diachrony of the same and the other in sensibility" (*Otherwise than Being* [1974], p. 71).

That is, and we would have to repeat this in various guises for Levinas, justice does not refer to the other 'as' other (as *Totality and Infinity* seems to do). Justice is no longer the institution of a time as the resolution of the elements to which it points. Justice is rather the term which follows after maternity, after the diachrony (which it references), and which does not seek to do other than maintain the diachrony. When he speaks of the approach of God in the other, the coming to mind of God, he is no longer theorizing violence and nonviolence in their irrecuperable play. Rather, he will speak of good and evil,[193] obedience and egoism, and the eternal return of skepticism (which is not evil, which is not the other, or the advent of the other, but the falling out of synchrony of saying and said—a dissolution that characterizes philosophy in opposition to reason).[194]

It seems to me that the extent to which Levinas is indebted to phenomenology at this point is greatly underestimated (and doubtless further obscured by the very different quality of the metaphorizations). In a late text, Husserl explains his understanding of transcendence and subject, and of the bases for intentional thematizations:

> Before all such accomplishments there has always already been a universal accomplishment, presupposed by all human praxis and all prescientific and scientific life. The latter have the spiritual acquisitions of this universal accomplishment as their constant substratum, and all their own acquisitions are destined to flow into it. We shall come to understand that the world which constantly exists for us through the flowing alteration of manners of givenness is a universal

193. Good and evil are already central themes in *Totality and Infinity* (see, for example, p. 261), but they do not play the same role precisely where living in the goodness of being-for-the-other in the first book implies an obedience to the other's meanings, to the other as immediately meaningful in the face. The work of the trace, introduced in 1963, reconceptualizes the immediacy in terms of a unique ego, through the metaphor of maternity, with the trace of the other serving as the mark within the economy by which the unique ego knows that the other is the one for whom the ego is (already) hostage.

194. To intelligibility as an impersonal logos is opposed intelligibility as proximity. But does the reason characteristic of justice, the State, thematization, synchronization, representation, the logos and being succeed in absorbing into its coherence the intelligibility of proximity in which it unfolds? Does not the latter have to be subordinated to the former, since the very discussion which we are pursuing at this moment counts but its said, since in thematizing we are synchronizing the terms, forming a system among them, using the verb to be, placing in being all signification that allegedly signifies beyond being? Or must we reinvoke alternation and diachrony as the time of philosophy. . . . The periodic return of skepticism and of its refutation signify a temporality in

which the instants refuse memory which recuperates and represents. Skepticism, which traverses the rationality or logic of knowledge, is a refusal to synchronize the implicit affirmation contained in saying and the negation which this affirmation states in the said. (*Otherwise than Being*, p. 167 [my ellipsis])

mental acquisition, having developed as such and at the same time continuing to develop as the unity of a mental configuration, as a meaning-construct [*Sinngebilde*]—as the construct of a universal, ultimately functioning subjectivity. It belongs essentially to this world-constituting accomplishment that subjectivity objectifies itself as human subjectivity, as an element of the world. (*Crisis of the European Sciences* [1937], p.113)

If we each work with others to constitute the world 'as' meaningful, if the form of that constitution corresponds to an openly indeterminate horizon of possible meanings which have as their reference point the earlier form of constitution, if in particular, part of that form has been the explicit turn toward a certain communicative rationality called scientific endeavor, responsive to an urge toward description, then the universal accomplishment need not be construed 'metaphysically', that is, in terms of an activity outside of the accomplishments to which we already have access. The "ultimately functioning subjectivity" is (is objectified as) "human subjectivity, as an element of the world," but is also more than that which it has objectified itself as. A world-constitution which (unlike Husserl's) was not oriented by a search for evidence (self-presence of the idea), however, might not find such an accomplishment to be 'universal', and might find its particular accomplishment to still be oriented by a finite horizon (by a given conceptual problem, historical epoch, or ideological presupposition, for example) and not by the infinite horizon of scientific endeavor. For Husserl, his insistence on the self-accomplishment of evidence is both unapologetically 'European' (in its spirit and pedigree) and universal in the sense that no human is precluded from access to the scientific horizon of meaning (insofar as someone 'communicated' with others, in no matter what lifeworld context, he or she would be oriented toward the universal horizon of communications about the world, would be participating in the universal constitution, even though not a part of the particular tradition, the European tradition, that has thematized the scientific problem as such spiritually).

Levinas, in a fundamentally original appropriation, is questioning that which is European, the drive towards description, or evidence, which is said to be the spiritual gift of our forebears,[195] but, somewhat surprisingly, he is questioning it in the name of the monotheism which is also part of (or encompasses) our tradition. The move toward an even more original form of human communication—of the ethical in speaking—as it creates both a drive toward speaking and finds its end in the spoken, is designed to avoid the presuppositions of Enlightenment humanism (although it doesn't preclude some of its more important results in terms of the law, respect, and individual rights). The 'form' of communication, its basic literalization in the lifeworld, now finds itself to be 'speaking to an other' and not speaking to oneself as—or in the place of—the transcendental describer; however, the one who speaks is still the transcendental ego who speaks (ethically, with humility), who is responsible for the whole world. That is, with Husserl, but clarifying that step beyond, the move away

195. This manner of clarifying history by inquiring back into the primal establishment of the goals which bind together the chain of future generations, insofar as these goals live on in sedimented forms yet can be reawakened again and again and, in their new vitality, be criticized; this manner of inquiring back into the ways in which surviving goals repeatedly bring with them ever new attempts to reach new goals, whose unsatisfactory character again and again necessitates their clarification, their improvement, their more or less radical reshaping—this, I say, is nothing other than the philosopher's genuine self-reflection on what he is *truly seeking*, on what is in him as a will coming *from* the will and *as* the will of his spiritual forefathers. (Husserl, *The Crisis of European Sciences* [1937], p. 71)

196. A trace would seem to be the very indelibility of being, its omnipotence before all negativity, its immensity incapable of being self-enclosed, somehow too great for discretion, interiority, or a self. And it was indeed important for us to say that a trace does not effect a relationship with what would be less than being, but obliges with regard to the infinite, the absolutely other. But this superiority of the superlative, this height, this constant elevation to power, this exaggeration or this infinite overbidding—and, let us

from humanism is a methodological move toward approximating the meaning of the human as such, finding a higher humanism than the one we inherited (as Europeans) from the Enlightenment.

What I am seeking here is a fundamental congruence that could result in an ethically grounded methodological approach that we could appropriate from Levinas. I don't believe that "attention to the claims of others" fully captures the methodological move away from epistemology and psychological relativism that Husserl already gave us (and which Levinas criticizes, grounds differently, but fundamentally takes up). One is, if we could take this citation of Husserl's slightly away from its scientific context, perhaps merely accentuating what we mean by 'human' subjectivity—that is, accenting the ways the necessity of identifying transcendental world-constitution in general demands that the 'human' be as literalization of the subject, be as the goal of that constitution. World-constitution, we remember, is always mine (my responsibility) and cannot be reduced to a world's effects on me. Not that we are positing an ontological solipsism; in fact, quite to the contrary, we are merely not demanding that the other be as anything other than an other (we are refusing the 'we' with which humanism is usually, and thoughtlessly, formed). Yet we also see that the other's presence is essential to the world which has been constituted, and, with Levinas, that the reference to the other (which justice as a reference to diachrony accomplishes without thematizing the other, even 'as' the one who is excluded, etc.) is essential to that constitution, even prior to the passive syntheses which, maternal, bodily, give the space of an affirmation to the diachrony between same and other.[196]

But here we come back to the problems we broached with Gandhi. If we take the body, the individual's ego 'as' literalized in its human garb, as the point of accessing a claim about the economy, as the point from which judgments arise as to the violence or nonviolence of the economy or some of its constituent parts, don't we have to take the origin of that body (its biology, its culture, its mother, etc.) as somehow instituting the capacity to recognize violence, *and* instituting the willingness to respond to the obligation? (I have heard people, on various occasions, respond to readings of Levinas by saying, "But how could you *force* me to respond to a face?") For Levinas, I think fairly clearly, the metaphorizations of humanism, including respect for the other and the third, necessarily result from the structures implied in the formal possibility of becoming 'as' a human (being literalized into human subjectivity) as that implies a certain being in reciprocity with others (who already believed themselves to be humans—or, more true to Levinas, who found themselves, too, to have been in a world already overfull with meaning) and a dependence on that reciprocity. (One is not forced to respond, one already is 'as' responding—

although, of course, one may be responding as an egoist, or technologist, and do one's best to ignore the claims of others.)

The difficulty here is what calls for Levinas's invocation of purity in the one-for-the-other of the maternal. Not, as we could too quickly assume, a purity in content; this maternity will always be literalized in the unique assignation of its humanity, of its historically lived body, arising from the pure structure of alterity in its impure manifestation within history. This is the strength of his appropriation of Merleau-Ponty, and of his emphasis on the historical: yet, as we have seen, Levinas consistently invokes a moment outside of the historical existence of the ego. This ego is not free to constitute the world in whatever way it pleases, but will always find that obligation to constitute a world in the presence of another human and as an anxiety over that other (which is, for Levinas, resonant with the metaphor of the maternal, of the ethical substratum which replaces the universal mind as the destination, and horizon, of all activities).[197] This will always, of necessity, result in a nonindifference toward the other, an anxiety in the face of these obligations—although this may not be recognized and translated into the respect which culminates with justice (or, more to my point, may only culminate in a respect that, as merely respectful, is unable to reach justice in its diachrony). What I will question is the necessity of the anxiety, question why the trace of the anxious in the face of God (the metaphorization of divinity in subjectivity) seems destined to determine the meaning of the obligation to the other as anxiety.

The flesh of Merleau-Ponty, one would

say the word, this divinity—are not deducible from the being of beings nor its revelation, even if it is contemporary with a concealment, nor with "concrete duration." These signify something on the basis of a past which, in a trace, is neither indicated nor signaled, but yet disturbs order, while coinciding neither with revelation nor with dissimulation. A trace is the insertion of space in time, the point at which the world inclines toward a past and a time. This time is a withdrawal of the other and, consequently, nowise a degradation of duration, which, in memory, is still complete. Superiority does not reside in a presence in the world, but in an irreversible transcendence. It is not a modulation of the being of entities. As *He* and third person it is somehow outside the distinction between being and entities. Only a being that transcends the world, an ab-solute being, can leave a trace. A trace is a presence of that which properly speaking has never been there, of what is always past. (Levinas, "Meaning and Sense" [1972], *Collected Philosophical Papers*, p. 105)

197. On the hither side of the zero point which marks the absence of protection and cover, sensibility is being affected by a non-phenomenon, a being put in question by the alterity of the other, before the intervention of a cause, before the appearing

of the other. It is a pre-origi-
nal not resting on oneself, the
restlessness of someone persecuted—Where to be? How to
be? It is a writhing in the
tight dimensions of pain, the
unsuspected dimensions of
the hither side. It is being
torn up from oneself, being
less than nothing, a rejection
into the negative, behind
nothingness; it is maternity,
gestation of the other in the
same. Is not the restlessness
of someone persecuted but a
modification of maternity, the
groaning of the wounded en-
trails by those it will bear or
has borne? In maternity what
signifies is a responsibility for
others, to the point of substitution for others and suffering
both from the effect of persecution and from the persecuting itself in which the perse-
cutor sinks. Maternity, which
is bearing par excellence,
bears even responsibility for
the persecuting by the perse-
cutor. (Levinas, *Otherwise
than Being*, p. 75)

198. It is clear that the verb *to be*,
or the verb *to consist*, is used
in the formulas from these
first pages that name the
hither side of being. It is also
clear that being makes its apparition, shows itself, in the
said. As soon as saying, on the
hither side of being, becomes
dictation, it expires, or abdi-
cates, in fables and in writing.
If being and manifestation go
together in the said, it is in
fact natural that if the saying
on the hither side of the said
can show itself, it be said al-

have to say here, is a metaphor (structuring
said), already on the plane of determinations, already destined to its expression. The
same would be true of corporeality in general, of the being open to being touched of
all the objects of the world. This general
structure of transcendence, of objects being
accessible in their meaning, speaks the election of man (and woman) to mankind—to a
life of need, obligation, and love. The
human is not, then, an a priori category, but
a necessary supplement, called into her/his
separation, elected into transcendence, as a
responding to the world. This election itself,
in its temporal structure as passivity, as a
maternity that bears the burden of susceptibility, demands the metaphorization of itself
in the terms of being, but also demands that
the diachrony of time follow and that the
structure of that demand for metaphorization itself be oriented towards a culmination
in an articulated justice (even as that justice
refers to the psyche as unthematizable).[198]
We are called to the work of justice. We are
called to judge. The metaphors follow each
other, and, for Levinas, it is necessary that
the human metaphor (the metaphor of humanism) precede the various metaphorizations of beings. His argument, as we have
seen, runs from a phenomenological analysis of the structure of sensibility or signification, insofar as it precedes intentional
thematizations, toward explicating the structure that lies at the base of that thematization in terms of the ethical relation. In his
later work, the ethical act remains as the determinant of justice, but justice (or the striving toward articulating justice) no longer
shapes the progress of time (as it did in *Totality and Infinity*). Does it still make sense to

call this time diachronic? The time of the psyche, of the maternal in *Otherwise than Being*, is a time of diachrony, characterized by its passivity and willingness to disintegrate. No moment of time belongs to its constructive activity; justice, instead, merely references the original time in the face of which the obligations were incurred. Husserl, for one, would not have seen any reason to characterize this time as diachronic. The horizons of constitution were open to interruptions, but the progress through time and space was not thereby staccato. Perhaps, taking a step back from the subtlety of the possible distinctions, we are merely dealing with a polemical distance, an aftereffect of the choice of metaphors.

The diachrony of time, for Levinas, is thought from the interplay of Good and Evil—an interplay which is not equivalent to the movement between saying and said (which, as skepticism, characterizes the "time of philosophy"). The saying is always ours, yet, in its justice, always references the structure of encountering another from out of my dissolution, always references the structure of alterity within world-constitution. This already involves an interpretation on Levinas's part, although clearly Levinas finds the interpretation to be motivated by a phenomenological look at the possibility of the socially constructed world. In either case, a necessity of metaphors is being invoked. The subject is opposed to its determinations just as the multiplicity, or alterity, of subjects intervenes in the singularity of apperception. The Same and the Other are a necessary pair, a couple, from which we will be able to think the progression of time, and the apparition of the Good and the apostasy

ready in terms of being. But is it necessary and is it possible that the saying on the hither side be thematized, that is, manifest itself, that it enter into a proposition and a book? It is necessary. The responsibility for another is precisely a saying prior to anything said. The surprising saying which is a responsibility for another is against "the winds and tides" of being, is an interruption of essence, a disinterestedness imposed with a good violence. But one has to say that the gratuity nonetheless required of substitution, that miracle of ethics before the light, this astonishing saying, comes to light through the very gravity of the questions that assail it. It must spread out and assemble itself into essence, posit itself, be hypostasized, become an eon in consciousness and knowledge, let itself be seen, undergo the ascendency of being. Ethics itself, in its saying which is a responsibility, requires this hold. (*Otherwise than Being*, pp. 43–44)

If we are to say that books should still be written, can we give up the imperative of phrasing, of insisting that they be said? In the schema of the metaphors offered us, the determination as humanist is already necessary, the metaphors must be phrased as on their way to the other, within being (and destined to a communication, meant to be understood). What if a metaphor could have a different destination? Or rather, what if the difference in destination could be expressed by a metaphor which wasn't representational? One need not endlessly multiply metaphors (although I don't think one would stop at any given point) simply because the sense of the metaphor would not lie in its numerical finitude (which is essential to its multiplication) but in its aesthetics (indeterminate in its simple being beyond the grasp of those words which would pretend to say what they meant).

that shows us Evil. From here, time will be thought. In an appreciative look at Nemo's work, Levinas recaps his own understanding of time, as he sees it in his later work:

> But the knowledge of the world, thematization, does not give up its efforts. It tries to reduce the disturbance of the Same by the Other, and succeeds. It reestablishes the order troubled by Evil and by the Other, through the history in which it accepts to enter. But cracks reappear in the established order. Our modernity seems then not only to rest on the certainties of history and nature, but on an alternation: recuperation and rupture, knowing and sociality. In this alternation the moment of recuperation is not more true than that of the break-up, the laws do not have more meaning than the face-to-face relationship with the neighbor. This does not attest simply to a lack of synthesis, but would define time itself, time in its enigmatic diachrony: a tendency without issue, an aim without coincidence. It would signify the ambiguity of an incessant adjournment, of the progression of prayer and possession. But also the approach of an infinite God, an approach which is his proximity. ("Transcendence and Evil" [1978], *Collected Philosophical Papers*, pp. 185–86).

Perhaps, if we wanted to be 'postmodern', if we were not to invoke such an alternation, we would have to approach the end of a grand opposition, structuring even time itself, between God and the creation, between saying and said. The philosophy of Merleau-Ponty, as we've already noted, eliminates that difference in the name of the said (at least this seems to be Levinas's understanding of Merleau-Ponty's approach to time and determination). If, in fact, Merleau-Ponty thinks of transcendence in terms of the collection of intentional thematizations, then Levinas is right—and a more subtle and detailed reading than we can embark on here, of both Merleau-Ponty and Husserl, would be required to decide the exegetical question. Levinas seems to feel that he has more accurately privileged the temporal, in his thinking of the Good, of the approach of God, of the breakup of the established order of things in the world. Yet he continues to think of that established order as determined; he cannot see thinking without the necessity of a moment of determination; he cannot think the said without violence and negation. Time will always alternate with its death in determination. The public will always be a field of violence (and a more or less violent imposition of law, and respect for the law, is justified in Levinas's thought). And further, the respect will again reference the individual on the other side of the violence, in a determined step away from the justice which references the unthematized movement of time.

With the hope of a metaphorization, or a literalization (and, I trust it is clear, these are not an opposed pair of concepts), which grants transcendence without instituting the conceptual pair of determinate/indeterminate, I have repeatedly introduced the aesthetics of refusing to describe, of refusing representation. Levinas himself seems to give us the methodological possibility of this very metaphorization, perhaps even more forcefully than Heidegger. However, in his humanism, Levinas is finding a necessity to the metaphor of speech that would interpret this progression as diachrony, as an interplay between subjects. Levinas, despite the brilliance of his interpretation of the meaning of transcendence, still thus thinks transcendence as a determination, even if that determination will always reference a dissolution. And that determination, eventually, is a metaphorization enacted by God (or inherent to the Good), that is, enacted, or articulated, by the very structure of passivity, susceptibility, or maternity, as the pure structure of any immediacy whatsoever—and as such an immediacy, no longer a metaphor, but a necessity. All of this is given when he too quickly identifies signification with transcendence:

> Transcendence as signification, and signification as the signification of an order given to subjectivity before any statement, is the pure one-for-the-other. Poor ethical subjectivity deprived of freedom! Unless this would be the trauma of a fission of the self that occurs in an adventure undergone with God or through God. But in fact this ambiguity also is necessary to transcendence. Transcendence owes it to itself to interrupt its own demonstration and

monstration, its phenomenality. It requires the blinking and dia-chrony of enigma, which is not simply a precarious certainty, but breaks up the unity of transcendental apperception, in which immanence always triumphs over transcendence. (Levinas, "God and Philosophy" [1973], *Collected Philosophical Papers*, p. 173)

But if that unity was never ideal, never organized by a said which meant separation or determination, which gained its sense by separation and diachrony, that is, which was still conceptual in the Hegelian sense, then there would be no sense to a breakup, no way one would go from public to private, private to public, since the transcendence is already thought in the existing of the world. That is, the breakup already occurs within the opening to time which is the unique ego, within the moment one has said 'Here I am', in response to the call of obligation, and would only go back to a diachrony, would only find the diachrony necessary, in that each unicity finds itself with other subjects (with whom the subject alternates) who are subjects because the universal mind in Husserl's sense has (also—and the difficulty of this 'also' is our difficulty here) literalized them; (the metaphor of humanism, of subjectivity, interprets metaphors as passing between multiple subjects, as a communication between similarly constituted subjects—and the abstraction of 'respect for the other' arises from recognizing the similarity, or unicity, in constitution). But the metaphor of humanism here is also a method, and we can choose, after the fact, to wager a different metaphor, one that thinks the subject differently. And, of course, Levinas already understands this, is merely already phrasing the polemical priority of his metaphor, or at least the necessity of a similar metaphor for the construction of a meaningful life, in general, and, specifically, for the collection of subjects who have heard God's call:

> Subjectivity in ageing is unique, irreplaceable, me and not another; it is despite itself in an obedience where there is no desertion but where revolt is brewing. These traits exclude one another, but they are resolved in responsibility for one another, older than any commitment. In such a resolution not a world but a kingdom is signified. But a kingdom of an invisible king, the kingdom of the Good whose idea is already an eon. The Good that reigns in its goodness cannot enter into the present of consciousness, even if it would be remembered. In consciousness it is an anarchy. The Biblical notion of the Kingdom of God—kingdom of a non-thematizeable God, a non-contemporaneous, that is, non-present, God—must not be conceived as a certain "époque" of the "history of Being," as a modality of essence. One has to go back from the Eon to the kingdom of God, which signifies in the form

of subjectivity, of the unique one assigned in the passive synthesis of life. It
signifies in the form of the proximity of
a neighbor and the duty of an un-
payable debt, the form of a finite condition. Temporality as ageing and death
of the unique one signifies an obedience where there is no desertion. . . .
The subject as a *one* discernible from
the other, as an entity, is a pure abstraction if it is separated from this assignation. (*Otherwise than Being* [1974],
p. 52 [my ellipsis])

Thus do we find an appeal to a certain kind
of humanism, the Judeo-Christian identification of man and divinity (which still inhabits secular humanism, for example), installed in the very definition of time as that
which makes openness to being an obligation (or an election). This assignation, as we
saw before, was always thought as the condition for the body's taking shape as a literalization of a set of concrete obligations.[199]
That is the sense in which, as a methodology which moves within phenomenology's
reduction to the transcendental ego without
also determining the telos of all activity in
meaning, Levinas's conception of unicity
(and of the passivity of the maternal) allows
us to better question the general structures
of oppression (and of liberation) we are
faced with without, in advance, giving in to
the supposed necessity of oppression in
general. We would ask, however, and in
terms of the metaphors, exactly what alternative to oppression we are offering. Must
we follow the turn in metaphors which
makes of the body a divinity? Or can we
take that divinity to be other than Judeo-

199. "Incarnation is not a transcendental operation of a subject
that is situated in the midst of
the world it represents to itself;
the sensible experience of the
body is already and from the start
incarnate. The sensible—maternity, vulnerability, apprehension—binds the node of incarnation into a plot larger than the
apperception of the self. In this
plot I am bound to others before
being tied to my body" (*Otherwise than Being*, p. 76).

200. The body, for the Aztecs, and only for one example, was very much the object of religious discourse and of violent controls (and nearly constant self-sacrifices or self-mutilations)—all of which were destined for the gods (the blood served as their food) and yet none of which either destined the individuals to a unity with divinity or expressed their own preexisting connection with divinity insofar as the humans were also, like the divine, spiritual (if anything, it emphasized the corporeal without any reference to the spiritual, or the historical in our sense—even if they still had something analogous to histories, as they still had something analogous to the noncorporeal). Their stories, in that vein (and only as far as I can tell; it's not clear what evidence would decide the issue in any case), did not lead to tragic, or cathartic, drama.

Christian (would each 'culture' have its own divine body)?[200] Can we think a body which is not destined to its god, its election (whether to toil or salvation)? As we have already noted, Levinas does not see this as a choice, does not see his activity as a metaphorization, but as—in a phenomenological sense—determined by the matters themselves. And perhaps, since to a large extent Levinas seems descriptively right (at least insofar as he describes how a body and a language could be destined for each other in the very possibility of subjectivity—in the first institution of a thought which could be called thematizing), what we are indeed questioning, now with the body, is whether matters are best defined in (or destined to) their determinations. Whether, perhaps, technology, science's determination of the world as the object of thematizing activity, does not coincide with the reign of a certain, unique, and jealous god?

That is, with the citation on the kingdom, we are replaying the polemic between Heidegger and Levinas that we saw earlier. And again, it is about a freedom in metaphorization. Before continuing, we should mark what Levinas has already given us in terms of the trajectory of my writing: the access to a domain of self-questioning that explicitly goes beyond the circle that is constrained by the form of the previous questions within which the present manifestation of an ego arises. That is, a variation on the horizons of Husserl's philosophy which lives toward, and defines life as the working toward, an ethical, not merely a descriptively true, future. Thus the desire of the other in Lacan, which always results in the tragedy of recognition for a finite self, can be thought through the possibility of a Good lying precisely in that (no longer tragic) structure of necessary otherness. To be responsible for the whole world is to be the one capable of addressing the justice of that world[201]—it is not an arrogance, but an empowerment, a recognition of a capacity to think the just in the world. It announces an order not defined by the opposition violence/nonviolence (nor even, activity/passivity). And before we too quickly try to formulate what that justice would look like, we should think about what the fact of that capacity, and its concurrent responsibility, mean for the possibility of knowledge and of thematization (especially as that justice still refers to an unthematized).

I can no longer speak from my position of authority (as author); I no longer have the right to speak. Justice, instead, if it is to happen, must happen in my attentiveness to its call (and to the unthematized diachrony it presupposes). This already announces a priority of thought over practice (or, rather, it renounces, and withdraws from, the economy which had found them opposed). One can no longer say, "I'm only doing my part— if I do it well enough, I have fulfilled my responsibility to the whole"; the banality of evil is denounced. One becomes responsible for thinking through the problem as a whole (and, with Levinas, this obligation also forces one to look for that type of indeterminism one would come to call human, to pay a special attention to that indetermination/infinitude in the other who approaches). Of course, as much could be said of the methodological consequences of Husserl's view of science or, with even more attention to the motivation of our feeling of

201. It is the reduction to restlessness in the literal sense of the term, or to its diachrony, which, despite all its assembled forces, despite all the simultaneous forces in its union, being can not eternalize. The subjective and its Good can not be understood out of ontology. On the contrary, starting with subjectivity in the form of saying, the signification of the said will be interpretable. It will be possible to show that there is question of the said and being only because saying or responsibility require justice. Thus only will justice be done to being, will the affirmation, the, to take it literally, strange affirmation that through injustice "all the foundations of the earth are shaken" be understandable. Thus alone will the terrain of disinterestedness that allows us to separate truth from ideology be given its truth. (Levinas, *Otherwise than Being* [1974], p. 45)

obligation (our anxiety) within the unthematized, Heidegger's *Being and Time*. What manifests the difference between Heidegger's thinking of anxiety and Levinas's restlessness in one's own skin—not considered by either thinker to be merely a metaphor, but still explicitly placed within their conceptions of a temporality that is not other than metaphorization—can be found in the fact that Levinas sees anxiety arising from the other, over the abundance of meaning (the fact that, immediately, meaning is already there and determinate), and Heidegger sees anxiety as stemming from anxiety over indetermination (over nothingness). Both thinkers will look for better metaphors, will even think of this search in terms of the possibilities of metaphors, but I want to sort out a little better both where this anxiety fits in with a general problem of approaching meaning (as a philosopher or as a human) and in what sense that anxiety was originally thought to be necessary, that is, not (merely) a metaphor.

In an interesting note (appended to the end of the text I used as my epigraph for this subsection), Levinas explains how he conceives of his difference from Heidegger at the time of *Otherwise than Being*:

> Heidegger's analysis describes anxiety over the limitation of being. Inasmuch as this analysis is not to be read as simply psychological or anthropological, it reaches us that form (which in our philosophical tradition defines a being) is always too small for a being. Definition, which, as form, "formosity," is beauty, lustre and appearing, is also strangulation, that is, anguish. The disproportion between Being and its phenomenality, the fact that Being is cramped in its manifestation, would then be produced in anthropological form in a being-existing-for-death. The measure of a determination would thus be the evil measurement of a Nessus tunic. But anxiety as being-for-death is also the hope to reach the deep of non-being. The possibility of deliverance (and the temptation to suicide) arises in death anxiety: like nothingness, death is an openness into which, along with a being, the anxiety over its definition is engulfed. But, on the other hand, anxiety as the tightness of "going forth into fullness," is the recurrence of the oneself, but without evasion, without shirking, that is, a responsibility stronger than death. (*Otherwise than Being* [1974], p. 194–95)

Clearly, this is a subtler reading of Heidegger than the one informing the citation we saw from *Totality and Infinity* in my last subsection. Even though the form of the criticism (opposing anxiety in the face of plenitude to anxiety in the face of nothingness) goes back at least to *Existence and Existents* [1940–45], his earlier thinking of time did not allow him to clearly delineate the similarities between himself and Heidegger in terms of their phenomenological description (the motivation of ontology in the individual's anxious uniqueness, in the anxiety that makes existence into a task), and led him to too starkly reduce Heideggerian ontology to thematization (since he felt anxiety must result in a thematizing act). "Going forth into fullness" better captures the futurity of our anxiousness (a Heideggerian theme, after all) but maintains the distinction which is indeed essential in terms of the death analysis. Opposed to Heidegger, one is not individuated in one's own death, but in the plenitude of obligations that fill the world. The individuation, for both philosophers, plays a quasi-methodological role in that without that individuation, and the anxiety that thematizes that individuation, one cannot make sense of the transcendence in its structure as a whole—as the transcendent world. From that understanding, and differentiating their responses in respect to the two different metaphorizations which they choose to define anxiety in its futural readiness for . . . , one could then approach the concrete problem of how to answer the ethical and political questions of our time.

Except that Heidegger, too, stops defining anxiety in terms of death and works within the problem of finitude more generally as early as *Kant and the Problem of Metaphysics* [1929]. And then, perplexingly, Heidegger almost completely stops talking about anxiety and starts talking about things like wandering down forest paths, poetry, dwelling, and thinking without technological manipulations. He multiplies his metaphors while talking, again somewhat enigmatically, about the 'Same' that all philosophizing is oriented towards (and we would not want to too quickly oppose this 'Same' to any 'Other', since—on analogy with Levinas's recurring dissolution of the said, but without implying a diachrony—Heidegger is calling for listening to a difference).[202] And, as anxiety clearly played a quasi-methodological role (not a technological method, but a key to the movement of thinking) in *Being and Time*, the very multiplication of metaphors, the poetic metaphor above all others speaking the possibility of that multiplication, plays a similar methodological role in his later thought—one now strives to become capable of the capable word (as in the epigraph to the introduction to this book). Which is why, earlier, I had taken the liberty of referring to Heidegger's thought as turning on a methodological freedom of metaphorization.

For example, despite the differences between the two metaphors Levinas offers for thinking the history of the said (passivity in the body and obedience to the Good or God), both are found to necessarily transcend, to be the outside, or the form, that makes the thematization of beings (history in our sense, including all determinate forms) possible. Thus, where Levinas speaks of the kingdom of God, "which signifies in the form of subjectivity" (above), he is invoking the necessity of God's humanism—placing God, and the Good, apart

202. Following out all of Heidegger's clues on the meaning of time would be a monumental task, and not one to be undertaken too quickly—and especially not one to be taken up here, at the already late stages of my work. I am tempted to say, although this could misrepresent the situation as being overly stark, that the anxiety threw everything back onto the methodological starting point (which Levinas embraces) which calls for a humanism, while a different attention to the type of 'call', anxiety producing or not, to which we, as humans, would respond, prevents Heidegger from interpreting the starting point as a repetition of the original religious instance of a subjective principle (which, in Hegel's extreme form, Heidegger had dubbed ontotheology). Perhaps the mere citation of a clue somewhat resonant with our trajectories will suffice:

> The calling of the dif-ference is the double stilling. The gathered bidding, the command, in the form of which the dif-ference calls world and things, is the peal of stillness. Language speaks in that the command of the dif-ference calls world and things into the simple onefold of their intimacy. *Language speaks as the peal of stillness.* Stillness stills by the carrying out, the bearing and enduring, of world and things in their presence. The carrying out of world and thing in the manner of stilling is the appropriative taking place of the dif-ference. Language, the peal of stillness,

from any metaphorization (and restricting the metaphor to its conceptual role). And, above all, he is claiming a necessity for our obedience to God, or the Good, insofar as they work as metaphors for the possibility of good, or divine, metaphorizations; in susceptibility (in the for-the-other of maternity) we have struck (the form of the) ground. But, then, from where does the necessity of an anxiety arise? In terms of our metaphors, it arises from the necessity of separation (the necessity of the said as a determination), which is best expressed in the anxious subjectivity called a son.[203] If we invoke the freedom of metaphorizations in order to speak of daughters, it is not because we are announcing our freedom to comprehend—rather the opposite, since it announces the liberation from a certain (and pervasive) anxiety, always structured towards determinations, anxious over its possessions, its comprehensions, and therefore, destined for words (in their turn destined for the comprehensions, etc., of others).

Anxiety occurs, in the tradition, in the face of the dissolution of wholeness. The presumption that the response to that anxiety is the just act—as in *Totality and Infinity*, and in a different but correlative sense, in Lacan—which rephrases the wholeness (and yet refers to no 'absolute' wholeness) is disrupted by *Otherwise than Being*'s insistence that justice refers to the dissolution itself—a dissolution which is still thought as diachronic, I am maintaining, because the metaphorization of subjectivity in terms of a human subjectivity anxious over its approach toward divinity (and it would be difficult to find atheists in our tradition at this level, thinkers who did not believe in either the divinity of the word or the divinity of the immediate) itself necessitates our thinking of anxiety as a move to resolve a rupturing (even if that resolution is a further dissolution, a reference back towards the maternal which makes that dissolution an obedience and a destiny). Life, for Levinas, is no longer tragic, no longer an unresolvable conflict between irreconcilable claims, but it remains arduous and without rest.

The possibility I am moving toward, through my various, often incommensurate, metaphorizations of art and women, is the literalization which is not *necessary,* which doesn't respond to an anxiety over the necessary (the necessary is, perhaps, the last anxiety; after having dispelled the anxieties of entities, of contradictions, and even of death, we still have the anxiety over the necessity of the word). Such a metaphor on my part need not imply irresoluteness, nor irresponsibility (both defined by their opposites, after all), for the time in which one lives is not the staccato of either conflict or diachrony, but the gradual approach of an attempt. (Levinas, too, announces this approach; he merely already interprets the meaning of that approach in terms of a rather well-known God).[204]

At the very end of *To the Lighthouse,* Lily is still trying to finish her painting (nonrepresentational, it is not 'of' Mrs. Ramsay). She has painted past, endured through, her anxiety[205] (see note 168 above)—and Mrs. Ramsay no longer sits, casting her shadow on the step, within the painting, within the said at all:

> Quickly, as if she were recalled by
> something over there, she turned to her

is, inasmuch as the dif-ference takes place. Language goes on as the taking place or occurring of the dif-ference for world and things. (Heidegger, "Language" [1950], *Poetry Language Thought,* p. 207)

203. We should remember that anxiety here remains a methodological move. Heidegger clearly saw this in *Being and Time* where anxiety was the only occasionally given mood within which the possibility of being-a-whole emerged. Likewise, for Levinas, anxiety is a moment that announces the changing of a time, and the threatening dissolution. Only anxiety can *see* the dissolution as a threat, in need of reparation, only from anxiety is the separation of the individual kept tied to the concretely given world, and only insofar as the purpose of that anxiety is to reestablish a 'said', an order, can we gain access to the methodological ground from which Husserl's phenomenology is thought. Our problem is to think that grounding without a tragic or cathartic separation, without the singularity of a separation, nor its accompanying anxiety.

204. And, perhaps, with a careful reading of the work of skepticism in *Otherwise than Being,* we could approach something like an irony toward god and anxiety in the face of god, toward the founding metaphors and their destinations/origins, which would be the freedom of an art called philosophy.

205. And the art of one of Stein's characters, so infrequently anxious

over the meaning which is so overabundant in her works, might give us even a better exemplar if we were searching for a completely new art—yet, not feeling, as writer, the necessity for a break with the tradition of anxiety, we can still speak of anxiety's presence in our world (as we might have spoken of any other violence), and of its overcoming (or undergoing).

canvas. There it was—her picture. Yes, with all its greens and blues, its lines running up and across, its attempt at something. It would be hung in the attics, she thought; it would be destroyed. But what did that matter? she asked herself, taking up her brush again. She looked at the steps; they were empty; she looked at her canvas; it was blurred. With a sudden intensity, as if she saw it clear for a second, she drew a line there, in the centre. It was done; it was finished. Yes, she thought, laying down her brush in extreme fatigue, I have had my vision. (*To the Lighthouse*, pp. 309–10 [the end])

I am not claiming that Woolf proposed a new (much less a coherent) philosophical *theory* of intersubjectivity. She did, however, and in a way that we shouldn't rush to understand, open us to a theory of the time of art which separates art from the constitutions of meaning we tend to call bodily (habit, communication, etc.) but doesn't thus go over into the instantaneity of the sublime creation (her vision, although one can indeed pinpoint the time of its conclusion, came after the resolution of anxiety, did not, of itself, cause the cessation of an anxious indetermination). As such, the painting must be nonrepresentational, just as her book as a whole, with its clearly allegorical contents (although one is never exactly certain about the destination of the allegorizations) also refuses the usual paradigm of representation (and, first of all, it must not will to be a father, to be the institution of a new aesthetic, hung in museums and sold at galleries). Her vision would have followed on her irony, her comportment toward anxiety, and not have caused it. This insight alone, still so difficult to follow, would explain the winding course of my sections on sisters and mothers. And it would also explain the reasoning behind choosing the conceit of metaphorization, and especially of the metaphorization of women, in that one can declare that the metaphors are not necessary exactly in using them again, without determining their truth beyond the given context of this metaphorization. Not that the determination was temporary, but that the metaphor wasn't determination, did not attempt to come to its term, or its exact reference in the world (I would not speak about women; they are not the target of this metaphorization; they are not determined by my metaphorization—which, properly speaking, remains indeterminate in its very self-referentiality, in its inability, or unwillingness, to reach the determinative, the diachronic).

Within our thinking of time, then, as it no longer mimics either the time of instantaneous apprehension or of diachronic alternation, the important point about a metaphor would be that it doesn't come all at once, the fit has to be worked out, the literalizing contact with each individual other bringing forth the question of whether it 'fits', questioning the justice of the fit (this is the sense of externality as a face in *Totality and Infinity*). Unless, further, we can question even this metaphor for metaphors, speak of a metaphor which is not judged by its fit, not destined for a 'just' fit; the nonrepresentational aspect of any art, if that 'non' makes any sense, might be the best example of this different metaphor, as Heidegger's turn towards poetry already suggests. This not fitting is not less 'something new', no less the advent of time, but, to extend a metaphor that has been building throughout this book, is more of a daughter than a son. And, to exactly that extent, and against the metaphors of modernity, against its continuity and fertility in the lineage which bears the patriarch's name, we will have been left with very little to say. No longer deciding between competing claims, no longer deciding meanings (including the meaning of justice), we must more slowly approach the possibility of speaking. Rather than too quickly designating a group of beings as human, and deciding which one has what right to what thing in the world, we must approach the very possibility of a humanism, or of a beyond to humanism—one which, as an open questioning, as a comportment towards the future, can pose the question of justice and not merely apply the results of previous decisions about some determinate set of facts (such as who already possesses the rights, or the power, in the situation as it was previously articulated).

# D) DAUGHTERS— part 2

*Paternity is the relationship with a stranger
who, entirely while being Other, is myself, the
relationship of the ego with a myself who is
nonetheless a stranger to me. The son, in effect,
is not simply my work, like a poem or an
artifact, neither is he my property. Neither the
categories of power nor those of having can
indicate the relationship with the child.
Neither the notion of cause nor the notion of
ownership permit one to grasp the fact of
fecundity. I do not have my child; I am in
some way my child. But the words "I am" here
have a significance different from an Eleatic or
Platonic significance. There is a multiplicity
and a transcendence in the verb "to exist," a
transcendence that is lacking in even the
boldest existentialist analyses.*

—Levinas, Time and the Other

$A$s I hope is clear, we stand with the possibility of *thinking* differently—the answers we give for even the simplest situations in our lives are soon to change—we stand with the possibility, insofar as we become capable of this possibility, of changing the foundations of the world. Which is only to say that we are at a point where we can change how we characterize that thinking which we have always done, that thinking which is most common. But we cannot take the difference between act and description as too easily understood exactly here, where we are trying to find appropriate metaphors for thinking itself. That is, and almost at the level of a metaphor, we begin with a summary of our negative findings: Thinking, apparently, is not isolated, nor isolating; thought is not a derivative of action, nor a species of violence, or abstraction (although it has been, to our collective detriment, interpreted as such). Thinking, then, is something else. It is, as a first approximation, a transcendence, a literalization of an approach, an "attempt at something," an art.

With Levinas's humanism, and at a certain level I would affirm this analysis in spite of any of my earlier critiques, we now understand—and this understanding itself is the withdrawal from a certain question of violence, and thus is to be understood as precisely having been available at any point in history, as the 'other' of history—the simple fact that we don't speak in order to express ourselves (self-expression, after all, is always more or less a tailored, that is, conceptual, illusion): we speak to someone else. Within this simple maxim, the death of representational thought is both perfectly explicable and not so frightening. After all, it is true that we have been speaking to others all along. To take this insight seriously, to use it against the various disguised and undisguised selfishnesses of contemporary society, of our contemporary selves, becomes, again, a daunting prospect—except (and is this not merely an extension of Levinas's thinking on transcendence and nonviolence?) that we are not called to a battle with the contemporary, our understanding is not a domination, our future is not a command issuing from our present.

The refusal of the metaphor of a command coincides with my preference for the metaphor of art over the metaphor of two subjects speaking to each other—especially insofar as we can accentuate art's own type of aesthetic indeterminism (an indetermination which is not akin to the simple lack of understanding we experience in the face of another human speaking a different language). This artistic creation would not be the institution of an anxiety, the threat of castration, but the approach of an art, an "attempt at something," which didn't need its reception within the public in order to validate its having been produced, an attempt that was not intended for another 'as' human but for that (not the self) which precisely is not captured within the metaphorization of subjectivity (and of subjects in community, participating in economies).

More broadly, we are still discussing the problems I began with. The question: what is poetry (or art of any sort) without metaphor, without the metaphor that represents, that declares the dependence of the metaphor on an outside of the metaphor? This is the same as the question of politics after nationalism, of sex without orgasm, of political commitment instead of marriage, of marriage as political commitment, of accessible philosophical discourse. In other words, given the imposition of violence on others around me—I am the witness of injustices directed by others towards others—is there some appropriate political activity required of (or even available to) me? Something beyond (my) mere innocence of intent which obliges (my) activity to take the direction of the political? Does that, in turn, oblige me to fight, to fight in all the various wars of domination, to strive, in my time, to dominate and kill—this time (and would it be the first time?) in the name of the weak? Too easily, as everyone sees, the recourse to war barters away all the ideas the war was supposed to win.

And thus we turn back to Gandhi's dilemma. He wished to withdraw

206. That is, to take responsibility for an ethics of questioning, for the responsibility of questioning, requires moving beyond the simplistic 'I believe' and toward the questions about the constructions of those beliefs.

We then understand ourselves, *not as subjectivity which finds itself in a world ready-made, as in simple psychological reflection, but as a subjectivity bearing within itself, and achieving, all of the possible operations to which this world owes its becoming.* In other words, we understand ourselves in this revelation of intentional implications, in the interrogation of the origin of the sedimentation of sense from intentional operations, as transcendental subjectivity, where, by "transcendental," nothing more is to be understood than the theme, originally inaugurated by Descartes, of a regressive inquiry concerning the ultimate source of all cognitive formations, of a reflection by the knowing subject on himself and on his cognitive life, the life in which all scientific formations valid for him have been purposefully produced and are preserved as available results. (Husserl, *Experience and Judgment* [1938], pp. 49–50)

from the violence of politics in such a way as to cause a judgment against violence to come from the other (who holds the institutionalized power). He wished to educate without saying too much, bring people to ask about what they were doing, to act as the humanity they wanted to be. Here, I believe, we have an opening onto a new type of political question, a question of political education and of consequent actions, but also a questioning which is not about the individual's (or the other individual's) desires. Gandhi, without invoking the coherence of a systematic philosophy, wishes to think through a style of political intervention which is not dependent on the coherence of a center, does not depend on the opposing claim, as claim, to find acceptance as just—rather, and we wonder if even Gandhi thought this through, he is thinking a withdrawal from all contingencies, from claims in the sense of the individual's interest expressed within an economy; only this withdrawal would correspond to the religious purity he sought. Clearly, however, this doesn't reach to any profound level of questioning on the part of the various political actors (those others with concrete power) in any given situation as long as it counts on their pregiven understandings of a situation (an innate humanism, a general feeling of good will, or a specific tradition of 'just' distributions, etc.). Rather, beyond any reference to the content of a tradition, and with the more complicated sense of the human that phenomenology gave us, we see that being thrown back from the economy, as a questioning of that economy, is far from a mere retreat away from the given situation and its intricacies.[206]

But how is one (the self or the other in power) taught the irony of a withdrawal that doesn't merely escape into a fantasy? This is the question of education, and of writing as a form of education, that grounds the stylistic hesitancies (and exuberances) of this book—for we are not certain of what will be produced in the reader, nor even of the reader's kindness, understanding, or goodwill, yet we write. To write, as I have attempted to do here, without the safety of a delineation, or a demarcation, seems to me to be required by the very paradoxes of art as writing—that is, that one must anticipate the openness of a community, the comportment of a multiplicity of readers, through an act that is neither exemplary in the sense of a model nor judgmental in the sense of a determination of the indeterminate. I would like to be read. I do not write to finish off the topic, to end the necessity of reading, or of future writing: I do not herald the end of time, an apocalyptic justice (or injustice).

Writing, at this level, has to do with a politics of pedagogy (and, indeed, the classroom—as student, fellow-student, and teacher—is where many of the questions of this book first arose for me concretely). For example, it is quite common to see a political agenda of one sort or another slipped into the curriculum of an English composition class. Most commonly, it is the generally humanist literary canon, with which the professors are usually most familiar in any case. Most students even expect this. However, when that political content is exceeded, in any of a variety of directions, one hears cries of 'injustice!' from the students, parents, or from other faculty. Often enough, it is even phrased as a question of rights. If I paid for a certain type of class, it is a breach of contract for me to be taught something I didn't pay for. Such an argument both avoids recourse to a direct confrontation over the material at stake and deftly takes advantage of our legalistic thinking concerning the nature of subjectivity, such that the accusation most frequently finds the overextended professor mumbling something about grammatical rules being taught on Tuesdays.

At this point, and as a conclusion to what I have been saying in the previous pages, we should see that our metaphorizations of subjectivity badly hinder not only a questioning about the world (education is reduced to a repetition of the commonly known), but stop us from thinking of justice outside of a contractual relation between opposing subjects, each possessing obligations and rights. That these two problems stem from the same metaphorization in terms of a continuity of individuals should be clear philosophically from what I've already said about the nature of time; however, I would like to follow that example a little further, especially as it should help us to enter into the question of daughters.

If we think of empowerment in the strictly polemical terms of learning to value what one already is (as the left, enamored of the idea of determining cultural metaphors, tends to structure the ideal pedagogical situation), then we have already tacitly agreed to a strategy by which a standard culture (or canonical idea of culture, such as a Christian humanism) is given as the measure of all others (we, of the center, are supposed to support alternative cultures since they have special areas of knowledge which may enrich 'our' culture). A strategy of 'respect' for other cultures indeed strikes us as an appropriate response to the simplistic (yet omnipresent) racism (if not to the sexism) of the usual reading list, but that respect is already burdened with an individualism that will demand that the greatest respect be given to the existing power structures and to that cultural tradition which itself codified the idea of respect for (and arising within) the individual. Even if it attained a perfect 'respect', only the existing structures would be accorded that deference (and such a deference allows, after all, many oppressions to continue unabated).

Thus, equally, someone who claims merely to teach the best literature, no matter what ethnic or cultural affiliation it holds, and someone who claims to be presenting the best literature from various cultures, would both have to open up the definition of 'best' and of 'literature' to examination. For whom? For themselves, before they begin teaching, but that is not the primary locus of the questioning. The classroom itself must be opened up to a new level of questioning (one usually consciously avoided by professional teachers at every level). Freire's *Pedagogy of the Oppressed* broaches these metatheoretical questions when he insists on grounding the pedagogical approach in the concrete needs of the students. The problem comes when these needs are too narrowly circumscribed by material concerns already interpreted through a metaphorization of individuals in competition (even if a class consciousness is engendered, it will arise as a variation of a technological approach to both society and education—which is, of course, not a critique where narrowly circumscribed technical and material questions are at stake; the problem would be ever establishing the 'grounds at stake' without a previous and guiding conceptualization of the question of value, or of the human as the site of value, which was dependent on an aestheticization of the human which would, for pragmatic reasons, remain beyond questioning).

To open the class to the question of the aesthetic, for courses both within the humanistic and technological traditions, is to open up a new type of question—albeit one which has always functioned at some level within all types of education. Instead of 'respecting' other cultures, one asks about how the metaphor of culture itself is politicized, how it functions within present political and aesthetic situations, and how it fits into the constitution of a world—a world which, as an ever present question, is always being pushed toward its future, toward new forms of justice (and injustice) and new questions which exceed the simplicity of choice, desire, and fulfillment, which exceed the economy named by the concept 'culture'.

To accomplish such a questioning within education is to violate the simple model of justice with which we began: the student cannot have paid in advance for a knowledge which she/he already wanted to own unless the education is merely formal (and/or repetitive). And, of course, it is the commonest of things to hear that one emerged changed after college, etc., without hearing of the injustice of that change. The difference is, perhaps, that we tend to equate the change the student undergoes with a maturation, with the reaching of a goal which had been buried in the genetic code from the day of conception (or within the cultural codes from the day of its foundation). Of course, with that selfsame conception we justify squelching all changes that are not clearly within our own view of the model (of maturity). With that conception we justify the condescension so pervasive at all levels of teaching. To open up the question of the purpose of school, beyond the mere technologies of control usually invoked (beyond getting a job), is to necessarily question the very model of maturity that has created our current school system. It is to question the reason for learning to read and write without merely acceding to the parental command, without blindly accepting the necessity of the present and "its stupid, 'that's the way it is.'"

The teacher's responsibility is thus made infinite, and urgent. Not for the improvement of the student's moral character, not for the student's benefit at all, education must be its own question (it must already be a thinking). Education must aspire to the aesthetic freedom of metaphorization which an art invokes. And, importantly, the necessity of education must be phrased as a question and must be a question which can sometimes be answered in the negative (although Levinas's conception of passivity would imply that the negative answer would be impossible if the question were phrased in its infinite form, that is, insofar as each student took on the responsibility of the whole, of the teacher—unfortunately, one is sometimes restricted, for institutional reasons, from taking the step toward the infinite, and one may need to find a different path, a different education; that is, a finite negation, a 'no' which is not suicide, is still possible; in fact, as a withdrawal, it makes all questions which refer back to the best construction of institutions, etc., possible). And here we have circled back to the question concerning Gandhi's political practice, especially as he proposes to teach the strength of nonviolence through a withdrawal from the economy of violence (through personal fasting, etc.). That is, as a question of our own political practice inside the classroom, as teachers and students, we must ask how to withdraw without separating, how to fast without starving to

207. And here, again, we would have to approach Nietzsche's presence within the metaphorizations, within the styles, of contemporary philosophy. The child is the metaphor which structures the largest arc within his *Zarathustra*, from the parable of the camel, lion, and child, to the childrens' voices after he leaves the 'last men' and the disturbed solitude of his mountain cave. The freedom of the metaphor he announced, the possibility of a style of philosophy that did not depend on the coherence of its references, on the transparence of its own intentions as art, gives my less ambitious use of metaphors something of a 'tradition', although Levinas's work uses the metaphors in a more philosophical vein, and better approximates my usage. For both Levinas and Nietzsche, the power of metaphorization is forefronted in both style and in terms of the philosophy itself, yet for Levinas, those metaphors return to the nonmetaphorical of the other human and Nietzsche's seems to return to the nonmetaphorical of the 'healthy body.'

death, alone on a mountain peak, without engendering any children.[207]

Personal escape, the refusal of participation, I think, would summarize the political statement the West as a whole is left with at this point—a withdrawal into the solitary aspect of an I commanded by a You (a student choosing a teacher over a parent, but still thinking of the choice in terms of role models). Roles, as roles, will always fail to specify the ethical content of education or politics; a rule-governed society is precisely not ethical. The broad-based resignation—masquerading as apathy—among so many of the relatively privileged peoples of the first world today seems to stem directly from the institutionalized separation of public and private realms. The strikingly odd facet of this resignation is how it's related to the obvious failure of the division between the two realms. By these lights, the public realm has been incarnated into an autonomous institution—of which even the most localized and grassroots organizations partake—which systematically, often tragically, infringes on the private realm. The discourse of rights being the only—and quite frail—protection of the private.

Not being able to escape the logic of inside and outside, each person is resigned to a personal escape, trying, perhaps, to minimize the negative impacts of their own consumption (withdrawing into an individual or communal unit), but the individual remains unable to see any possibility for political activity which is not merely an addition to the weight of an institution—variously figured as Capitalism, Marxism, Bureaucratism, or Fundamentalism—gone mad. An ethics which sees obligations merely as

incurred duties, costly results of previous noninnocent actions, mine and others's, will always idealize absolute withdrawal from the economy as the only
form of nonviolence. Supposedly, if I do not agree with the politics of coffee
production, I should forego my morning coffee (perhaps even abstain completely). But would we thus be doing more than feigning nonparticipation?
Only if we concurrently threw the larger system into question (nonviolence
must perform an interruption in the continuity of violences—an interruption
that is not violent because continuity is not the definition of the same; continuity is not the locus of rights, is no longer itself the definition of nonviolence).

In brief, this typical withdrawal, an abstention of some sort, only leaves
the economy in order to ensure *itself* a better return, only thinks in terms of its
own moral purity; not being able to answer the problem of the other's obligation in its totality, one pretends to answer the problem of the obligation to the
self as literalized in/as a moral (human) agent—the call toward personal stability, toward a self-complacency in the personal innocence of particular deeds,
undercuts the claims of sacrifice imposed by others. The radical exteriority of
meaning, on the other hand—which eventually denies the division of public
and private—an exterior language as the conveyor/conveyance of the transcendental ego, the other's face as the marker of the infinite desire to leave oneself, prescribes meaning precisely as speaking to the other, transcending toward infinity, productively participating in the others' creation (as giving up
the pretension to the completion of meaning, to possession of an answer). We
do not stop at the given formality of reciprocal respect—the obligation is infinitely 'for-the-other', with a reciprocity in claims only coming as a late and
contingent addition, if it would be established at all.

In the terms of our earlier analogy, the role of the teacher is also transformed. Responsible for every student's learning, the teacher must withdraw
from the site of education, from the facts which constitute, supposedly, a discourse, so that the student's questioning can form those questions into a discourse into which facts may come to appear meaningful. To read Shakespeare
as a model of humanism, as one who makes us all ask essential questions on
a par with Hamlet, is thus still a step short of the education that fulfills its re-
ponsibilities. To read the play "Hamlet," one must stop identifying with the
title character and start thinking through the question of characterization in a
play; that is, one must think through the artistic procedures by which the
artistic presentation is polemically, politically, personally, and aesthetically
possible (this is not a new fact about reading: it has always been true of the
process).

Such questions, it should be clear, are already being asked with even the
simplest reading; this questioning already exists, yet because it is threatening,

because it always implies burgeoning responsibilities for the teacher as the reading explodes past the limits of the canonically construed text, the teacher usually falls back on (and insists on) the point of control (the exigetical determination of Shakespeare's original intentions) and then (sometimes) opens up to a responsible (respectful) criticism—which has already agreed to the terms of control (which has already agreed to take Shakespeare's intentions as fixed bearers of meaning). I am not advocating the elimination of the teacher, the freeplay of students who already think they know what they need to know ('I think Hamlet stands for . . . '). Rather, students—and teachers, although one cannot justly differentiate between them in a classroom—must take on the task of thinking through Shakespeare as an artist, must take on the choices of writing, and of presentation, which make the previous understandings (Hamlet's supposedly fixed metaphorical content) tremble under the possibility of new aesthetic (including critical/historical) appropriations and interventions. So that, with Hamlet, we must not only ask what tropes represent his anxiety (or Shakespeare's anxiety) to us, and whether Hamlet's anxiety in fact resembles our own, but also (for one privileged example of questioning) begin to ask of the origins, and necessity, of anxiety in familial relations, in our own world and in Shakespeare's, and—most importantly for us, and for our future aesthetics—we must question whether such an anxiety is to be our destiny as much as it was Hamlet's.

That this was not Shakespeare's 'theme', or intention, would only be a criticism if we thought of artistic choices only as determinations (and as arising from previous determinations) which had been available as determinant. Our questioning, then, insofar as it asked of the play of indeterminations which make determinations possible, would again invoke the problem of why critics had praised this presentation and, concurrently, why it was being read in that particular classroom. That is, in terms of the very structure of the indeterminate in its orientation towards a future, its refusal of the present, I am responsible for Hamlet, for a fictional character who cannot exceed his given presentations except through me—and I am responsible for the infinity of possible future readings which my readings, insofar as they are to be ethical, must engender. Hermeneutics, as Levinas already clearly suggested in the metaphor of maternity, becomes childbearing (and childbearing is already transcendence). Further, childbearing, without the linearity of a single story of maturation, stops being the condescension it has so often been. Education is no longer measured by right answers, but through the generation of interesting questions.

Precisely at this level one might wish to read an author who shares a more immediately accessible context (culturally, temporally, etc.) in order to make these very questions resonate as questions (rather than instill a distanced respect toward either some 'other' set of answers or toward a canonical answer—or even toward a canonically formulated question). Similarly, where Gandhi was most successful was not in setting up an alternative form of government (although one might well see a call for such a move) but in setting up a new type of question within the political, a question which highlights the necessity of finding alternatives to the present system without reducing all those alternatives to a repetition of the same violence under different rulers. To sit at a lunch counter and be served food equally with all others is a privilege that fundamentally differs from the right to exclude someone else from being served (the latter does not emerge from a right, but from a prejudice phrased as a right). The reciprocity of the abstract right to service was granted as a response to a questioning (the nonviolent sit-ins) which should have reached further than the abstraction of reciprocity. Perhaps what remains of racism will require more positive interventions than an application of our current conception of rights could provide, or perhaps an intervention even beyond the scope of a government (like our own) that claims to only judge between competing claims (which thinks of humans as always merely a step away from war) and only distributes scarce resources (always projecting, and reinstituting, the scarcity, the economy of violence, itself). Which is not to argue with the form of government as much as with its content. Thus, to make a new government, or approach a new art, requires questioning the very bases of the world, and the aesthetic's location within that world (for justice is an aesthetic concern), even if the questioning is not thematized as 'radical', as opening up a new public space, etc., even if it is merely an "attempt at something."

Levinas has metaphorized this open questioning in terms of an anxiety felt at the restrictiveness of given roles and in terms of a more primal inability to speak as if you spoke to yourself (or your transcendental self) alone. Does this mean that you can find no meaning in monogamous marriage, or by yourself alone in the woods? Not at all—these may, in fact, be the points at which you come to terms with yourself as a transcending self. Still, meaning, which admittedly you may have clarified in solitude, does not come from these roles as wife, husband, or hermit but from the excess of these goals, the directedness of these goals away from the self. It is what Levinas uses the metaphor of paternity to describe, a father having sons—his problem is still his inability to conceptualize the position of the daughter. He cannot see the woman who actively seeks justice, just as he has only begun to see the man who might listen, who might display the patience to live in/for justice.

In Günter Grass's *Show Your Tongue*, Grass admirably knows that he is not in a position to represent the life—to appropriate the experience—of the urban poor of India. The categories of experience are, perhaps, too Western; more, the categories of Western rights—of the representative divinity made abstract—have already failed them. There is no individual to be portrayed in such a way as to evoke sympathy; there is only our (privileged) shame—our shameful selfishness and our shameful failures. Shame constitutes an interesting possibility of withdrawal, for it doesn't claim to be pure, even as a withdrawal. It doesn't stem from the innocence of the individual as a 'human', innocently becoming a world from the privileged purity of divine election. There is a moment in the book when he transcends the boundaries of his vision and adumbrates the contours of the circle in which he, an artist and a wealthy Westerner, is implicated:

> If you lent (for a fee) one of these slum hovels, created from bare necessity, to the city of Frankfurt am Main, and had it set down next to the Deutsche Bank highrise, where the hewn granite sculpture by the artist Bill says yes, always yes to the towering bank, because as an endless loop it loves only itself, is incontrovertibly beautiful and immaculately endorses the circulation of money stamped valid for eternity—if, I say, you replaced that granite celebrating its flawless self, and set down instead one single slum hovel, as authentic as want has made it, right next to the glassy arrogance of the Deutsche Bank, beauty would at once be on the side of the hovel, and truth too, even the future. The mirrored art of all those palaces consecrated to money would fall to its knees, because the slum hovel (each hovel in its own way) belongs to tomorrow. (*Show Your Tongue* [1988], p. 21)

The hovel is not mirrored, it does not represent—it points, instead, to the failure of representation. Instead of saying yes, it asks why—of every individual, of the entire system that distributes wealth, the systems of representation which are the institution of the hierarchies of caste and poverty.[208] We don't reach our truth in art by pretending to some type of social realism. There is no sensuously immediate bare existence to which we all refer, in some long-forgotten essential nature. Stories about third-world women seen from the point of view of first-world peoples—even if the third-world women *see themselves* within similar categories—fail to see the individuality and efficaciousness of their conscious, active lives precisely because such stories interpret the world as if it were something merely viewed. To treat these women, or anyone, as individuals would require not only the relatively recent admission that they already inhabit a world of meaning—meanings which they may or may not wish to escape—but that the responsibility for our collective tomorrow lies hard upon them, as it does upon us. Which doesn't make the truth of their (or our) existence their anxious worry over their future. Our response to them need not be the materiality of comfort; it may be, instead, the very invocation of their power, our release from our anxiety in the face of their power. But doesn't their otherness, and their 'other' power, actually threaten me (us)? Only within a metaphor of humanism that doubts whether they agree with us, that finds it important that they agree (or at least agree to be part of the same 'we'), that already sets everything into a competition, or war, between individuals and their 'claims'.

Grass probably intends his found sculpture to make a point to the observing German populace—a worthy pedagogic goal. I think the same sculpture could mean something else, something to the hovel dweller (whom we can't seem to hear). The German, presumedly, would see the opulence of Germany and the poverty of India in relation for the first time (and feel shame, and maybe even *do* something). The Indian builder, in authentic need, has already seen this opulence. Grass's sculpture would serve no (direct) purpose for the one 'in need'. Most writers have, like most anthropologists, refused to see, simply, that the ones we look at are looking back at us. Too polite to stare, perhaps (or we are just too dense to understand their staring or our shame). But when Grass refers to the future, he is adumbrating the fact that a different power rests with those whom we have always only seen as 'others', as 'the' poor, and as victims.

With this reference to a future which is not ours, his pedagogical goals extend beyond recognitions of injustice, and reach

208. "To defend and illustrate philosophy in its differend with its two adversaries: on its outside, the genre of economic discourse (exchange, capital); on its inside, the genre of academic discourse (mastery). By showing that the linking of one phrase onto another is problematic and that this problem is the problem of politics, to set up a philosophical politics apart from the politics of 'intellectuals' and of politicians. To bear witness to the differend" (Lyotard, *The Differend* [1983], p. xiii).

209. It is with subjectivity understood as self, with the excid-
ing and dispossession, the
contraction, in which the ego
does not appear, but immo-
lates itself, that the relationship with the other can be
communication and transcendence, and not always an-
other way of seeking cer-
tainty, or the coinciding with
oneself. Paradoxically
enough, thinkers claim to derive communication out of
self-coinciding. They do not
take seriously the radical reversal, from cognition to solidarity, that communication
represents with respect to inward dialogue, to cognition of
oneself, taken as the trope of
spirituality. They seek for
communication a full cover-
age insurance, and do not ask
if inward dialogue is not be-
holden to the solidarity that
sustains communication. In
expiation, the responsibility
for the others, the relationship with the non-ego, precedes any relationship of the
ego with itself. The relationship with the other precedes
the auto-affection of certainty,
to which one always tries to
reduce communication. (Levinas, *Otherwise than Being*,
pp. 118–19)

toward the eyes of others, where our shame
will be found. The body-less knower of
Kantian apperception is not an impossible
ideal because we never lose our prejudices,
as sometimes claimed. It's not that simple;
we are able to efface our body, our contexts,
as far as our eyes (our world views or our
perspectives) are concerned. It is the other
whose gaze we cannot escape (without the
violence of a suppression).[209] Our desire,
our writing, reaches out to the others, the
other, the infinite. This collective gaze from
the oppressed doesn't mean anything to our
past—they are precisely the ones we have
been excluding from the structures of meaning all along—they can only mean something to our future (and it's not clear if we
even still want to reconstrue meaning in
terms of economies either past or future).
Better, trying to speak without economies,
these others have meaning, they mean, as
subjects of a gaze opposite of me, before I
am. But in that precedence, if we can think
through a new aesthetics of philosophical
writing, our anxiety need not be individual,
or individuating; in a thinking of transcendence which is not already 'human', no
competition would make the other's meaning either a determination or a violence.

If this poor person has borrowed
wealthy eyes—which we, the wealthy, are
always encouraging them, the poor, to bor-
row—then she or he sees that the system
has deprived them of the opulence they are
supposed to want. Rather, and borrowed
eyes won't work here, we need to see that
the mirrored privilege of the Deutsche Bank
is empty. The inability of the Deutsche
Bank, in all of its glassy splendor, to dominate the hovel is not some lesson learned

from history (or even from future history)—we are not asked to see that all oppressed classes will eventually rise up in a red tide. Domination is as meaningless, as brittle, as glass; with our own eyes, with eyes of the poor or eyes of the rich, with the strength which belongs to those who are willing to look for justice, we see this.

# Daughters in time

*Days I have held,*
*days I have lost,*

*days that outgrow, like daughters,*
*my harbouring arms.*

—D. Walcott, *"Midsummer, Tobago,"*
Collected Poems

This book—I—asks to be read as a piece of fiction (and only looks toward, somewhat wistfully, the possibility of being read like a poem, or a piece of art). Not that I have pretensions to a mastery of any narrative style, but, like a fiction, the proper judgment rests not with how well my writing represents reality, how faithful the son is to the father, but with how well it implicates the audience in its questions, how well, as written, these questions are able to produce—and live—the sociality (the indetermination and justice) of the written word. Thus I neither pretend to be alone, like a primary source, nor do I pretend to be merely subservient to another's will and decisions, like a secondary source. One thus refuses the distinctions between teacher and student, author and reader. Thus we all approximate, and repeatedly, the problem of the child who comes to consciousness already in a world of meanings (of shames, joys, privileges, and oppressions) and like any child, we must take the time to learn to find our own way in a world already filled with the paths of others, already filled with others' expectations.

Husserl's infinite horizons of intelligibility found the world to be the correlate of an ego's endlessly multiple possible intentions, all of which could eventually be thematized, corrected, and brought to evidence such that one could separate genuine from spurious beliefs.[210] The difference between my position and Husserl's is the lack of any determinate, eternal, and abstract

327

formal measure (such as the structure of evidence, or givenness) which announces the appropriateness of a question or set of questions (for example, fleshing out all possible objects of knowledge as pieces of knowledge—that is, enacting Science). Rather, questions are measured, in content and in form, by the given problems of an existing world: the question of science and art, "genuine and spurious," is posed, but not yet answered. Thus an emphasis on the ethics of questioning does not necessarily decide in favor of funding social programs over research in high energy physics, but it can, in ways that the existing emphasis on descriptive science cannot, ask the question of this hierarchy. To take some time to consider what questions we should be asking is to refuse the simple identification of justice with a correct answer (or an ethical act).

Levinas, if one were to divide the world into only idealists and materialists, is an idealist. He is also, as Derrida points out, a radical empiricist. He is no more sexist than the division between content and form itself— exactly as sexist as the division of questions of society and questions of the self (and Levinas himself has taught us new ways to question these very divisions, to see why and how these divisions literalize a sexism). He is not a sexist at the level of separating woman's tasks from man's—he neither believes (as far as his writing goes at least) that a woman's place is in the home nor that a biological man, as a biological being, is less feminine than a biological woman. There does seem to remain in Levinas a preference, however, and perhaps only at the level of the metaphor, for heterosexual desire and its ramifications within the structure of the

210. *Radical* sense-investigation, as such, is at the same time criticism for the sake of original clarification. Here original clarification means shaping the sense anew, not merely filling in a delineation that is already determinate and structurally articulated beforehand. Nowhere indeed is such a quite determinate predelineation of sense essentially possible, except as a secondary consequence of clarity previously obtained. After the living evidence of clarity has passed, the effect this evidence produced in the realm of habit persists, along with the possibility of a restoration, which at first is empty but contains, in empty form, the determinate sense-predelineation. This predelineation brings with it, then, the certainty of possible clear restoration, as renewal of the evidence. If, as in our case, such clarification is out of the question, then original sense investigation signifies a combination of determining more precisely the vague indeterminate predelineation, distinguishing the prejudices that derive from associational overlappings, and cancelling those prejudices that conflict with the clear sense-fulfillment [*mit der besinnlichen Erfüllung*]—in a word, then: critical determination between the genuine and the spurious. (Husserl, *Formal and Transcendental Logic* [1929], p. 10)

family and of society. In a 1979 preface to a 1947 book, Levinas puts his 'idealism' within the framework of a certain privileged concept (albeit already a concept of difference):

> The notion of a transcendent alterity—one that opens time—is at first sought starting with an *alterity content*—that is, starting with femininity. Femininity—and one would have to see in what sense this can be said of masculinity or of virility; that is, of the differences between the sexes in general—appeared to me as a difference contrasting strongly with other differences, not merely as a quality different from all others, but as the very quality of difference. This idea should make the notion of the couple as distinct as possible from every purely numerical duality. The notion of the sociality of two, which is probably necessary for the exceptional epiphany of the face—abstract and chaste nudity—emerges from sexual differences, and is essential to eroticism and to all instances of alterity—again as quality and not as a simply logical distinction—borne by the "thou shalt not kill" that the very silence of the face says. Here is a significant ethical radiance within eroticism and the libido. Through it humanity enters into the society of two and sustains it, authorizes it, perhaps, at least putting into question the simplicity of contemporary paneroticism. (*Time and the Other*, p. 36)

The materialist critique of idealism is quick to recognize the sentimentality and nostalgia here. By materialist lights, we are asking, with Paul McCartney, what's wrong with silly love songs? The answer, for the materialists, is that the discourse of romantic love obscures the actual bases of society and prevents a coherent critique of the society (or the self). Levinas hears this critique and agrees, maintaining, just the same, the priority of interiority. He is not willing to say that man should go home to his woman and take care of the small shop of the petite bourgeoisie. He is maintaining that before one speaks, one is spoken to (the humanity of receiving a "thou shalt not kill" emerges as a command)—this priority itself then constitutes an ideal, an above (or an otherwise) from which, or as which, meaning comes (although we are not to take that meaning as being already filled with a content beyond our apprehensions, beyond the form of the for-the-other in signification). Who speaks to us? Better, for now, to ask what desire has in common with the need for the sociality of two, the need to end a solitude. Must that sociality be heterosexual? I don't see why, unless we are back on the grounds of the necessity of a particular humanity instituted in the maternal relation (such as Freud's—which does, of course, reflect a metaphor many people actually strive to live through).

Recalling the position of the mother, metaphorically more than actually (although there is a simple sense to the actuality of this as well), my engenderment as a child, as a subject in the world, was preceded by a world that constituted me, that gave me no choice of possession. That is to say, as the object of a language, I am constituted as a subject and as a subject I am obliged to speak. From whence do I speak? I speak from the point of contact with the feminine other of the home—that is, I speak as the engendering of future children. This is, clearly, as much Hegel as Levinas. The differences will be hard to stake.

The withdrawal the Marxist, or any materialist, makes is based on the possibility of an earlier withdrawal, a withdrawal that materialism as such is unable to theorize, a withdrawal from the paradigm of society based on productive exchange (which constitutes all possibilities as already within the material). Levinas, as we have seen, is trying to rethink the meaning of this withdrawal. It would be tempting, especially with *Totality and Infinity* (1961) and less so with *Otherwise than Being* (1974), to claim that Levinas has merely reinvented the preexpressive silence which grounds sensibility, susceptibility, itself—that is, albeit now as an invention, he has reintroduced the reified, and inviolable, first-person subject.[211] Although Levinas's language seems to authorize such a critique, a careful analysis of his use of Husserl's transcendental ego, in the contexts of his conception of time, frees us from either an oversimplified subjectivity merely coming up with idiosyncratic names or of a world-historical progress where the present moment is abstractly equal to, and materially determined by, the first moment of time.

Here we should recognize not only the

211. Levinas addresses this criticism in the last paragraph of the book: "In this work which does not seek to restore any ruined concept, the destitution and the desituating of the subject do not remain without signification: after the death of a certain god inhabiting the world behind the scenes, the substitution of the hostage discovers the trace, the unpronounceable inscription, of what, always already past, always 'he,' does not enter into any present, to which are suited not the nouns designating beings, or the verbs in which their essence resounds, but that which, as a pronoun, marks with its seal all that a noun can convey" (Levinas, *Otherwise than Being* [1974], p. 185).

discussion in "Mothers" about the transcendental ego but the analysis of desire in "Sisters." To begin, and at this point only haltingly, to think the discourse of desire outside of the simple oppositions of lack and satisfaction—outside of economies—is the moment that separates the self-absorption of romantic love from what Kierkegaard would call the love of God—the existence of creative forces which transcend our simple solitude, and our concurrent stagnation.[212]

Philosophy as love of truth aspires to the Other (*l'Autre*) as such, to a being distinct from its reflection in the I—it searches for its Law, it is heteronomy itself, it is metaphysical. According to Descartes, the I who thinks possesses the idea of the infinite: the otherness of the Infinite is not deadened in the idea, as is the otherness of finite ideas of which according to Descartes, I can give an account through myself. The idea of the Infinite consists in thinking more than one thinks.

This negative description assumes a positive sense which is no longer literally Cartesian: a thought which thinks more than it thinks— what is this, if not Desire? It is a desire which distinguishes itself from the privation of need. The Desired does not fill it, but deepens it. (Levinas, "Signature," *Research in Phenomenology* [1978], 8:184–85)

To see "in what sense this can be said of masculinity or of virility" would require conceptualizing ourselves as the ambiguous objects of the Other's desire. Or, as objects of

212. "But also, with the putting into me of the idea of the Infinite, the prophetic event beyond its psychological peculiarity is the throbbing of primordial time where, for itself, of itself, deformalized, the idea of the Infinite signifies. God-coming-to-mind as the life of God" (Levinas, "The Old and the New" [1980], *Time and the Other*, p. 138).

language, we are obliged to subjectivity, required to speak. This move is not beyond the philosophical resources of Levinas's position—but neither is it beyond the resources of Heidegger's. My claim to originality is—as with fiction—a question of emphasis, a structure of implication, which is obscured in these primary texts because of their own insistences on primacy, on a hierarchical distance of author from reader, an insistence on the difficult task, the difficult character, of their own work. Rather, we are asked to replace the dead creator, to fill the space Christ's crucifixion left in the world—not by assuming the cross, but through our horror at the continuing crucifixions, not by becoming gods, but by becoming mortals. We take the cross as the end of the divine and not its beginning—even if it is an end, in the infinity of subjective creation, that we share.

Or rather: perhaps here, with our thinking about the subject, we are precisely still within the sexism of humanism's unwillingness to really rethink the basic metaphors of our humanity (and its traditionally given structures of possible meaningfulness). The son is literalized in 'my future', even as a future not possessed by me (I remain ambiguously—as an ideal of difference, or as a non-ideal, bodily unicity—beyond any particular literalization), yet destined to a 'human' creation—that is, destined to create meaningfully, to communicate meanings to others. The daughter who refuses marriage, who doesn't accept another's gods either, would be the woman who can literalize indeterminacy, who can think a justice beyond the formalization, or enactment, of previous justices as determinations. The daughter imag-

213. The intimacy which familiarity already presupposes is an *intimacy with someone*. The interiority of recollection is a solitude in a world already human. Recollection refers to a welcome. But how can the separation of solitude, how can intimacy be produced in the face of the Other? Is not the presence of the Other already language and transcendence? For the intimacy of recollection to be able to be produced in the oecumenia of being the presence of the Other must not only be revealed in the face which breaks through its own plastic image, but must be revealed, simultaneously with this presence, in its withdrawal and in its absence. This simultaneity is not an abstract construction of dialectics, but the very essence of discretion. And the other whose presence is discreetly an absence, with which is accomplished the primary hospitable welcome which describes the field of intimacy, is the Woman. The woman is the condition for recollection, the interiority of the Home, and inhabitation. The simple living from . . . the spontaneous agreeableness of the elements is not yet habitation. But habitation is not yet the transcendence of language. The Other who welcomes in intimacy is not the *you* [*vous*] of the face that reveals itself in a dimension of height, but precisely the *thou* [*tu*] of familiarity: a language without teaching, a silent language, an understanding

without words, an expression
in secret. The I-Thou in
which Buber sees the category
of interhuman relationship is
the relation not with the interlocutor but with feminine
alterity. This alterity is situated on another plane than
language and nowise represents a truncated, stammer-
ing, still elementary language.
On the contrary, the discretion of this presence includes
all the possibilities of the
transcendent relationship
with the Other. It is comprehensible and exercises its
function of interiorization
only on the ground of the full
human personality, which,
however, in the woman, can
be reserved so as to open up
the dimension of interiority.
And this is a new and irreducible possibility, a delight-
ful lapse in being, and the
source of gentleness in itself.
(Levinas, *Totality and Infinity*
[1961], p. 155)

214. And Levinas, already in
1961, helped us phrase this question (even if we are not following
his answer):

I can indeed recollect myself
in the midst of my life, which
is life from . . . However, the
negative moment of this
*dwelling* which determines
possession, the recollection
which draws me out of sub-
mergence, is not a simple
echo of possession. We may
not see in it the counterpart
of presence to things, as
though the possession of
things, as a presence to them,
dialectically contained the

ines a justice otherwise than in greater and
greater production—otherwise than in the
resolution of fights over property—and only
thus do we encounter a justice that doesn't
fall back on the supposed truism that what's
good for the economy is good for the people
in the economy.

Does this indeterminism in justice mark
an idosyncratic escape from meaning? No. It
merely marks the difficulty of forming a 'we'
once we have abandoned the too facile recourse to 'we subjects', or 'we humans', who
share the meanings (the determinations) of a
world.[213] We (the readers of this book) are
constantly within differing discourses, inhabiting an unstable space. Allegorically,
this is still because we have not yet come to
terms with the feminine: we haven't left the
space of being a masculine subject dependent on (yet demanding) feminine kindness;
we haven't learned (and here, too, we would
have to see in what sense this could be said
of the masculine as well as the feminine) to
live this kindness from the side of the
giver.[214] Levinas leaves us at the point of
saying that truth lies in questioning passive
syntheses but reinstitutes the priority of an
appropriate question coming from the self—
from the ego, as human, as moral agent,
constituted by passive synthesis. This is still
an obvious advance for Levinas, but he
seems thereby to reappropriate responsibility—blame and praise—for bearing the
child back to the masculine subject who
works outside the home, who lives in, and
to some extent believes in the necessity of,
the economy of, the 'said'. To think the
metaphor of the daughter here together with
the metaphor of art (the metaphor which is
not destined to its communication, to its

being received as meaningful) is to see the gradual appropriation that makes saying not a violence. In this sense, the metaphor of sociality (more primal than the metaphor of subjectivity that Levinas's invocation of the kingdom seems to place at the base of any society) is the most common and most difficult of literalizations to achieve. Here we would speak of the daughter who neither breaks with the order of the father (like a son who separates) nor accepts the father 'as' governor (like the wife who raises sons). She does not see the father as identical to his rules/roles, but accepts him as he (in his modernity) would not have been willing to accept his father; that is, she accepts him as one accepts a work of art, a gift which is more than its giving. In that 'more' of giving we approach (and we have not yet reached) a thinking that does not begin from a dichotomy between a subject and his/her tradition.

The key here for Levinas, as for Husserl and Heidegger before, is to reconceptualize our understanding of time. Levinas chooses the metaphor of patrilineal descent—and this is where he trusts he can rediscover (or at least displace) the problem of the fidelity of passive synthesis.[215] For Hegel, the case was fairly simple. The feminine represents the ethical unconscious, all those things we believe without knowing we believe them. Truth (the son) comes from a reflection, from saying of the ethical unconscious (the mother) that it, too, must submit to the laws of reason—the laws of the publicly verifiable, of the light. If we were to map this same framework on to Levinas, as is tempting within the tradition Levinas belongs to, he is guilty of the same sexism. It doesn't fit,

withdrawal from them. This withdrawal implies a new event; I must have been in relation with something I do not live from. This event is the relation with the Other who welcomes me in the Home, the discreet presence of the Feminine. But in order that I be able to free myself from the very possession that the welcome of the Home establishes, in order that I be able to see things in themselves, that is, represent them to myself, refuse both enjoyment and possession, I must know how *to give* what I possess. (Levinas, *Totality and Infinity,* pp. 170–71)

215. I should like finally to stress a structure of transcendence that in *Time and the Other* has been caught sight of starting with paternity: the possible offered to the son and placed *beyond* what is assumable by the father still remains the *father's* in a certain sense. Precisely in the sense of kinship. The father's or non-indifferent—is a possibility that another assumes: through the son there occurs a possibility beyond the possible! This would be a non-indifference that does not issue from the social rules governing kinship, but probably founds these rules—a non-indifference through which the "beyond the possible" is possible for the Ego. This is what, starting with the—nonbiological—notion of the Ego's fecundity, puts into question the very idea of *power* [*pouvoir*], such

as it is embodied in transcendental subjectivity, the center and source of intentional acts. (Levinas, preface [1979] to *Time and the Other*, pp. 36–37)

My point against Levinas is merely that there is no reason that the possible and the beyond the possible should be both thought in their trajectory toward a determinate transcendence (and further, in Levinas's version of the ethical, it would be a transcendence which is anxious over the justice of those determinations as determinations).

216. "The caress aims at the tender which has no longer the status of an 'existent,' which having taken leave of 'numbers and beings' is not even a quality of an existent. The tender designates *a way*, the way of remaining in the *no man's land* between being and not-yet-being. A way that does not even signal itself as a signification, that in no way shines forth, that is extinguished and swoons, essential frailty of the Beloved produced as vulnerable and as mortal" (Levinas, *Totality and Infinity* [1960], p. 259).

however. Within Hegelianism, as construed by Levinas, there is nothing which corresponds to the feminine. Hegel's feminine has a positive content; it is embodied in the mother—or the wife/sister as potential mother—whom Hegel knows to have a voice and a consciousness (although he assumes she can never question that voice). The feminine is of primary importance to the little boy still ensnared in the life of the home.

For Levinas, and here is where he approaches his own brand of idealism, the sensual caress itself becomes important: the feminine is no longer something merely to be dominated, no longer merely a point of (possible) control within the production of economies.[216] It is difficult, to begin with, to point to the division between a description of gender relations and a too casual use of gendered metaphors. If one construes oneself in terms of typifications, the philosophical determination of those typifications—even if meant as relatively innocent metaphors—becomes part of the concrete relations of humans. That reason alone will be enough to make some people condemn Levinas's work as sexist. However, given the way these metaphors, on the whole, have been allowed to play themselves out in terms of the male domination of the given world (as in fact organized around an anxiety toward determinations), it is equally irresponsible, equally sexist, to ignore the gendered metaphors that already exist, to pretend that all that need be done is declare all nouns neuter and decree that soon everyone will forget.

Certainly, and I say this without the reservations I hold above, there is at least one sexist aspect to Levinas's work: the feminine, woman, is always literally figured in the place of the other; his work is *literally* androcentric. Here we have the most difficult problem for my thinking of metaphorization and literalization. There is a freedom within these metaphors which I have already tried to enact through a nonsystematic appropriation of various metaphors from various sources. I am not freely creating 'new' metaphors, but asking metaphorizations to do work within horizons that are not originally predelineated by the horizon of that metaphor (as a humanism, or a science, would claim to do, bringing the metaphorization and the literalization into exact correlation due to their common origin in the nature of the speech act or of description, etc.). In terms of a Lévi-Strauss, I am enacting the structural role of the daughter who lives within a different line, who perhaps even serves other gods, without abandoning my parents. Yet, exactly in that role, the priority of roles is contested. We would not want to take the necessity of this metaphor of daughters (and their exchange by foreign powers) for granted, would not want to implicate either a heterosexuality or an exchange between cultures approximating a universal structural truth about cultures (or culturing) in general—rather, we are approaching words within which a proximity with thinking is possible,[217] within which it is no longer necessary for a woman to get married at all.

And here we mark the inextricability of words and the things they name, and yet the distance which they always maintain. The metaphorizations of our language, in terms of vision, sex, daily life, etc., are all we have

217. In his "Conversation on a Country Path" (1944–45), Heidegger has the scientist hazard a definition of thinking as the "coming-into-the-nearness of distance," but then finds the scientist unwilling to hazard more in the uncertain vocabulary with which the scientist seems uncomfortable (anxious at the possible rebuke of the others). At that point, the scholar reassures the scientist by saying that, within the conversations, they "see to it that [they] move freely in the realm of words." And the teacher adds: "Because a word does not and never can re-present anything; but signifies something, that is, shows something as abiding into the range of its expressibility" (Heidegger, *Discourse on Thinking*, pp. 68–69).

218. And here I would like to retain the critique from the previous section concerning Levinas's humanism, concerning the necessity of some determination, or some said, within all thinking. His thinking of women would be controlled by that necessity, toward some set of provisional, always quickly abandoned, determinations, and thus would still be anxious in the face of a more fundamental indeterminism. My invocation of a daughter, metaphorically, was simply to avoid that anxiety over the necessity of metaphorization. Yes, we live within metaphors, but as Antigone showed in her sacrifice, life is not necessary. As Woolf's artist showed us, not even the body is necessary. To live the ambiguity of the metaphor, to live the strange interior of a circle only defined in its exterior points, is to live by thinking, to literalize as thinking—no longer dependent on the necessity of a thought (or the description of a thought).

available to us and already structure the way in which we speak about the objects of our world (including the objects of science). That these metaphors can be found to be metaphors, that we can 'discover' that our everyday understanding of simultaneity won't work at the very high speeds of relativistic physics, for example, is a key factor underlying the possibility of new thinking. How we characterize the fact of finding a metaphor to be inexact is what lies at stake here. To simply opt for an outside of the metaphor (that is, for the necessity of a particular metaphor of the metaphor which would guide all others) ignores the difference between the metaphor and the thinking which lives within the metaphor; the necessity of a metaphor would announce that, for at least some moment, it fit, it actually determined what was. Rather, we would want to mark the proximity as a time within which nothing was ever said to fit, in which the indeterminacy was not structured by a pregiven idea of what could be true. In that sense, like Heidegger and Levinas, we are still trying to think through the Husserlian insight into the transcendental ego and the horizons within which it lives.

Thus the question of sexism would be asked differently of Levinas precisely in his acknowledgment that the feminine does not determine a woman (as it still did for Hegel).[218] With questions of sexism, with the difference between Levinas and Hegel in mind, we turn back toward Levinas's reworking of the metaphors and facts of language use, of his theory of signification.

Let us recall what is involved in signification. The first instance of signification is produced in the face. Not that the face would receive a signification *by relation* to something. The face signifies by itself; its signification precedes *Sinngebung*. A meaningful behavior arises already in its light; it spreads the light in which light is seen. One does not have to explain it, for every explanation begins with it. In other words, society with the Other, which marks the end of the absurd rumbling of the *there is*, is not constituted as the *work* of an I giving meaning. It is necessary to already be for the Other—to exist and not to work only—for the phenomenon of meaning, correlative of the intention of a thought, to arise. Being-for-the-Other must not suggest any finality and not imply the antecedent positing or valorization of any value. To be for the Other is to be good. The concept of the Other has, to be sure, no new content with respect to the concept of the I: but being-for-the-Other is not a relation between concepts whose comprehension would coincide, or the conception of a concept by an I, but my goodness. The fact that in existing for another I exist otherwise than in existing for me is morality itself. (Levinas, *Totality and Infinity* [1961], p. 261)[219]

I begin here by remarking a distance within Levinas's thinking. As I tried to sketch out before, a clearer understanding of the ways in which Husserl's phenomenology was not reducible to the cliché that every object is the object of an intentional grasping led Levinas to better ground the necessity of the Other—no longer as the

219. Language does not exteriorize a representation preexisting in me: it puts in common a world hitherto mine. Language *effectuates* the entry of things into a new ether in which they receive a name and become concepts. It is a first action over and above labor, an action without action, even though speech involves the effort of labor, even though, as incarnate thought, it inserts us into the world, with the risks and hazards of all action. At each instant it exceeds this labor by the generosity of the offer it forthwith makes of this very labor. The analyses of language that tend to present it as one meaningful action among others fail to recognize this *offering* of the world, this offering of contents which answers to the face of the Other or which questions him, and first opens the perspective of the meaningful. The 'vision' of the face is inseparable from this offering language is. To see the face is to speak of the world. Transcendence is not an optics, but the first ethical gesture. (Levinas, *Totality and Infinity*, p. 174)

220. The separated being can, to be sure, shut itself up in its interiority. Things can not counter it absolutely, and Epicurean wisdom lives from this truth. But the will, whereby a being wields itself by somehow holding in its own hands all the strings that operate its being, is by its work exposed to the Other. Its exertion is

seen as a thing, if only by virtue of the insertion of its body in the world of things. Corporeity thus describes the ontological regime of a primary self-alienation, contemporaneous with the very event by which the self ensures, against the unknown factor of the elements, its own independence, that is, its self-possession or its security. The will equivalent to atheism—which refuses the Other as an influence being exerted on an I or holding it in its invisible meshes, which refuses the Other as a God inhabiting the I—the will which tears itself from this possession, from this enthusiasm, as the very power of rupture, delivers itself over to the Other in its work, the very work which permits it to ensure its interiority. Interiority thus does not exhaust the existence of the separated being. (Levinas, *Totality and Infinity*, p. 226)

221. A model which, especially at the time of his earlier work, still moved fundamentally within a play defined by the conflict with violence:

This inversion is more radical than sin, for it threatens the will in its very structure as a will, in its dignity as *origin* and identity. But at the same time this inversion is infinitely less radical, for it only threatens, is indefinitely postponed, is consciousness. Consciousness is resistance to violence, because it leaves the time necessary to forestall it. Human freedom resides in the future,

source of the particular meanings that will be discovered, the Other must come as the very trope of subjectivity as it has been passed down to us. The necessity of that metaphorization would ground the necessity of the morality that would precede intentionality. Which does not undercut the strength of the metaphors already operating through *Totality and Infinity*: "The fact that in existing for another I exist otherwise than in existing for me is morality itself." As signifying, as being conscious, we are called to be for another; we may attempt to efface that relation by claiming an inherent selfishness, or enlightened selfishness, in our thought, but all possible modes of consciousness will exist as a violence to our selves, will be like Oedipus at Colonus, traversed by an alien discourse.[220] Consciousness resides with Antigone, with the woman who is not yet married, who decides which discourse to submit to; here we have the Levinasian model of free consciousness.[221] This allegory, too, would have to be modified in terms of the creativity entailed by the withdrawal of god. With Levinas, the road to the modification of the modern project is reconceptualizing our relation to time, to the future, in terms of the other, not just in terms of the other who leaves a meaning in our world for us to pick up, but the other who will make of our actions new meanings.

Every will separates itself from its work. The movement proper to action consists in issuing in the unknown—in not being able to measure all its consequences. The unknown does not result from a factual ignorance; the unknown upon which action issues resists all knowledge, does not stand out in the light, since it represents the meaning the work receives from the other. (Levinas, *Totality and Infinity* [1961], p. 227)

Recapitulating a series of positions: signification, expression, language itself, all come into being as the future-oriented response/gesture of an individual to the need, the fragility, of the other.[222] This happens as a relation to the fact of the other's subjectivity, as an acknowledgment of my dependence on the interiority of the sensuous relation itself, my dependence on a sensuality that precedes names and numbers, the interior self which is constantly in front of the self,[223] and offers these meanings to me. And perhaps what is most questionable for us here is the interpretation of the giving in terms of meaning, in the terms of determinations. Perhaps, as in our example concerning education, the strange gift that is only as a withdrawal from the economy (the teacher who doesn't just give an answer) is itself the giving of a new possibility for thought. On this ground, Irigaray questions exactly how well Levinas has conceptualized the role of passive synthesis:

> Intuition without an end, intuition that does not mark out but inscribes itself in an already insistent field. A prehensive intuition, which inhales from the air something of what is already there to come back to itself?
>
> The loved one would be she who keeps herself available in this way. Offering to the other what he can put to his own use? Opening the path of his

always still minimally future, of its non-freedom, in consciousness—the prevision of the violence imminent in the time that still remains. To be conscious is to have time— not to overflow the present by anticipating and hastening the future, but to have a distance with regard to the present: to relate oneself to being as to a being to come, to maintain a distance with regard to being even while already coming under its grip. To be free is to have time to forestall one's own abdication under the threat of violence. (Levinas, *Totality and Infinity,* p. 237)

222. We can say it yet otherwise: exteriority defines the existent as existent, and the signification of the face is due to an essential coinciding of the existent and the signifier. Signification is not added to the existent. To signify is not equivalent to presenting oneself as a sign, but to expressing oneself, that is, presenting oneself in person. The symbolism of the sign already presupposes the signification of expression, the face. In the face the existent par excellence presents itself. And the whole body—a hand or a curve of the shoulder—can express as the face. The primordial signifyingness of the existent, its presentation in person or its expression, its way of incessantly upsurging outside of its plastic image, is produced concretely as a temptation to total negation, and as the infinite resistance

to murder, in the other qua other, in the hard resistance of these eyes without protection—what is softest and most uncovered. The existent qua existent is produced only in morality. Language, source of all signification, is born in the vertigo of infinity, which takes hold before the straightforwardness of the face, making murder possible and impossible. (Levinas, *Totality and Infinity*, p. 262)

223. The Beloved, at once graspable but intact in her nudity, beyond object and face and thus beyond the existent, abides in virginity. The feminine essentially violable and inviolable, the "Eternal Feminine," is the virgin or an incessant recommencement of virginity, the untouchable in the very contact of voluptuosity, future in the present. Not as a freedom struggling with its conqueror, refusing its reification and its objectification, but a fragility at the limit of non-being wherein is lodged not only what is extinguished and is *no longer*, but what is not yet. The virgin remains ungraspable, dying without murder, swooning, withdrawing into her future, beyond every possible promised to anticipation. (Levinas, *Totality and Infinity*, p. 258)

224. This essay has also been translated in Irigaray's *An Ethics of Sexual Difference* (pp. 201–2).

225. Thus Irigaray is accentuating something of the same

return to himself and of his own future? Giving him back time?

When the loved one perceives the lover in this way, does she inscribe herself in a moment of her trajectory as he arrives at a moment of his own? He believes that she is drawing him down into the abyss; she believes that he is cutting himself off from her to constitute his transcendence. Their paths cross but achieve neither an alliance nor a mutual fecundation. Except for the lover, whose double is—the son. (Irigaray, "The Fecundity of the Caress," *Face to Face with Levinas* [1986], p. 244)[224]

Irigaray, here, would rather reappropriate the work of Levinas than dismiss it. As Homans said when we started this book, the woman has to learn to enter the symbolic order gradually—only then does she understand that she is traversed by a destiny that is not her choosing, but of her own making. To be feminine, at this point, becomes to recognize the space of fecundity within oneself, to submit oneself to a future order and not a destiny mapped out in the past. This is what I already pointed to, in the last section, thinking through Levinas's use of the maternal as a metaphor for signification.[225]

Our task, then, is to think the birth of the daughter, of one also capable of the strange affirmations, the giving, that maternity requires. And here I must be most hesitant. Perhaps it is the daughter, the metaphor for a woman who will not bear 'my' child, who will not institute the anxiety we blame on the mother—who does not institute the play of presence and absence, but is rather a pure affirmation of the fact that there are always other possibilities, other metaphors—perhaps, even, it is the daughter who will thus (and "There is a multiplicity and a transcendence in the verb 'to exist', a transcendence that is lacking in even the boldest existentialist analyses") exist the future.[226]

And perhaps that daughter will show us that thinking was always other than separation and anxiety over the threat of separation. Will show us that the myth of a separation (of a necessary violence) and of a full presence (a perfection in Being) are only artifacts held over from a millennias-old tradition of thinking the essence of the human (of the 'we') in terms of man's fight for recognition in the public, in man's invocation of the importance of his work (his 'I') in the constitution of the 'we'. The other of this myth has always been available to us; it's not a new development in the possibilities of thought, merely the recognition that our hierarchies of essential and trivial had missed the point about the relation of thoughts to words, forms to matter, men to their children. From the woman's point of view, everything but the child (which, in its way, in this metaphor, is everything) comes from the outside. The child, in fact, does not come of its own, but only as the strange tensing of time the woman is capable of. Literally, for man and woman, we are speaking of the desire to have a conscience, the desire to do justice or speak the truth—the desire not to be alone.

If that desire is no longer anxious in front of the possibility of its completion, haven't we thereby abandoned any motivation it might engender toward justice in-

metaphorical insistence which *Otherwise than Being* gives us over *Totality and Infinity*:

Before orality comes to be, touch is already in existence. No nourishment can compensate for the grace, or the work, of touching. Touch makes it possible to wait, to gather strength, so that the other will return to caress and reshape, from within and from without, flesh that is given back to itself in the gestures of love. The most subtly necessary guardian of my life being the other's flesh. Approaching and speaking to me with his hands. Bringing me back to life more intimately than any regenerative nourishment, the other's hands, these palms with which he approaches without going through me, give me back the borders of my body and call me back to the remembrance of the most profound intimacy. As he caresses me, he bids me neither to disappear nor to forget but rather, to remember the place where, for me, the most intimate life holds itself in reserve. Searching for what has not yet come into being, for himself, he invites me to become what I have not yet become. To realize a birth still in the future. Plunging me back into the maternal womb and, beyond that, conception, awakening me to another—amorous—birth. (Irigaray, "The Fecundity of the Caress," *Face to Face with Levinas* [1986], pp. 232–33 [*An Ethics of Sexual Difference*, p. 187])

226. The relation borne to the child must also be rethought. One trend of current feminist thought tends to denounce a trap in maternity that would consist of making the mother-woman an agent who is more or less the accomplice of re-production: capitalist, famil-ialist, phallocentric reproduc-tion. An accusation and a caution that should not be turned into prohibition, into a new form of repression. Will, you, too, discounting everyone's blindness and pas-sivity, be afraid the child might make a father and hence that the woman mak-ing a kid plays herself more than one dirty trick, engen-dering the child—the mother—the father—the family all at the same time? NO, it's up to you to break the old circuits. It will be the task of woman and man to make the old relationship and all its consequences out-of-date; to think the launching of a new subject, into life, with defamilialization. Rather than depriving woman of a fascinating time in the life of her body just to guard against procreation's being recuper-ated, let's de-mater-paternal-ize. Let's defeteshize. Let's get out of the dialectic that claims that the child is its par-ents' death. The child is the other but the other without violence. The other rhythm, the pure freshness, the possi-ble's body. Complete fragility. But vastness itself. (H. Cixous, "Sorties," *The Newly Born Woman* [1975], pp. 89–90)

stead of injustice? For an answer, again, we only have recourse to the metaphor of edu-cation (and wasn't it always more of a meta-phor than an example?): that is, only insofar as the question of justice can be phrased be-yond the supposed necessity of its answers can we expect that questioning to resonate in those who are coming to question. In the daughter we find the full impact of the questioning which gives us a future other-wise thought than as a play between Good and Evil, God and Man; in the daughter the aesthetics of religion, of the just and good life, becomes a question of aesthetics, a question to be phrased explicitly and not just assumed, not just taken as a given within the cultures from which we believe ourselves to emerge—and, most impor-tantly, not just to be answered in the con-ceptual pairing which believes itself to know the purpose behind all questioning (that is, not a questioning which would be satisfied with an answer).

Perhaps what we should think of, in terms of the daughter, is the way we can all belong to a tradition, to a 'we', by virtue of a questioning held in common, a questioning given its loose form by its opposition to the supposed reign of given facts (and thus ex-tending back to Descartes) but which has in-creasingly doubted if it knew even what it was looking for. This increasing self-doubt, the willingness to turn against even a previ-ous incarnation of the self (to doubt our own paternal voice), is perhaps what would best characterize the 'community' of literary and philosophical writers who appear in my writing.

# ii)                                    Politics

> *You stand at midday in the marketplace*
> *Before your life: to see is to have spoken*
> *—Yet to see, Blind One, is to be alone.*
>
>                 —R. Jarrell, *"The Sphinx's Riddle to*
>                 *Oedipus,"* The Complete Poems

Marjorie Perloff's *The Futurist Moment* poses the question of poetry versus prose in terms of the Futurists who—in an attempt to aestheticize the political—pitted a prose aesthetics against the ruling aesthetics of poetry. The Futurists remain interesting to us now because of precisely this move to aesthetics; the ambiguity lies in their blind trust of progress, their machine aesthetics, their love of war (and its determinations, its new nouns):

> "This war," Cendrars wrote to a friend in September, on his way to the front, "is a painful delivery, needed to give birth to liberty. It fits me like a glove. Reaction or Revolution—man must become more human. I will return. There can be no doubt.". . . Seventy years and two world wars later, it is almost impossible to understand this particular mixture of radicalism and patriotism, of a worldly, international outlook and a violently nationalist faith. Yet we find this paradox everywhere in the arts of the *avant guerre*. Before we dismiss as a contemptible proto-Fascist the Marinetti who declared, in the first Futurist manifesto [1909], "We will glorify war—the world's only hygiene," we must look at the context in which such statements were made. (Perloff, *The Futurist Moment* [1986], p. 6 [my ellipsis])

History's multiplicity too often still eludes our memory, since in order to

227. Although Derrida continues to think of that politics as a mediation between a necessary violence (thought in determinations) and a justice in approach. Thus, in the article which has seemed to engender the most discussion of late, Derrida attempts "to show why and how what is now called Deconstruction, while seeming not to 'address' the problem of justice, has done nothing but address it, if only *obliquely*, unable to do so directly. *Obliquely*, as at this very moment, in which I'm preparing to demonstrate that one cannot speak *directly* about justice, thematize or objectivize justice, say 'this is just' and even less 'I am just,' without immediately betraying justice, if not law (*droit*)" (Derrida, "Force of Law: The 'Mystical Foundations of Authority'" [1989], *Deconstruction and the Possibility of Justice*, p.10). This oblique address rests, perhaps, on a "deconstructive affirmation" (p. 63.), and it is that affirmation which would have to be otherwise than violent, otherwise than either right or wrong, in order to bear progeny. To think the indeterminate from the side of the one who approaches, which places Derrida within a Husserlian problematic (as Derrida himself teaches us in "Violence and Metaphysics"), and think the determinate as that which stands there, now, ready for deconstruction, is to betray the always already of transcendence (of a futurity not to be my own) which I have tried to invoke with the metaphor of daughters.

remember we have to look with a different and still unaccustomed eye—instead of merely seeing the marching progress of triumphant (and ever-cleansing) war. This new mode of vision would even be necessary to the extent that peace had triumphed over war—peace may be the most violent in its reduction of all to one. This remembrance, as a structure of writing, or conscience, is the political meaning of deconstruction.[227] Accordingly, we must see that the historical moment of the Futurists (as of any moment) contained missed opportunities, missed in ways that we may yet learn from, missed in more ways than we can presently name. Missed, perhaps, for having said too much (and who hasn't been guilty of the somewhat mad attempt to fill in all the gaps, misunderstandings, silences). At the turn of the last century, it was already, although seldom admitted, a question of feminism, of industrialization, of economic organization, of the efficacy of cities and the morality of the farm, and of art.

Ezra Pound is interesting to me here because he is so obviously a political poet—and so few of this century's canonized poets in English have been. His personal life is interesting because it transcends any one movement, of which he helped define several; yet his life is even more interesting to me, perhaps perversely, because of its failures. Perloff sees Pound as a transitional figure, yet a Futurist:

> Pound was right at the center of what we might call the Futurist vortex. However irritating he may have found Marinetti's posturing, as well as his obsession with "automobilism" and the

new technology and the Futurists' simplistic rejection of tradition, Pound nevertheless absorbed the more specifically aesthetic doctrines of Futurism. The first axiom in the 1909 manifesto is, "We intend to sing the love of danger, the habit of energy and fearlessness." "Vortex. Pound." begins with the sentence, "The vortex is the point of maximum energy," a point made even more emphatically in "The Serious Artist" [1913]: "We might come to believe that the thing that matters in art is a sort of energy, something more or less like electricity or radioactivity, a force transfusing, welding, and unifying" (LE 49). (Perloff, *The Futurist Moment* [1986], p. 173)

Energy, the machinations of progress—usually in the form of endless war—finds its focus in the word, like Christ finding his telos on the cross. This continues to be apparent in Pound's *Guide to Kulchur* where he insists on one principle, traced by Pound to Confucius, containing everything necessary to a person's life: 'call people and things by their names'. This art of prose names— Pound had an encompassing preference for the noun—unifies the threads of the past in a triumphant now, regulated by an appropriate word. This can take the vacuous—and common—stand that the now is appropriate because it is triumphant, or that truth is somehow stronger than lies and the necessary result of applied energy—of aesthetics—would be an appropriate (beautiful, just, truth-filled) now.

Pound, believing enthusiastically in the wrong side of WWII, found himself a prisoner of the American occupying forces in Pisa. His disappointment with the conclusion of WWI (of which he had been on the winning side) had led him to write an epic on the model of Dante. Thirty years later, it was time to write the Heaven Cantos and he was in the first stages of a personal hell of confinement in prison and asylum. In short, a peculiar vantage on the failures of a lonely (and arrogant) energy to find an appropriate aesthetic. His writing becomes more sparse, less anxious in the face of its silences, in the face of its inability to simply name the words. Of course, his failure was to a woman, further a woman of ancient Troy:

> Cassandra, your eyes are like tigers,
> with no word written in them
> You also have I carried to nowhere,
> to an ill house and there is
> no end to the journey
> The chess board too lucid
> the squares are too even . . . theatre of war . . .
> "theatre" is good. There are those who did not want
> it to come to an end.

And Pound comforts her, in this, the fifth of the Pisan Cantos:

> there
> are
> no
> righteous
> wars.
>
> (Pound, "Cantos LXXVIII" [1948],
> *The Cantos of Ezra Pound*, pp. 477, 483)

It's interesting that the failure here is figured as the inability to find the words in the other's gaze—like (ourselves) the mute audience unable to respond to Iphigenia's eyes. Derrida, sketching the death of the modern project, gives us the same:

> In Strasbourg, I had wanted to tell her that I love her all the while being afraid of her seer's lucidity, which is frightening because she sees true (juste), but she is mistaken because she is just, like the law. I did not dare say it to her, and moreover we have never been alone together. (Derrida, *The Post Card* [1980], p. 192)

Insofar as she is just, she is both mistaken and loved. Insofar as she sees, she is never alone—and never speaks. He is recognizing the feminine seer (and we should recognize Cassandra's structural complicity with Antigone), and, like Pound, he is announcing the failure of that search for a justice that could be encapsulated in the noun. The problem, for Pound and Derrida, is that the woman remains the other, inaccessible to man. We can begin to renounce the transcendental justice of our sexual desires, as men, which would be quite a step itself, but, and it would seem this is somewhat true of men and women, we cannot live the political space of a Cassandra. We cannot live the transcendence of a daughter who sees the whole situation but cannot name it for others—yet still attempts the words. Cassandra does not take to the type of resignation our present-day humanism would require (a retreat to safer grounds), but becomes a seer, a new type of daughter.

Here, with Derrida, I believe, and I am far more tentative now, is the same problem we began with. There are only two officially sanctioned avenues to a meaningful life—the private (feminine) values of individual connection and the public (masculine) values of production and the transcendence of individuality. Derrida has told the feminine other not to see for him, not to be passively faithful to him—he has no desire (nor nostalgia) which is strong enough to cause him to be actively faithful to her. He doesn't know what she would say—although he presumes to know her intention to be true (knows himself to be her audience).

This places us back within the question of the violence of language—the inescapable conclusion of the negativity of language, of presence. To see with the seer's eyes, the dangerous eyes of great cats, the desiring eyes of infinite patience, is to understand the obligation of appearance, not its fleeting endurance in the now, but the weight of the infinite desire, the infinite reaching out, which says 'I am here, waiting'.

As we have already seen, but always bearing repeating, the answer to injustice is to recognize the time of injustice, the activity of violence, as always directed toward the other, toward the possible murder of the future. Precisely in this locatability, in the face of injustice, the eyes that call for justice, does the call to an overwhelming obligation take place; my obligation for the responsibiliy of others. At first this seems to place violence in the public sphere— which Derrida does, extending this public sacrifice to all realms of meaning— and gentleness in the private (or, with Derrida, in the affirmative approach of a deconstruction). But it is precisely the conception of justice as written which speaks against this, and this is where I speak against Levinas as well. The said—what had been construed as the public violence, the necessity of a moment of violence, even as that violence bore the trace of the other's saying within it—as the necessity of a certain type of metaphor (or violence), does perhaps inhabit the very base of dwelling, but the creative act of writing, a private love affair, not yet given over to the 'human' and its necessities, precedes, precisely as the always indeterminate other, all the personal enjoyment of public violence. This is merely to say that the bare fact of understanding is not economic, but ethical, not determinate, but indeterminate; the activity of consciousness is a reading and not a writing; freedom is feminine and not masculine.

Our question, with Pound, after the modern theory of war, is how to ensure an end to war's theater, an end to the representational farce of art and politics. His failure, the failure of his boundless energy, speaks the frail justice of writing, always hostage to the other's laws, to the other's energy—leaving nothing to call my own, nothing to expect in return. Still I (he) write(s). Why? Is it just the simple inertia of a lifetime of eating (of violence)? No and yes. When we look at that lifetime's activity closely, everything resolves back into the same answer, into the same endless, infinite, unfulfillable desires. And when we look at the failures of our energy? Yes, it's true, we neither redeem the past nor escape time through our activity. The question, rather, is why we were trying to escape; escaping our obligations is escaping the possibility of a meaningful

228. When asked to describe herself, this woman says that she values "having other people that I am tied to, and also having people that I am responsible to. I have a very strong sense of being responsible to the world, that I can't just live for my enjoyment, but just the fact of being in the world gives me an obligation to do what I can to make the world a better place to live in, no matter how small scale that may be on." Thus while Kohlberg's subject worries about people interfering with each other's rights, this woman worries about "the possibility of omission, of your not helping others when you could help them." (C. Gilligan, *In a Different Voice* [1982], p. 21)

life;[228] escape itself, always alone and blind, constitutes the failure as irredeemable.

# Bibliography

Abrams, Meyer Howard. *Natural Supernaturalism*. New York: Norton, 1971.

Adorno, Theodor. *The Jargon of Authenticity*. (1964). Trans. K Tarnowski and F. Will. Evanston, Ill.: Northwestern University Press, 1973.

Anouilh, Jean. "Antigone." (1944). Trans. L. Galantiére. In *Anouilh (Five Plays)*. New York: Hill and Wang, 1958.

Arendt, Hannah. *The Human Condition*. Chicago: University of Chicago Press, 1958.

Bataille, Georges. *Guilty*. (1943, 1961). Trans. B. Boone. San Francisco: Lapis, 1988.

———. "The Notion of Expenditure." (1933). *Visions of Excess*. Trans. and ed. A. Stoeckl. Minneapolis: University of Minnesota Press, 1985.

Baudrillard, Jean. "Fetishism and Ideology." (1970). In *For a Critique of the Political Economy of the Sign*. Trans. C. Levin. St. Louis: Telos, 1981.

———. "The Ideological Genesis of Needs." (1969). In *For a Critique of the Political Economy of the Sign*. Trans. C. Levin. St. Louis: Telos, 1981.

———. *Seduction*. Trans. B. Singer. New York: St. Martin's Press, 1990.

———. "Toward a Critique of the Political Economy of the Sign." (1972). In *For a Critique of the Political Economy of the Sign*. Trans. C. Levin. St. Louis: Telos, 1981.

Beauvoir, Simone de. *The Second Sex*. (1949). Trans. and ed. H. M. Parshley. New York: Knopf, 1953.

Blanchot, Maurice. "Literature and the Right to Death." (1949). In *The Gaze of Orpheus and Other Literary Essays*. Trans. L. Davis, ed. P. Adams Sitney. Barrytown, N.Y.: Station Hill, 1981.

Blumenberg, H., *The Legitimacy of the Modern Age*. (1966). Trans. R. Wallace. Cambridge, Mass.: MIT, 1983.

———. *Work on Myth*. (1979). Trans. R. Wallace. Cambridge, Mass.: MIT Press, 1985.

Buck-Morss, S. *The Dialectics of Seeing*. Cambridge, Mass.: MIT Press, 1989.

Butler, J. *Bodies that Matter*. New York: Routledge, 1993.

Certeau, Michel de. "The Arts of Dying." (1975). In *Heterologies Discourse on the Other*. Trans. B. Massumi. Minneapolis: University of Minnesota Press, 1986.

Chodorow, Nancy. *The Reproduction of Mothering*. Berkeley: University of California Press, 1978.

Cixous, Hélène. "Extreme Fidelities." In *Writing Differences*. Ed. S. Sellers. New York: Open University Press, 1988.

———. "Sorties." In *The Newly Born Woman*. Trans. B. Wing. Minneapolis: University of Minnesota Press, 1986.

Deleuze, Gilles and Félix Guattari. *Anti-Oedipus Capitalism and Schizophrenia*. (1972). Trans. R. Hurley, M. Seem, and H. Lane. Minneapolis: University of Minnesota Press, 1983.

Derrida, Jacques. "Afterword." (1971). In *Limited Inc*. Trans. S. Weber. Evanston, Ill.: Northwestern University Press, 1988.

———. "Différance." (1968). In *Margins of Philosophy*. Trans. A. Bass. Chicago: University of Chicago Press, 1982.

———. *Dissemination*. (1972). Trans. B. Johnson. Chicago: University of Chicago Press, 1981.

———. "The Ends of Man." (1968). In *Margins of Philosophy*. Trans. A. Bass. Chicago: University of Chicago Press, 1982.

———. "From Restricted to General Economy." (1967). In *Writing and Difference*. Trans A. Bass. Chicago: University of Chicago Press, 1978.

———. *Given Time: I. Counterfeit Money*. (1991). Trans. P. Kamuf. Chicago: University of Chicago Press, 1992.

———. *Glas*. (1974). Trans. J. Leavey and R. Rand. Lincoln: University of Nebraska Press, 1986.

———. *Of Grammatology*. (1967). Trans. G. Spivak. Baltimore: Johns Hopkins University Press, 1974.

———. "Otobiographies." In *The Ear of the Other*. Trans. P. Kamuf, ed. C. McDonald. Chicago: University of Chicago Press, 1985.

———. "The Pit and the Pyramid: Introduction to Hegelian Semiology." (1968). In *Margins of Philosophy*. Trans. A. Bass. Chicago: University of Chicago Press, 1982.

———. *The Post Card*. (1980). Trans. A. Bass. Chicago: University of Chicago Press, 1987.

———. "Signature Event Context." (1971). In *Limited Inc*. Trans S. Weber and J. Mehlman. Evanston, Ill.: Northwestern University Press, 1988.

———. *Specters of Marx.* Trans. P. Kamuf. New York: Routledge, 1994.

———. *Speech and Phenomenon.* (1967). Trans. D. Allison. Evanston, Ill.: Northwestern University Press, 1973.

———. *Spurs.* Trans. B. Harlow. Chicago: University of Chicago Press, 1978.

———. "Structure, Sign, and Play." (1966). In *Writing and Difference.* Trans. A. Bass. Chicago: University of Chicago Press, 1978.

———. *The Truth in Painting.* (1978). Trans. G. Bennington and I. McLeod. Chicago: University of Chicago Press, 1987.

———. "Violence and Metaphysics." (1964). In *Writing and Difference.* Trans. A. Bass. Chicago: University of Chicago Press, 1978.

Descartes, René. "Discourse on Method for Rightly Conducting One's Reason and Seeking Truth in the Sciences." (1637). Trans. and ed. M. Wilson. New York: New American Library, 1964.

Donne, John. "A Valediction: Forbidding Mourning." (1611). In *John Donne's Poetry.* New York: Norton, 1966.

Duras, Marguerite. *India Song.* (1973). Trans. B. Brae. New York: Grove, 1976.

Erikson, Erik. *Gandhi's Truth.* New York: Norton, 1969.

Euripides. "From the *Iphigenia of Aulis* in Euripides." Trans. H.D. In *H.D.: Collected Poems.* Ed. L. Martz. New York: New Directions, 1983.

Felman, Shoshana. *Jacques Lacan and the Adventure of Insight.* Cambridge, Mass.: Harvard University Press, 1987.

Foucault, Michel. *The History of Sexuality.* Vol. 1. (1976). Trans. R. Hurley. New York: Random House, 1978.

Gallop, Jane. *Reading Lacan.* Ithaca, N.Y.: Cornell University Press, 1985.

Gandhi, M. K. *Non-violent Resistance.* New York: Schocken, 1951.

Gilligan, Carol. *In a Different Voice.* Cambridge, Mass.: Harvard University Press, 1982.

Girard, René. *The Scapegoat.* (1982). Trans. Y. Freccero. Baltimore: Johns Hopkins University Press, 1986.

Graham, Jorie. "New Trees." In *Hybrids of Plants and of Ghosts*, Princeton, N.J.: Princeton University Press, 1980.

Grange, Joseph. "Lacan's Other and the Factions of Plato's Soul." In *Question of the Other.* Ed. A. Dallery and C. Scott. Albany: State University of New York Press, 1989.

Grass, Günter. *Show Your Tongue* (1988). Trans. J. Woods. New York: Harcourt Brace Jovanovich, 1989.

Habermas, Jürgen. "Between Eroticism and General Economics: Bataille." (1983). In *The Philosophical Discourse of Modernity.* Trans. F. Lawrence. Cambridge, Mass.: MIT Press, 1987.

———. "Hegel's Concept of Modernity." (1983). *The Philosophical Discourse of Modernity.* Trans. F. Lawrence. Cambridge, Mass.: MIT Press, 1987.

———. "On Leveling the Genre Distinction between Philosophy and Literature." (1983). In *The Philosophical Discourse of Modernity*. Trans. F. Lawrence. Cambridge, Mass.: MIT Press, 1987.

———. *The Structural Transformation of the Public Sphere*. (1962). Trans. T. Burger. Cambridge, Mass.: MIT Press, 1989.

———. *The Theory of Communicative Action*. Vol. 1. (1981). Trans. T. McCarthy. Boston: Beacon Press, 1984.

———. *The Theory of Communicative Action*. Vol 2. (1981). Trans. T. McCarthy. Boston: Beacon Press, 1989.

Hass, Robert. "Meditation at Lagunitas." In *Praise*. New York: Ecco, 1979.

H.D. "From the *Iphigenia of Aulis* in Euripides." Trans. H.D. In *H.D.: Collected Poems*. Ed. L. Martz. New York: New Directions, 1983.

Hegel, G. W. F. *Hegel's Phenomenology of Spirit*. (1807). Trans. A. V. Miller. Oxford: Oxford University Press, 1977.

———. *The Philosophy of History*. (1831). Trans. J. Sibree. New York: Dover, 1956.

———. *Hegel's Philosophy of Nature*. Trans. A. V. Miller. Oxford: Oxford University Press, 1970.

———. *Hegel's Science of Logic*. (1812). Trans A. V. Miller. Atlantic Highlands, N.J.: Humanities Press, 1989.

Heidegger, Martin. "The Age of the World Picture." (1938). In *The Question Concerning Technology*. Trans. W. Lovitt. New York: Harper and Row, 1977.

———. *Basic Problems of Phenomenology*. (1927). Trans. A. Hofstadter. Bloomington: Indiana University Press, 1982.

———. *Being and Time*. (1927). Trans. J. Macquerrie and E. Robinson. New York: Harper and Row, 1962.

———. "Conversation on a Country Path." (1944–45). In *Discourse on Thinking*. Trans. J. M. Anderson and E. H. Freund. New York: Harper and Row, 1966.

———. *Hegel's Phenomenology of Spirit*. (1930–31). Trans. P. Emad and K. Maly. Bloomington: Indiana University Press, 1988.

———. *History of the Concept of Time*. (1925). Trans. T. Kisiel. Bloomington: Indiana University Press, 1985.

———. *Introduction to Metaphysics*. (1935). Trans. R. Manheim. New Haven, Conn.: Yale University Press, 1959.

———. *Kant and the Problem of Metaphysics*. (1929). 4th ed. (1973). Trans. R. Taft. Bloomington: Indiana University Press, 1990.

———. "Language." (1950). *Poetry Language Thought*. Trans. A. Hofstadter. New York: Harper and Row, 1971.

———. "Letter on Humanism." (1947). Trans. F. Capuzzi. In *Basic Writings*. Ed. D. Krell. New York: Harper and Row, 1977.

————. *The Metaphysical Foundations of Logic.* (1928). Trans. M. Heim. Bloomington: Indiana University Press, 1984.

————. "Nietzsche's Fundamental Metaphysical Position in Western Thought: The Doctrine of Eternal Recurrence of the Same." (1937). In *Nietzsche.* Vol. 2. Trans. D. Krell. San Francisco: Harper and Row, 1984.

————. "The Origin of the Work of Art" (1935). In *Poetry Language Thought.* Trans. A. Hofstadter. New York: Harper and Row, 1971.

Heidegger, Martin, and Eugen Fink. *Heraclitus Seminar.* (1969). Trans. C. Seibert. Evanston, Ill.: Northwestern University Press, 1979.

Homans, Margaret. *Bearing the Word.* Chicago: University of Chicago Press, 1986.

Hurston, Zora Neale. *Their Eyes Were Watching God.* Chicago: Illini Books, 1978.

Husserl, Edmund. *Cartesian Meditations.* (1929). Trans. D. Cairns. The Hague: Martinus Nijhoff, 1960.

————. *Crisis of the European Sciences.* (1937). Trans. D. Carr. Evanston, Ill.: Northwestern University Press, 1970.

————. *Experience and Judgement.* (1938). Trans. J. Churchill and K. Ameriks, ed. L. Landgrebe. Evanston, Ill.: Northwestern University Press, 1973.

————. *Formal and Transcendental Logic.* (1929). Trans. D. Cairns. The Hague: Martinus Nijhoff, 1969.

————. *Ideas Pertaining to a Pure Phenomenology and to a Phenomenological Philosophy, First Book.* (1913). Trans. F. Kersten. The Hague: Martinus Nijhoff, 1983.

————. "The Origin of Geometry." (1936). In *Crisis of the European Sciences.* Trans. D. Carr. Evanston, Ill.: Northwestern University Press, 1970.

————. *The Phenomenology of Internal Time Consciousness.* Ed. M. Heidegger, trans. J. Churchill. Bloomington: Indiana University Press, 1964.

Irigaray, Luce. "The Envelope." In *An Ethics of Sexual Difference.* (1984). Trans. G. Gill and C. Burke. Ithaca, N.Y.: Cornell University Press, 1993.

————. "The Fecundity of the Caress." In *Face to Face with Levinas.* Ed. R. Cohen. Albany: State University of New York Press, 1986. (Also in *An Ethics of Sexual Difference*).

————. *Speculum of the Other Woman* (1974). Trans. G. Gill. Ithaca, N.Y.: Cornell University Press, 1985.

Jarrell, Randall. "The Sphinx's Riddle to Oedipus." In *The Complete Poems.* New York: Farrar, Strauss, Giroux, 1969.

Kahler, Erich. *The Inward Turn of Narrative.* (1957). Trans. R. Winston and C. Winston. Evanston, Ill.: Northwestern University of Press, 1987.

Kant, Immanuel. *The Critique of Judgment.* (1790). Trans. J. C. Meredith. Oxford: Oxford University Press, 1952.

Kierkegaard, Søren. *The Concept of Irony.* (1841). Trans. L. Capel. Bloomington: Indiana University Press, 1965.

———. *Concluding Unscientific Postscript.* (1846). Trans. D. Swenson and W. Lowrie. Princeton, N.J.: Princeton University Press, 1941.

———. *Either/Or.* 2 Vols. (1843). Trans. H. Hong and E. Hong. Princeton, N.J.: Princeton University Press, 1987.

———. *Works of Love.* (1847). Trans. H. Hong and E. Hong. New York: Harper and Row, 1962.

Kristeva, Julia. *Tales of Love.* (1983). Trans. L. Roudiez. New York: Columbia University Press, 1987.

Lacan, Jacques. "The Direction of the Treatment and the Principles of its Power." (1958). In *Écrits A Selection.* Trans. A. Sheridan. New York: Norton, 1977.

———. *The Four Fundamental Concepts of Psycho-Analysis.* (1973). Trans. A. Sheridan. New York: Norton, 1978.

———. "The Function and Field of Speech and Language in Psychoanalysis." (1953). In *Écrits A Selection.* Trans. A. Sheridan. New York: Norton, 1977.

———. "Guiding Remarks for a Congress on Feminine Sexuality." (1958). In *Feminine Sexuality.* Trans. J. Rose. New York: Norton, 1982.

———. "The Mirror Stage as Formative of the Function of the I as Revealed in Psychoanalytic Experience." (1949). In *Écrits A Selection.* Trans. A. Sheridan. New York: Norton, 1977.

———. *The Seminar of Jacques Lacan: Book I.* (1953). Ed. J.-A. Miller, trans. J. Forrester. New York: Norton, 1991.

———. "The Signification of the Phallus." (1958). In *Écrits A Selection.* Trans. A. Sheridan. New York: Norton, 1977.

———. "The Subversion of the Subject and the Dialectic of Desire in the Freudian Unconscious." (1960). In *Écrits A Selection.* Trans. A. Sheridan. New York: Norton, 1977.

Lacoue-Labarthe, Philippe. "The Caesura of the Speculative." (1978). *Typography.* Trans. R. Eisenhauer. Cambridge, Mass.: Harvard University Press, 1989.

Laing, R. D., and D. G. Cooper. *Reason and Violence.* London: Tavistock, 1964.

Lauterbach, Ann. "Revenant." In *Clamor.* New York: Viking, 1991.

Leibniz, Gottfried. *Monadology.* (1700–15). Trans. G. Montgomery. La Salle, Ill.: Open Court, 1902.

Lévi-Strauss, Claude. *The Elementary Structures of Kinship.* (1947). Trans. J. Bell and J. von Sturmer, ed. R. Needham. Boston: Beacon, 1969.

———. *The Savage Mind.* (1962). Chicago: University of Chicago Press, 1966.

Levinas, Emmanuel. "Apropos of Buber: Some Notes." (1982). In *Outside the Subject.* Trans. M. Smith. Stanford, Calif.: Stanford University Press, 1994.

———. "The Ego and the Totality." (1954). In *Collected Philosophical Papers.* Trans. A. Lingis. The Hague: Martinus Nijhoff, 1987.

———. *Existence and Existents.* (1940–45). Trans. A. Lingis. The Hague: Martinus Nijhoff, 1978.

———. "Freedom and Command." (1953). In *Collected Philosophical Papers.* Trans. A. Lingis. The Hague: Martinus Nijhoff, 1987.

———. "God and Philosophy." (1975). In *Collected Philosophical Papers*. Trans. A. Lingis. The Hague: Martinus Nijhoff, 1987.

———"Humanism and An-archy." (1968). In *Collected Philosophical Papers*. Trans. A. Lingis. The Hague: Martinus Nijhoff, 1987.

———"Language and Proximity." (1967). In *Collected Philosophical Papers*. Trans. A. Lingis. The Hague: Martinus Nijhoff, 1987.

———. "Meaning and Sense." (1972). In *Collected Philosophical Papers*. Trans. A. Lingis. The Hague: Martinus Nijhoff, 1987.

———. "The Old and the New." (1980). In *Time and the Other*. Trans. R. Cohen. Pittsburgh: Duquesne University Press, 1987.

———. "On Intersubjectivity: Notes on Merleau-Ponty." (1982). In *Outside the Subject*. Trans. M. Smith. Stanford, Calif.: Stanford University Press, 1994.

———. *Otherwise than Being*. (1974). Trans. A. Lingis. The Hague: Martinus Nijhoff, 1981.

———. "The Pact." (1982). Trans. S. Richmond. *The Levinas Reader*. Ed. S. Hand. Cambridge: Basil Blackwell, 1989.

———. "Preface." (1979). In *Time and the Other*. (1947). Trans. R. Cohen. Pittsburgh: Duquesne University Press, 1987.

———. "The Rights of Man and the Rights of the Other." (1985). In *Outside the Subject*. Trans. M. Smith. Stanford, Calif.: Stanford University Press, 1994.

———. "Signature." Trans. M. Petrisko, ed. A. Peperzak. *Research in Phenomenology* 8 (1978): 175–89.

———. *The Theory of Intuition in Husserl's Phenomenology*. (1930). Trans. A. Orianne. Evanston, Ill.: Northwestern University Press, 1973.

———. *Time and the Other*. (1947). Trans. R. Cohen. Pittsburgh: Duquesne University Press, 1987.

———. *Totality and Infinity*. (1961). Trans. A. Lingis. Pittsburgh: Duquesne University Press, 1969.

———. "Transcendence and Evil." (1978). In *Collected Philosophical Papers*. Trans. A. Lingis. The Hague: Martinus Nijhoff, 1987.

Levinas, Emmanuel, and P. Nemo. *Ethics and Infinity*. (1981). Trans. R. Cohen. Pittsburgh: Duquesne University Press, 1985.

Lingis, Alphonso. *Deathbound Subjectivity*. Bloomington: Indiana University Press, 1989.

Löwith, Karl. *Meaning in History*. Chicago: University of Chicago Press, 1949.

Lukács, Georg. *The Young Hegel*. (1938). Trans. R. Livingstone. Cambridge, Mass.: MIT Press, 1975.

Lyotard, Jean-François. *The Differend*. (1983). Trans. G. Van Den Abbeele. Minneapolis: University of Minnesota, 1988.

———. *Lessons on the Analytic of the Sublime*. (1991). Trans. E. Rottenberg. Stanford, Calif.: Stanford University Press, 1994.

———. "Newman: The Instant." Trans. D. Macey. In *The Lyotard Reader*. Ed. A. Benjamin. Cambridge: Basil Blackwell, 1989.

————. "Scapeland." Trans. D. Macey. In *The Lyotard Reader*. Ed. A. Benjamin. Cambridge: Basil Blackwell, 1989.

————. "The Sublime and the Avant-Garde." (1984). Trans. C. Liebman. In *The Lyotard Reader*. Ed. A. Benjamin. Cambridge: Basil Blackwell, 1989.

Mahasweta Devi. "Stanadayini." Trans. G. Spivak. *In Other Worlds*. New York: Methuen, 1987.

Marx, Karl, and Frederick Engels. *The German Ideology* (1846). Ed. and trans. C. J. Arthur. New York: International Publishers, 1947.

————. *The Holy Family or Critique of Critical Critique*. (1845). Trans. R. Dixon. Moscow: Foreign Languages Publishing House, 1956.

Merleau-Ponty, Maurice. "The Child's Relations with Others." (1960). In *The Primacy of Perception*. Trans. W. Cobb., ed. J. Edie. Evanston, Ill.: Northwestern University Press, 1964.

————. *Phenomenology of Perception*. (1945). Trans. C. Smith. London: Routledge and Kegan Paul, 1962.

Nancy, J.-L. "The Inoperative Community." In *The Inoperative Community*. (1986). Trans. P. Connor et al. Minneapolis: University of Minnesota, 1991.

Natanson, Maurice. *Anonymity*. Bloomington: Indiana University Press, 1986.

Nicholas of Cusa. *God as Not-Other*. (1461). 3rd ed. Trans. J. Hopkins. Minneapolis: Banning, 1987.

————. *Learned Ignorance*. (1440). 2d ed. Trans. J. Hopkins. Minneapolis: Banning, 1985.

————. *The Vision of God*. (1453). Trans. J. Hopkins, with interpretive study, *Nicholas of Cusa's Dialectical Mysticism*. Minneapolis: Banning, 1985.

Nietzsche, F. *Beyond Good and Evil*. Trans. H. Zimmern. New York: Boni and Liveright, 1917.

Nussbaum, Martha. *The Fragility of Goodness*. Cambridge: Cambridge University Press, 1986.

Olafson, Frederick. *Heidegger and the Philosophy of Mind*. New Haven, Conn.: Yale University Press, 1987.

Olsen, T. *Silences*. New York: Delacourte Press, 1978.

Pelikan, J., *The Christian Tradition:* Vol. 1, *The Emergence of the Catholic Tradition (100–600)*. Chicago: University of Chicago Press, 1971.

Perloff, Marjorie. *The Futurist Moment*. Chicago: University of Chicago Press, 1986.

Plato. *The Republic*. Trans. P. Shorey, ed. E. Hamilton and H. Cairns. Princeton, N.J.: Princeton University Press, 1961.

Pound, Ezra. "Cantos LXXVIII." In *The Cantos of Ezra Pound*. New York: New Directions, 1971.

Ricoeur, Paul. *Freud and Philosophy*. (1961). Trans. D. Savage. New Haven, Conn.: Yale University Press, 1970.

Sartre, Jean-Paul. *Critique of Dialectical Reason*. (1960). Trans. A. Sheridan-Smith. London: Verso, 1982.

————. *Saint Genet*. (1952). Trans. B. Frechtman. New York: Braziller, 1963.

Schmidt, Dennis. *The Ubiquity of the Finite*. Cambridge, Mass.: MIT Press, 1988.

Schürmann, Reiner. *Heidegger on Being and Acting: From Principles to Anarchy*. (1982). Trans. C-M. Gros. Bloomington: Indiana University Press, 1987.

Schutz, Alfred. "Common Sense and Scientific Interpretation of Human Action." (1953). In *Collected Papers*. Ed. M. Natanson. The Hague: Martinus Nijhoff, 1962,

Shakespeare, William. *Troilus and Cressida*. Ed. A. Walker. Cambridge: Cambridge University Press, 1957.

Shapiro, Ian. *The Evolution of Rights in Liberal Theory*. Cambridge: Cambridge University Press, 1986.

Shepard, Sam. *Fool for Love and Other Plays*. New York: Bantam, 1984.

Sophocles. "Oedipus at Colonus." In *The Three Theban Plays*. Trans. R. Fagles. New York: Viking Penguin, 1982.

Spivak, Gayatri. "A Literary Representation of the Subaltern: A Woman's Text from the Third World." In *In Other Worlds*. New York: Methuen, 1987.

Stein, Gertrude. *Ida*. New York: Random House, 1941; Vintage, 1972.

Taminiaux, Jacques. "Hegel and Hobbes." (1982). In *Dialectic and Difference*. Trans. and ed. R. Crease and J. Decker. Atlantic Highlands, N.J.: Humanities Press, 1985.

Theweleit, Klaus. *Male Fantasies*. Vol. 1, *Women, Floods, Bodies, History*. (1977). Trans. S. Conway. Minneapolis: Minnesota University Press, 1987.

———. *Male Fantasies*. Vol. 2, *Male Bodies: Psychoanalyzing the Terror*. (1978). Trans. E. Carter and C. Turner. Minneapolis: Minnesota University Press, 1989.

Ulmer, Gregory. *Applied Grammatology*. Baltimore: Johns Hopkins University Press, 1985.

Vernant, Jean-Pierre. "Tension and Ambiguities in Greek Tragedy." (1972). In *Myth and Tragedy in Ancient Greece*. Trans. J. Lloyd. New York: Zone, 1988.

Walcott, Derek. "Midsummer, Tobago." (1976). In *Collected Poems*. New York: Farrar, Strauss, Giroux, 1986.

Warren, Mark. *Nietzsche and Political Thought*. Cambridge, Mass.: MIT Press, 1988.

Whitman, Walt. "A Sight in Camp in the Daybreak Gray and Dim." In *Complete Poetry and Selected Prose of Walt Whitman*. Ed. J. Miller. Boston: Houghton Mifflin, 1959.

———. "A Song of the Rolling Earth." In *Complete Poetry and Selected Prose of Walt Whitman*. Ed. J. Miller. Boston: Houghton Mifflin, 1959.

Wittgenstein, Ludwig. *Philosophical Investigations*. Trans. G. E. M. Anscombe. New York: Macmillan, 1953.

Wolf, Christa. *Cassandra*. (1983). Trans. J. Van Heurck. New York: Farrar, Strauss, Giroux, 1984.

Woolf, Virginia. *To the Lighthouse*. London: Hogarth Press, 1927.

# I n d e x

## A

Abrams, M. H., 56

activity: Derrida, 136; existence, 51; judgment, 16–17, 120–21; Pound, 345–47; vs. question, 23, 39; signification, 165; value, 84, 125

Adam, 56–57, 125

Adorno, Theodor, 38–40

Aeschylus, 9, 14

Agamemnon, 8–10, 13, 214

allegories. *See* metaphors

animal: eating, 94–95, 192; vs. human, 49–50, 62–63, 239

Anouilh, Jean, 68, 73, 241

answers: ontotheology, 96; postponing, 11; questions, 14, 19, 24, 172, 216

Antigone, 29, 207, 256, 337, 339; active, but not tragic, 67–70, 91, 224; audience, 59–61, 70; Christ, 83; complex virtue, 55; death, 248–49; freedom, 71–77; vs. Lacan, 246–47; memory, 249; suicide, 241

anxiety: contraction inwards, 286; face, 338; Hamlet, 321; non-indifference towards

other, 298; Levinas and Heidegger, 307; as method, 309–10; mother and tradition, 278, 280–81, 343; presence, 183; son, 309; Stein, 254, 312; Woolf, 312

appropriation: consciousness, 94; deformation in différance, 102–3; form, 99; vs. Heidegger, 119; objectification, 146; tradition, 4, 7, 18, 23, 31–32, 57, 85, 145, 194, 321, 343

Arendt, Hannah, 65–66, 71

Aristotle: good life, 66; matter, 31–32, 124; tragedy, 60–61

arpeggio, 291

art: beautiful fruit, 88, 104–5, 209; vs. experience, 33, 150, 207; giving, 209; irony, 207; politics, 34, 195, 197, 344–47; power, 22; representation, 257, 311; sublime, 205; transcendence, 201–2

articulation: Christ, 126, 143; unity, 101; in writing, 93. *See also* determination

atheism: hard to find, 309–10; vs. 'Here I am', 144; in this book, 86, 126–27, 147, 151

audience: absent, 134; freedom, 61; future, 246; gift, 105; historical trajectories, 85; multiplicity, 153; promise, 55; reading, 14; not